THE CANADIAN FEDERAL ELECTION OF 2025

The Canadian Federal Election of 2025

EDITED BY JON H. PAMMETT
AND CHRISTOPHER DORNAN

McGill-Queen's University Press
Montreal & Kingston • London • Chicago

ISBN 978-0-2280-2875-8 (paper)
ISBN 978-0-2280-2876-5 (ePDF)
ISBN 978-0-2280-2877-2 (ePUB)

Legal deposit third quarter 2026
Bibliothèque nationale du Québec

Printed in Canada on acid-free paper that is 100% ancient forest free (100% post-consumer recycled), processed chlorine free.

This book has been published with the help of a grant from Carleton University.

Funded by the Government of Canada | Financé par le gouvernement du Canada | Canada
Canada Council for the Arts | Conseil des arts du Canada

We acknowledge the support of the Canada Council for the Arts.
Nous remercions le Conseil des arts du Canada de son soutien.

McGill-Queen's University Press in Montreal is on land which long served as a site of meeting and exchange amongst Indigenous Peoples, including the Haudenosaunee and Anishinabeg nations. In Kingston it is situated on the territory of the Haudenosaunee and Anishinaabek. We acknowledge and thank the diverse Indigenous Peoples whose footsteps have marked these territories on which peoples of the world now gather.

Library and Archives Canada Cataloguing in Publication

Title: The Canadian federal election of 2025 / edited by Jon H. Pammett and Christopher Dornan.
Names: Pammett, Jon H., 1944– editor | Dornan, Chris, editor
Description: Includes bibliographical references.
Identifiers: Canadiana (print) 20260180726 | Canadiana (ebook) 20260180734 | ISBN 9780228028758 (paper) | ISBN 9780228028765 (ePDF) | ISBN 9780228028772 (ePUB)
Subjects: LCSH: Canada. Parliament—Elections, 2025. | LCSH: Political campaigns Canada. | LCSH: Political parties—Canada.
Classification: LCC JL193.C35883 2026 | DDC 324.70971—dc23

This book was designed and typeset by Sayre Street Books in Sabon Pro.
Copyediting by Louise Piper.

McGill-Queen's University Press
Suite 1720, 1010 Sherbrooke St West, Montreal, QC, H3A 2R7

Authorized safety representative in the EU: Mare Nostrum Group BV, Doelen 72, 4831 GR Breda, the Netherlands, gpsr@mare-nostrum.co.uk

Contents

Tables and Figures | vii

Preface | ix

1 Reversal of Fortune | 3
Christopher Dornan

2 From Oblivion to Victory: The Stunning Liberal Turnaround | 23
Brooke Jeffrey

3 Poilievre's Conservatives Make Gains but Fall Short of Victory | 50
Faron Ellis

4 Fighting for Relevance: The NDP Campaign | 76
Daniel Westlake and Jacob Robbins-Kanter

5 The Bloc Québécois and the Anti-System Dilemma | 100
Eric Montigny and Katryne Villeneuve-Siconnelly

6 Campaigning from the Outside: The Other Parties | 121
Gala Palavicini

7 Electoral Legislation 2015–25: The Conventional Wisdom Returns | 145
Louis Massicotte

8 The Pragmatist and the Disruptor: The Unexpected Role of Leadership in the Election | 169
Jonathan Malloy

9 Foreign Interference and the 2025 General Election | 186
Lori Turnbull

10 The Media Narratives that Defined the Mainstream Election Coverage | 205
Brett Popplewell, Adrian Harewood, and Patrick White

11 Polling's Ups and Downs | 235
Christopher Adams

12 Competence Versus Change: The Role of Valence Politics in the Election | 257
David Coletto and Richard Jenkins

13 The Future of Minority Government in Canada | 283
Jon H. Pammett and Lawrence LeDuc

Appendix: Results of the 2025 Canadian Federal Election | 299

Contributors | 301

Tables and Figures

TABLES

10.1 Content of election coverage of party leaders in Quebec and English Canadian media, 24 March to 27 April 2025 223
11.1 Accuracy of final polls in the 2025 election 246
11.2 Seat projections by pollsters and aggregators, 2025 249
12.1 Vote flow from 2021 to 2025 270
12.2 Flow of the vote, 2021–25, among voters who voted for change 271
12.3 Changes in probability for Liberal and Conservative parties associated with changes in statistically significant predictors 277
13.1 Preferred outcomes of the last three federal elections 293

FIGURES

4.1 Trend in party support from January 2024 to the 2025 election 81
4.2 Esquimalt-Saanich-Sooke strategic voting literature 91
4.3 Percentage of 2021 NDP vote lost by candidates in ridings the NDP won in 2021 92
11.1 Aggregated polls from 21 September 2021 to 23 March 2025 239
11.2 Aggregated campaign polls from 23 March to 27 April 2025 241
11.3 Regional accuracy of polling, 2025 247
12.1 Perceptions of the state of the Canadian economy 260
12.2 Top three issues and single most important issue 261

12.3 Party best able to handle most important issue 262
12.4 Federal government approval 2021 to 2025 264
12.5 Leader impressions, 2015 to 2025 265
12.6 Perceived leadership traits during final week of the campaign 266
13.1 Turnout in Canadian federal elections, 1965–2025 288
13.2 Estimated voting by age groups, 2025 federal election 289
13.3 Are minority governments good or bad? 294

Preface

A Canadian federal election is a remarkable exercise in civic competence. On 28 April 2025, across the six time zones of the second-largest country in the world, 19.8 million people cast their ballots, and their votes were counted and reported that very day and into the next, delivering an outcome within hours of the polls closing (the Liberals would remain in government) and by the following day an answer to whether it would be a majority government (it would not).

This was an unusual election, not least because what only months before was expected to happen did not happen, and yet by the end of the thirty-six-day campaign the result was not unexpected. It was particularly unusual because of an external factor that distorted what otherwise would likely have been the outcome.

The editors thank the contributing authors of this volume for bringing their expertise to bear on a determining moment in Canadian political history. Each chapter insightful in its own right, together they make the election reveal itself.

We thank our external reviewers for their comments and suggestions. We are indebted to Emily Andrew and the team at McGill-Queen's University Press for their support throughout and for bringing this study to press. Thanks also to Neil Erickson and Louise Piper for their meticulous work in compiling and copyediting the volume.

We are grateful to Prof. Jonathan Malloy, who provided helpful funding from the Hon. Dick and Ruth Bell Chair for the Study of Canadian Parliamentary Democracy at Carleton University.

David Coletto of Abacus Data not only used his company's data for the voting chapter he wrote with Richard Jenkins but provided the data for other chapters as well.

We especially thank Micaal Ahmed, our research and editorial assistant, who assembled the volume with a discerning eye and without whom the editors would still be chasing lost files and correcting the wrong proofs.

Jon H. Pammett and Christopher Dornan
Ottawa, December 2025

THE CANADIAN FEDERAL ELECTION OF 2025

1

Reversal of Fortune

Christopher Dornan

It was as certain as anything ever is in politics. Power was coming to Pierre Poilievre and the Conservative Party of Canada. The polls said it, the pundits said it, and for more than a year before the election it was what the country believed. The governing Liberals were a spent force led by a charismatic prime minister whose charisma had worn off. The Conservatives would sweep to a majority, the government of Canada would take a sharp ideological turn, and in a Commons of 343 members the Liberals would be reduced to forty seats, perhaps thirty, as they had been in the 2011 election. After a decade in opposition, the right wing of Canadian federal politics was irreversibly ascendant.

That did not happen. And the space of time over which it did not happen was remarkably short. On 9 January 2025, three days after Prime Minister Justin Trudeau announced he was stepping down, Abacus Data reported that the Conservative lead over the Liberals had increased to its largest margin, at twenty-seven points. Of committed voters, 47 per cent would vote Conservative while only 20 per cent would vote Liberal.[1] Fourteen weeks later, as the election drew to a close, all the major pollsters were anticipating a Liberal majority government.[2] But that, too, did not happen.

On election night, the TV anchors and their panels of analysts went to bed not knowing exactly how many seats each party had won or whether the Liberals would be able to form a majority. The number of seats needed to do so was 172. In the small hours of the morning, the Liberal total stalled at 168, flickered higher, and then dropped back down. There were multiple ridings in which the vote was so close the TV networks declared them back and forth for one party or another as different polling stations reported.

In the end, in the largest voter turnout in thirty-two years, the Conservatives won 41.3 per cent of the vote and the Liberals 43.7 per cent – more than either party had received in the 2021 election. Between them, the two parties accounted for more than 85 per cent of total votes cast. After all the validation procedures[3] and official recounts, the result was that the Liberals won 169 seats, seventeen more than they had won in 2021 but three shy of a majority, while the Conservatives won 144, a gain of twenty-four over their 2021 results, but their leader lost his own riding.

Before the election, the Liberals were a minority government on their way out. Afterward, for all their gains in seats and the popular vote, they remained in the outcome a minority government. The Conservatives went into the election not just as the official opposition but as the government-in-waiting, yet for all their gains in seats and the popular vote they ended up still in opposition, still waiting. Even the diminished other parties, for all their losses in seats and the popular vote, came out of the election as they went in, as the balance of power. Had the Liberals won 172 seats, the other parties – NDP, the Bloc Québécois, the Greens – would not have to be factored into the governing strategy. But there is an arithmetic to a minority government.

The Liberals won 169 seats, but one of their MPs became Speaker of the House, leaving them in command of 168 votes on the floor of the Commons. The NDP lost seventeen seats, including the leader's, along with their official party status and its substantial parliamentary resources and financial support, leaving them with seven votes in the House.[4] The Bloc lost eleven seats, leaving them with twenty-two. The Greens held one seat and lost one. So, the election produced a parliament that can only stay a parliament as long as the governing Liberals can carry the confidence of either the NDP (168 + 7 = majority) or the BQ (168 + 22 = majority). But if both the Bloc and the NDP were to vote with the Conservatives (144 + 22 + 7 = 173), the government would fall.[5] An election that produces a minority government leads in the long run to political bartering and brinksmanship.

The ready explanation of the 2025 election is that there were three determining factors from which everything else flowed. First, Trudeau announced his resignation (6 January). Second, Donald Trump, who had won the 2024 US election the previous November, officially became president for the second time (20 January), began his tariff war with the world, and voiced his imperialist fantasies of Anschlussing Canada by beggaring the country into submission. Third, Mark Carney won the leadership of the Liberal Party of Canada, became prime minister (9 March), and two weeks later called the election. The ready explanation is that Poilievre's Conservatives were elbowed aside by history, denied power because circumstances overtook them.

Not necessarily. These were all crucial developments that shaped the course of the election, but there was nothing in any of them that made the outcome inevitable. The reality is more complicated, more interesting, and more telling, as the contributors to this volume make clear.

This was not an election decided by policy platforms, or even a sharp choice between left and right. Those things mattered and they influenced voting intention, but only broadly, not narrowly or specifically. Voters did not make up their minds by weighing the policy platforms of the parties against one another. (This tax cut versus that tax cut? This spending promise versus this promise to slash spending?) Instead, the decisions of the 19.8 million people who cast a vote, argue David Coletto and Richard Jenkins in chapter 12, were made on the basis of valence politics, "the idea that elections turn on judgments of competence, leadership, and broadly shared goals rather than what parties stand for." And in the main these decisions were taken in light of Trump's aggressions toward Canada and the spectacle of how he was transforming the United States, the country with which Canada shares the world's longest undefended border.

THE DEMAGOGUE NEXT DOOR

Foreign affairs and foreign policy almost never figure as ballot questions in Canadian elections. But nor has any nation posed an external, perhaps existential, threat to Canadian prosperity and sovereignty since the Second World War or the Cold War, and even then, Nazi Germany and the Soviet Union were half a world away. As Lori Turnbull points out in chapter 9, the messy machinery of democratic politics (party membership drives, nomination procedures, opponents slinging mud at one another) and the tools made available by the twenty-first century social media provide opportunities for malicious foreign actors to try to tip the outcome, undermine the legitimacy of the vote, or just roil things up. But those malign foreign actors – China, India, Russia – try to do so stealthily, so as not to betray their hand, and they are still half a world away. The real foreign influence on the course of the election was conducted in full view at the top of its lungs and from the ally right next door. The calls were coming from inside the hemisphere.

It is difficult to make sense of Trump's tariffs on international trade, since they are nonsensical, especially as he appears unshakeably convinced that his tariffs are paid by the companies or countries exporting goods to the United States, rather than the American companies importing them. In the bold thinking of Trumpism, tariffs are both a revenue stream for America and punitive to other countries. All this squabbling over tariffs and counter-tariffs would disappear overnight if Canada just dropped its border and signed over its territory to the United States. Trump has had it in his head for quite some time that this could be his crowning achievement, his mark on history – a real estate deal of epic proportions.

Trump broached the idea in a meeting at Mar-a-Lago with Prime Minister Justin Trudeau and a small Canadian contingent on 29 November 2024, nine days after he had been re-elected president. He confirmed he would be imposing 25 per cent tariffs on Canada but said there would be no tariffs if Canada were part of the US. No border, no levies. Dominic LeBlanc, then minister of public safety who had been present at the meeting, laughed nervously on behalf of Canada when he insisted to the media that the president was only teasing.[6] Trump made clear he was not. Four days later he posted to his Truth Social and Instagram accounts an AI generated image of himself standing at the summit of a mountain (incongruously in a business suit) looking out over a range of snow-capped peaks receding into the distance (one of which was incongruously the Matterhorn), as an enormous Canadian flag streamed beside him in the wind. It did not take long for LeBlanc's diplomatic nervous laughter to harden into a nation's rather angry resolve.

The resolve got a rallying cry and a hashtag on 1 March, three weeks before the election was called, when comedian and national treasure Mike Myers appeared on the US comedy program *Saturday Night Live*, playing Elon Musk. At the closing credits, when the cast assembled onstage, Myers revealed a T-shirt reading "Canada Is Not for Sale," flexed his elbow at the camera, pointed to it, and mouthed "Elbows up!" He made the same #elbowsup! gesture the following week.

It is a hockey phrase, dating back to Gordie Howe, Mr Hockey from half a century ago, who was seemingly a gentleman but if you crossed him on the ice, he met you in the corner and his elbow came up. You got your jaw rattled and the ref saw nothing. Most of Canada – it is, after all, a country of immigrants and new arrivals – was not immediately familiar with the term, but by the following week, when Myers did it again, Canadian popular culture had enthusiastically embraced the idea of responding to Trump with sharp elbows. Peace by Chocolate, the company created in Halifax in 2016 by immigrants from war-scarred Syria, rolled out a flavour called Elbows Up. The day before the election was called, the Liberals released a campaign video of Carney and Myers in hockey jerseys talking about Canada while leaning on the boards at a rink.

This was in contrast to another national treasure, Wayne Gretzky, the greatest hockey player in the history of the NHL, who almost overnight fell out of national favour for reasons he could not understand but were obvious to everyone else. He was a friend of Trump's. Gretzky had prominently endorsed Stephen Harper in the final days of the losing Conservative campaign of 2015, and that might have irritated progressives, but it did not make him a pariah. Trump, though, offered him up as the governor of a future fifty-first state of Canada, posting to the world just before Christmas 2024 that he'd had dinner with Gretzky at Mar-a-Lago.

"I said, 'Wayne, why don't you run for prime minister of Canada, soon to be known as the governor of Canada – you would win easily, you wouldn't even have to campaign.' He had no interest." Gretzky may have had no interest but neither did he do anything to speak out against the very idea that Canada should be absorbed into the US. By February, Trump felt compelled to come to Gretzky's defence. "Wayne is my friend, and he wants to make me happy, and is therefore somewhat 'low key' about Canada remaining a separate Country, rather than becoming a cherished and beautiful 51st State, paying much Lower Taxes, a Free and Powerful Military, NO TARIFFS, and having a Booming Economy," Trump posted to Truth Social.[7]

Curiously, although the election churned with reaction to Trump's repeated goading, Trump barely mentioned Canada once the election was underway. He railed against Canada throughout March, complaining about the weak border that he falsely claimed allowed fentanyl and dangerous aliens to flood into the US and about Ontario's threat to impose a surcharge on electricity sold to the US. But the last time before the election that he openly referred to Canada's annexation was on 26 February, when he came to Gretzky's defence, and the last time he referred to the Canadian prime minister as "governor" was on 5 March. Carney became prime minister four days later.

On 27 March, four days into the election, Trump threatened even more trade-inhibiting tariffs against the European Union and Canada if they conspired between them to do "economic harm to the USA," but the next day, in an uncharacteristically respectful post, he said he had spoken with Carney, referring to him as "Prime Minister Carney," said they agreed on many things, and seemed to assume Carney would win the election, as they would "be meeting immediately after Canada's upcoming Election." Other than that, Trump kept his mouth shut about Canada over the course of the campaign, and the longer he did so the more Conservative prospects improved. With only three seats making the difference, Trump may have prevented a Liberal majority by not raging against one. In the end, of course, he could not contain himself, and on the day of the election he urged Canadians to vote for him and for joining the United States, as though he was their leader.

LEADERSHIP MATTERS

In chapter 8, Jonathan Malloy explores why leadership – or at least the projection and perception of the leader's persona – has come to be so important in the machine politics of democracy, and why in this election it was especially a category in play.

Pierre Poilievre won the leadership of his party handily in 2022. A career politician first elected to the House in 2004 at the age of twenty-five, he was an attack dog whose time had come round at last. The party machine and the enthusiasm of its base were now his. He was in charge of their anger – though, as Faron Ellis points out in chapter 3, he was deliberate in ensuring he was not indebted to the social conservative wing of the party, an anger he wanted nothing to do with. Hence the importance of his overwhelming victory on the first ballot. He neither courted nor needed the support of the social extremists and all their liabilities.

His national campaign to win the next election began immediately, and he waged it for the next two-and-a-half years. He travelled the country. He inspired and motivated large, enthusiastic crowds. He said he was "running to be prime minister." He made YouTube videos that were both admired and mocked but found viewers. Short on specific policy proposals but fierce with determination, what Poilievre stood for was a hostility toward an infrastructure of institutions and regulations Conservatives see as intrusive, wasteful, and rigged against them, and that they would eliminate or reconfigure upon taking power. Poilievre pledged to do away with English language CBC and was openly contemptuous of the news media. He thought judges were too lenient. He said he would fire the governor of the Bank of Canada. What he and his people were so angry about was the establishment, the Laurentian elite, a power structure they vowed to dismantle.

Carney was the embodiment of all that. You could not get a more establishment man if you built him in a laboratory. Harvard and Oxford educated, he had worked in private sector banking at Goldman Sachs, been governor of the Bank of Canada, and governor of the Bank of England. He sold himself as a crisis manager of the highest echelon, having steered the Bank of Canada through the financial crisis of 2008 and the Bank of England through Brexit in 2020. Which was all very impressive, said the media commentators, but he never had to win an election. How was Mr Bank Man going to perform ringing doorbells, charming grandmas, and handling angry voters who wanted to give him a piece of their mind? Carney had no experience in partisan politics, while Poilievre had no experience that wasn't partisan politics.

All political ambition is a form of hubris, and there is no greater hubris than scheming to occupy the top political office, to run the government of a nation. Poilievre could at least tell himself that his ambition to be prime minister was grounded in reality because a plurality of the country approved. All the polls confirmed it. But what could Carney tell himself as he contemplated pursuing the leadership of this party Canadians so plainly wanted out of power? Especially since the Liberal Party has a history of betting poorly on brainy outsiders to rescue them from defeat. Stéphane Dion and Michael Ignatieff both led the Liberals into elections against the Conservatives, and both left nothing behind but their bleached bones. In chapter 2, Brooke Jeffrey charts Carney's course to the party leadership and electoral victory, but one might pause to consider why he entertained the idea at all, when everyone else was certain the Conservatives were going to win in a landslide.

Everyone except those in some offline, backroom, high-oxygen Liberal Party discussion chambers, where the candidacy of Mark Carney was engineered and his electoral triumph imagined, if not foreseen. Conversations about a possible role Carney might play in the Liberal Party and a Liberal government had been going on behind closed doors for some time, but crucially Carney never joined the Trudeau government, which allowed him to present himself to the electorate as not-Trudeau, even as he took control of Trudeau's caucus, Trudeau's cabinet ministers, and the infrastructural machinery of the Liberal Party – everything except the circle of Trudeau's closest PMO staff. Almost nothing about the party changed, except for the leader. The takeover was so swift and complete it suggested Carney was not recruited by the Liberals so much as he recruited them. The Liberal Party was a political machine in search of a leader. Carney was a leader who needed a machine.

Still, one wonders at the initial calculation made by Carney and the top party insiders who negotiated his entry into the Liberal leadership race. Clearly, the expectation was that he would win the party leadership as decisively as Poilievre had won his. But beyond that, what? In early January, besieged by the polls, were they genuinely confident that Carney as leader would deliver them the party's fourth plurality in a row? Or was the calculation more ruthless? If the Liberals under Carney were routed in the federal election, well, they were going to be routed anyway, so no great loss except the rebuke to Carney's ego, and the party could set about looking for another leader. If they lost, but still held around a hundred seats, this could be credited to Carney, and the party could rebuild under his leadership. And if they managed to defeat Poilievre's Conservatives, that would be a triumph beyond anyone's expectations attributable entirely to Carney and a campaign apparatus ready to capitalize on the opportunity they were given.

CAMPAIGNS MATTER

In an election in which the Liberals were three seats short of a majority, there were four official recounts. The margin between minority and majority government was exceedingly slim. There were numerous ridings that were likely decided by which party turned out their vote more efficiently. Results might have tipped in different ways if people who didn't vote had voted. Campaigns matter.

But even a superb party machine can labour against electoral headwinds. The after-ballot question for the Conservatives was why so many people decided that Carney was the one to deal with Trump rather than Poilievre. In chapter 3, Faron Ellis considers how the Conservative Party processed their loss. How did they explain to themselves what happened to their 25 per cent lead in the polls?

After all, Trump was elected in November 2024, but this did not noticeably alter the nation's assessment of the Liberal government, whose support and popularity continued to decline the longer Trudeau insisted he intended to stay on as PM and fight the next election. If Poilievre's politics (tough on crime, sceptical about immigrants, big on cops, hates taxes, detests government bureaucracy, etc.) aligned with Trump's, this did not damage Poilievre's prospects of forming a government, not at first.

Going into the election, the primary concern of a plurality of the electorate was affordability. Rents and house prices were going up, the cost of groceries kept rising, inflation was a persistent worry. Month-to-month income was being eaten away. And of those who just wanted things to be more affordable, the Conservatives were the favoured party. Even after Trump started in with his tariffs and his annexation trash talk, for a third of Canadians the cost of living was still their number one issue, as against 21 per cent who saw Trump as the foremost priority.[8] So, why did Trump's threats drive a Liberal Party resurgence?

Trump's tariff war was a direct assault on Canadian industry, and therefore on Canadian prosperity. It was an economic issue, which was a Conservative Party strength. Rightly or wrongly, most Canadians judged the Conservatives to be better stewards of the country's treasury. And for all that the Liberals and the other parties attempted to portray him as Trump-adjacent, Poilievre, unlike Gretzky, was no friend of Trump's. In fact, Trump had gone out of his way to disparage the Conservative leader, telling the British magazine The Spectator in late February that Poilievre's "biggest problem is he's not a MAGA guy ... I don't like what he's saying about me. It's just not positive about me."[9] Four days before the election was called, Trump suggested to Laura Ingraham of Fox News that he would rather have a Liberal government in Canada because "it's easier to deal ... with a Liberal," and reiterated that "the Conservative that's running is stupidly no friend of mine. I don't know him, but he said negative things."[10]

If what Canadians wanted was a combative leader to stand up to Trump, Poilievre came already equipped with an elbows-up personality. He was aggressive, abrasive, confrontational – so much so that as the prospect of an election loomed (but before Trump began his annexation talk), Ellis points out that his handlers attempted to soften his image, to make him more palatable to voters beyond the nucleus of Conservative Party supporters who wanted a leader as angry as they were.

Still, among those voters who had given the Conservatives their twenty-five-point lead in the polls, it was the technocratic Carney who was seen as best qualified to deal with Trump. The Conservatives conducted their campaign hammering away at issues of affordability but never managed to effectively link those pocketbook concerns to the macro-economic threats posed to Canadian industry by Trump's bullying. Could their campaign have been conducted differently? Some in the conservative movement certainly thought so. Kory Teneycke, Ontario premier Doug Ford's campaign manager, had been arguing since before the election that the Poilievre team had not adjusted their strategy to account for Trump. By the middle of the campaign, on one of his regular appearances on the Curse of Politics podcast, Teneycke exploded, accusing the federal Conservatives of "[expletive] campaign malpractice at the highest [expletive] level."[11]

Poilievre, meanwhile, was waging two campaigns simultaneously. There was the national campaign, jetting back and forth across the country to fire up rallies of supporters, but there was also the local campaign for his own riding of Carleton, an outer belt of Ottawa against which the riding of Nepean nestles, where Carney was running to win a seat in the House for the first time. Back when all the polls proclaimed a Poilievre victory, there were two people who believed he could be beaten. One was Mark Carney. The other was a retired marketing executive named Bruce Fanjoy who, like Carney, had never before run for political office.

Poilievre began his national campaign two and a half years before the election was called. Fanjoy, the Liberal candidate in Poilievre's riding, was not far behind, ringing his first doorbell two years before the vote. One of the most remarkable things about the 2025 election is that Fanjoy, a political unknown, defeated one of the most recognizable figures in the country, the man at the head of a political machine whose purpose is to win elections.

Political leadership in a parliamentary democracy starts with the doorbell. In Canada, no matter how many seats a party wins, if the party leader is not first-past-the-post in their own riding, they have no seat in the House.

The riding that Carney won and the riding that Poilievre lost may be neighbours, but they are very different. They have roughly the same number of eligible voters. Nepean, the riding Carney won, had 93,244; Carleton, Poilievre's home riding, had 105,881. But Nepean is a riding of suburban tracts, while Carleton is mostly farmland. Nepean is 86 square kilometres in area; Carleton is more than twenty times that, at 2,000 square kilometres. In Nepean, the population density per square kilometre is 1,428 people. In Carleton, it is 62.6. Knocking on doors is very different in a riding where the doors are so far apart. Fanjoy estimates he rang fifteen thousand doorbells. In the end, this was not one of the ridings where a recount was required. The margin of defeat was unambiguous. Poilievre lost to Fanjoy by more than 4,500 votes.

It was a serious embarrassment for Poilievre to lose a seat he had held for twenty years. He did not campaign in the riding much during the election, but neither did Carney in the riding next door. They both had national campaigns to run. It may have been a rebuke to his ego for Poilievre to lose his seat, but more than that it complicated his position within his party and threw his leadership off kilter. He had not delivered the victory the party had been expecting. He would remain as party leader at least until a mandatory leadership review in January 2026, but he could not serve as leader of the official opposition as he had no parliamentary standing, so the party named Andrew Scheer, a former leader, to that position in the interim. Though he was required to close his constituency and Parliament Hill offices, Poilievre continued to reside at public expense in Stornoway, the official residence of the leader of the official opposition; according to the Privy Council Office it was up to the Conservative Party to decide who should occupy the residence. And immediately following the election, when ideally Poilievre should have been visible in Ottawa, focused on Carney's government and Trump's posturing, for the next three months much of his time was spent campaigning to win a seat in the Commons in a byelection in the Alberta riding of Battle River-Crowfoot, a safe Conservative constituency that covers almost 52,000 square kilometres, where the doorbells are even further apart than in his former riding.

ELECTORAL INTEGRITY

An electoral system is a living thing, forever subject to change and adjustment. Voting districts get redrawn, new constituencies are added and others removed to reflect population growth, shift, or decline, in an ongoing attempt to ensure that the expression of the vote is an accurate and fair reflection of the popular will. Poilievre's loss of his own seat immediately prompted online suspicion that the system had been rigged against him. The boundaries of the riding had been redrawn in 2022. Perhaps this had been done to change its character, to include more urban and immigrant voters in order to disfavour Poilievre? No, it had not. The reconfiguration of the riding made it more rural, not less,[12] but the persistence of rumours that Poilievre's defeat was somehow illegitimate prompted the Canadian Press to issue a fact-check report debunking the claims that the redrawn boundaries of the riding made Poilievre's defeat inevitable, though this hardly quashed the online conspiracy theorists.[13]

It is not enough for democracies to hold free elections. It is essential that the electorate has confidence in the outcome, otherwise elections are not moments of political legitimation but occasions for legitimation crises. Every government elected is an artifact of the system by which it was elected, but among all the things essential to a politically stable free society, the first is that all votes are counted scrupulously. The second is that the outcome of the tally, whatever the imperfections of the system, is accepted by the people as broadly representative of their political will. These two together amount to a promise made to the polity that every vote counts.

When a national election comes down to a handful of local contests that mean the difference between majority or minority government – between a government with near absolute authority and one that must somehow broker the support of rival parties – then the system that produces the outcome is surely a factor in the outcome. If three seats could make all the difference, to what extent was that because of the first-past-the-post system? Would the result have been different under a ranked ballot system, or proportional representation? If so, how different? Would it have been different had the boundaries of certain ridings been drawn along different lines? In chapter 7, Louis Massicotte explains the electoral system we have, how its legislative framework has evolved over forty years, and how it gives expression to Canadian democracy.

Elections Canada is the independent crown agency charged with the integrity of the ballot process, administering, tabulating, and reporting the vote. It has a superb reputation and is a model to the world. But out of 19.8 million votes cast, Elections Canada managed to misplace one, in a riding where the result turned on a single vote.

Terrebonne is an electoral district on the north side of the river from Montreal. It was one of those ridings that got counted, counted again, and then recounted. At first, the Liberal was ahead by thirty-five votes. After the validation procedure, the Bloc candidate led by forty-four votes. This triggered an automatic judicial recount, which ruled that the Liberal had won by a single vote. Until a Bloc voter reported that her mail-in ballot had been returned to her, unopened and therefore uncounted. Elections Canada admitted this was their fault – an error in the postal code on the envelope – but said election law prohibited them from counting the vote after the fact.[14] The Bloc launched a court action to contest this, but the case would not be considered until months after the election.[15] Though a serious embarrassment for Elections Canada, the incident only proved the agency's integrity. It is an organization that can account for every single vote cast in a riding, right down to the ones it mislaid. It is honest and open about its mistakes.

Nonetheless, Masicotte reports that a disconcerting proportion of the electorate lacks confidence in the legitimacy of the outcome. A Leger poll found that less than 65 per cent of voters trusted that the election results were accurate, while 13 per cent said they did not trust the results at all. Trust varied sharply according to party affiliation. Some 96 per cent of Liberal voters had confidence in the results, but only 44 per cent of Conservatives. It is not clear how many of those who distrust the outcome do so because they believe votes are not accurately recorded or counted (i.e. the fault lies with Elections Canada), or whether the system itself is skewed to produce results that are not a true register of the country's political will, or whether they simply disavow any result that does not align with their preferred outcome.

THE POLLS, THE NEWS MEDIA, THE OTHER PARTIES

In late 2024, preparing themselves for a 2025 election, all the opposition parties gamed out their strategies based on the expected collapse of the Liberal vote. Jagmeet Singh, leader of the NDP, presented himself as the alternative to Poilievre, a credible candidate to form a government. He, like Poilievre, said he was running to be prime minister. Yves-François Blanchet, the Bloc leader, spoke openly of how his party would conduct itself as the official opposition. The Greens hoped to pick up seats in a wave of anti-Poilievre votes. The NDP, the Bloc, and the Greens all counted on harvesting the votes of people abandoning the Liberals but looking to vote against the Poilievre Conservatives. How many seats this might have yielded each of them in a first-past-the-post system when one party is storming to a majority is impossible to say, but certainly they would have received a greater share of the popular vote.

When Liberal support did not collapse – when, on the contrary, it surged with support drawn from the NDP, the Bloc, and the Greens – each of the smaller parties was forced to recalibrate its hopes and tactics. Singh dropped his talk of running for prime minister and Blanchet no longer mentioned becoming leader of the official opposition. In chapter 6, Gala Palavinci examines the Green campaign, along with the range of other smaller parties that make up the electoral tapestry of Canadian democracy. In chapter 4, Daniel Westlake and Jacob Robbins-Kantor suggest that the very ambition of the NDP proved costly, when the party was too slow to redirect resources to defending seats it already held, rather than hoping to take ridings from the Liberals. In chapter 5, Eric Montigny and Katryne Villeneuve-Siconelly note how Trump's talk of annexation caused the Bloc – and indeed Quebec voters en masse – to take cover behind a "Canadian shield." Absorption into the notoriously ethnocentric and xenophobic United States, particularly a Trumpist authoritarian US of far-right extremism and lawlessness, would be a far greater threat to Quebec culture and self-determination than anything posed by the province's complicated political entanglement with English Canada.

This rather begs the question of what might have happened had Trump spoken of annexing only English Canada. What if he had promised Quebec that it would be allowed to exist as a French-speaking nation at the top of North America, just as Mexico is a Spanish-speaking nation at the bottom of North America? If Trump had offered Quebec its independence, albeit as an enclave surrounded by a greater United States, how would the parties have reacted? How would Quebec voters have responded? It would certainly have complicated Canada's response to Trump and sowed the sort of chaos in which Trump revels.

With the Liberals and the Conservatives between them accounting for 85 per cent of the vote, there was some talk among media commentators about Canada inching toward a two-party system, but this is unlikely. Certainly, the 2025 election became an almost two-party race, but Canada can never have a two-party system in the manner of the US if only because of Quebec. As long as there is a Canada that includes Quebec, the province will complicate confederation with a strain of politics that will not be absorbed into a brute binary choice, especially since, as chapter 5 points out, the Bloc are not in lockstep with the provincial Parti Québécois by any measure, and neither are in any alliance with the Coalition Avenir Québec. Canadian federal politics without the Bloc, or a party to give voice to Quebec nationalism, unaffiliated with the federalist Liberals or Conservatives, is now as implausible as a Canada without the NDP, or an equivalent party in the tradition of Canadian politics that gave us Medicare.

In chapter 10, Brett Popplewell, Adrian Harewood, and Patrick White trace like a seismograph how the election was presented to the public by and through the news media, along with the ways in which the attentions and emphases of the media in English Canada differed from those in Quebec. For all that they claim to be objective, news journalism organizations are invariably politically inflected. No one needs a media literacy course to see the difference between the perspectives of the right-leaning *National Post* and the environmentally conscious Narwhal. And as the traditional news media have lost their revenue base, they have turned increasingly to political commentary over political reporting (opinion is cheaper to produce than chasing down sources and cross-checking facts), and much of this commentary is exhortatory rather than analytical, an instrument of one political stripe or another. One of the noteworthy incidents in the election occurred during the leaders' debates, in what amounted to a dispute within the media over who was a legitimate journalist and who was not.

The new media environment has given rise to a number of far-right media outlets, including Rebel News, True North, and Juno, that adopt the trappings of news journalism but are really provocateurs in the service of their ideologies. (There are also forthrightly left-wing media outlets, such as rabble.ca, the Tyee, and Ricochet, but these adhere to a discipline of responsibility in their coverage. They provide reliable reporting whatever their political bent, they do not invent content for political ends.) Because they are opinion mongers and agitators, not news providers, Rebel News, True North and Juno are not considered journalism organizations by the Canada Revenue Agency and so are not eligible for tax measures designed to support the Canadian news media.[16] When Rebel News and True North were curtly denied press accreditation to pose questions to the party leaders following the leaders' debates in 2019 and 2021, they sought redress in the courts, which found the rationale provided by the Leaders' Debates Commission to be unpersuasive, as other outlets, such as the *Toronto Star*, also engage in political advocacy but had been accredited.[17]

By the 2025 election Rebel News and its confederates argued they should each be accredited more than one journalist, just as the *Toronto Star* had an accredited photographer and a journalist who typed on a keyboard. The Leaders' Debate Commission, figuring there was no point in spending more public money to fight this in court only to give the alt-right more publicity, threw up its hands and conceded. The result was that at the first debate there was a contingent of alt-right true believers and agitators in the press room who cannily stacked the queues to the microphones (one for English, one for French) and dominated the post-debate questioning of the party leaders. Known for their stunts designed to cause maximum political discomfit and wrest the attention of the legacy news media, by the ambitions of the alt-right media this was a triumph. They had discredited the Leaders' Debate Commission, shoved aside the so-called legitimate news media, and made a spectacle of themselves.

The next night, at the second debate, the alt-right crowd were gunned up and the legitimate news media had had enough. Ezra Levant, founder of Rebel News, tried to barge his way into a CBC live broadcast. In the press room, there were heated exchanges between the alt-right and the legitimate media. Things got to the point that it would have been irresponsible to send the party leaders into a room of people angrily yelling at one another about who was a journalist and who was not. The debate commission scrubbed the post-debate press scrum, and in doing so probably conceded that trying to draw a distinction between legitimate and illegitimate political journalism is a lost cause.

The polling companies also have their political colourations – like the news media, they interpret the findings in different ways – but at least the polling companies have a standard against which they can measure their reputations. Any polling company that gets things wrong discredits itself. There were more publicly published polls over the course of the 2025 campaign than in any previous election, and probably more conducted privately for the parties than in any election. As Christopher Adams points out in chapter 11, new tech. and new ways of assembling representative samples have lowered the cost of public opinion polling, meaning more players in the market. Meanwhile, steady updates of poll results are irresistible to the news media. Reporting on poll results is easy content, and to some extent replaces actual reporting.

The thing about polling – and journalism for that matter – is that it can be right in the moment but wrong in the outcome. Were the polls wrong in December 2024 when they said Poilievre was all but certain to become prime minister? No, that is what people believed at the time. But then they changed their minds.

At a Poilievre rally in Brampton mid-campaign, some supporters showed up wearing hoodies reading "Do you believe the polls?" This was quickly, and oddly, seized upon by the media as a foreboding indication that the Conservatives were prepared to disbelieve the outcome of the election if they lost, as though scepticism about what the polling industry might be saying any given week equated to a refusal to accept the results of the vote.[18] The party immediately disavowed the hoodie-wearers and declared its confidence in the veracity of the pollsters.[19] Chapter 11 details how remarkably accurate the polling companies and the aggregators were in predicting how many people would vote for each party, but how every single one of them still got the big question wrong. All the pollsters anticipated a majority government. The hoodie people[20] just could not believe that would happen, and they were right.

GOVERNMENTS TO COME

The 2025 election produced the third minority government in a row. In chapter 13, Jon Pammett and Lawrence LeDuc spell out why this, rather than a majority, is the increasingly likely outcome of Canadian elections. Minority governments are frustrating for the party in power, which is one of the things to their credit. And they are not unpopular with the public. They provide a version of what the advocates of ranked ballots and proportional representation want: a voice for minority interests in the formation of government policy and decisions.

The Liberal government of Mark Carney, having come to power on a surge of votes from people who would otherwise have supported the NDP, the Bloc, and the Greens, and which even then only managed to win a minority government, is surely poorly positioned to win a majority in the next election. Too many of those NDP, Bloc, and Green votes are only on loan. They will drift back as Carney disappoints them.

Although Poilievre articulated few specific policies, the thrust and attitude of what a Poilievre government would look like was clear. That was not true for Carney, who carried himself as a free-floating Liberal, perhaps more in favour of large-scale infrastructure building projects than the previous prime minister, who leaned toward spending on social programs such as day care, dental care, and pharmacare. A vote for Poilievre was a vote for a clearly defined political intention and direction. A vote for Carney was for something less so, something more vague.

On the way to power, Carney vowed to cancel the consumer carbon tax ("Axe the Tax" had been a Conservative Party priority) and deliver middle class tax cuts (another Conservative priority). Once in power, he committed to a massive increase in defence spending (a Conservative priority) and to slashing the size of the federal government (a Conservative priority). Poilievre wanted to defund the CBC. Carney instructed the CBC to find ways to defund itself.

In heated circumstances this complex political contraption called Canada managed to elect a conservative Liberal government.

NOTES

1 David Coletto, "Abacus Data Poll: Post-Trudeau Resignation, Conservative Lead Grows To 27. Freeland And Carney Well Ahead of Others on Recognizability, Familiarity, and Net Favourable Impression," Abacus Data, 9 January 2025, https://abacusdata.ca/canadian-politics-abacus-datapost-trudeau-resignation/.

2 See Christopher Adams's chapter 11 in this volume.

3 An account of how Elections Canada tabulates and validates elections results can be found here: "Results, Validation, Recounts, and Contested Elections: What Happens After Voting in a Federal Election," *Elections Canada*, 14 August 2024, https://www.elections.ca/content.aspx?section=vot&dir=bkg&document=ec90565&lang=e.

4 A party must hold at least twelve seats to maintain official party status. A quick accounting of the financial and other benefits that come from official party status is provided here: Chris Knight, "What Does It Mean for the NDP to Lose Official Party Status in Parliament?" *National Post*, 29 April 2025, https://nationalpost.com/news/politics/federal_election/what-does-it-mean-for-thendp-to-lose-official-party-status-in-parliament.

5 Although Canadian MPs are subject to amongst the most stringent party discipline in any parliament in the free world, such numbers are not set in stone. MPs can abstain or switch parties, both of which happened when the first Carney Liberal budget came to a confidence vote on 17 November 2025. The Conservatives and the Bloc both voted against it, but the budget bill passed 170 to 168 because Nova Scotia MP Chris d'Entremont, elected as a Conservative, crossed the floor to the Liberals, two NDP MPs tactically abstained, as did two Conservative MPs, while Green Party leader Elizabeth May voted with the government.

6 John Paul Tasker, "Trump's Quip About Canada Becoming 51st State Was a Joke, Says Minister Who Was There," CBC News, 3 December 2024, https://www.cbc.ca/news/politics/trudeaupoilievre-leader-briefing-mar-a-lago-1.7399534.

7 Michelle Butterfield, "Trump Defends Gretzky, Says 'The Great One' Wants Canada to Remain Canadian," Global News, 27 February 2025, https://globalnews.ca/news/11051987/donaldtrump-wayne-gretzky-51st-state/.

8 See David Coletto and Richard Jenkins's chapter 12 in this volume.

9 Kelly Geraldine Malone, "Trump Says Poilievre 'Not A MAGA Guy,' Calls Freeland a'Whack,'" Global News, 28 February 2025, https://globalnews.ca/news/11055372/donald-trumppierre-poilievre-chrystia-freeland-comments-tariff-threat/.

10 Stephanie Ha, "Trump Weighs in on Federal Election, Would 'Rather Deal With a Liberal Than a Conservative,'" CTV News, 19 March 2025, https://www.ctvnews.ca/politics/article/trump-sayshe-would-rather-deal-with-a-liberal-than-a-conservative-calls-poilievre-no-friend-of-mine/.

11 Curse of Politics, "Do You Believe the Polls?" *Air Quotes Media*, 10April2025,https://www.youtube.com/watch?v=KgznczbZv2I&list=PLiz4-vaadmZQ8xegyZKopD_Q6ocybrYhY&index=24.

12 The Wikipedia entry on this addresses, and debunks, complaints that the ridings had been redrawn to disadvantage Poilievre. Wikipedia contributors, "Carleton (Ontario Federal Electoral District)," *Wikipedia*, 13 July 2025, https://en.wikipedia.org/wiki/Carleton_(Ontario_federal_electoral_district).

13 Marissa Birnie, "A Look At Misleading Claims About Poilievre's Riding After His Election Loss," *The Canadian Press*, 2 May 2025, https://www.thecanadianpressnews.ca/fact_checking/a-lookat-misleading-claims-about-poilievres-riding-after-his-election-loss/article_1b8a8dd0-e5b3-5d26-8e65-58ae095292ba.html.

14 Catherine Morrison, "Vote in Terrebonne Riding Is Final Despite Uncounted Mail-In Ballot That Would Make It a Tie, Elections Canada Says," *National Post*, 14 May 2025, https://nationalpost.com/news/canada/vote-in-terrebonne-riding-is-final-despite-uncounted-mailin-ballot-that-would-make-it-a-tie-elections-canada-says.

15 On 13 February 2026, the Supreme Court of Canada annulled the result of the election in Terrebonne, forcing a byelection in the riding.

16 Maura Forrest, "Rebel News Not Eligible for Journalism Tax Credits, Federal Court Rules," CBC News, 19 September 2024, https://www.cbc.ca/news/politics/rebel-news-federal-court-1.7328047.

17 *Lawton v. Canada* (Leaders' Debates Commission), 2019 FC 1424 (CanLII), https://canlii.ca/t/j3c37.

18 Olivia Stefanovich, "Some Conservative Supporters Question Whether the Polls Can Be Trusted," CBC News, 10 April 2025, https://www.cbc.ca/news/politics/do-you-believe-the-pollspoilievre-supporters-ask-1.7507437.

19 Laura Stone, "Conservative Party Distances Itself from Supporters Questioning Election Polls," *Globe and Mail*, 11 April 2025, https://www.theglobeandmail.com/politics/federalelection/article-conservative-party-distances-itself-from-supporters-questioning/.

20 Katherine Declerq and Jessica Smith Cross, "Mississauga Group Claims Credit for Those 'Do You Believe The Polls' Hoodies," *Trillium*, 10 April 2025, https://www.thetrillium.ca/news/politics/mississauga-group-behind-those-do-you-believe-thepolls-hoodies-10507271.

2

From Oblivion to Victory: The Stunning Liberal Turnaround

Brooke Jeffrey

Canadians delivered a rare fourth mandate to the Liberal Party in this election, a significant achievement in itself, and all the more remarkable because the party had faced the threat of electoral devastation only three months earlier. Instead, the Liberals increased both their seat count (from 160 to 169) and their share of the popular vote (from 32.6 to 43.7 per cent) from the 2021 election and came tantalizingly close to forming a majority government. Just 611 more votes in three ridings would have delivered three more seats to the Liberals, putting them at 172 seats or a majority. Moreover, this stunning result capped a federal election in which a host of unprecedented developments overturned almost all the conventional norms of electoral behaviour in Canada.

In almost all respects the 2025 Canadian federal election was the most extraordinary in living memory, far surpassing even the landmark elections of 1988 and 1993. To begin with it took place in the context of an economic war with the United States, triggered by newly elected president Donald Trump shortly after his inauguration in late January. In addition, it was launched immediately after the dramatic announcement by Prime Minister Justin Trudeau on 6 January that he intended to resign, and the extraordinary Liberal leadership race that followed. That race ended in early March with the selection of Mark Carney, a technocratic outsider with no political experience and no seat in the House of Commons. Despite this highly unusual resumé, Carney won the contest in an unprecedented landslide and quickly became Canada's forty-fifth prime minister. Then, after only nine days in office, the new prime minister called a federal election for 28 April, at five weeks the shortest possible campaign allowed by legislation.

As if these developments were not remarkable enough, professional pollsters had been at a loss to adequately describe the incredible roller coaster of public opinion they had been witnessing in the weeks leading up to the election call.[1] Only three months earlier the Liberals – whose political fortunes had been in a steep decline since the summer of 2023 – had sunk to a record low in popular support[2] and appeared almost certain to lose even the status of official opposition to the Bloc or NDP. At the same time the Poilievre Conservatives, which had maintained a twenty-point-plus lead over the Liberals for more than a year, were on track to obtain the largest majority in Canadian history.

The Liberals' dire electoral straits began to improve shortly after Trudeau's announcement.

By the time Carney was sworn in as prime minister on 14 March the Liberals were actually slightly ahead of the Conservatives in the polls. The Liberal surge continued and by 23 March the party was considered to have a solid chance of not merely winning the upcoming election but obtaining a majority. On that day the newly minted prime minister made a second trip to Rideau Hall, this time to request the governor general dissolve parliament and launch the election.

The party's dramatic reversal of fortune was all the more significant since both the NDP and the Conservatives had been calling for a federal election and had vowed to bring down the Liberals' minority government as soon as Parliament resumed from its prorogation on 24 March. Consequently, they could hardly complain that an election was now underway. Yet both parties appeared to be caught flat-footed by the fact that the election they had long desired would now be fought with a different Liberal leader, and on a far different election issue than either had expected. It is in this context that the results of the 2025 election must be seen.

PRELUDE TO THE ELECTION: THE DRAMATIC DECLINE IN LIBERAL SUPPORT AND THE CAUCUS REVOLT

The events leading to the collapse in Liberal support during 2024, and to the unprecedented hostility of many voters towards then prime minister Justin Trudeau personally, played a crucial role in the party's sudden change of leaders in January 2025 and to its eventual resurrection in the 2025 election.

After nine years in office virtually any government is likely to have reached its best before date. After nearly a decade in power, the Liberals had certainly had their share of perceived scandals and blunders, although they had also introduced a host of progressive social, environmental, and cultural policies that were widely supported. Perhaps most important, the Liberals had already been elected three times and faced an even greater challenge if they hoped to secure a rare fourth consecutive term of office.

Nevertheless, by the fall of 2024 the level of vitriol directed at the Liberals, and at the prime minister personally, was unprecedented.[3] Many observers pointed to the negative fallout from the global pandemic of 2020–23 for an explanation, even though the Liberal government was widely viewed as having managed the pandemic itself exceptionally well.[4] They noted that virtually every western economy was hit by many of the same supply chain issues, interest rate increases, housing and employment problems that plagued Canada as the world emerged from the pandemic. This global disruption deepened with the Russian invasion of Ukraine, further damaging national economies and creating uncertainty in international markets.

As a result, in 2024, a year in which most western liberal democracies were scheduled to hold elections, governing parties of all political stripes were blamed for forces largely beyond their control and suffered the consequences. The Trudeau Liberals, observers argued, could therefore be seen as just another casualty of this widespread discontent.

But while these external factors went some way towards explaining the party's steeply plummeting popularity, they did not account for the deeply personal and extreme resentment among a significant portion of the Canadian electorate. Instead, as historian and journalist Mark Bourrie, among others, has outlined in detail,[5] it was only after Pierre Poilievre became leader of the Conservative Party in September 2022 that dislike of the Trudeau government accelerated in such an uncharacteristic manner. This was exemplified by the Conservative leader's frequent references to the prime minister as a liar and a traitor[6] and his flagrant disdain for civil discourse in parliament, accentuated through his skillful use of social media and his party's financial wherewithal to conduct a permanent campaign.

Chief amongst Poilievre's policy targets for attack was the Liberals' carbon pricing plan, an initiative supported by environmentalists and economists alike. Yet within less than a year, Poilievre had managed to vilify the plan to such an extent that even environmentalists were concluding it was a lost cause. Similarly, the image of the Liberal prime minister had been so diminished by Conservative attacks that his approval rating tanked, the party lost several by-elections, ministers began resigning rather than stay on to fight another election, and some members of the Liberal caucus were in open revolt.

The final straw proved to be the government's handling of the economic update scheduled for 16 December 2024. On the morning of that day, Finance Minister Chrystia Freeland shocked Liberals, and the country, with a devastating resignation letter published on social media, accusing Trudeau of undermining her position and criticizing the proposals outlined in the statement. Chaos ensued. Trudeau hastily appointed new cabinet ministers and assigned his house leader, Karina Gould, to simply table the document in the House before adjournment for the Christmas break.

For the Liberals this was now a full-fledged crisis. Unlike the Conservatives, who had a long tradition of unceremoniously dispatching leaders from John Diefenbaker to Erin O'Toole, the Liberal Party had traditionally maintained an image of party unity and ensured smooth leadership transitions. Some transitions have been successful, such as from Lester Pearson to Pierre Trudeau, while others, such as from Pierre Trudeau to John Turner have been less successful, but all had been accomplished through a leader's voluntary resignation and a subsequent leadership race. It was only with the hostile internal takeover of the Jean Chrétien government by the Paul Martin Liberals in 2003 that party disunity became a public feature, and it cost the Liberals mightily in the 2006 election.[7] By their return to power in 2015 under Justin Trudeau, the lesson about the importance of party unity had become deeply ingrained. Trudeau himself had taken measures through amendments to the party constitution to ensure that no such debilitating internal putsch would re-occur. And so, despite the alleged turbulence inside the Liberal caucus[8] and Freeland's highly public act of rebellion, there was no formal mechanism available to replace the leader, and only a very small minority of Liberal MPs were willing to publicly call for Trudeau to step down.[9]

Over the holidays Liberals therefore waited anxiously to see what the prime minister would do, since he had given every indication that he intended to stay on as leader and fight the next election despite these developments. But on 6 January Trudeau called a press conference at which he announced he would indeed be resigning and asked the governor general to prorogue parliament until 24 March in order to facilitate a Liberal leadership race.

THE UNPRECEDENTED LIBERAL LEADERSHIP RACE

With Trudeau's announcement that he would be stepping down, the Liberal Party was obliged to organize a full-fledged leadership race in record time. After the party's executive met on 9 January, it announced that all candidates must indicate their interest by 23 January and pay a total of $350,000 in entrance fees in four installments. A maximum expenditure of $5 million per candidate was also set. To be nominated, a candidate must have collected three hundred signatures from registered Liberals, with at least one hundred each coming from three different provinces or territories. For some potential candidates these limitations were a bridge too far. There was quiet criticism of the high entrance fees and the short time to establish leadership teams. Karina Gould, who announced her intention to run despite the hurdles, went further and argued that the "aggressive fundraising limitations" had been set deliberately to exclude some candidates and limit the diversity of participants.[10]

Apart from these financial and technical limitations, the number of candidates in the race was also informally limited by American threats concerning tariffs and Canadian sovereignty. Due to this unexpected crisis, several prominent Trudeau cabinet ministers, including Mélanie Joly, François-Philippe Champagne, and Dominic LeBlanc, announced they would not be candidates because they believed they should stay in their posts to handle the government's response to these threats.

Meanwhile the party's executive announced that individuals must be registered with the party by 27 January in order to vote for the leader. The three criteria for eligibility were that an individual must either be a Canadian citizen or permanent resident of Canada or have status under the Indian Act; must not be a member of another political party; and must be a minimum of fourteen years old. Voting would take place between 26 February and 9 March by preferential ballot. By 27 January approximately 400,000 registered voters were eligible to cast ballots.

The party organizing committee was also challenged by the additional expectations for voting procedures outlined in the final Hogue

Report on Foreign Interference, tabled 28 January. (This report was the end result of more than a year of debate over the issue of foreign interference). Since the one-member, one-vote system replaced the Liberals' delegated leadership conventions in 2009, voting for the Liberal leader would take place online. In the climate of heightened concern over foreign interference, the issue of secure voter identification became a major issue for the first time. The party ultimately chose the Canada Post Identity+ platform used by Canada Post, which party spokesperson Parker Lund described as "the most secure and accessible voting process in Canadian history."

In the end there were only four candidates for the Liberal leadership, an unusually low number. They included Chrystia Freeland, (former minister of finance and deputy prime minister) and Karina Gould (house leader and former minister of international development), along with Mark Carney, (former governor of the Banks of Canada and England and private sector financier), and former MP Frank Bayliss, (a well-known Quebec businessman and the first Black Canadian to seek the Liberal leadership). Three little known Liberals – former MP Ruby Dhalla and sitting MPs Jaime Batiste and Chandra Arya – had also put their names forward, but Batiste soon withdrew. Both Dhalla and Arya were disqualified from running by the party executive, the former for alleged procedural infractions and the latter for issues related to foreign interference.[11]

From the beginning much was made of the fact that Carney had never been elected to any political office. Moreover, few Canadians knew Carney except by reputation. While his name had surfaced on several occasions as a potential finance minister, and most recently as the indirect cause of Chrystia Freeland's resignation, he remained an unknown quantity.

One effort to rectify that problem saw Carney participating in an interview with host Jon Stewart on the US Comedy Central satirical news program the *Daily Show* a few days before he officially announced that he was entering the race. The appearance was widely viewed in Canada and generally seen as positive. But many critics noted the friendly chat format did not demonstrate how Carney would perform in a hostile political environment such as an election campaign. At his campaign launch on 16 January, it also became clear that Carney was not as fluent in French as has come to be expected of a Liberal leader, something many considered to be a serious impediment.

There were also critics who compared him with Michael Ignatieff, who had led the party to unprecedented defeat in 2011 after returning to Canada from prestigious postings in the UK and Harvard. However Carney immediately demonstrated one significant difference between himself and Ignatieff, who famously had been unable to answer the question of why he wanted to be Liberal leader and prime minister.[12] Carney did not wait to be asked. He told his audience at his campaign launch in Edmonton that he had "put his hand up" to help out in this time of existential threat to Canada because he wanted to give back to the country that had given him so much.

Chrystia Freeland was recognized as Justin Trudeau's second in command. Her extensive political pedigree as former deputy prime minister, minister of finance and chief negotiator of the trade agreement (CUSMA) signed with the first Trump administration, was considered by some to be an obvious advantage. Others worried it was actually a disadvantage, since it too closely associated her with the Trudeau government to represent the change that the party needed to demonstrate to make progress in the polls.

Gould was seen as the standard bearer for "social" Liberals, the sole candidate from the party's left wing. At thirty-seven she was also the youngest candidate in the race and seen as a role model for younger generations. Bayliss, as a wealthy entrepreneur, was presumed to be a "business" Liberal of the party's right wing like Carney and was essentially unknown at the start of the race.

Initially Carney and Freeland were seen as the clear frontrunners in a two-horse race. But with the general public's growing concern over Trump's menacing threats, that situation rapidly began to change. By the mid-point in the campaign polls showed a hypothetical Carney-led party pulling even with the Conservatives, while one led by Freeland still trailed significantly.[13] Shortly before the leadership debates it was reported that Carney had raised eight to ten times more money for his campaign than Freeland, whose campaign was floundering.

Two leadership debates were held on 24 to 25 February. The French-language debate highlighted the fact that Carney's French was rusty, and his responses were the weakest of the four. In one instance his comment supporting a reply Bayliss had given, about the situation in Gaza, appeared to suggest that Carney was in favour of Hamas, rather than of Bayliss's position on Hamas. This potentially damaging gaffe was immediately pointed out by Freeland and was subsequently reported extensively in both English and French media. However, Carney did score some political points with his defence of Canadian sovereignty and his repeated use of the classic Quebec phrase "Maîtres chez nous."

The English-language debate was dominated by Carney and Gould, who put forward the competing business and social Liberal perspectives on a range of issues. However, Carney clearly appeared the most effective of the candidates in explaining his approach to the Trump tariff threat. In a calm, measured fashion he stressed the importance of the federal government focusing on those factors that could be controlled domestically, given the unpredictable nature of the external threat.

Voting for the next Liberal leader began 26 February and concluded 9 March. As some had feared, despite the lengthy timeline the new enhanced voting process proved a challenge for many potential voters. The party had provided detailed instructions to registered participants, but it was soon clear that the many stages involved in the vetting process presented unanticipated difficulties. Although leadership camps were reluctant to criticize party organizers, concern over the voting process soon became public and a major rescue operation was launched by the party to ensure as many eligible voters as possible were able to participate. In the end the party reported some 40 per cent of the original 400,000 individuals who registered had actually voted, but party spokesperson Parker Lund noted that any leadership race will initially attract many individuals who fail to follow through and vote, and he stressed that 93 per cent of those who completed the authentication process had voted.

The results of the race were announced at an in-person event in Ottawa that was televised nationally. It began with remarks by outgoing prime minister Justin Trudeau and former prime minister Jean Chrétien. Both men delivered well-received speeches highlighting their most significant accomplishments. Both also underlined the importance of defending Canadian sovereignty in the face of the American president's threats. In what would prove a precursor of things to come, several commentators noted that Trudeau's handling of the Trump threat during the leadership race had actually seen his own approval rating rise to 47 per cent, far higher than Pierre Poilievre at 35 per cent.

The results were as unprecedented as many other features of the race. Mark Carney won by a landslide on the first ballot. He received a stunning 85.9 per cent of the vote and took every electoral district including those of Freeland and Gould. Chrystia Freeland trailed badly with a mere 8 per cent, followed by 3.2 per cent for Karina Gould and 3 per cent for Frank Bayliss. Many observers were shocked by the lack of support for Freeland. Almost everyone agreed the perceived American threat had prompted social liberals to vote for Carney, someone they would normally never have considered. Apparently recognizing this, Carney delivered a brief victory speech in which he not only committed to maintaining a strong and united Canada in the face of the "existential crisis" posed by Trump but stressed the importance of reinforcing social cohesion and Canadian values.

PRIME MINISTER CARNEY'S FIRST NINE DAYS

The new prime minister had his work cut out for him in crafting a new cabinet. He needed to make major changes in order to demonstrate a real shift from the Trudeau era, while also keeping a number of veteran ministers in place to handle the American crisis. Carney also had to navigate these pressing considerations on top of the pre-existing set of constraints faced by all federal leaders when forging a cabinet – such as gender parity, diversity, and regional representation – making it an even more daunting challenge. If all of these factors are to be accommodated, a Canadian cabinet will almost inevitably be far larger than the norm elsewhere. The 2023 Trudeau cabinet, for example, contained thirty-seven ministers, up from thirty in 2015 and only slightly below the high of forty last reached under Prime Minister Stephen Harper. In this context Carney's decision to limit the size of his cabinet to a mere twenty-four ministers was nothing short of breathtaking. It was also an obvious attempt to demonstrate change, through a new, leaner look to government. All told, Carney dropped eighteen Trudeau-era ministers from cabinet. But despite the smaller size, both gender parity and diversity were seen to be adequately respected.

The newly minted prime minister's first act was to sign a directive reducing the so-called consumer carbon tax to zero, while allowing individuals to receive a final scheduled rebate on 1 April. With one stroke of the pen, Carney had deliberately neutralized the principal campaign strategy of Conservative leader Pierre Poilievre, who could no longer frame the election question around his theme of "Axe the Tax."

Carney and his cabinet then wasted no time trying to demonstrate they were competent and hard at work crafting a response to the threatened tariffs, which would be the focus of their campaign strategy. Cabinet ministers held meetings with Trump associates and announced a variety of potential retaliatory measures, while Carney spent his first week in office appearing prime ministerial. He left almost immediately on trips abroad to meet with Canada's closest European allies, in an effort to cement support for Canada's position vis-a-vis Trump's increasingly outrageous threats. He began in France, where he met President Emmanuel Macron, and then moved on to the United Kingdom, where he held meetings with both Prime Minister Keir Starmer and King Charles III. All of these meetings were well-publicized and presented Carney in a positive light.

On his return, Carney went directly to Nunavut to meet with premier P.J. Akeeagok and announce funding for enhanced military and infrastructure spending in the Arctic, in a move designed to emphasize his commitment to northern security in the context of the American threat.

Only three days after these travels Carney held a virtual first ministers' conference in which he and the premiers agreed to pursue a cooperative approach to the Trump crisis. For his part, Carney announced a suite of measures the federal government would implement to support workers and businesses, and to "develop a national trade and economic corridor that will drive investment, create jobs, and build economic growth."[14]

Meanwhile the prime minister had issued a number of policy statements over the week, including decisions to rescind the Trudeau government's proposed capital gains tax, a 1 per cent tax cut for Canadians in the lowest income bracket, and a set of proposals to remove any federal barriers to interprovincial trade by Canada Day.

By now Canadians were becoming familiar with Carney, who in many respects was the complete opposite of Trudeau in temperament, calm and reserved rather than extroverted. Where Trudeau obviously enjoyed campaigning, Carney was not merely inexperienced but lacked the instinctive ability to connect with voters. He was not a charismatic speaker, and his somewhat ponderous delivery of early speeches emphasized his lack of political experience, as did his occasional flashes of impatience with media questions. (As many of those who knew him well would readily admit, Carney is not someone who tolerates fools gladly.[15]) At the same time his evident self-confidence about the issues under discussion lent him an air of gravitas that Trudeau had been lacking, especially on economic issues. As Carney himself would later say, he was far more comfortable governing, as prime minister, than he was campaigning as Liberal leader. Luckily for the Liberals the striking contrast between the two men actually appeared to be another advantage in the context of the Trump crisis.

By 23 March most observers were declaring Carney's first nine days as prime minister a public relations success. In any event he had run out of time. With Parliament scheduled to return from prorogation the following day, Carney headed to Rideau Hall Sunday afternoon to request that the governor general dissolve parliament and set in motion the federal election to be held on 28 April. In a brief speech outside Rideau Hall, Carney said the election was necessary so that the government would have a strong mandate from Canadians to stand up to the American president and to implement the changes necessary to enhance the efficiency and independence of the Canadian economy. In short, the speech made it crystal clear that the Liberal campaign strategy was to focus on the "existential threat" Canada was facing from Trump, hopefully undermining any attempts by the Conservatives to frame the election question around issues such as cost-of-living and housing which they had been stressing for the past year. It also made it clear that the Liberals considered this election to be a two-horse race, with much less attention paid to the NDP who increasingly appeared to be in freefall.

ORGANIZING THE CAMPAIGN UNDER PRESSURE

While Carney was laying down the policy framework for the Liberals' election campaign a large number of unusual organizational challenges also had to be addressed. To begin with, since he did not have a seat in the House of Commons, Carney needed to find a riding in which to run in the upcoming election. The party executive had recently decided that Arya Chandra, the Liberal MP disqualified for the leadership, would not be allowed to run again as a Liberal candidate. Since Chandra's riding was in west end Ottawa in Nepean, and was considered a relatively safe seat, this vacancy presented an obvious opportunity for the Liberal leader, whose home is in the city, and he took it.

Carney was also under pressure to finalize his election campaign team. Given his outsider status in the party, he had lacked his own group of supporters for the short leadership campaign, another unusual situation since leadership hopefuls typically rely on loyal longtime staff and volunteers. For the most part Carney's leadership team consisted of veterans from past campaigns and the staff in the offices of various ministers who were supporting him. It was to these individuals that he now turned to forge his election campaign team as well. Fortunately, his early popularity during the leadership race, and ongoing positive fortunes of the party, had attracted a wide range of experienced campaign personnel.

Most noteworthy was the absence of senior Trudeau advisers such as Katie Telford and Jeremy Broadhurst, another obvious attempt to demonstrate change rather than continuity, since Telford in particular was so well-known and closely associated with Trudeau. Instead, veteran Liberal strategist Andrew Bevan was appointed campaign director when Broadhurst resigned at the end of 2024. Bevan was well known as a former adviser to the provincial Liberal government of Kathleen Wynne, but he had also served as chief of staff to Liberal leader Stéphane Dion and most recently as chief of staff to Finance Minister Chrystia Freeland. Reflecting the importance of information technology (IT) to any modern party's campaign team, Tom Pitfield, CEO of the firm Data Sciences, a longtime Liberal (and close friend of Justin Trudeau), was named executive national campaign director and chief strategist.

Andrée-Lyne Hallé, a former Parliament Hill staffer, and Braeden Caley, a former senior party operative who ran Carney's leadership campaign, were named co-directors along with Andrew Bevan. Mike Maka, a former adviser to several ministers, was named tour director, with another former ministerial aide, Jamie Kippen, organizing the ground game. Communications would be led by Parker Lund, the former party spokesperson, while Jane Deeks led digital operations. Jeff Costen led the issues team and Terry Guillon, former chief of the parliamentary press gallery, served once again as a wagon master. Other Quebec members of the team included Audrey Champoux, Ann-Clara Vaillancourt, Laurie Bouchard, and Marie-Pascale Des Rosiers.

In the end several veterans of previous Liberal election campaigns pronounced the team "impressive." One commented on the speed with which it had been drawn together, while another cited the "broad depth" of federal and provincial experience.[16]

Fortunately, the campaign team was not hampered by a lack of financial support, as had happened so often during the Liberals' lengthy periods in the wilderness in the 1980s and 2000s, and might have been expected this time given the party's disastrous prospects at the start of the campaign. Shortly after the announcement of Trudeau's resignation and the launch of the leadership race, donations to the party's coffers poured in. In early March the party's national director, Azam Ishmael, announced the Liberals had achieved their best first quarter fundraising results ever. In anticipation of the party's campaign strategy, the press release accompanying this announcement also doubled down on the party's chosen theme. "While Pierre Poilievre follows Donald Trump's playbook, Liberals are ready to fight and win this next election, so that we can stand up against Trump's threats to our economy and sovereignty and build a better future for all Canadians."

One advantage of this increased revenue was the party's ability to fight back against the Conservatives' relentless advertising campaign. The Conservatives' apparently bottomless coffers had led to the phenomenon of the "permanent campaign" and the use of social media to attack the Liberal government and former prime minister Trudeau on an ongoing basis for much of the past two years. Now the Liberals, under the direction of Tom Pitfield and his team of digital gurus, were able to mount an aggressive campaign of their own. In March alone the party launched 4,430 campaign ads on Facebook and Instagram, compared with only forty-four new ads by the Conservatives, and they even outspent the Tories by a small margin.[17] All of the ads emphasized the threat posed by Trump, and the fact that Mark Carney was the only party leader willing and able to respond to it, a message that analysts concluded was resonating well with voters.[18]

SMOOTH SAILING: THE EARLY LIBERAL CAMPAIGN

The Liberal campaign unfolded surprisingly smoothly in the early innings, given Carney's complete lack of political experience and the party's plan to focus on the tariff and national security threats was front and centre from the start. One minor glitch involved the leader's incorrect identification of a Liberal candidate in Montreal as a victim of the 1992 shooting at Concordia, rather than the 1989 massacre at the École Polytechnique, something that reinforced the lingering fears of those Liberals who saw Carney as a potential Ignatieff who was "just visiting." However, the incident quickly faded from view as the Trump factor reclaimed the spotlight.

The mid-week announcement by President Trump on possible tariffs for the auto sector allowed Carney to pause the campaign for a day in order to hold a cabinet meeting and prepare plans for more retaliatory tariffs. Since the Liberals' skyrocketing climb in the polls was attributed by most analysts to their perceived advantage in handling this crisis, the image of prime ministerial competence was widely considered helpful to the Liberal campaign. In addition, Carney had his first phone call with Donald Trump. The prime minister subsequently noted the president had been "respectful" of Canada and that the two had agreed to discuss renegotiating the CUSMA after the election was over. Trump later referred to the discussion as "productive."

In what could only be described as another early gift to the Liberals' campaign strategy, former NDP leader Tom Mulcair posted a lengthy article on X on 24 March titled "Trump's Threat to Canada Means This Election Must be a Choice between the Liberals and the Conservatives."[19] In it, Mulcair argued voters had no choice but to cast their ballots strategically for the Liberals, the only party that could reasonably be expected to stand up to Trump and defend Canada's economic sovereignty.

As if that were not enough, reports began circulating that Alberta's United Conservative Party premier Danielle Smith had rejected the Team Canada approach and participated in an interview with the far-right American news and opinion website Breitbart in late March. There she had reassured MAGA Republican listeners that "Pierre" was more "in sync" with Trump's policies and urged the president to hold off on tariff measures until after the election.[20] One senior Liberal staffer was heard to remark, "with friends like that, Pierre doesn't need enemies."

Meanwhile candidate nominations, which had been an original area of concern to Liberal organizers in preparing for the election, were soon completed. With the Liberals' death spiral in the polls over the course of late fall 2023 and early winter 2024, a record number of sitting Liberal MPs and cabinet ministers had either resigned or announced their intention not to run in the next federal election. As a result, by 18 March the party had only nominated 185 individuals, while the Conservatives had already selected 275 and the NDP had 217. Fortunately, the party's greatly improved electoral chances encouraged many individuals to come forward and in the end the party nominated 342 candidates, only one short of a full slate, a situation replicated by the Conservatives and NDP, who also were one candidate shy due to administrative errors in paperwork.

ROOKIE ERRORS AND THE QUEBEC ISSUE POSE SOME CHALLENGES

The initial good news for the Liberals was quickly tempered by extensive negative coverage of remarks made by one of their sitting MPs, Paul Chiang (Markham-Unionville) about his Conservative rival, Joe Tay, who had been born in Hong Kong. Evidently tone deaf to the high level of public concern over the issue of foreign interference, Chiang publicly suggested, "If you can take him (Tay) to the Chinese Consulate General in Toronto, you can get the million-dollar reward,"[21] referring to the bounty Hong Kong authorities has placed on Tay's head under the new and widely criticized national security law imposed by Beijing. Instead of immediately removing Chiang as expected, Carney inexplicably allowed the MP to remain a candidate, noting Chiang had apologized to both Tay and the Liberal leader for his "completely unacceptable" remarks.

This misstep resulted in two days of negative coverage for Carney, with many observers questioning his judgment and apparent lack of concern over the foreign interference issue. Although Chiang voluntarily withdrew as a candidate, there was still concern the Liberal campaign might have been damaged in other ridings with significant Chinese Canadian communities. (The Liberals did in fact go on to lose Chiang's riding to the Conservatives.) More importantly, the affair temporarily distracted Canadians, and the media, from the tariff threat message so central to the Liberal strategy.

Carney's position on Quebec's Bill 96 on the French language soon became an issue as well. The bill had originally surfaced as an election issue because the Trump administration specifically listed it as an unfair trade practice because foreign-based companies were obliged to comply with requirements for signage and packaging in French. But Carney addressed that issue effectively by making it clear his government would never negotiate with the United States on any matters related to Quebec language and culture. However, the Bloc Québécois attempted to make the Liberals' position on the French language into an election issue for a different reason. Leader Yves-François Blanchet noted that Carney had indicated the federal government would intervene if a challenge to the bill reached the Supreme Court. In reply Carney stressed that this was in order to defend the Charter of Rights, because the Liberal government was opposed to the provincial government's pre-emptive use of the notwithstanding clause. Nevertheless, the Bloc leader continued to argue the Liberals could not be counted upon to defend the French language.

The issue of Carney's competence in French also returned when the Liberal leader met with three Radio-Canada interviewers for "Five Leaders, One Election."[22] After answering questions on a wide range of policy issues in somewhat stilted French, Carney was pointedly asked how he would grade his capability in his second language.

But with Liberal fortunes improving dramatically in Quebec at the expense of the Bloc, the language issue had seemingly become less important for francophone Quebec voters in this election than previously. Experts agreed this was primarily because Quebecers viewed the Trump threat even more seriously than other Canadians. For them, the issue was not only economic but linguistic and cultural.[23] Trump had recently accentuated their concern by signing an executive order declaring English the only official language of the United States. At the same time commentators also noted that the leaders' debate in French might be an opportunity for both the Bloc and Conservative leader to regain lost ground if Carney's French proved inadequate.[24]

On the Sunday before the leaders' debates, Carney appeared on the popular Quebec program "Tout le monde en parle." This represented another opportunity for Carney to reinforce what he saw as the urgency of the existential crisis posed by Trump, to remind Quebec listeners of Poilievre's right-wing populist policies, and also to demonstrate his improved French language skills and knowledge of Quebec culture. His advisers also saw this as a dry run leading up to the leaders' debate in French, and they were pleased to see that most analysts, and notably Chantale Hébert of the *Toronto Star*, concluded his performance – and his French – had been better than expected and that they felt he would not likely lose support because Quebecers were willing to "cut him some slack" on language.

Despite these challenges the Liberal numbers continued to soar. By the third week the party was projected to win a solid majority.

Needless to say, this was a remarkable turnaround, and one that appeared to be driven almost exclusively by the flight of NDP voters to the Liberals across Canada and of the Bloc vote to the Liberals in Quebec. Since the Conservatives were now holding steady at slightly lower than their pre-election levels, this meant the election had indeed become a two-horse race.

DUELLING CAMPAIGNS

This two-party race was being conducted by the principals on the basis of two quite different assumptions about the main election question. For the Liberals, the economic crisis arising from the American president's upheaval of the global trading system predominated. Mark Carney painted a stark picture of the challenge the country faced. "Trump is trying to break us so that America can own us," he repeatedly warned, but then assured voters "that will never happen."[25]

Carney also emphasized ways his government would not only counter this perceived threat but strengthen the Canadian economy and enhance national unity. He argued there was an opportunity afforded by this crisis to not only shore up but expand and diversify Canada's economy and ultimately make it more productive and resilient. "We must focus on what we can control, not what we cannot," he repeated at every possible occasion.

The Poilievre Conservatives continued to emphasize many of the same issues they had been raising over the past two years, including cost of living and housing concerns and tough-on-crime, anti-drug policies. For them, the so-called existential crisis of Donald Trump's tariffs and other attacks on Canadian autonomy were clearly a secondary matter. For some observers this dichotomy represented a contrast between fear (the Liberal approach) and hope (the Conservative approach), while for others it was a contest between political pragmatism (the Liberals) and rigid ideology (the Conservatives).

It was in this context of duelling campaign strategies that the Liberals were handed another gift when internal Conservative discord spilled over into the public domain. With polls showing the Conservatives now had little chance of forming a government, rumours of serious conflict in Poilievre's inner circle of advisers grew. Then former Harper strategist Kory Teneycke, now a close adviser to Ontario Conservative premier Doug Ford, gave several interviews in which he argued the federal Conservatives needed to change direction immediately and focus on the Trump issue if they were to have any hope of winning the election. Poilievre dismissed the criticism and made it clear there would be no change in his approach. Asked about his views on Teneycke's comments, Ford delivered the coup de grâce when he replied, "Sometimes the truth hurts."[26]

At this point the Liberals had taken a commanding ten-point lead over the Conservatives in Ontario and Premier Ford had already declared he would remain neutral in the federal campaign. This meant Ford's Big Blue Machine would not be offering any assistance to Poilievre's team. Since the third-place provincial Liberals were seriously limited in their ability to help Carney, this lack of on-the-ground support for Poilievre's candidates was particularly helpful to the Liberals.

Meanwhile Poilievre had gone even further on his tough-on-crime agenda with a pledge to invoke the notwithstanding clause of the charter (s. 33) in order to override decisions of the Supreme Court on the sentencing of mass murderers. Carney immediately rejected this proposal, noting that no federal government had ever used this clause, calling it a "dangerous move" that could "lead Canada down a slippery slope."[27] Carney also used the opportunity to emphasize the similarities between Poilievre's position and that of Donald Trump, who was involved in several outright battles with the American Supreme Court, thereby again casting the Conservative leader as "Trump-lite" and reminding voters of Poilievre's right-wing tendencies.

In addition, conscious of the need to retain the strategic voters from the NDP and Greens who were flocking to the Liberals, Carney attempted to reassure them that he was still committed to the social liberal programs introduced by his predecessor. He emphasized that his approach to dealing with the Trump threat depended on the protection of existing social programs, government aid to workers negatively affected by the tariffs, and public sector investment in a range of areas, from housing and transportation to energy and infrastructure, that would also help to ensure Canada's long term economic self-sufficiency. This was meant to provide a stark contrast with the Conservative approach, which Carney repeatedly noted depended not on government intervention but on a laissez-faire approach that focused on removing constraints on the private sector.

SURVIVING THE LEADERS' DEBATES

Some in the Liberal campaign team were anxiously holding their breath as the two official leaders' debates drew near. They believed that Carney would be the target of all of the other leaders, attacked from all sides by increasingly desperate opponents, and were unsure as to how well he could stand up to this type of onslaught. There was also some concern that Carney's French could still trip him up at a critical point.

In this context the French language debate, held 16 April in Montreal, was a success. A widely recognized professional performance by moderator Patrice Roy of Radio-Canada, and a tightly controlled format, allowed all of the leaders to express their views on a range of topics. Despite some occasional hesitation, Carney performed well in French and was viewed as holding his own and avoiding any pitfalls. Perhaps most importantly, he again was able to underline his commitment to the French language and culture and assure viewers that his government would never negotiate with the Americans on these matters.

Responding to criticism from Poilievre that he was simply another version of Justin Trudeau, Carney also scored points by noting once more that he was not Trudeau and had only been prime minister for a month. Then he outlined his record during that time, noting he had cut the carbon tax, struck a deal with the provinces to break down interprovincial trade barriers, started trade talks with France and the UK, and negotiated a military partnership with Australia. "We've done all of that in this short time – we've done all of that in a month," he said.[28]

Somewhat surprisingly, both NDP leader Jagmeet Singh and Bloc leader Yves-François Blanchet spent much of their allotted time questioning and criticizing the Conservative leader instead of Carney. Moreover, Blanchet made it clear that as Bloc leader he was neither interested nor able to form a government, and NDP leader Jagmeet Singh also appeared to have accepted that the NDP had no chance of forming a government. Instead, Singh focused on the important role his party could play influencing the policies of the next government. This dynamic essentially allowed the Liberal leader to stand back and watch as many of the most confrontational exchanges took place without him.

This was certainly not the case during the English language leaders' debate the following night. From beginning to end it was seen as a full-frontal attack on the Liberal leader by all three of the opposition party leaders. But Carney had the advantage here, both in terms of language and in terms of his relevant knowledge and experience on the issue he had framed as the campaign question. Remaining calm and in control, Carney was able to project the mature prime ministerial image so essential to the Liberal campaign theme. In addition, he avoided any potential pitfalls and made no significant gaffes. For the Liberals, this was better than good enough.

At the same time, Bloc leader Blanchet appeared to change course during this debate, repeatedly offering to cooperate with Carney if he formed the government, and not only on the tariff issue. Meanwhile NDP leader Singh actually helped Carney when the Liberal leader was pressed by Poilievre on the issue of pipelines, pointing out it was Liberal prime minister Justin Trudeau, not Conservative prime minister Stephen Harper, who had purchased the Transmountain Pipeline to aid Alberta.

At the end of the day there was no obvious winner in either contest. Observers concluded the debates had not likely influenced voting intentions very significantly, if at all, and subsequent national polls suggested they were largely correct, although some observers felt Blanchet and the Bloc had benefited slightly from the French debate.

Nevertheless, the Liberal lead nationally appeared to have peaked and was now declining slightly. Several analysts speculated this apparent slide might be due to the unusually quiet situation south of the border in terms of the American threat, since Donald Trump and his team had lately refrained from any references to making Canada the fifty-first state and turned their focus to other international issues in Europe, Latin America, and especially China.[29] Some members of the Carney team worried that voters might feel the threat had subsided, and shift their focus to the cost-of-living issues Pierre Poilievre was continuing to hammer home. Other advisers worried that a perceived decline in the threat might lead some NDP and Green voters to return to the fold, thereby splitting the progressive vote and depriving the Liberals of a majority.

THE HOME STRETCH: THE RACE TIGHTENS

As promised during the leaders' debates, the Liberals released their costed platform on the Saturday of the Easter weekend, in the middle of advance polling. This late release was widely criticized by the media, but since the Conservatives had not even indicated when their platform would be publicly available, the fallout was negligible. It was also more than compensated for by the fact that there was so little time left for any critical analysis of the various planks.

Entitled "Canada Strong," the contents of the document were predictably focused on the "existential" threat to Canadian sovereignty and the "unjustified trade war" launched by the American government. Organized in four major sections – "Unite, Secure, Protect and Build" – the platform included such terms as "nation-building," and committed a future Liberal government to a wide range of interventionist measures that would both ensure the continuation of Canadian social and cultural distinctiveness and promote the economic growth and diversification necessary to support them.

Although there were some similarities in other areas, in this respect the Liberal platform was in stark contrast to the Conservative platform released several days later, which focused instead on removing government from many policy areas in order to encourage the private sector to flourish. Two notable examples of this different approach were to be found in the areas of housing and Canadian culture. Among the measures proposed to address the housing shortage, the Liberals planned to create a new government program, Build Canada Homes, that would "get government back in the business of building," reinforce the government-sponsored regulatory initiatives under the Housing Accelerator Fund introduced by the Trudeau government, and focus on ensuring affordable housing for lower-income Canadians. Meanwhile the Conservatives planned to cancel the Accelerator Fund, eliminate the GST on first time home purchases under $1 million, and promote private sector construction.

A second equally stark distinction could be found in the Liberal proposal to inject some $150 million in additional funds into the CBC and introduce legislation to create a statutory obligation for funding, in order to "protect Canadian voices." The Conservatives pledged to withdraw all government funding from the English CBC, leaving it to depend on private donations.

When the Conservative platform was finally released, Liberals quickly pointed out that despite Poilievre's routine criticism of their fiscal failings, the Conservatives' platform also did not expect to eliminate the deficit for four years, nor did it expect to repair Canada's longstanding failure to meet NATO expectations for spending 2 per cent of GDP on its military until 2030. Adding insult to injury, an analysis of the two platforms by the Institute of Fiscal and Democratic Studies, led by former Parliamentary Budget Officer Kevin Page, awarded an overall assessment of "Good" to the fiscal framework of the Liberal platform, and only a bare "Pass" to the Conservatives. Nevertheless, in the final days of the campaign Liberal strategists' concerns about their slipping numbers appeared to be well founded. The Liberal lead over the Conservatives declined from more than 6 per cent to barely 3 per cent and pollsters began to speak openly of a "tightening" of the race.

Despite this, pollsters Éric Grenier and Philippe Fournier concluded the Liberals were still on track to win, and probably to obtain a majority because their vote was so much more efficient than that of the Conservatives,[30] meaning that the Conservatives would win many ridings in western Canada with far more votes than necessary, while the Liberals, by contrast, would win many more ridings right across the country but with much lower margins of victory. In addition, the unprecedented collapse of the NDP and decreased Bloc support still appeared sufficient to avoid the split in the progressive vote that typically prevented substantial Liberal majorities. But the polls in the last few days of the campaign also showed a slight but concerning increase in support for the NDP, especially in BC, and for the Bloc in Quebec.

Not surprisingly the Liberal team's emphasis was on ensuring they maintained their support among progressives and on getting out their vote. Here the skills of Tom Pitfield's IT support and "Big Data" approach, first instituted in 2015, once again came into play, with the sophisticated voter identification technology helping those in the trenches to know where to focus their message and their volunteers. Meanwhile the Liberals' advertising continued to emphasize the leader's strengths as a manager of crises, and the fact that a Carney government represented change, not merely the continuation of previous Liberal governments as Pierre Poilievre had argued. In particular, the Liberals' "This Election is Different" ad was seen as epitomizing their two campaign objectives.[31]

RESURRECTION: THE LIBERALS RETURNFOR A FOURTH MANDATE

For the Liberals this election result was a source of jubilation and relief. Although they had not managed to break through to a majority, they had come extremely close, and they had obtained a rare fourth consecutive mandate. The handful of surviving NDP MPs were sufficient to ensure passage of government bills, although the Bloc likely could be counted on for support in many cases as well. Given the Liberals' dire prospects only a few months earlier, their situation was unbelievably positive, and they knew it.

Moreover, the huge gamble the Liberals had taken in choosing Mark Carney as leader, rather than an experienced politician, had proven to be inspirational. In politics timing is everything, and for Mark Carney – who had decided to take the plunge *before* the Trump crisis had really taken hold – the stars had aligned. Carney easily won his own riding as well and now had a seat in the House of Commons. Many analysts were already concluding it was Carney's presence as Liberal leader, and his unusual profile, that had won the election for them. He was, they argued, the right man for the times.

Many Liberals also felt this election result provided a clear answer to their original question during the leadership race. For them, the vote demonstrated it was the singer (Trudeau) and not the song (the Liberal Party) that was the principal problem. Others were not so convinced, arguing this had been an extraordinary election in so many ways that it was too soon to tell. In particular, they argued that for many Canadians this had been as close to a single-issue election as possible, far more than even the 1988 so-called free trade election, and this was what had driven many NDP and Bloc voters to the Liberals. They argued the party could not count on this lack of competition for progressive votes in future.

At the same time there clearly were two competing narratives for the election, not one. Although the Liberal version had won, the Conservative perspective – focusing on affordability issues – had also appealed to a significant percentage of the population. Nowhere was this more evident than in Ontario, the one province where the national polls included in the CBC Poll Tracker had failed to predict so many Conservative victories, primarily in the "905" suburban region surrounding Toronto and in the southwest. While Quebec and BC had performed as expected, with greatly increased seat counts for the Liberals, Ontario had unexpectedly denied the Liberals a majority by delivering twenty more seats to the Conservatives than any of these polls had projected, including four they did not lose as expected and sixteen they were not expected to win.[32]

From a broader perspective, many observers argued that in this election the Liberal Party did what it had so often done in the past, namely, re-invent itself. After all, it is this ability that has made the party the most successful in the Western democratic world.[33] Coincidentally, one of the enduring elements of the Liberal Party has been its image as promoter of national identity and protector of national unity, an image tailor-made to fit the American sovereignty threat.

Despite this advantage, it can be argued that the hard part is still to come, for the party and for Prime Minister Carney's government, as they face so many challenges in uniting a divided nation. The election results could be seen as a reprieve for the party, but the ongoing American threat, the internal strains posed by the rigid ideological bent of the Alberta government, the concerns of so many voters with cost-of-living issues and notably housing, the ongoing issues related to Indigenous rights and reconciliation, and the other "existential" threat posed by climate change, will all have to be confronted in an era of reduced resources and heightened expectations. They will also be confronted by a prime minister who as a former CEO is accustomed to having control of situations, but who will undoubtedly learn quite quickly about the need for compromise and consensus in Canadian politics. How the new Liberal government handles all of these deep-seated problems may well determine whether the party continues to dominate Canadian politics.

NOTES

1 "The Liberal Party's Polling Surge Is Canada's Largest Ever," *Economist*, 3 April 2025, https://www.economist.com/the-americas/2025/04/03/the-liberal-partys-polling-surge-is-canadas-largest-ever.

2 "The Federal Liberals' New Year's Eve Nightmare: Party Vote Intent Sinks to 16%, Trudeau Approval at All-Time Low," *Angus Reid Institute*, 30 December 2024, https://angusreid.org/liberals-prime-minister-trudeau-resign-election-2025-poilievre-singh/.

3 Although Prime Minister Brian Mulroney and his government were also highly unpopular by the end of their time in office in 1984, the personal animus directed towards Trudeau was of a markedly different and far more worrisome order, as several commentators have noted. See for example: Ian Pattison, "Toxicity Takes Its Toll: Challenges of Modern Public Life Highlighted by Vitriolic Attacks on Trudeau," *Chronicle Journal*, 5 August 2023, https://www.chroniclejournal.com/opinion/toxicity-takes-its-toll-challenges-of-modern-public-life-highlighted-by-vitriolic-attacks-on-trudeau/article_14b55ea8-33ac-11ee-bfe8-

ab1d245e7c2d.html; "The Ugly Face of Right-Wing Extremism in Canada," *Charity Report*, 2 September 2021, https://www.thecharity-report.com/photo-essay/the-ugly-face-of-right-wing-extremism-in-canada/; and Mark Kingwell, "Can We Rescue Civility in Public Discourse?" *Globe and Mail*, 22 February 2024, https://www.theglobeandmail.com/opinion/article-can-we-rescue-civility-in-public-discourse/.

4 Marieke Walsh, "More Than Half of Canadians Polled Say Liberals Did a Good Job on COVID-19 Pandemic Management," *Globe and Mail*, 13 July 2021, https://www.theglobeandmail.com/politics/article-more-than-half-of-canadians-say-liberals-did-a-good-job-on-covid-19/.

5 Mark Bourrie, *Ripper: The Making of Pierre Poilievre* (Toronto: Biblioasis, 2025).

6 Noah Fry, "From Dog Whistles to Blaring Horns, Poilievre Makes His Case," *Conversation*, 16 January 2025, https://theconversation.com/from-dog-whistles-to-blaring-horns-poilievre-makes-his-case-246970.

7 For a detailed account, see Brooke Jeffrey, *Divided Loyalties: The Liberal Party of Canada 1984–2008* (Toronto: University of Toronto Press, 2010); and Brooke Jeffrey, *The Road to Redemption: The Liberal Party of Canada 2006–19* (Toronto: University of Toronto Press, 2021).

8 Amy Peng et al., "Relative Pandemic Severity in Canada and Four Peer Nations during the SARS-Cov-2 Pandemic," *Canada Communicable Disease Report* 49, no. 5 (2023): 197–205, https://www.canada.ca/en/public-health/services/reports-publications/canada-communicable-disease-report-ccdr/monthly-issue/2023-49/issue-5-may-2023/sars-cov-2-pandemic-severity-canada-peer-nations.html.

9 John Paul Tasker, "Some Liberal MPs Repeat Calls for Trudeau to Quit After Freeland Debacle – But He Still Has Defenders," CBC News, 17 December 2024, https://www.cbc.ca/news/politics/liberals-renew-calls-trudeau-resign-1.7412642 and Rachel Aiello, "We're Not United': Liberal Caucus Meets, as PM Trudeau Faces Fresh Calls to Resign in Light of Freeland's Departure," CTV News, 16 December 2024, https://www.ctvnews.ca/politics/article/were-not-united-liberal-caucus-meets-as-pm-trudeau-faces-fresh-calls-to-resign-in-light-of-freelands-departure/.

10 Catharine Tunney and Holly Cabrera, "Gould Calls Out 'Very, Very High' Liberal Leadership Fee Ahead of Fundraising Deadline," CBC News, 6 February 2025, https://www.cbc.ca/news/politics/baylis-gould-policy-announcements-1.7452516.

11 Robert Fife and Steven Chase, "Ousted Liberal MP Chandra Arya Barred from Running under Party's Banner over Alleged Ties to India," *Globe*

and Mail, 26 March 2025, https://www.theglobeandmail.com/politics/article-liberal-mp-chandra-arya-ousted-alleged-foreign-interference-india/.

12 Micahel Ignatieff, *Fire and Ashes* (Toronto: Vintage Canada, 2015), 8.

13 The Canadian Press, "Leger Poll: Carney as Leader Would Have Liberals Tied with Conservatives," CTV News, 11 February 2025, https://www.ctvnews.ca/politics/article/leger-poll-carney-as-leader-would-have-liberals-tied-with-conservatives/.

14 Canada, "Prime Minister Carney Meets with Premiers and Shares His Plan to Build One Strong Canadian Economy," Prime Minister of Canada, 21 March 2025, https://www.pm.gc.ca/en/news/news-releases/2025/03/21/prime-minister-carney-meets-premiers-and-shares-his-plan-build.

15 Michael Taube, "Michael Taube: Heed Britain's Stern Warnings about Mark Carney," *National Post*, 21 March 2025, https://nationalpost.com/opinion/britains-stern-warnings-about-mark-carney.

16 Laura Ryckewaert, "Who's Who on Mark Carney's 2025 Liberal Campaign Team," *Hill Times*, 2 April 2025, https://www.hilltimes.com/story/2025/04/02/whos-who-on-mark-carneys-2025-liberal-campaign-team/455672/.

17 Catherine McIntyre and James Temperton, "The Liberals Launched Thousands of Facebook Ads in the First Week of Campaigning," Logic, 4 April 2025, https://thelogic.co/news/facebook-instagram-ads-canada-election/.

18 McIntyre and Temperton, "Liberals Launched Thousands Of Facebook Ads."

19 Tom Mulcair, "Tom Mulcair: Trump's Threat to Canada Means This Election Must Be a Choice between the Liberals and Conservatives," CTV News, 24 March 2025, https://www.ctvnews.ca/federal-election-2025/article/tom-mulcair-its-a-two-horse-race/.

20 Catherine Cullen, "House Party: Is Pierre Poilievre Really 'In Sync' with Donald Trump?" CBC Radio, *House*, 26 March 2025, https://www.cbc.ca/listen/live-radio/1-64-the-house/clip/16136169-house-party-is-pierre-poilievre-really-in-sync.

21 The editorial board, "The Price of Paul Chiang's Unacceptable Comments," *Globe and Mail*, 31 March 2025, https://www.theglobeandmail.com/opinion/editorials/article-the-price-of-paul-chiangs-unacceptable-comments/.

22 Verity Stevenson, "What We Learned from Radio-Canada's 'Cinq Chefs' Party Leader Interviews," CBC News, 4 April 2025, https://www.cbc.ca/news/politics/canada-election-cinq-chefs-french-language-party-leaders-interviewed-src-1.7501815.

23 The Canadian Press, "Will Carney's French Flubs Matter to Quebec Voters?," CTV News, 29 March 2025, https://www.ctvnews.ca/federal-election-2025/article/will-carneys-french-flubs-matter-to-quebec-voters/; and Francine Pelletier, "On Guard with Thee: A Rapprochement between French Quebec and English Canada," *Canadian Geographic*, 24 June 2025, https://canadiangeographic.ca/articles/on-guard-with-thee-a-rapprochement-between-french-quebec-and-english-canada/.

24 Robert Benzie, "Mark Carney's Liberals Consolidate Lead over Pierre Poilievre's Conservatives, Polls Suggest," *Toronto Star*, 5 April 2025, https://www.thestar.com/politics/federal/mark-carneys-liberals-consolidate-lead-over-pierre-poilievres-conservatives-polls-suggest/article_edeb2694-88a2-4be8-86ed-bded23221126.html.

25 Catharine Tunney, "Carney Vows to Govern for All Canadians after Winning Election Upended by Trump," CBC News, 28 April 2025, https://www.cbc.ca/news/politics/carney-poilievre-federal-election-vote-1.7518649.

26 Sarah Petz, "Ford Says 'Truth Hurts' When Asked about Criticism of Federal Conservative Campaign," CBC News, 14 April 2025, https://www.cbc.ca/news/canada/toronto/ford-responds-teneycke-criticism-poilievre-campaign-1.7510103.

27 CBC News, "Carney Calls Poilievre's Plan to Use Notwithstanding Clause a 'Dangerous Step,'" CBC News, 14 April 2025, https://www.cbc.ca/player/play/video/9.6722922.

28 John Paul Tasker, "Front-Runner Carney Faces Jabs from All Sides at French-Language Debate," CBC News, 16 April 2025, https://www.cbc.ca/news/politics/french-language-debate-main-file-1.7512429.

29 Mallen Baker, "Why Did Trump Suddenly Stop Attacking Canada?," 17 April 2025, https://www.youtube.com/watch?v=_ZsyHhDX6V8.

30 CBC News, "Poll Tracker," CBC News, last updated: 27 April 2025, https://newsinteractives.cbc.ca/elections/poll-tracker/canada/.

31 Mario Canseco, "Conservative Golf Ad Missed Mark with Most Canadian Voters," Research Co., 5 May 2025, https://researchco.ca/2025/05/05/ads/.

32 Mark Gollom, "How the Liberals Came up Short in Ontario – and Lost Their Majority Bid," CBC News, 1 May 2025, https://www.cbc.ca/news/politics/liberal-vote-ontario-majority-conservatives-1.7523038.

33 Note the numbers have actually improved since these two texts were written: Stephen Clarkson, *The Big Red Machine* (Vancouver: UBC Press, 2005) and R. Kenneth Carty, *Big Tent Politics: The Liberal Party's Long Mastery of Canada's Public Life* (Vancouver: UBC Press, 2015).

3

Poilievre's Conservatives Make Gains but Fall Short of Victory

Faron Ellis

Early in 2025 the Conservative Party of Canada (CPC) was recording its greatest support in public opinion polls since its founding twenty years before.[1] Indeed, analysts had already been cautioning about the perils of "winning too big" in the upcoming election, citing the difficulties of managing an unwieldy super-majority caucus.[2] After a decade in opposition resulting from three disappointing election losses, under three different leaders, the Conservatives were ready to end what they characterized as the "lost Liberal decade" and usher in a new government that would "put Canada first, for a change." But the Conservatives' standing in the polls was not just due to hard work and the relative popularity of their new leader, Pierre Poilievre. It was also the result of the very poor standing of the governing Liberals and the extreme unpopularity of its once celebrated leader, Prime Minister Justin Trudeau.

When Trudeau resigned and was replaced by the Mark Carney, the Conservative-favourable comparisons diminished. When Carney jettisoned the most unpopular policies from the government he was inheriting, he effectively neutralized what would have been the most important planks of the Conservative platform. Further, newly elected US president Donald Trump included Canada in his trade wars and began attacking Canadian sovereignty, shifting the election ballot question dramatically from a focus on the economy, rising cost of living, and resulting desire for a change in government, to a competing narrative focused on a reinvigorated sense of nationalism, patriotism, and fear of annexation. Combined, these two exogenous developments moved the Conservatives' fortunes from an election they could not lose, to an election that was likely unwinnable.[3] After having successfully cultivated an image and style for their leader, and having developed an election strategy based on conditions that no longer existed, Conservatives adjusted their campaign strategy within the parameters of what was realistic and credible, as best they could. They ran a professional, relatively mistake-free campaign with a consistent message, tweaked as it was to adjust to the circumstances. But reframing a message crafted for different circumstances was not enough to produce an overall win, even after generating substantial increases in vote percentage and seat totals.

THE 2022 CONSERVATIVE LEADERSHIP ELECTION: EMBRACING POILIEVRE-CONSERVATISM

Despite Erin O'Toole's desire to remain Conservative leader after the disappointing 2021 election loss, in early February of 2022 thirty-five Conservative MPs presented caucus chair Scott Reid a letter demanding a vote on his leadership. In doing so, they were the first party to adopt, and then use the leadership removal provisions[4] of Conservative MP Michael Chong's Reform Act.[5] These 2015 amendments to the Parliament of Canada Act require newly elected parliamentary caucuses to decide if they want to empower themselves with the authority to expel or readmit caucus members, elect or remove caucus chairs, elect interim leaders, and remove the party leader, thereby triggering a party leadership selection process. When seventy-three Conservative MPs voted to remove O'Toole, versus only forty-five voting to retain him, O'Toole's tenure as leader ended. Manitoba MP Candice Bergen was selected interim leader and in mid-February the party announced that Ian Brodie, University of Calgary political scientist amd former chief of staff to Prime Minister Stephen Harper, would chair the twenty-member Leadership Election Organizing Committee (LEOC). In early March he confirmed that the modified one-member one-vote, single transferable ranked ballot used in the 2017 and 2020 leadership contests would again be used and votes would be tabulated for each of the country's 338 electoral districts with each contributing one hundred points to the total. Candidates would be awarded a share of points based on their percentage of votes in the district. An entry fee of $200,000 was established, as well as a $100,000 refundable compliance deposit. Candidates would have until 19 April to apply to enter the race and until 3 June to sell memberships. The winner would be announced in September of 2022.

Pierre Poilievre waited for none of this and announced his candidacy to become Canada's next prime minister just days after O'Toole's ouster. Observers noted the presidential aspects of his announcement in as much as he was prioritizing his candidacy for prime minister above his candidacy to be leader of the Conservative Party and Canada's official opposition. The focus – Poilievre before party – would also characterize the Conservatives' approach to the antebellum parliament and the 2025 election campaign, at least until the final weeks of the contest. A born and raised Calgarian and graduate of the University of Calgary's political science program, Poilievre was active in Reform Party politics as a teenager and landed a job as a Canadian Alliance Parliament Hill staffer during Stockwell Day's leadership, prior to graduating from university. When the Alliance merged with the Progressive Conservative Party (PC) to form the CPC, the then twenty-five-year-old Poilievre was elected MP in the 2004 campaign.[6] He was re-elected six more times with an increasing percentage of the vote, topping out at 49.9 per cent in 2021.

Poilievre served in various parliamentary secretary roles once the Conservatives formed government in 2006, including secretary to the prime minister. He was elevated to cabinet in the final Harper government, serving as minister for democratic reform (2013–15) and briefly as minister of employment and social development (2015). Once back in opposition he rose to prominence as a member of the finance committee during the Trudeau government years, distinguishing himself as a forceful interrogator and cross-examiner of witnesses, particularly Liberal cabinet ministers appearing before parliamentary committees. He developed a style of interrogation, endearing to some, frustratingly irritating to others, that consisted of posing a question designed to ensure the only possible responses cast the witness in a negative light and then demanding a yes or no answer to the question. Described as prosecutorial, he brought that style, albeit with altered tactics, with him to the House of Commons as leader of the opposition.

Poilievre had considered seeking the leadership after the 2019 election but declined based on family considerations. In 2022, his team, led by longtime Reform-Alliance-CPC organizer and strategist Jenni Byrne and national campaign novice Jeremy Liedtke, raised more funds and sold more memberships than all of his competitors combined, clearly demonstrating his ability to organize, fundraise, and recruit supporters at an unparalleled level. They sold 312,000 new memberships and raised nearly $10 million; spending less than $8 million they finished the campaign with a $2-million surplus.[7] His closest rivals, former federal Progressive Conservative (PC) leader and Quebec Liberal premier Jean Charest and social Conservative favorite Ontario Conservative MP Leslyn Lewis raised approximately $3.5 million and $2.5 million respectively. Former Ontario PC MPP Roman Baber raised an impressive $1.3 million while Parry Sound-Muskoka MP Scott Aitchison collected nearly $730,000.[8]

Charest represented the diminishing Progressive Conservative wing of the party while Poilievre represented some but not all of the old Reform elements. Poilievre championed libertarian and populist conservatism while eschewing social conservatism, leaving those votes for others, primarily Lewis. Poilievre's goal was to recruit enough support to win on the first ballot without requiring second ballot support from any other candidate's Red-Tory or social conservative ("so-con") members, and therefore not be beholden to any factions, particularly social conservatives, within or outside of the party. Unlike Andrew Scheer,[9] a social conservative himself who openly campaigned for so-con support in the 2017 leadership contest, or Erin O'Toole in 2020[10] who, while not a social conservative still attempted to accommodate so-con positions in an effort at picking up second ballot support, Poilievre openly disavowed social conservative support, drawing the ire of their organizations,[11] but avoiding the social conservative dilemma encountered by his predecessors.[12]

He succeeded. The Poilievre campaign juggernaut won over 70 per cent of the votes on the first ballot, winning the leadership handily. The overwhelming result impacted the party and its preparation for the 2025 election campaign in a number of ways. Initially, it reinforced the strategy of adopting the all-Poilievre-all-the-time approach they would pursue in parliament and in preparation for the election. It also effectively marginalized social conservative issues ensuring he owed no policy concessions and, unlike his two immediate predecessors, distanced him from social conservatism more generally thereby defusing it for opponents to use as a wedge against the Conservatives on the campaign trail. Some insulation was an important consideration given Poilievre's background with Reform and some controversial positions he had previously taken, not least of which was his recent support for the Ottawa-occupying Freedom Convoy, a position that Charest and others claimed disqualified him from being prime minister.

POILIEVRE PROLOGUE

That the leader would be the focal point of all things Conservative through to the next election campaign became evident immediately and was illustrated through one of Poilievre's most effective means of communication – video storytelling, particularly long-form video. Although the CPC YouTube channel had a relatively robust selection of short, commercial-length videos among its selections, Poilievre's leader's YouTube channel was extensively developed, populated with hundreds of videos ranging from short, thirty-second conventional ads featuring Poilievre narrating over unflattering clips of his main opponents, "trust-fund Trudeau" and "Maserati Marxist" Jagmeet Singh, to long-form, single camera, single-take productions with Poilievre giving his pitch while walking through Canadian neighborhoods. Poilievre was not the first Conservative leader to attempt to bypass the legacy media and communicate directly to voters through his own productions. From 2006 to 2011 the Harper Conservatives maintained a permanent campaign war room dubbed the "fear factory" that included a production studio.[13] During his final two years in office, his Prime Minister's Office (PMO) produced weekly "Stephen Harper 24 Seven" videos in its ongoing efforts at narrative control.[14] Poilievre's techniques, debuting with his fifteen-minute "Housing Hell: How We Got Here and How We Get Out" mini-documentary released in late 2023, refined and enhanced political video storytelling while supercharging its exposure primarily, but not exclusively, to millennials by way of his extensive social media reach – he boasted 1.4 million followers on X and 1.2 million on Instagram. Panned by critics as providing overly simplistic solutions to complex problems,[15] the polished, graphics heavy, video rendition of his developing stump speech broke new ground in political communications, immediately garnered millions of views while earning him extensive secondary publicity from the very legacy media the video was designed to circumvent.[16]

With neither the Liberals nor NDP launching media campaigns aimed at negatively branding Poilievre early in his leadership, the

Conservatives had the opportunity to craft an image for him as they saw fit. Two examples illustrate their strategy. Both demonstrate Poilievre's skill as a political communicator, and therefore his appeal as a leader, but also some of the weaknesses the Conservatives were building into his brand. Soon after becoming leader, Poilievre launched a campaign around the theme of "Canada seems broken." It began with him sitting on a downtown Vancouver beach with a homeless encampment in the background, speaking to the camera explaining how "Trudeau's Liberal drug and crime policies" created a crisis leaving many Canadians to feel the country is broken. While not the most popular of his missives, garnering only a quarter-million views compared to others with millions, it was effective political communication in that it galvanized supporters around a theme they believed reflected their lived experiences. It was also a lightning rod for opponents who accused him of being derisive in his description of the country, and unpatriotic once Trump began his fifty-first state attacks and Canadian nationalism emerged as a central campaign ballot question.

In a much more widely viewed posting from October of 2023 entitled "How Do You Like Them Apples," Poilievre jousts with a local journalist after speaking with fruit growers in BC's Okanagan valley prior to holding one of his many campaign-style rallies. When Don Urquhart, editor of the Oliver-Osoyoos Castanet, prefaced some of his questions by using a selection of what Conservatives viewed as the legacy media's banal framing of contemporary Canadian conservatism, Poilievre took exception. Challenging Urquhart's unsupported prefaces such as "some people say" that Poilievre was taking a populist page out of "Trump's playbook" and using "polarizing ideological rhetoric," an obviously prepared Poilievre calmly munched on an apple and demanded Urquhart provide specifics such as who are "some people" and "what pages?" When the frustrated Urquhart could not provide specifics, he gave up pursuing that avenue of questioning, reported that Poilievre had turned "acerbic" and allowed him to provide his stock responses on the topics.[17] The exchange, and the reaction to it, captured the polarizing approach that would characterize Poilievre's leadership style and branding heading into the 2025 election. Opponents, including those in the national and parliamentary media corps, viewed his antics as shameful thuggery, the bullying of an unprepared local journalist. Conservatives, on the other hand, roared their approval, lauding Poilievre for having the courage and skill to challenge and effectively dismantle the biases they believed were endemic in the legacy media's portrayal of conservatism.[18]

Emboldened by his success in reaching potential supporters directly through his videos and social media communications, Poilievre accelerated hostilities with the media by promising to defund the CBC and end many of the federal taxpayer supported subsidies for what he described as the bought-and-paid-for Liberal media organizations.[19] He was nevertheless able to earn media coverage by repeating his messages in catch-phrases such as that the government needed to "axe the tax," "build the homes," "stop the crime" and end the "Justinflation" by removing the Liberals and their gatekeeping accomplices.

CANDIDATE RECRUITMENT

Conservatives began their candidate recruitment process in the spring of 2023, soon after Poilievre was elected leader. Incumbent MPs would generally have their candidacies secured without a constituency nomination process so long as they met some minimal donation and contribution thresholds. With the party climbing in public opinion polls, the prospect of many highly competitive constituency nomination contests in ridings where the Conservatives had no incumbent presented the party with opportunities to further expand its membership base while building strong local campaign organizations. However, CPC nominations have been ripe for takeover by social conservative candidates since its Reform Party days, leading to parliamentary caucuses that are often much more socially conservative than is the party base itself, and certainly more so than the contemporary Conservatives' target segment of the electorate.[20] Further, unmanaged CPC nomination contests can attract many fringe candidates who, even if they do not win the nomination, can generate a great deal of negative publicity for the party. Neither of these possibilities was acceptable to a leadership team determined to control both the caucus and the publicity arising from its nomination processes. Complicating matters, however, was the long-held ethos within conservative parties, particularly the Reform-Alliance stream from which Poilievre and his senior advisers hail, that the leadership should not interfere in the local nomination process. Indeed, the CPC constitution places the authority to nominate candidates with the local constituencies, but using rules and procedures established by the National Council. Further, under delegated authority, a National Candidate Selection Committee (NCSC) has the ability to disallow any person before or after the nomination on any grounds it sees fit.[21] Also, the National Council can appoint candidates if an election writ has been issued and it determines the timelines would not allow for a credible local nomination process to be carried out. Poilievre's team was determined to use all of the levers at their disposal to manage the process, and in some cases, the outcomes.

Conservative candidate selection proceeded in one of three ways: immediately and at times by acclimation; through a local, but NCSC-managed, process; or by appointment once the election was imminent.[22] Initially, in ridings where only their preferred candidate was registered, the party set very short deadlines thereby limiting any potential rivals' ability to effectively organize a credible challenge.[23] Next, they began opening nomination contests in manageable stages, four to ten per week during 2023–24, and used the NCSC's authority to weed out undesirable contenders, particularly social conservatives,[24] and sometimes to the advantage of their preferred candidate as had happened for a number of by-elections prior to the 2025 vote.[25] The NCSC's actions led to some negative publicity as rejected candidates or emasculated constituency association executives[26] shared their complaints with the media, but the Conservatives were willing to endure this in order to maintain control over the process.[27] In a few circumstances rejected candidates ran as independents but ultimately did not impact the election results.[28]

By mid-February, only a month before the election call, the Conservatives had nominated the vast majority of their candidates by way of the normal MP or candidate selection process, putting them well ahead of the Liberals and NDP, but with still more than ninety positions to fill. Once the election was officially called, the party began exercising its prerogative to quickly call nomination meetings or appoint candidates. Although only a couple of dozen Conservative candidates were appointed during this final phase of nominations, complaints from members contributed to the early election narrative that the Conservative campaign was overly centralized, disorganized, or dysfunctional. Once candidate registration closed, the Conservatives would field a slate only one short of full after their Québec Centre candidate had last-minute paperwork filing issues.[29]

CAMPAIGN ORGANIZATION

Poilievre staffed the 2025 Conservative campaign primarily with organizers, strategists, and communications personnel who had served on his leadership campaign and had been promoted to positions within his opposition leader's office (OLO) or the CPC organization. Many had experience in the Harper prime minister's office (PMO), extensive previous campaign experience with the federal Conservatives, or with provincial parties, particularly the Ontario Progressive Conservatives, Alberta's United Conservatives, or Quebec's Coalition Avenir Quebec. Others gained their credentials working for the Canadian Taxpayers Federation (CTF) or the defunct Sun News TV. Principal among these was his campaign manager, longtime confidant, and leadership bid organizer Jenni Byrne. Like Poilievre, Byrne began her political career with the Reform Party while in her youth, and ascended to more senior positions in CPC campaigns and the Harper government, serving as deputy to campaign director Doug Finley in the CPC's 2006 and 2008 campaigns, and as chair in the 2011 and 2015 campaigns until she was sidelined late in that campaign due to conflicts with other senior campaign staffers over policy and some questionable strategic decisions on her part.[30] While temporarily ostracized from federal Conservative politics she worked for Ontario premier Doug Ford but left that position amid conflict with other members of the Ford team.[31] Known as talented, at times strategically brilliant, but demanding and often difficult, Byrne developed a reputation for vindictiveness rather than rapprochement that impacted her ability to work with other Conservatives with whom she had crossed swords. Bruised egos, grudges, and threats of revenge characterized many of her political relationships and some of those conflicts were about to erupt on the 2025 campaign trail, particularly in Ontario and Nova Scotia.

The leader's tour was organized from the Ottawa war room by former PMO staffer Stephen Staley. OLO press secretaries joined Poilievre on tour but without the national media who were not invited to travel on the leader's tour plane. Also joining Poilievre on tour was his wife Anaida, often accompanied by their children. Having worked for years as a Parliament Hill staffer before meeting Poilievre, she showcased some of her communication talents when she delivered a passionate speech introducing Poilievre after he won the CPC leadership. The trilingual, immigrant mother of three also provided considerable feedback on policy, communications, and strategy. She was featured prominently in Conservative campaign ads, including its pre-election attempted softening of Poilievre's image, as well as introducing him and speaking about Conservative policy at most campaign rallies.

Overall campaign messaging was crafted by Ben Woodfinden, chief architect of the populist, gatekeeper narrative,[32] while policy development was led by CTF veteran Aaron Wudrick with input from former Harper PMO staffer Howard Anglin, a vocal critic of Canada's progressive institutions.[33] Together they implemented a national media relations strategy designed to be coordinated with policy position announcements, culminating in a late-campaign platform release. A distinct Quebec messaging strategy was developed by former Harper PMO staffer and CTF veteran Carl Vallée, including a Quebec platform released on the first full day of the campaign.[34] Designed to be tightly scripted and centralized within the national campaign's war room, the messaging strategy culminated in a gag order for caucus and candidates who were barred from conducting unapproved interviews with local media.

Financing the campaign would not be a problem. For over a decade the CPC out-fundraised the Liberals, typically accumulating 25 per cent more in donations during the later Harper years, increasing during his two successor leaders to 29 per cent under Scheer and 31 per cent for O'Toole.[35] But after Poilievre's team revamped fundraising to focus more on social media, with less reliance on phone calls and email, costs were reduced while donations skyrocketed. The party regularly generated approximately $10 million per quarter, totalling nearly $42 million in 2024 from over sixty-two thousand individual contributions, more than double what the Liberals collected. The strong CPC finances enabled executive director Michael Crase to revamp the party's voter ID and management systems, considered leading edge during the Harper years but which had more recently fallen behind the other parties.[36] Key would be integrating social media data inputs for two-way information sharing between the party central office and local campaigns, allowing volunteers arriving at voters' doors to be pre-equipped with profiles, knowledge of voters' interests, and issues the party could address on their behalf. So flush with cash were the Conservatives that they could also afford to spend rather extravagantly on media when introducing Poilievre to the country as the party's new leader and on pre-election advertising aimed at negatively framing their opponents, while still spending within the election writ limit.

ADVERTISING

Long before the election call and without competing campaigns from the other parties, the Conservatives were provided an open field to supplement their social media communications,[37] spending $8.5 million on paid advertising in 2023 alone. Included was a $3 million campaign aimed at reintroducing Poilievre as a family-man, much less combative than the attack dog Canadians had become accustomed to from his parliamentary performances. All the advertising was Poilievre-centric, featuring him as star or narrator, or both, increasingly presenting him without his glasses, wearing blue-jeans, blazers, and tight-fitting tee-shirts rather than his familiar business suite attire. Conservative ads, like most CPC pre-election communications, originated from themes explored in Poilievre's longform videos, with the messages shortened for repurposing on other platforms.

As 2024 drew to a close, the Conservatives released six negative ads on their YouTube channel; one targeting the New Democratic Party while the others zeroed in on the Liberals. They also released a one-minute ad called "Mountain" that summarized their strategy heading into the new year. It continued the attempted softening of Poilievre's image by illustrating the issues that concerned Conservatives about the country and its direction, emphasizing the need for change, while moderating the sharp tone and dropping the overt references to Canada being "broken."

The ad featured a softspoken, soothing Poilievre narrating over images of the Rocky Mountains. He describes a vision of Canada from his childhood home while he and Ana prepare to raise a Canadian flag. Poilievre discusses how he was adopted by schoolteachers and how he grew up believing that "if you worked at it, you can climb any mountain." However, he continued, nine years of Liberal government has led to higher debt, a crumbling immigration system and a government consumed by divisive "woke obsessions" that dishonour Canada's history while destroying its military and education system. The ad concluded with the flag raising and the "Pierre – Bring it Home – Poilievre" logo that would be the standard brand for the Conservatives for the first two-thirds of the election campaign.

More aggressively, as the Liberals were completing their leadership contest Conservative ads began targeting the presumed front-runner directly, claiming that if "Carney Wins, Canada Loses," portraying him as "Sneaky Carney," borrowing from his pre-launch appearance on US comedian Jon Stewart's *Daily Show*. This was followed by another shorter ad claiming "Nobody's Weaker," which accused Carney of "[selling] out Canada" for his role in Brookfield Asset Management moving its headquarters from Canada to New York. The party was careful to not include Poilievre in this ad campaign, instead making a rare use of Conservative MPs, having them hold news conferences to present the more negative attacks against their eventual election foe.

In the first weeks of the campaign, the Conservatives attempted to reframe their messaging by linking Carney to Trudeau's record, claiming he was simply an incarnation of the unpopular former prime minister. But when Carney declared he would end the consumer carbon tax and the planned increase in capital gains taxes, and conceded the government had grown too large, that taxes need to be lowered, and that crime was a problem, Conservative branding of him as Trudeauesque did not resonate with non-Conservative voters. Rather than continue to question his credibility by highlighting the contradictions between his campaign promises and the principles he espoused in his recently published autobiography *Values*,[38] Conservatives calculated that attacking Carney too harshly on personal matters, even if they were not having Poilievre do it directly, would contradict their softening initiative and result in a net loss for both their campaign momentum and for votes. For example, in another ad they emphasized that Carney had never held elected office, implying Poilievre's twenty-year parliamentary career was a virtue, but it primarily served to highlight Carney's impressive résumé, something Conservatives acknowledged later in the campaign by arguing that a résumé is not a plan. Further, attacking him for allegedly under-referencing bits of his doctoral dissertation only reminded or informed voters that he holds an Oxford PhD in economics.

Understanding that Poilievre could not compete directly with Carney on many leadership measures, and on dealing with Trump in particular, but understanding they nevertheless had to provide voters with a position on how they planned to deal with the American president, the Conservatives would again attempt to turn negatives into virtues. In an ad directed at Quebecers, Poilievre admitted that his blunt style could be grating on some, but that was what made him best equipped to stand up to Trump. In others he addressed the sovereignty issue with slogans such as "Canada First, Canada Last, Canada Always," and proposing to rebuild the Canada-US relationship. Although Poilievre was clear in stating Canada would never be the fifty-first state, and he echoed a message about bearing any burden and paying any price to defend Canadian sovereignty,[39] the optics were clear: Carney's more aggressive stance was viewed by voters as more appealing than Poilievre's softer positioning. Paradoxically, on this issue Canadians were looking for a warrior with Poilievre's more aggressive parliamentary persona at the very time Conservatives were attempting to moderate that image.

By the final weeks of the campaign the Conservatives understood they had lost the leadership battle and completely removed Poilievre from their broadcast advertising. One odd spectacle saw Conservatives attempting to win back support from older white men. In an ad featuring two of them on the golf driving range, talking about their kids' futures, Conservatives openly acknowledged how far they had fallen behind with boomers, particularly older men who were traditional bedrock supporters. In another, they enlisted Harper to endorse Poilievre after he had previously done so at a large Edmonton rally where he reminded voters that he was once the boss of both men campaigning to run the country and, in his evaluation, he recommended Poilievre. Unlike all previous CPC branding since Poilievre became leader, neither his image nor his name was mentioned in either ad. By that stage in the campaign, gone too were the once ubiquitous Pierre Poilievre signs, now replaced with more conventional Conservative Party-branded signage at events and rallies.

CAMPAIGN DYNAMICS

Poilievre launched the Conservative campaign from Gatineau, Quebec, with Parliament Hill across the Ottawa River in the background, ready to present a clear message early in the contest: time for change because the Liberals have failed Canadians on the most important economic and security issues. Conservatives planned to accomplish two strategic objectives during the early weeks of the campaign: first, to shore up Poilievre's weaknesses by flooding the campaign trail with policy initiatives while presenting him as less aggressive and polarizing, and therefore more prime ministerial; and second, link Carney to the Liberal Party to demonstrate that he did not represent a significant change from the previous government. If they could accomplish both goals by the time the debates rolled around, they believed Poilievre could close the deal, with or without a major mistake from Carney. They would then finish the campaign by releasing their costed platform and presenting a leader ready to govern. Or so it was planned. But the dramatic changes in the Canadian political landscape altered the situation. Instead of a big lead, the Conservatives were sitting at 37 per cent in public opinion polls when the election began, relatively robust, but down 8 per cent from their recent peak of 45 per cent. More importantly, the 25 per cent lead they had over the Liberals in January had evaporated. The optics were clear. The Liberals were resurgent and the Conservatives were retrenching, even though CPC support had not moved significantly from its 2024 average, nor would it fluctuate more than a few per cent during the entire campaign. Rather, Liberal support had surged nearly 20 per cent from its January lows and would continue to move upward for the first half of the campaign due in large part to that party capturing a larger share of the collapsing NDP, and to a lesser extent Green and Bloc support. To prevail, Conservatives needed to immediately change the momentum. Shoring up their leader's policy credentials was the response.

One of the ongoing critiques of Poilievre was that although he could turn a phrase and deliver catchy slogans, he was weak on actual policy proposals. Hence, policy would be Poilievre's focus during the first phase of the campaign. However, with Carney conceding and therefore neutralizing the Conservative's signature "axe the [consumer carbon] tax" policy, as well as its secondary signature policy that government has grown too large and must therefore be reduced, the Conservatives were left with the minutiae of economic policies upon which they could campaign. But detailed niche or boutique policy proposals do not typically galvanize votes during election campaigns. Nevertheless, Conservatives strategized that if they released a blitzkrieg of tax reduction proposals, they could recapture their natural advantage on economic issues that Carney was significantly eroding. To that end, in the first week of the campaign Poilievre announced no fewer than six tax reduction pledges. What would become their new signature tax cut, a reduction of the lowest tax rate from 15 per cent to 12.75 per cent was followed by promises of boutique cuts to the GST on new homes, tax breaks for seniors, an increase to tax-free savings account (TFSA) contribution limits, capital gains tax breaks, and a tax write-off for expenses incurred by travelling trades people. Designed to present a comprehensive tax reduction message, nothing stood out as particularly galvanizing, especially since the Liberals were promising similar cuts to income tax and the GST on home purchases. Further, the TFSA and capital gains measures would primarily help the wealthy, not the economically distressed and dislocated voters Conservatives were targeting. And although the micro-targeting of travelling trades people is an example of the kind of tax policy Canadian Federation of Taxpayers staffers appreciate, it appeared somewhat trivial as a policy-of-the-day announcement when the Liberal leader and the national media were predicting economic Armageddon and the demise of national sovereignty.

When Poilievre was not talking tax policy during the early days of the campaign he was mostly talking about crime and security issues, particularly while campaigning in southern Ontario and BC. His first crime policy announcement included a "three strikes you're out" slogan, an awkward, American analogy, particularly for a leader being accused of appearing too much like the US president. It was also a curious choice to associate the party's opening crime and order proposal with one of the US's most discredited justice policies of the past half century. He also proposed life sentences for those convicted in serious cases of fentanyl dealing, gun smuggling, or human trafficking. He would later add planks promising to give police the power to dismantle illegal homeless encampments and judges the option to order mandatory drug treatment. While campaigning in Quebec City he unpacked his Quebec platform, promising to reduce the number of temporary immigrants coming to Quebec and practise responsible federalism by respecting Quebec as a nation. Despite his promise to defund the CBC, he pledged to preserve Radio-Canada, thereby ensuring cross country access to French language programing. And he again promised to resurrect the Quebec Liquid Natural Gas (LNG) project. Clearly the Conservatives had a plan for their Quebec campaign efforts, both in an effort at securing votes and to ensure they had a comprehensive Quebec policy foundation to fall back upon should unpredicted events in that region emerge. They were not nearly as prepared for unexpected developments in other regions.

Like previous Conservative campaigns, the 2025 effort had to deal with distractions from people otherwise considered friends. In 2021, the O'Toole campaign had been taken off-message for days because of Alberta premier Jason Kenney's COVID-19 pandemic response. This time it was Premier Danielle Smith who, after having been described as traitorous for not signing the Carney-led joint Team Canada communiqué on responding to Trump, took it upon herself to visit Trump at his Mar-a-Lago estate to make her own case for Alberta and Canada. She also made repeated appearances on right-wing US media, exclaiming that Trump's antics were helping Carney even though Poilievre was more "in sync" with the US president, an image Poilievre was unsuccessfully trying to shed. At the same time, other Conservative premiers, particularly Ontario's Doug Ford and Nova Scotia's Tim Houston, were actively working with Carney on the Team Canada plan, with Ford particularly exuberant in his praise of Carney and former finance minister Chrystia Freeland. Meanwhile, Kory Teneycke, former Harper communications director and recent successful Ontario PC campaign manager, delivered a blistering attack from the sidelines demanding, among other things, a pivot in strategy to more directly address the Trump threat. He declared the campaign was making Poilievre look too much like Trump, later adding it was in chaos and accusing it of campaign malpractice. At the same time dozens of local Conservative riding associations were being told their candidate would be appointed by the national party. Those who had been organizing nomination campaigns were mostly rejected without explanation and their associations told only that there was not sufficient time to conduct a proper contest. Poilievre's question and answer session with the media on 27 March, just three days into the campaign, was illustrative. With the Conservative leader trying to sell his "Bring it Home, Canada First Tax Cuts," the national broadcast media was having none of it and universally pursued the campaign chaos narrative. CBC prefaced its question by stating the party had blown a twenty-five-point lead, before asking, what went wrong? CTV cited Teneycke saying Poilievre sounds too much like Trump, before asking how Poilievre could then stand up to the American president. Global provided a list of aggrieved constituency associations and asked why so many upset Conservative members were contacting the media. Poilievre capably deflected by stating that the party would have quality candidates and returned to one component or another of his core message in response to each question. But the external framing of the CPC campaign was clearly not positive. Teneycke's intervention, and then Ford's follow-up defending his campaign manager while disparaging the national Conservative campaign, fuelled the chaos narrative and likely stalled a Conservative recovery in the polls.

Although the Conservatives' eventual response to the Trump threat was too muted to be considered a pivot, they did engage in a slow reframing of many of their economic planks to mollify some of their traditional voters, particularly those who were more interested in supporting a national protector than a tax cutter. Understanding that they were not going to beat Carney on leadership with respect to this issue, they nevertheless had to appear more attentive to it. To that end, following Trump's announcement of 25 per cent tariffs on auto imports Poilievre described the trade war as unjustified and unacceptable. He reiterated his position that Canada must respond to such attacks by imposing counter-tariffs and began reframing much of his economic messaging in the context of undoing a decade of Liberal-induced damage to the economy as a defence strategy against Trump's threats. But voters and the media wanted more. Hence, ten days into the campaign, in a speech to a Bay Street audience, Poilievre assembled his economic policies into a package he claimed would build a "economic fortress" to defend Canada against Trump. He added that he would immediately begin renegotiation of CUSMA and promised a Keep Canadians Working Fund to help companies retain workers during trade war-induced shocks. And with that, the Conservative campaign would attempt to switch narratives as much as the external dynamics would allow. The Conservatives knew, as did pollsters, that although the Trump threat was significant, the national media's myopic focus on that issue was not an accurate reading of the full campaign dynamic. Affordability and other economic issues regularly topped Canada-USA relations in importance.[40] The Conservatives correctly understood that their prospects would improve if the campaign focus shifted back to the economy and the desire for change.

To that end, Poilievre went back to revealing his platform, plank by plank on a daily basis before its eventual full release in the final week of the campaign. Central to much of that effort was Poilievre's successful ongoing appeal to labour and working-class voters through his "boots not suits" initiative.[41] Labour leaders were featured at Conservative rallies in multiple provinces with Conservatives eventually revealing endorsements from nearly a dozen union locals or associations.[42] He promised jobs that would flow from creating a national energy corridor and enacting policy recommendations from Canada's energy sector, including a "one-and-done" approval process and a 25 per cent reduction in regulations throughout the Canadian economy more generally. He pledged to crack down on tax cheats, get tough on intimate partner violence, end federal funding for opioids, shut down drug dens, and create recovery programs for over fifty thousand Canadians. He pledged to protect seniors from fraudsters. And in response to a question about one of his candidate's past stances on abortion, he repeated his position that a Conservative government would make no laws restricting reproductive rights. This was one of the few times in the entire campaign that Poilievre had to respond to a social conservative issue and the immediate acceptance of his position demonstrated how successfully Poilievre had distanced himself from that element of Canadian conservatism. More controversial, Conservative strategists anticipated, was Poilievre's vow to use section 33 of the Canadian Charter of Rights and Freedoms, known as the notwithstanding clause, to override the courts and ensure those convicted of multiple murders serve consecutive sentences. He made the announcement in Montreal just prior to the leaders' debates, trying to create a wedge issue juxtaposing the Conservatives' law-and-order positioning against all of the other "hug a thug" parties.

With Conservative polling numbers stabilizing, Poilievre headed into the two leaders' debates encouraged. His demeanor was calmer, less prosecutorial, and more engaging than usual, although his awkward smile at inopportune moments appeared forced. During both encounters he characterized Carney as being too similar to Trudeau to represent real change. In good French during the first debate, he used housing to make the case that Carney was proposing the same policies the previous government had undertaken for a decade and that they only built bureaucracy, not homes. He also had a heated exchange with Bloc leader Yves-François Blanchet over pipelines during which Poilievre declared there is no social licence for the status quo, that economic and energy sovereignty require a pan-Canadian pipeline, and that majority rule should prevail when questions of consent arise. And he duelled with Jagmeet Singh in both English and French over housing and Poilievre's track record while a Harper cabinet minister. But his main target was Carney, repeatedly calling him Trudeau's economic adviser and therefore culpable for the inflation the government had caused. He pointed out that some of Trudeau's former staff were physically present in Montreal, helping Carney with debate preparation. Importantly, Poilievre kept his emotions in check while he endured attacks from the other leaders, particularly Singh over the environment, border security, and Poilievre's crime policies. Overall, Poilievre performed admirably, but with no clear debate winner he and all of the leaders prepared to close the campaign by releasing their costed platforms and making a final-week sprint to election day.

All of the parties waited until very late in the campaign to release their complete platforms, indicating none placed a great deal of strategic weight behind the platform document as a campaign communications tool. Rather, they viewed it as a minimal requirement to be completed before the campaign ended. The CPC document – "Change. For an Affordable Life. For Safe Streets. For Canada First" – organized the party's platform planks into six categories each with a subtitle appended by the statement: "For a Change." Visually the document was populated with plenty of images of Poilievre, typically hugging or shaking hands with voters, and was clearly designed prior to their late-campaign shift away from having his images dominate. In one subtle shift, however, Poilievre was again featured building a map of Canada jigsaw puzzle, just as in his 2023 ad blitz, but this time he was accompanied by two senior citizens rather than his young family.

Poilievre spent the final days of the campaign crisscrossing the country, making stops in key ridings Conservatives knew would be close, and in other normally safe Conservative areas such as Saskatoon and Calgary where the Liberals were attempting to make gains. While attempting to boost support for his Nova Scotia candidates at a Halifax rally, Poilievre was joined by provincial political legends former MPs Elmer and Peter MacKay, but not current premier Tim Houston. Rather than attend in person to support his federal counterparts, Houston released a self-promoting video and the rivalry between the federal team, particularly campaign manager Byrne, and the provincial Conservatives reemerged, sowing further doubts among some voters searching for stability about the Conservatives' ability to deliver. When former Reform Party leader Preston Manning intervened by declaring Carney a threat to national unity and that a Liberal victory would reignite western separatist sentiments,[43] Poilievre distanced himself as much as he could, but had to again endure the spectacle of Conservatives sniping at each other in the media rather than rallying behind the leader in one final push to secure votes.

Poilievre held four Ontario events on the final day of the campaign; the last one in his own riding which the party was aware he was in danger of losing. Poilievre had won his seat in seven consecutive elections primarily by personally knocking on thousands of doors and campaigning energetically for most of the writ period in his own riding. Conservatives assumed that this time his position as leader would carry the day but became aware of difficulties when 41 per cent of all eligible voters cast ballots at the advance polls, and knew they were not responsible for delivering very much of that. When nearly 82 per cent of the electorate worked their way through the country's "longest ballot,"[44] Poilievre garnered a respectable 45.7 per cent of votes cast but had indeed lost to his Liberal challenger who won over half the Carleton vote.

OUTCOME

Disappointing, but not disastrous, again, is a familiar but not inaccurate description of the Conservative Party of Canada's 2025 general election results. The party secured 144 victories, twenty-five more than in 2021, but still lost to a resurgent Liberal Party for the fourth consecutive time. They kept the liberals to a minority, but only barely. They picked up seats in some crucial areas but also lost ground in others. Most of their preferred candidates and frontbench talent won their seats, but their leader lost his. Their strategy of recruiting the economically alienated, youth, and labour was at least partially successful, but their lack of a competitive response to the Trump threat cost them among voters who were more concerned about national sovereignty than economic security.

Aside from Carleton, undoubtedly the most significant losses occurred in Nova Scotia. The Conservatives managed to increase their vote share by 6 per cent over their 2021 totals, but they still lost two seats when the Liberals increased their vote count by 15 per cent. This was a pattern that occurred throughout the Maritimes, and in Nova Scotia it left only one Conservative MP elected in that province. They did secure two additional seats in Newfoundland and Labrador where Conservatives added slightly more votes to their total than did the Liberals, bringing the CPC parliamentary contingent from one to three from that province. The party increased its vote share in New Brunswick by 7 per cent, leading to four victories, the same number as in 2021. In Prince Edward Island they gained 5 per cent in vote share, but lost all of that province's four contests, again. Given the number of very close contests throughout the Atlantic provinces, the emergence of the late-campaign feud with the provincial PCs likely cost the party a seat or two in Nova Scotia. The lack of a regionally specific sub-tour or Atlantic campaign featuring local MPs and candidates likely had an impact as well.

In Quebec, Conservatives won 23 per cent of the vote, nearly five points better than in 2021, but that netted them only one additional seat for a total of eleven, all in the Quebec City region. The party was predictably shut out of Montreal, but also lost in Quebec City proper, winning its suburbs but losing all three of its most urban ridings. A similar pattern emerged for Conservatives in Manitoba where the party won 46 per cent of the vote, but the 7 per cent improvement on their 2021 results did not produce more wins, leaving the party with no urban Winnipeg wins. Conservatives increased their overall support to nearly 65 per cent and swept all but one of the Saskatchewan's seats, winning thirteen in total. In Alberta, Conservatives withstood a Liberal push to secure major inroads into Edmonton and Calgary. They increased their vote share in Poilievre's home province to nearly 64 per cent, 8 per cent more than in 2021 and won thirty-four of Alberta's thirty-seven seats, a gain of four over their 2021 total.

British Columbia saw the Conservatives increase their vote share to 41 per cent, an eight-point gain over 2021, leading to nineteen victories, six more than in 2021. However, when the Liberals captured more of the collapsing NDP and Green vote than did the Conservatives, the Liberals won an additional five seats and bested the CPC in BC seats. But Conservatives made breakthroughs by winning three Vancouver Island ridings, also taking back Richmond and two Langly ridings. Clearly, Conservatives were picking up some former NDP and Green voters, but the Liberals were the net winners in that province.

Undoubtedly, the Conservatives' greatest gains came in Ontario where they won nearly 44 per cent of the total vote, 9 per cent more than in 2021, leading to fifty-three Ontario seats, sixteen more than in 2021. Most of their new seats came at the expense of the

Liberals, but Conservatives picked up substantial numbers of NDP votes, notably in Windsor, where they won all three seats, and in the Hamilton region where they picked up one win. They won two of the four London area ridings and two of four in Kitchner-Waterloo. Indeed, aside from those and losses in Guelph and St Catharines, the Conservatives swept all of southern Ontario including most of the coveted 905 area code surrounding Toronto. In the Greater Toronto Area, Conservatives flipped eight Liberal seats, winning all but two "905" contests. They also won a seat in Brampton and came within less than a thousand votes of winning in five others in that region. In eastern Ontario, however, not only was Poilievre defeated but other Conservative incumbents lost in Peterborough and Bay of Quinte, tarnishing an otherwise successful Ontario campaign effort.

After their fourth consecutive election loss, but their best showing since their 2011 majority government victory, Conservatives will have much to evaluate as they conduct a postmortem on their improved but ultimately unsuccessful 2025 election campaign.

NOTES

1 This chapter reflects, in part, interviews conducted with several individuals associated with various aspects of the Conservative campaign. Interviews were arranged and completed based on a commitment to ensure the anonymity for all participants. The author sincerely thanks all those who consented to provide their insights, as well as the anonymous reviewers for their suggestions in helping make this a more accurate and complete analysis. The author assumes responsibility for any errors in interpretation.

2 Ian Brodie, "The Thursday Question 2:23: Minimum Winning Coalitions," Substack, 11 July 2024, https://thethursdayquestion.substack.com/p/the-thursday-question-223-the-minimum.

3 Nelson Wiseman, "Polls, the Campaign, and Pierre Poilievre," *Hill Times*, 15 May 2025, https://www.hilltimes.com/story/2025/05/15/polls-the-campaign-and-pierre-poilievre/459912/.

4 Adelina Petit-Vouriot, Michael Morden, Paul EJ Thomas, "Assessing the Reform Act as a Tool of Parliamentary Reform: One Step Forward, One Step Back," *Canadian Parliamentary Review* 43, no. 2 (Summer): Article 3 / 11. With a review of the Samara Centre for Democracy's analysis of the *Reform Act* in practice.

5 After the 2015 election, the Conservative caucus adopted all of the *Reform Act* provisions except the authority over initiating a leadership review. After the 2019 election they adopted only the caucus membership and chair provisions. Following the 2021 election they adopted all of the measures. Ironically, the first use of any *Reform Act* provisions occurred only a year earlier when O'Toole was forced to seek caucus authority to remove troublesome MP Derek Sloan in January of 2021.

6 For a more complete biography see Andrew Lawton, *Pierre Poilievre: A Political Life* (Toronto: Sutherland House, 2024).

7 Elections Canada, "Leadership Contestant Campaign Returns. Conservative Party of Canada," 10 September 2022, https://www.elections.ca/WPAPPS/WPF/EN/LC/DetailedReport?act=C76&selectedEvent=10397&returnStatus=1&reportOption=2&selectedReportType=10&queryId=2bbd87b504cb44139 67de393e0c5c3f7&selectedPart=1.

8 Baber, Aitcheson, and Lewis would all contest and win their seats for the Conservatives in the 2025 election.

9 Faron Ellis, "The Conservative Campaign: An Opportunity Squandered," in Jon H. Pammett and Christopher Dornan (eds.), *The Canadian Federal Election of 2019* (Montreal and Kingston: McGill-Queen's University Press, 2020): 43–72.

10 FaronEllis, "The Conservative Campaign: Erin O'Toole and the Conservative Dilemma," in Jon H. Pammett and Christopher Dornan (eds.), *The Canadian Federal Election of 2021* (Montreal and Kingston: McGill-Queen's University Press, 2022): 36–59.

11 Jack Fonseca, "Can Pro-Lifers Support Pierre Poilievre?," *Campaign Life Coalition*, 15 February 2022, https://www.campaignlifecoalition.com/clc-blog/id/168/title/can-pro-lifers-support-pierre-poilievre-.

12 Faron Ellis, "Twenty-First Century Conservatives Can Continue to Succeed," in Mark Charlton and Paul Barker (eds.), *Crosscurrents: Editors' Choice*, 8th edition (Toronto: Nelson, 2015): 17–36.

13 Faron Ellis, "Stephen Harper and the 2015 Conservative Campaign: Defeated but Not Devastated," in Jon H. Pammett and Christopher Dornan (eds.), *The Canadian Federal Election of 2015* (Toronto: Dundurn Press, 2016): 23–56.

14 See, Mireille Lalancette and Sofia Tourigny-Koné, "24 Seven Videostyle: Blurring the Lines and Building Strong Leadership," in Alex Marland, Thierry Giasson, and Anna Lennox Esselment, (eds.), *Permanent Campaigning in Canada* (Vancouver-Toronto: UBC Press, 2017): 259–77.

15 Gary Mason, "Poilievre's Hosing Hell Video Offers a Lousy, Dine-Store Analysis of Our Housing Crisis," *Globe and Mail*, 5 December 2023,

https://www.theglobeandmail.com/opinion/article-poilievres-housing-hell-video-offers-a-lousy-dime-store-analysis-of/.

16 Stuart Thomson, "Poilievre Releases 'Housing Hell' Mini-Documentary, Testing New Ground in Political Communications," *National Post*, 2 December 2023, https://nationalpost.com/news/politics/poilievre-releases-housing-hell-documentary.

17 Don Urquhart, "Pierre Poilievre Was in Town Wednesday Capping the Visit Off with a Rally in Oliver," *Oliver Times Chronicle*, 13 October 2023, https://www.castanet.net/news/Oliver-Osoyoos/451775/Pierre-Poilievre-was-in-town-Wednesday-capping-the-visit-off-with-a-rally-in-Oliver.

18 Gabriel Hays, "Conservative Canadian Leader Goes Viral for Munching on Apple While Calmly Batting down Reporter's Questions," Fox News, 17 October 2023, https://www.foxnews.com/media/conservative-canadian-leader-goes-viral-munching-apple-while-calmly-batting-down-reporters-questions.

19 Peter Menzies, "Subsidized Journalists Are Praising the Government Hand That Feeds," *Hub*, 18 August 2024, https://thehub.ca/2024/08/18/peter-menzies-subsidized-journalists-are-praising-the-government-hand-that-feeds/.

20 Faron Ellis, *The Limits of Participation: Activists and Leaders in Canada's Reform Party* (Calgary: University of Calgary Press, 2005).

21 Conservative Party of Canada, *Constitution of the Conservative Party of Canada*, (section 14.1) and Conservative Party of Canada, "Rules and Procedures for Candidate Nominations," (section 2(c) and section 3(t)), as amended by the delegates to the National Convention (virtual), 18–20 March 2021, as consolidated by the National Constitution Committee and approved by the National Council, https://cpcassets.conservative.ca/wp-content/uploads/2026/02/27102601/47f659ed94424a5.pdf.

22 Abbas Rana, "In Anticipation of a Potential Spring 2024 Election, Conservatives Start Nominations in 221 Unheld Ridings," *Hill Times*, 14 August 2023, https://www.hilltimes.com/story/2023/08/14/in-anticipation-of-a-potential-spring-election-conservatives-start-the-candidate-nomination-process-in-221-unheld-ridings/394884/.

23 As was the case for leadership contender Baber in York Centre.

24 Ian Bailey, "Anti-Abortion Groups Angered by Ouster of Candidate for Conservative Nomination," *Globe and Mail*, 20 March 2023, https://www.theglobeandmail.com/politics/article-anti-abortion-groups-angered-by-ouster-of-candidate-for-conservative/.

25 Of the eleven by-elections that were held from the time Poilievre was elected CPC leader until the 2025 federal election, the Conservatives won six.

26 Calvi Leon, "Hijacked': Riding Officials Quit after Heated Conservative Nomination Fight," *London Free Press*, 28 March 2023, https://lfpress.com/news/local-news/hijacked-party-officials-quit-after-heated-conservative-nomination-fight.

27 Catherine Lévesque, "Second Tory Nominee Candidate Alleges Irregularities in Nomination Process," *National Post*, 23 May 2024, https://nationalpost.com/news/politics/second-tory-nominee-candidate-alleges-irregularities-in-nomination-process.

28 Rejected by the NCSC as unqualified, former BC cabinet minister and thirty-year MLA Michael de Jong ran unsuccessfully as an independent in Abbotsford-South Langley.

29 The Conservatives dismissed and replaced four candidates prior to nominations closing, primarily for social media indiscretions.

30 See Simon Lewsen, "Jenni Byrne's Big Gamble: The Ruthless Tactician behind Pierre Poilievre's Campaign Has Spent Decades Shaping Canadian Conservatism from behind the Scenes," *Maclean's*, 31 March 2025, https://macleans.ca/longforms/jenni-byrnes-big-gamble/.

31 Adam Radwanski, "Jenni Byrne's Redemption Story in Doug Ford's Government Comes to a Disconcerting End," *Globe and Mail*, 11 January 2019, https://www.theglobeandmail.com/canada/article-jenni-byrnes-redemption-story-in-doug-fords-government-comes-to-a/.

32 Ben Woodfinden, "The Conservatives Lost, but the Poilievre Coalition Is Only Growing Stronger," Hub, 10 May 2025, https://thehub.ca/2025/05/10/ben-woodfinden-the-conservatives-lost-this-election-but-the-poilievre-coalition-is-only-growing-stronger/.

33 Howard Anglin, "Conservatives Must Stop Putting up with Canada's Obviously Biased National Institutions," Hub, 30 September 2024, https://thehub.ca/2024/09/30/howard-anglin-conservatives-must-stop-putting-up-with-canadas-obviously-biased-national-institutions/.

34 For a much more comprehensive list of senior campaign staff see Laura Ryckewaert, "Key Hands behind Pierre Poilievre's 2025 Conservative Campaign," *Hill Times*, 7 April 2025, https://www.hilltimes.com/story/2025/04/07/key-hands-behind-pierre-poilievres-2025-conservative-campaign/456254/.

35 Éric Grenier, "Why Pierre Poilievre's Fundraising Edge Is Different: Conservatives Have a Massive Fundraising Advantage over the Liberals," *Weekly Writ* 8/7, 7 August 2024, https://www.thewrit.ca/p/weekly-writ-87-why-pierre-poilievres.

36 Ian Campbell, "Poilievre's Executive Director Pick Hints New Data System a 'Primary Focus' for Conservatives," *Hill Times*, 22 September 2022, https://www.hilltimes.com/story/2022/09/27/poilievres-executive-director-pick-hints-new-data-system-a-primary-focus-for-conservatives/284608/.

37 Conservatives spending on Meta (Facebook and Instagram) outpaced the Liberals prior to the campaign but Liberals caught up and eventually out-spent the CPC. See Stuart Benson, "Conservatives Spent Campaign 'Fending off Attacks on All Sides' as Liberals, Third Parties Dominated Meta Election Ads, Says Expert," *Hill Times*, 30 April 2025, https://www.hilltimes.com/story/2025/04/30/conservatives-spend-campaign-fending-off-attacks-on-all-sides-as-liberals-third-parties-dominated-meta-election-ads-says-expert/458349/.

38 Mark Carney, *Values* (Toronto: Penguin-Random House Canada, 2022).

39 Tyler Dawson, "'Any Level Of Damage': How Far Stephen Harper Would Go to Keep an Independent Canada," *National Post*, 12 February 2025, https://nationalpost.com/news/canada/any-level-of-damage-how-far-stephen-harper-would-go-to-keep-an-independent-canada.

40 Darrell Bricker, "Conservatives and Liberals Tied on Who's Best on #1 Issue: Affordability; Liberals Dominate on #2 Issue: Relationship with the US," Ipsos, 30 March 2025, https://www.ipsos.com/en-ca/conservatives-and-liberals-tied-whos-best-1-issue-affordability.

41 Martin Lukacs, "How Pierre Poilievre's Conservatives Seduced Working-Class Voters," Breach, 4 May 2025, https://breachmedia.ca/how-pierre-poilievres-conservatives-seduced-working-class-voters/.

42 Conservative Party of Canada, "Poilievre Thanks Labour Unions for Historic Endorsements, Unveils Plan to Fix Canada's Port," 23 April 2025,https://www.conservative.ca/poilievre-thanks-labour-unions-for-historic-endorsements-unveils-plan-to-fix-canadas-ports/.

43 Preston Manning, "Mark Carney Poses a Threat to National Unity," *Globe and Mail*, 2 April 2025, https://www.theglobeandmail.com/opinion/article-mark-carney-is-a-threat-to-national-unity/.

44 Darren Major, "Longest Ballot Protest Targets Conservative Leader Pierre Poilievre's Riding," CBC News, 7 April 2025, https://www.cbc.ca/news/politics/longest-ballot-protest-candidates-carleton-riding-poilievre-1.7503993.

4

Fighting for Relevance: The NDP Campaign

Daniel Westlake and Jacob Robbins-Kanter

The 2025 election was one of the most challenging in the NDP's history. The party had spent much of the last four years in a supply and confidence agreement with the Liberal Party, making it difficult for them to present themselves as distinct from an increasingly unpopular government. Then, the election of Donald Trump and the resultant battles over tariffs and threats to make Canada the "51st State" left the NDP struggling in an election that looked increasingly focused on whether a Conservative or Liberal prime minister could better handle the volatile US presidential administration. Finally, the selection of Mark Carney as Liberal leader helped to drive a Liberal recovery, at the NDP's expense. As a result, on the eve of the election, the NDP found itself low in the polls and facing the threat of losing official party status. Ultimately, on election night, the party won just 6.3 per cent of the vote and seven seats.

This was not the first time under Jagmeet Singh's leadership that the NDP went into an election with seemingly bleak prospects. Selected as NDP leader in 2017, Singh immediately struggled to return the party to the level of popularity it had enjoyed under leaders Jack Layton during the 2011 campaign and Thomas Mulcair during the 2015 campaign. In 2019, Singh's first campaign, the party struggled to reach 15 per cent in opinion polls and lagged well behind its major competitors in nominating local candidates. As a practicing Sikh, Singh faced challenges connecting to Quebec voters in an election where legislation to restrict the wearing of religious symbols was a salient political issue.[1] To make matters worse, the Greens appeared at that time to be a serious threat, with polls at the outset of the election placing the NDP below the Greens in Quebec and with several New Brunswick NDP executives defecting to the Greens just before the campaign began. Yet the 2019 election was not the disaster that many in the NDP might have feared, as the party managed a respectable performance, winning twenty-four seats and roughly 16 per cent of the vote. In 2021, the party largely held its 2019 seats and slightly increased its popular vote total but was again relegated to a supporting role in an election fought primarily between Liberal and Conservative leaders in the shadow of the COVID-19 pandemic. At the outset of the 2025 election, NDP strategists and sympathizers were likely left hoping the NDP could achieve a recovery like that seen in 2019 and ideally hold most of their incumbent seats.

This chapter examines the NDP's strategic dilemmas in the 2025 election campaign. We draw primarily from campaign news stories, polling data, and eight original interviews conducted with 2025 local candidates and campaign managers, as well as two additional interviews with NDP strategists. It shows that the NDP faced challenges in drawing attention to its preferred issue set, on which the party might typically mount an argument for the support of centre-left voters. To make matters worse for the party, it struggled to develop a coherent message that matched its strategic circumstances. Early in the campaign, the message pivoted from asking voters to elect an NDP government to conceding they would not win, but that a strong contingent of NDP MPs would be needed to hold a Liberal government accountable and make progressive policy gains. Crucially, this message largely failed to resonate because the Liberals remained locked in a competitive race with the Conservatives, particularly towards the final two weeks of the campaign. This meant that these target progressive voters, who planned to vote strategically for the Liberals to prevent a Conservative victory, remained out of reach for the NDP. As a result, the NDP won the lowest share of the popular vote and seat share since its predecessor party, the Cooperative Commonwealth Federation (CCF), was created in 1935. With just seven seats, the NDP fell below the twelve seats necessary to obtain official party status and the research funds, places on parliamentary committees, and extra questions during question period that come with such status. In the election aftermath, the NDP entered discussions with the Liberal Party about potentially obtaining a larger parliamentary role, despite its lack of party status. These discussions, however, did not lead to any form of special recognition.

SETTING THE CONTEXT: FROM STABILITY TO VOLATILITY

In 2021, the Liberals were returned to government with a minority and the NDP were the natural option for the Liberals as a partner to help pass legislation. A third party[2] in such a position faces a potential trade-off. By working closely with the government, it can exert substantial influence over the government's policy agenda. However, a party in this situation risks tying itself to an unpopular government and losing the ability to meaningfully critique it. Moreover, its policy influence may be overlooked or undervalued by voters in the following election. The NDP chose the former option, accepting the risk that this could make it more difficult for the party to distinguish itself from the Liberals. In March 2022, in the wake of the trucker convoy protests in Ottawa, the NDP signed a confidence and supply agreement with the Liberals. While the agreement was not a formal coalition, it committed the NDP to supporting the government on budget and other confidence motions. In exchange, the Liberals agreed to make progress on dental care and pharmacare programs that the NDP had committed to introducing over the previous couple of elections as well as to a one-time top-up of the Canada Housing Benefit.[3]

The policy consequences of the confidence and supply agreement were substantial. Under the agreement the government passed legislation banning federally regulated workplaces from using replacement workers during strikes, introduced a housing accelerator fund to support municipalities trying to increase housing construction, introduced a program to provide dental care to low-income Canadians, and took first steps towards a pharmacare program by covering diabetes medications and contraception.[4] The impact of the agreement on NDP support is difficult to detect. For its duration, NDP support on the polling aggregation website 338 Canada (which takes a weighted average of publicly available polls) hovered between 18 and 20 per cent, never climbing higher than 21 per cent nor falling below 16 per cent.[5] On the one hand this suggested that the agreement had not cost the NDP. Indeed, a senior NDP strategist contends: "I would be really hard pushed to say that the supply and confidence agreement hurt Jagmeet's brand in so far as our numbers after ending the confidence-and-supply agreement were as strong as they have been since Jack Layton."[6] On the other hand, the NDP did not appear to make gains as support for the Liberals collapsed.

Between the middle of 2023 and end of the agreement in September 2024, the Liberals fell from 31 per cent in the polling average to 25 per cent, yet NDP support was relatively static. Rather than pushing voters away from the NDP, the cost of the confidence and supply agreement may have been that it prevented the NDP from picking up voters who were unhappy with the Liberals.

The confidence and supply agreement came to an end on 4 September 2024, when the NDP pulled out of the agreement. Leader Jagmeet Singh announced its end in a video posted to social media, saying that he had "ripped up the supply and confidence agreement" and that "the Liberals had let people down, they don't deserve another chance."[7] Despite this, the NDP said they would not force an election, and less than a month later voted against a Conservative non-confidence motion, keeping the Liberals in power.[8] Singh did not commit the NDP to voting no confidence until after Chrystia Freeland's resignation from cabinet in mid-December 2024.[9] Nonetheless, NDP polling numbers hovered continually around 18 per cent through much of the fall and winter 2024. Withdrawing from the agreement did not appear to help the NDP capitalize on the Liberals' unpopularity.

There were warning signs for the party as the 2025 election approached. Over the first two decades of the twenty-first century the Liberal Party had steadily shifted leftward. This started to become clear under the leaderships of Stéphane Dion and Michael Ignatieff and continued under Justin Trudeau.[10] This shift meant that the Liberals and NDP were increasingly competing for the same voters.[11] A decline in the popularity of the Liberals should have left the NDP as the natural choice of disaffected Liberals but was of no help to the NDP. It may have been the case that the confidence and supply agreement left the NDP tied too closely to the Liberals for them to have benefited from a decline in Liberal support. Why would a voter unhappy with the Liberals shift to the party that had spent the last two years helping to keep the Liberals in power? It may have also been the case that issues driving the Liberal decline simply favoured a shift to the Conservatives, despite its polarizing leader. For much of this period, public discourse was driven by concerns over the economy and cost of living. The Conservative emphasis on making life more affordable, especially by promising to repeal the increasingly unpopular carbon tax, may simply have resonated more with voters attentive to these things than NDP proposals.

Events in early 2025 dramatically altered the political landscape. Mark Carney replaced the unpopular Justin Trudeau as Liberal leader, seeking to establish new policy and stylistic approaches, while Donald Trump repeatedly threatened Canadian sovereignty and the Canadian economy. These developments posed problems for the NDP. Without the unpopular Trudeau as leader, Liberals could make a stronger case to progressive voters. This was especially the case with respect to voters scared about the possibility of a Poilievre-led government. As the Liberals' polling improved, the notion of a Conservative victory seemed less inevitable. Therefore, the Liberals could make a much stronger case that voting strategically for them could stop the Conservatives. Trump's threats of tariffs, however, were the bigger problem for the NDP.

All parties prefer to contest elections around the issues where they enjoy the greatest public credibility or "issue ownership." In the NDP's case, social programs such as health care are the party's preferred issue set.[12] An election framed around the intersection of US-Canada relations and the economy foregrounds issues on which the Conservatives and Liberals tend to be given substantially more credibility.[13] To make matters worse for the NDP, the question of who could best handle Trump was largely a question of personality. There was a near consensus amongst the major parties in Canada that Trump's tariffs should be met with retaliation aimed at lifting the tariffs and restoring the trade relationship as much as possible. Much of the debate going into the election campaign revolved around whether Carney or Poilievre would be more effective at dealing with Trump and getting tariffs removed. It was unclear where Jagmeet Singh fit into this debate when the NDP could not credibly claim it could form government.

The impact of Trudeau's resignation and the tariffs was clearly reflected in public opinion. Figure 4.1 shows the unweighted average of polling estimates from nine different firms[14] running from January 2024 to the day before the election. The shifts in Liberal and NDP support are near mirror images of each other and match both Trudeau's resignation and the tariff threats. Liberal gains and the NDP decline start to develop when Trudeau announced that he would resign but they did not become substantial until Trump was inaugurated and imposed his first set of tariffs. The timing of these shifts leaves no doubt about their impact on NDP support. By the

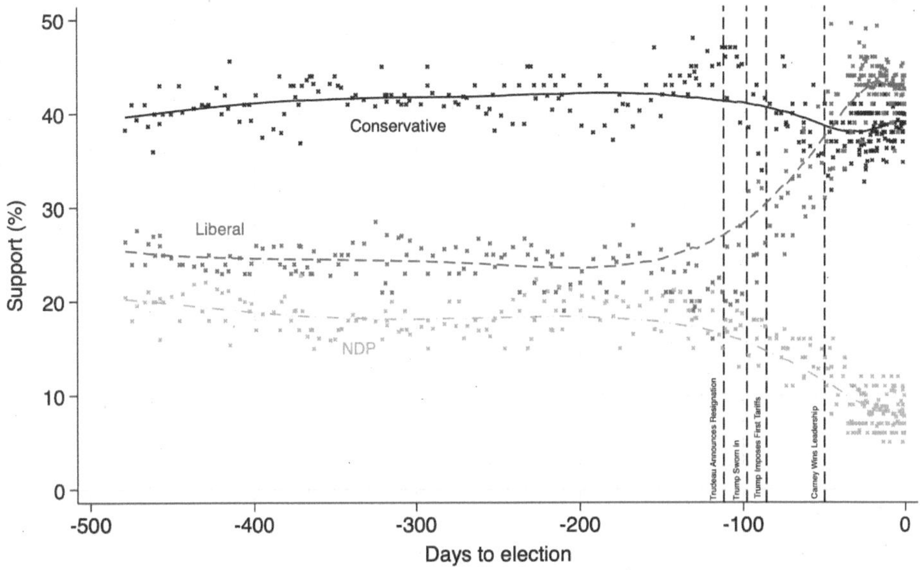

Figure 4.1 | Trend in party support from January 2024 to the 2025 election

Note: X's show estimated vote shares from polls. Lines show a LOESS trend.

Source: Links to the polls used to create this figure can be found on the Wikipedia page for polling in the lead up to the 2025 Canadian election. "Opinion Polling for the 2025 Canadian Federal Election," Wikipedia, https://en.wikipedia.org/wiki/Opinion_polling_for_the_2025_Canadian_federal_election.

time the election was called, the NDP had gone from around 17 per cent before Trudeau's resignation to just 9 per cent.

This was the context in which the NDP embarked on the 2025 campaign. Over the course of the election, it would have to fight to demonstrate its relevance to voters, speaking to issues around Canada's relationship with the US, while doing what it could to draw attention to issues where it had greater credibility, such as health care and social spending. The 2025 campaign thus presented one of the most challenging elections the NDP has faced to date.

THE CONTOURS OF THE NATIONAL CAMPAIGN

An Unfavourable Issue Environment

The overall shape of the national campaign was largely defined by the events that took place before it. Compared to the dramatic pre-election shifts, changes in support during the campaign were relatively small. This was as true for the NDP as it was for the other federal parties. The NDP hovered around 8 to 10 per cent through much of the campaign and then slightly underperformed its polling numbers on election night, finishing with 6.3 per cent of the popular vote. This is suggestive of a national campaign that had a limited impact on broader public opinion.

The campaign period presented an unfavourable issue environment for the NDP, driven by economic anxiety and sensationalist statements from the US president. In this context, the party could do little to change the issues viewed as most important by voters (see chapter 12). The cost of living and inflation, as well as the relationship with the United States, were seen as the top election issues. At the beginning of April, 50 per cent of voters listed cost of living and inflation as their most important issue, followed by 38 per cent listing the United States and tariffs as their top issue.[15] As some political commentators noted, these issue sets are linked, as the threat from the US also caused anxieties about cost of living.[16] In the campaign's final week, polling found Canada-US relations to be the top issue for 26 per cent of voters, followed by a variety of other issues.[17] The apprehension around Canada-US relations and the broader global environment was underscored by a late April poll showing that 84 per cent of respondents felt the world to be more dangerous than it had been five years previously, and 83 per cent seeing economic threats as Canada's greatest security concern.[18]

The NDP struggled to find ways to take positions that set them apart from the Liberals and the Conservatives. Debates over the Canada-US relationship were particularly challenging. The rhetoric from the different parties about the need to stand up to the US was fairly similar, though the Liberals and the NDP tried to paint Poilievre as unreliable on the issue. On policy, the differences between the three parties were limited. Both the Conservatives and the Liberals made commitments to invest in defence and security while the Liberals also prioritized strengthening internal trade. In contrast, the NDP committed to use money from counter tariffs to support workers and to overhaul federal procurement policies to buy Canadian materials.

A major problem the NDP faced in its positions on Canada-US relations is that most voters did not believe that Singh would be the person negotiating with Trump. Given this, and absent a highly distinctive position on the Canada-US relationship, this election-defining issue looked very much like a choice between the Liberals and Conservatives. This was a difficult predicament for the NDP, and it is not clear what they could have done to change this. Canada's economy is so closely tied to that of the US that there are few viable policy responses to the tariff threats.

The cost of living and housing offered the NDP slightly more fertile ground. As a social democratic party, these issues should have offered space for the NDP to advocate for greater government intervention to address rising costs. Here, the party committed to establishing a fund to help cities build housing quickly, to introduce rent control and price caps on essential food items, and to remove the GST on essential goods such as diapers, internet, and home heating bills.[19] As has often been the case in recent elections, many of these commitments involved policy areas in provincial jurisdiction.[20] Again, however, the NDP faced challenges in trying to distinguish themselves from the other parties. The Conservatives committed to cutting the GST on new homes, and to rewarding cities for increasing their homebuilding, while the Liberals promised to create a program called Build Canada Homes that would allow the federal government to support efforts to increase housing supply. All three parties offered a variation on a low-income-bracket tax cut. The Conservatives committed to cutting the lowest income bracket rate from 15 to 12.75 per cent, the Liberals promised to cut the tax on the lowest income bracket by 1 percentage point, and the NDP promised to raise the basic personal amount on which Canadians do not pay tax from $15,705 to $19,500.[21]

The NDP's policy proposals may not have been sufficiently distinctive for voters to be left with a clear idea of how and why the party differed from its competitors. The Conservative commitment to eliminate the carbon tax (sold as "axe the tax") stands out as a clear example of presenting a policy that was easy for voters to understand, to remember, and (at least until the Liberals reversed their position on the consumer carbon tax) set them apart from their competitors. It is not clear that any of the NDP's policies on the cost of living or housing served that purpose.

From Seeking to Grow the Party to Saving the Furniture

Faced with a difficult issue environment, the NDP shifted their strategic approach early in the campaign. The NDP began by saying that it aspired to expand its vote and seat shares, with Singh even starting the campaign saying that he was running to be prime minister.[22] Singh's leader's tour also began in areas where the NDP hoped to pick up seats, with the first stop of the campaign in downtown Montreal. Here, Singh appeared at the campaign office opening for a prominent local candidate, Julie Girard-Lemay in Hochelaga-Rosemont-Est. The leader was flanked by neighbouring Rosemont MP Alexandre Boulerice and two other prominent candidates: long-time Montreal city councilor Craig Savué, who had nearly won a recent by-election in Lasalle-Émard-Verdun, and epidemiologist Nimâ Machouf, who had come close to unseating Liberal cabinet minister Steven Guilbeault in the riding of Laurier-Sainte Marie in 2021. According to those present at the event, the NDP was in expansion mode, hoping to start building back a presence in Quebec, particularly by targeting districts held by the left-wing Québec Solidaire in the provincial legislature. Each of these candidates felt the dynamics in their particular riding presented an opportunity for NDP gains. Nimâ Machouf argued that voters in her environmentally conscious district might reward her third outing against Steven Guilbeault: "It's a race between the Liberals and Conservatives to see who can invest more in pipelines ... all projects that Quebecers don't want. The population has made that clear ... I think I have a good chance here despite the rise of Mark Carney. Here in Laurier-Sainte Marie there is no chance the Conservatives will be elected ... people don't have to worry about voting strategically. Not voting Liberal doesn't mean another Conservative will be in Parliament. People can vote their conscience, which I think will favour us."[23]

Similarly, Julie Girard-Lemay stated that in her left-leaning district, "people are very satisfied with the policies espoused by the NDP, and by the policy gains the party brought about in recent years. They are tired of the Liberals."[24] For his part, Craig Sauvé recalled that "I was there for the 2011 'Orange Wave.' We started like 13 per cent, 15 per cent in Canada. We went down to lows and, like a basketball that bounced, went back the other way."[25] Drawing on the NDP's core issue set, Sauvé contended that: "[Carney] is not talking about the health sector, in fact, he's talking about cutting the operations budget ... That's health transfers, that's social services transfers ... [we will be] talking about the things that matter to us, that even in the worst crisis, we must be fully operational and strong. For us, that is a social safety net. That's housing, that's our affordability, that's our ability to keep ourselves together, and have that solidarity."[26]

In Sauvé's case, he had received 26 per cent of the vote in a 2024 by-election in his district, only 2 per cent less than the winning candidate. In 2021, Machouf received 33 per cent versus 38 per cent for Guilbeault. And Girard-Lemay's progressive-leaning neighbourhood borders the NDP's incumbent Quebec seat in Rosemont-La Petite-Patrie. In this respect, during the early days of the campaign, the NDP aimed to expand their Quebec foothold.

Overall, the leader's tour spent the first week of the campaign in Quebec and Ontario, splitting time between places like Hamilton, London, and Windsor where the party was trying to hold on to seats, and Montreal and Toronto where it was trying to make gains. Notably, Singh did not spend any time during the first week in British Columbia, where more than half the NDP caucus in the previous parliament had been elected. Indeed, prior to the debates, Singh made just four stops in British Columbia. It is difficult to square this early expansionist approach with where the NDP stood at the beginning of the campaign. As noted in figure 4.1, the NDP began the campaign polling well below the 18 per cent it won in the 2021 election. Polling aggregators such as Philippe J. Fournier's 338.com had the NDP in particular trouble in BC, at risk of losing all but one of its seats in the province.

Eventually, the NDP campaign refocused to trying to hold as many seats as possible. This came through when, two weeks into the campaign, Singh dropped the messaging that he was running to be prime minister, instead arguing that voters should elect NDP MPs in order to hold the Liberals accountable.[27] After the debates, the NDP also changed the focus of their leader's tour, making fifteen stops in BC, largely in ridings where they had incumbents under pressure. These included multiple stops in places like Victoria, Nanaimo, and Burnaby. When the campaign made stops outside of BC post-debate, they largely went to places where they had incumbents, such as Edmonton, Winnipeg, London, and Windsor. Where the campaign had made a large number of stops in Montreal and Toronto prior to the debates, after the debates it restricted itself to just two stops in Toronto. It also made just one stop in Quebec after the debates, in Yamachiche where former MP Ruth Ellen Brosseau was running to regain the Berthier-Maskinongé riding that she held in 2011 and 2015.

There is evidence the campaign knew from the outset that it was facing these challenges. A senior NDP campaign staffer noted that this campaign had an unprecedented strategic voting dynamic:

> Insofar as this campaign, more than any I've been engaged with before, and I've worked as a senior staffer in maybe about a half dozen campaigns … had this really unique quality of strategic voting being not just an underlying factor as it often is … and more of an overtone, people were talking explicitly about strategic voting … [our data] it indicated that people were saying I like Jagmeet Singh … I appreciate what you do. You align closely with my values, but it's just too bad I feel like I have absolutely no choice but to vote Liberal in order to keep Pierre Poilievre from becoming prime minister. I just have no choice. I don't like it. It's not what I want to do, I'm not sure I'm totally comfortable with it, but it is what I have to do.[28]

In this respect the NDP faced a potentially fatal combination of fear – a fear of Donald Trump and a fear of Pierre Poilievre – which marginalized the party and pushed centre-left voters to the Liberals.

This dynamic was also felt at the ground level. A campaign manager in Ontario explains: "So much now we get to the door and they're like, 'Yeah, I'm just scared.' I would say it's like a level of fear. The fear is insane. It's both fear of Trump and America and an uncertainty and trade wars and tariffs and stuff, but it's also fear of Poilievre and that type of politics."[29] The campaign manager further highlights fear of the Conservative leader as rallying voters and resources to the Liberals: "Poilievre threw a regional rally here … [where] 3,000 people showed up to go see him at a hall, and then the Liberals got $10,000 in donations the day after that … we got $10,000 in donations over like weeks of begging people [we struggle] because I think it's fear. You knock on the door and you're like, 'Hey, I'm here for the election' and they gulp and they're like, 'Yeah, I'm sorry. I like the NDP … but I'm so scared right now.'"[30]

NDP candidate Daria Juüdi-Hope, who ran in Kingston and the Islands, notes that this strategic voting dynamic was not limited to competitive ridings: "Our riding is safe, Liberal-wise, as a traditionally, forever, unfortunately, Liberal riding."[31] Nonetheless, she said,

"I know that folks in our riding see that, yes, there is a fear that, 'Oh, my goodness, if we vote for you, we may allow for Poilievre to be the prime minister.'"[32] A local campaign official in Toronto suggested similarly that: "There's a lot of ... scared of Trump slash scared of Poilievre voters. You know, I wish it were a rollover [from the Ontario election]. It doesn't make sense. We have so many seats provincially, and I don't know if we'll have any seats federally in Toronto."[33]

Even worse for the NDP, as a senior strategist reported, the NDP was also hearing voters say they felt they had to strategically vote Liberal "in ridings where the NDP would [normally] be the strategic vote."[34] The strategist describes the essence of the party's argument on the need to have NDP MPs in Parliament: "I'm running for prime minister ... that was not going to work. And so fairly early on, you saw a pivot in the language from the leader, but also right down to the doorsteps, in language that matched where people were at. And that was to say, in most places ... [we need to] avoid giving one party all the power. We need New Democrats to actually make progress. Under minority governments with a strong New Democrat group, you get things like Medicare, dental care, and pharmacare legislation. We don't need to be the government, you just need to elect enough of us so to be a real force for good and to force progress because we know the Liberals don't do it on their own."[35]

As the strategist recalled, once they had adopted this message, the NDP campaign faced challenges adapting it to different ridings: "Trying to square the circle of how to deliver that message in ridings that we wanted to pick up and could pick up ... versus ridings where we had an incumbent but the Liberals were strong, versus ridings where we had an incumbent but the Conservatives were strong, that's a little bit of 3D chess that requires a lot of work on the ground on how to deliver that message in the most effective way. And it requires a lot of work in the central campaign to figure out how to deliver materials including ads and leaflets that will work for those multiple audience groups."[36]

The pre-campaign shift in support had also created challenges for the NDP in that key assumptions about target seats had to change. Prior to Trudeau's resignation and the Trump tariffs, the Conservatives were the likely main competitors in a number of ridings, particularly in Western Canada. This changed as the Liberals gained ground and started to look competitive in places where they had not been in recent elections. Saskatoon West NDP candidate Rachel Loewen

Walker described preparing for a campaign in which they expected to be fighting a "blue storm" and then "after week two [they] weren't even thinking about the Conservatives because [they] were so focused on the Liberals."[37] This was in a riding where the Liberals had never finished higher than third, and in the past two elections had won less than 10 per cent of the vote. NDP candidates in ridings such as Churchill-Keewatinook Aski, Esquimalt-Saanich-Sooke, Nanaimo-Ladysmith, and Victoria likely faced similar challenges as they ended up facing Liberal candidates who were suddenly competitive in ridings where the Liberals had not been competitive for a long time. In some cases, such as Victoria, this left New Democrats fighting to hold on to districts that historically had been safe NDP ridings. In others, like Nanaimo-Ladysmith and Saskatoon West, it left three-way races where a year before they would have reasonably expected to be in two-way fights with the Conservatives.

This dynamic clearly changed how some NDP candidates approached their campaigns, Loewen Walker describes going into the campaign expecting to work against a Conservative Party that was dominant in the polls but who voters were not excited about and whose leader "was not popular in Saskatoon West."[38] Instead, the NDP ended up in a three-way race that included a Liberal Party with a leader who was seen as someone who could stand up effectively to the threat from the US. Adjusting to these changing circumstances ended up presenting a challenge to NDP campaigns both national and local.

At the local level, the party also appears to have struggled to recruit volunteers. A Toronto-area campaign manager jokingly suggested having to ask volunteers, "Would you like to help us retain party status, maybe?" Fundraising was also a challenge, according to a party strategist: "because people just gave provincially [in the 2025 Ontario election]."[39] The NDP's limited prospects for success also conceivably made fundraising more difficult.

There were messier parts of the NDP campaign that may have betrayed the party's dire situation. In the middle of the campaign, Singh accused polling aggregators of being "massively wrong" without providing any evidence.[40] The NDP also ended up pressuring a strategic voting organization, Smart Voting, to change its data or models in instances where the organization had the NDP in the third place. Hamilton Centre candidate Matthew Green went so far as to suggest the organization was "Liberal-paid."[41] The NDP has certainly faced challenges associated with strategic voting in the past and has had to make the argument that voters should either not strategically vote or that it is the strategic option in some ridings. In the past, these efforts have rarely gone so far as to target or cast doubt on the veracity of polling and aggregators or strategic voting organizations. It is telling that in this campaign the NDP decided to try to discredit those providing data that could be used for strategic voting instead of making a principled argument against the practice.

The NDP's national campaign thus faced a number of challenges, some of which were beyond their control and some of which were not. The NDP could do little to change the issues that were important in the election or the fact that many voters felt they had to vote strategically. More within its control, the NDP could conceivably have had a clearer and more distinctive message on issues that cover more favourable terrain than Canada's relationship with the US. As well, the party could have planned from the outset to do everything possible to save incumbent-held seats. This would have required a much more tailored campaign focused on these districts, more efficient resource allocation, and a clear message of what NDP legislators would accomplish, including on cost-of-living issues. On the latter, NDP messaging on affordability issues had been forgettable. Despite natural openings for a left-of-centre party to champion causes such as building affordable housing, raising the minimum wage, or reducing tax burdens on workers, it was the Conservative Party that seemed to capture attention on issues of affordability and housing. It should be acknowledged that, compared to the Liberals and Conservatives, the NDP faces greater difficulty attracting media coverage and has a smaller budget for paid advertising. Moreover, in an election dominated by US-Canada relations, it was even more difficult than usual for NDP messaging to break through to voters, which is all the more reason why such issues needed to be emphasized before the start of the campaign.

Illustrating the challenges of resource allocation and central party priorities, a post-campaign news story reported that NDP headquarters allocated substantial numbers of staffers to Jagmeet Singh's riding of Burnaby Central, even though their polling would have showed the seat was out of reach for the NDP.[42] Indeed, Singh placed a distant third there, losing by more than twelve thousand votes, whereas an allocation of resources to closer races might have been better advised.

TURNING VOTES INTO SEATS – BATTLING ELECTORAL SYSTEM GEOGRAPHY

The NDP always faces a challenge translating votes into seats. Single member plurality systems tend to work against smaller parties with geographically dispersed voters, and the NDP has been no exception. In every election except for 2011 the NDP has won a lower percentage of seats than its percentage of votes. For the NDP to maximize its seat share it needs to ensure that its votes are as concentrated as possible in competitive ridings. This requires strong local campaigns in the party's geographic pockets of strength. This was especially the case in an election with a smaller number of seats to defend; accounting for retiring incumbents, the NDP had only seventeen incumbent-held seats.

Local campaigns matter, but their influence should not be overstated. Studies on local campaigns and candidates suggest that such campaigns can influence between 4 and 10 per cent of voters.[43] In this respect, the NDP had the advantage of having multiple incumbent MPs with strong local reputations. These included Alexandre Boulerice in Rosemont-La Petite-Patrie, Brian Masse in Windsor West, Niki Ashton in Churchill-Keewatinook Aski, and Peter Julian in New Westminster-Burnaby-Maillardville. However, many of these candidates faced challenges as a result of the NDP's weak position in national polls and the problems with the NDP's national campaign. To hang onto their seats, they would have needed to substantially outperform the NDP's national vote share.

There were certainly efforts on the part of local candidates to make strategic voting arguments in ridings where they felt they could make a compelling case that the NDP was in a better position to stop a Conservative from winning than the Liberals. Candidates such as Laurel Collins in Victoria and Tanille Johnston in North Island-Powell River made use of signs and online imagery with the tagline "BC votes NDP to stop Conservatives."[44] The kinds of strategic voting arguments some local campaigns were making comes through in the leaflet from Maja Tait's campaign in Esquimalt-Saanich-Sooke, shown in figure 4.2. Even in ridings that the NDP had not won in the 2021 election, but had finished second, such as in Saskatoon West and Saskatoon-University, NDP candidates made arguments that they were the strategic option.

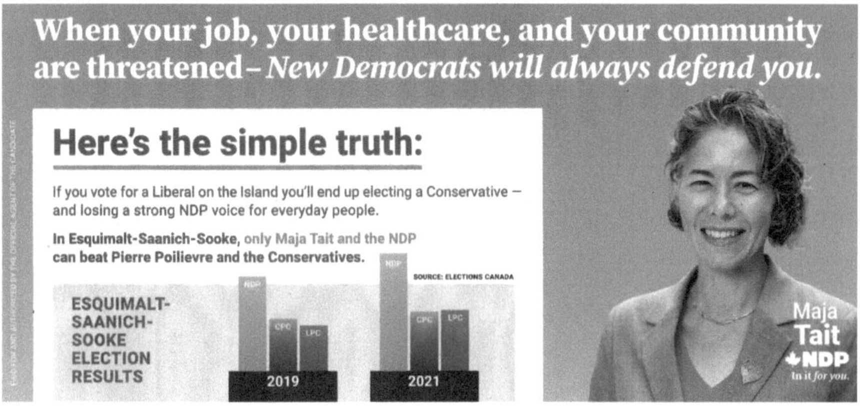

Figure 4.2 | Esquimalt-Saanich-Sooke strategic voting literature

Given the party's struggles in national polling, it is worth focusing on where the NDP had its best prospects to retain seats. The NDP's ability to hold on to its vote in incumbent ridings varied considerably. Figure 4.3 shows the percentage of its 2021 vote that the party lost in 2025. Of these candidates, Gord Johns in Courtney-Alberni and Taylor Bachrach in Skeena-Bulkley Valley held on to the largest proportion of their vote, losing less than 10 per cent of their 2021 vote. Other candidates that did notably well in this regard were Alexandre Boulerice in Rosemont-La Petite-Patrie, Blake Desjarlais in Edmonton Griesbach, and Tanille Johnston in North Island-Powell River. Despite holding on to more of the party's 2021 vote than other NDP candidates, three of these candidates (Bachrach, Desjarlais, and Johnston) lost their seats. Taylor Bachrach was in a challenging situation because he was running against a star candidate for the Conservatives in Ellis Ross, a prominent Indigenous leader in the riding and former provincial MLA. Desjarlais and Johnston were running in ridings where the NDP had won by 4 percentage points or less in the previous election, and so neither could afford even small losses.

A number of prominent NDP candidates performed relatively poorly compared to 2021. Peter Julian, Brian Masse, and leader Jagmeet Singh all lost a greater percentage of the 2021 vote than the

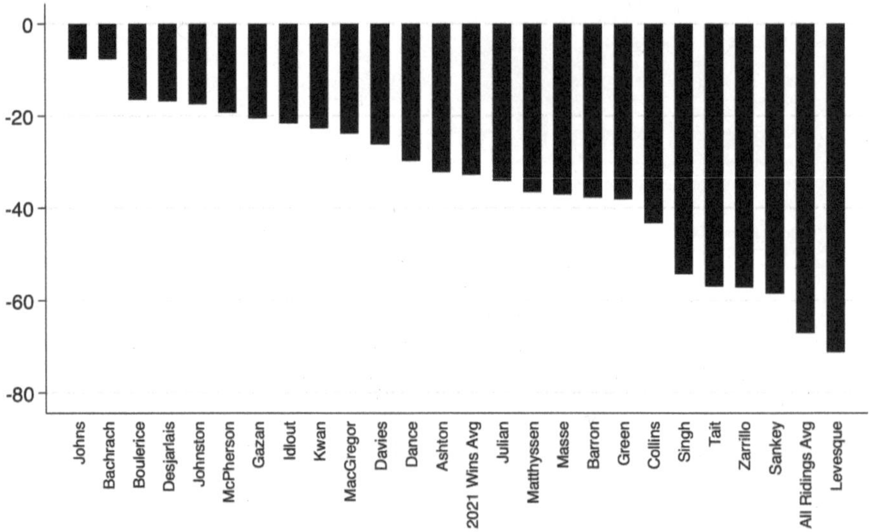

Figure 4.3 | Percentage of 2021 NDP vote lost by candidates in ridings the NDP won in 2021

average NDP candidate running in a district the party had won in 2021. The relatively high profiles of long-serving MPs Don Davies and Niki Ashton did not protect those candidates from losing substantial shares of their 2021 vote. Such instances suggest that the NDP's attempt to argue that they were the strategic choice in certain regions and incumbent-held ridings did not work. The riding of Victoria is illustrative of this. Laurel Collins had been a city councillor before winning the riding for the first time in 2019. The NDP has also held Victoria since 2006, almost always winning it by at least 10 percentage points. Despite this, Collins lost 43 per cent of her 2021 vote. Candidates who were running in ridings the NDP won in 2021 but were not themselves incumbents did particularly poorly. Of the four candidates to lose the largest shares of the party's 2021 votes, three were replacing retiring incumbents. These were Maja Tait replacing Randall Garrison in Esquimalt-Saanich-Sooke, Linda Sankey replacing Richard Cannings in Similkameen-South Okanagan-West Kootenay, and Nicole Fortier Levesque replacing Charlie Angus in Kapuskasing-Timmins-Mushkegowuk. Tanille Johnston was the only candidate replacing a retiring incumbent who did well relative to other NDP candidates, suggesting that incumbency did help some candidates to hold on to some of their vote share.

It is difficult to know if the NDP could have done more to ensure their vote was distributed more efficiently. Singh made multiple stops in London, Hamilton, and Windsor. Despite this, the three NDP incumbents in those cities all fared quite poorly, finishing third. It is remarkable, however, that losses in five British Columbia ridings that had previously been relatively safe NDP seats (Burnaby Centre, Cowichan-Malahat-Langford, Esquimalt-Saanich-Sooke, New Westminster-Burnaby-Maillardville, and Victoria) made up the difference between the NDP winning seven seats and the party getting the twelve seats it needed to maintain official party status. One wonders if investing more time in those ridings early in the campaign might have helped the NDP hold on to official party status.

WHERE TO FROM HERE? THE LESSONS OF THE 2025 ELECTION FOR THE NDP

Moving forward, the NDP faces substantial challenges and some potential opportunities. That the party suffered its losses to a Liberal Party that had shifted rightward and benefitted from strategic voting in a unique election issue environment suggests space for the NDP to grow its support. If the next election is less focused on Canada's relationship with the United States, the NDP may be able to get more attention paid to issues where it can make potentially compelling and credible arguments. These may include health care, social programs, affordability, and the environment. To do this, the NDP will need to do a better job distinguishing themselves from the Liberals and making these issues clear and memorable in their messaging. Compared to Justin Trudeau, Mark Carney has moved the party rightward, as seen in decisions to eliminate the consumer carbon tax and a scheduled capital gains tax increase, as well as a greater openness to the oil and gas sector. This may provide space for the NDP to win back more left-of-centre voters. Polling conducted in May 2025 also showed that 38 per cent of Canadians state they are open to voting for the NDP.[45] Nonetheless, the poor performance of incumbents in ridings where the NDP should have been the strategic option suggests that the effectiveness of riding-based strategic voting arguments is limited. While voters are generally attentive to national polling trends and unpersuaded by such arguments, the NDP might instead focus on messaging that convinces voters it is worth forgoing a strategic vote by supporting the party.

Further, despite such a significant defeat, the 2025 election left the NDP sharing the balance of power in parliament with the Bloc Québécois. After having fallen just short of a majority, the Liberals will need partners in order to pass legislation, and that gives the NDP some policy influence. A formal agreement of the kind that was negotiated in the last parliament is unlikely, but there may be opportunities for the NDP to negotiate legislative concessions with the Liberals, especially if the Conservatives and Bloc are unwilling to support the government.

Having lost official party status, the NDP faces significant resource challenges. This is true both with respect to funding, as the NDP will not receive the public funding for paid research staff that parties with official status in parliament enjoy, and with respect to media attention. With fewer questions in question period and without guaranteed places on committees it will be more difficult for the NDP to circulate its message in the media. That said, since it is increasingly difficult to reach voters through the traditional news media, this raises the importance of paid advertising. Here, the NDP also lacks crucial funds to achieve goals such as introducing a new party leader to voters through a digital advertising campaign. The party will also face resource challenges that result from lost reimbursement for local campaigns. Local campaigns get 60 per cent of their spending reimbursed by the federal government if they manage to win at least 10 per cent of the vote. In this election, 297 of the NDP's 342[46] candidates fell below this threshold for partial expenses reimbursement. This loss of reimbursements could be a significant blow to the party's ability to run competitive local campaigns.

There is also the danger of internal fragmentation following such a poor result. With a leadership race following Singh's resignation, different factions within the party will have competing ideas of why the party lost and proposals for how it should move forward. In particular, the party may have to decide if it wishes to pursue a bolder left-wing vision or accept ideological compromises with the aim of competing for government. Along these lines, that three of the seven remaining MPs wrote a letter expressing concern with the lack of consultation by the party head office before appointing Don Davies as interim leader gives credence to concerns of significant infighting

(Bailey, 2025).[47] Leadership candidates will also have to raise funds to compete in the leadership contest, which may crowd out desperately needed local and national fundraising efforts.

Finally, while the timing of the shifts of Liberal and NDP support suggest the Liberals are the bigger threat to the NDP, the challenges the Conservatives present should not be discounted. Polacko et al. demonstrate that the Conservatives have made gains over the past couple of decades amongst working-class voters with socially conservative views.[48] Westlake et al. also show that members of construction unions are more likely than other union members to vote Conservative.[49] That the Conservatives pose a threat to the NDP in ridings with large numbers of working-class voters is reflected in the results in Windsor-Tecumseh-Lakeshore and Windsor West. In Windsor-Tecumseh-Lakeshore the NDP vote declined by 24 percentage points compared to 2021 while the Conservative vote share increased by 18 percentage points. In Windsor West, the NDP vote share declined by 16 percentage points while the Conservative vote share increased by almost twenty. The threat the NDP faces from the Conservatives matches what other social democratic parties face. In their edited volume, Häusermann and Kitschelt show that, while social democratic parties are losing some votes to right-wing parties, they are losing more to liberal, green, and other left parties.[50] As a result, social democratic parties that adjust their positions to prevent defections to the right risk losing even more voters to other liberal and left parties. The NDP faces similar challenges. Any attempt to adjust to win back voters lost to the Conservatives risks making it harder to win back the larger number of voters they have lost to the Liberals.

How the NDP deals with these challenges will inform whether the party can regain the substantial ground that it lost in the 2025 campaign. To do so, it will need to be more strategic and disciplined in its use of resources and messaging. It must demonstrate to target voters that it offers a unique and politically viable alternative to the Liberals.

NOTES

1 CBC News, "Jagmeet Singh Hopes To Change Quebecers' Views On Religious Symbols," CBC News, 24 September 2025, https://www.cbc.ca/news/politics/singh-religous-symbols-own-identity-bill-21-quebec-1.5294265.

2 By third party we mean a party in the House of Commons that is neither in government nor the official opposition.
3 Aaron Wherry et al., "How the Liberals and New Democrats Made a Deal to Preserve the Minority Government," CBC News, 27 March 2022, https://www.cbc.ca/news/politics/liberal-ndp-accord-confidence-supply-agreement-1.6397985.
4 Darren Major, "What Was Left Undone by the Liberal-NDP Governance Agreement?," Radio Canada, 5 September 2024, https://ici.radio-canada.ca/rci/en/news/2102269/what-was-left-undone-by-the-liberal-ndp-governance-agreement.
5 Philippe J. Fournier, "338canada Federal Projection," 338Canada, https://338canada.com/federal.htm.
6 Interview with author.
7 Sean Boynton and Jillian Piper, "NDP Pulls Out Of Supply-and-Confidence Deal with Liberal Government," Global News, 4 September 2025, https://globalnews.ca/news/10732510/ndp-pulls-out-of-liberal-deal/.
8 Darren Major, "Liberals Survive First Confidence Vote after the End of Governance Agreement with NDP," CBC News, 25 September 2024, https://www.cbc.ca/news/politics/conservative-confidence-motion-result-1.7333819.
9 Rahim Mohamed, "Jagmeet Singh Promises Non-Confidence Motion When Parliament Returns," *National Post*, 20 December 2024, https://nationalpost.com/news/canada/jagmeet-singh-promises-trudeau-government.
10 Richard Johnston, "Canada Is Polarizing – and It Is Because of the Parties," in Daniel J. Hopkins and John Sides (eds), *Political Polarization in American Politics* (New York: Bloomsbury Academic, 2015); Royce Koop and Amanda Bittner, "Parties and Elections After 2011: The Fifth Canadian Party System?" in Amanda Bittner and Royce Koop (eds), *Parties, Elections, and the Future of Canadian Politics* (Vancouver: UBC Press, 2013); Daniel Westlake, "Electoral Politics and the Working Class: The Case of the Liberal Party," in Jacob Robbins-Kanter, Royce Koop, and Daniel Troup (eds), *The Working Class and Politics in Canada* (Vancouver: UBC Press, 2025).
11 Westlake, "Electoral Politics and the Working Class"
12 Éric Bélanger and Bonnie Meguid, "Issue Salience, Issue Ownership, and Issue-Based Vote Choice," *Electoral Studies* 27, no. 3 (2008): 477–91.
13 Richard Nadeau and Frédérick Bastien, "Political Campaigning," in Alain G-Gagnon and A. Brian Tanguay (eds), *Canadian Parties in Transition Fifth Edition* (Toronto: University of Toronto Press, 2024).

14 The firms we included are Abacus Data, Angus Reid, EKOS, Innovative Research, Ipsos, Leger, Mainstreet Research, Nanos Research, and Research Co.
15 Angus Reid Institute, "Election 45: Carney Preferred on Top Issues; Canadians Divided on Spend Vs Cut; Concern over Foreign Interference," Angus Reid Institute, 2 April 2025, https://angusreid.org/election-45-top-issues/.
16 David Coletto, "Abacus Data Poll: Defining the Ballot Box Question," Abacus Data, 25 March 2025, https://abacusdata.ca/2025-federal-election-poll-ballot-question-2/.
17 Mario Canseco, "No Minor Shifts Seen in the Final Weeks of Canada's Federal Election," Research Co., 27 April 2025, https://researchco.ca/2025/04/27/cdnpoli-lateapril2025/.
18 EKOS Politics, "Profound Shifts in Canadian Outlook on the World and Our Place in It," EKOS Politics, 25 April 2025, https://www.ekospolitics.com/index.php/2025/04/profound-shifts-in-canadian-outlook-on-the-world-and-our-place-in-it/.
19 NDP, *Made for People. Built for Canada*, 2025, https://www.ndp.ca/campaign-commitments.
20 Federal parties often make commitments that affect policy areas in provincial jurisdiction. This does not necessarily hurt them with voters as voters rarely have an in-depth understanding of the policy areas that fall under federal jurisdiction and those that fall under provincial jurisdiction. It does, however, complicate the ability of parties to deliver on their commitments once they are elected.
21 NDP. *Made for People. Built for Canada.*
22 David Thurton, "NDP's Singh Drops 'I'm Running for Prime Minister' Messaging Two Weeks into the Campaign," CBC News, 6 April 2025, https://www.cbc.ca/news/politics/canada-election-singh-ndp-campaign-week-3-pm-messaging-1.7502671.
23 Interview with author. Translated from French by the author.
24 Interview with author. Translated from French by the author.
25 Interview with author.
26 Interview with author.
27 Thurton, "NDP's Singh Drops 'I'm Running For Prime Minister' Messaging Two Weeks into the Campaign."
28 Interview with author.
29 Interview with author.
30 Interview with author.
31 Interview with author.

32 Interview with author.
33 Interview with author.
34 Interview with author.
35 Interview with author.
36 Interview with author.
37 Interview with author.
38 Interview with author.
39 Interview with author.
40 Thurton, "NDP's Singh Drops 'I'm Running for Prime Minister' Messaging Two Weeks into the Campaign."
41 Isaac Peltz, "NDP Faces Harassment Allegations And An Internal Collapse," *Rover*, 12 April 2025, https://therover.ca/ndp-faces-harassment-allegations-and-an-internal-collapse/.
42 David Thurton, "Inside The NDP's Last Ditch Efforts To Save Jagmeet Singh And His Riding," CBC News, 24 May 2025, https://www.cbc.ca/news/politics/jagmeet-singh-riding-burnaby-central-election-1.7542379.
43 André Blais et al., "Does the Local Candidate Matter? Candidate Effects in the Canadian Election of 2000," *Canadian Journal of Political Science.* 36, no. 3 (2003): 657–64; Jason Roy and Christopher Alcantara, "The Candidate Effect: Does the Local Candidate Matter?," *Journal of Elections, Public Opinion, and Parties.* 25, no. 2 (2015): 195–214; Benjamin Allen Stevens et al., "Local Candidate Effects in Canadian Elections," *Canadian Journal of Political Science.* 52, no 1 (2019): 83–96.
44 Laurel Collins, "Our Wonderful Sign Wave Crew Was In Quadra Village This Afternoon," Facebook, 26 April 2025, https://www.facebook.com/photo/?fbid=1073252944618990&set=a.291532109457748; Tanille Johnston, "Reminder! Advance Polls Close at 9 p.m. Tonight!," Instagram, 21 April 2025, https://www.instagram.com/p/DIuX7wihc2k/.
45 David Coletto, "Four Myths (and One Truth) about the 2025 Federal Election," Hub, 11 June 2025, https://thehub.ca/2025/06/11/david-coletto-four-myths-and-one-truth-about-the-2025-federal-election/.
46 The NDP did not run a full slate of 343 candidates as the party did not have a candidate in South Shore-St Margarets.
47 Ian Bailey, "NDP Caucus Members Dispute the Appointment of Interim Leader Don Davies," *Globe and Mail*, 16 May 2025, https://www.theglobeandmail.com/politics/article-ndp-caucus-members-letter-interim-leader-don-davies/.
48 Matthew Polacko, Simon Kiss, and Peter Graefe, "The Changing Nature of Class Voting in Canada, 1965–2019," *Canadian Journal of Political Science.* 55, no 3 (2022): 663–86.

49 Daniel Westlake, Larry Savage, and Jonah Butovsky, "The Labour Vote Revisited: Impacts of Union Type and Demographics on Electoral Behaviour in Canadian Federal Politics," *Canadian Journal of Political Science*. 58, no. 3 (2025): 642–65.

50 Silja Häussermann and Herbert Kitschelt, *Beyond Social Democracy: The Transformation of the Left in Emerging Knowledge Societies* (Cambridge: Cambridge University Press, 2024).

5

The Bloc Québécois and the Anti-System Dilemma

Eric Montigny and Katryne Villeneuve-Siconnelly

At the end of 2024, Yves-François Blanchet, the leader of the Bloc Québécois (BQ), could have dreamed of repeating Lucien Bouchard's 1993 feat of occupying the seat of leader of the opposition in the House of Commons. Various polling aggregators had the Bloc aspiring once again to the title of "His Majesty's Loyal Opposition" and its leader taking the keys to an official Ottawa residence, Stornoway. The previous summer, the Bloc Québécois had even managed to wrest a riding from the Liberals in Montreal's West End. It was a different world, long before Justin Trudeau's departure, Donald Trump's swearing-in, and his threats to annex Canada to the United States.

In an interview with Canadian Press, Blanchet outlined the attitude he would adopt as leader of the official opposition in Ottawa: "If that happens, I can only tell you that we respect institutions ... even though we've already said that the Senate should be abolished, that the monarchy in Canada should be abolished, but we're not here to break toys,"[1] he said.[2] He added that he would have a "positive and constructive attitude," while reiterating that Quebecers should choose sovereignty. He also told the rest of Canada that it had nothing to fear from the Bloc Québécois.

Only a few months earlier, the Bloc had chosen to break with the strategy it had adopted since Blanchet took over as leader, and to put a greater emphasis on the independence project. After the Coalition Avenir Québec (CAQ) formed the provincial government in 2018, the BQ adopted a more autonomist discourse.[3] Without officially renouncing the goal of Quebec independence, the party would instead emphasize defending Quebec's interests. What's more, independence was not even on Blanchet's 2021 agenda.[4] This was in stark contrast to the downright anti-system, resolutely pro-independence stance adopted only a few years earlier by Martine Ouellet, who had led the party in 2017–18.

In January 2025, when the Parti Québécois (PQ) was leading the polls in Quebec with its promise of a referendum on Quebec sovereignty, Blanchet didn't hesitate to see the election of the federal Bloc Québécois as a prelude to the election of the PQ provincially, and then to independence. He even used the metaphor of the three hockey periods once used by Jacques Parizeau: as a columnist from *Le Devoir* recalled, the first period was the 1993 federal election, won handily by Lucien Bouchard's newly formed Bloc Québécois; the PQ's 1994 victory was the second; the 1995 referendum the third.[5]

In this chapter, we will examine how, in this election campaign, the leader of the Bloc behaved like a tightrope walker. Since its founding, the relationship between the Bloc and the Parti Québécois has proven complex. Considered sister parties, the Bloc Québécois often has to follow the Parti Québécois' lead when it comes to Quebec's independence. However, in its electoral strategies, it must take into account that it is running in a federal parliament. And this time, the particular context imposed by American threats to Canada's independence made this balancing act even more complex, caught between the PQ's promise of an early referendum if elected to power in the next provincial election in 2026, and the sudden and unexpected rise of Canadian nationalism in Quebec in response to Donald Trump's threats. Then, as if he wanted to mobilize a traditional segment of his electorate, he made provocative statements at the end of the campaign about the artificial nature of Canada.

On the one hand, Blanchet sought to develop a much more anti-system rhetoric than in his previous election campaigns. On the other hand, he also sought to reassure, while reiterating his desire to cooperate within Canada's federal institutions. We will therefore analyze his positioning vis-à-vis the leader of the Liberal Party of Canada. We will explain that this must be understood through the prism of a "quest for the balance of power." We will then analyze the complex relationship between the Bloc Québécois and the leader of the Parti Québécois, Paul Saint-Pierre-Plamondon. In that regard, we will examine the anti-system nature of the Bloc Québécois' electoral platform. We will then look at the campaign dynamics and results. But first, it is important to appreciate the extraordinary context of this election.

THE TRUMP EFFECT: A CANADIAN SHIELD

In recent election cycles, many Quebecers have seen the Bloc as a safe bet: it was possible to vote for the Bloc Québécois without too many consequences. The Bloc's mission to defend the consensus positions adopted by the Quebec National Assembly, or its willingness to defend Quebec's specificity, had the merit of reassuring a segment of the electorate. In short, for many voters, if what the other parties had to offer wasn't to their liking, they could always fall back on the Bloc.

Indeed, one of the reasons behind the Bloc's creation in the wake of the failure of the Meech Lake Accord in 1990 was to avoid dual legitimacy.[6] The architects of the Bloc wanted to avoid history repeating itself. In the 1980 referendum, Pierre Elliot Trudeau had urged Quebecers to vote no to the sovereignty-association project and promised change. This change took the form of the unilateral patriation of the constitution, without Quebec's consent. He justified this action by pointing to the large number of Liberal seats in Quebec. In so doing, he even called into question the legitimacy of the Quebec National Assembly to speak on behalf of Quebecers. The creation of the Bloc Québécois, reminding everyone that the Quebec constitutional question was not yet settled, was one way of countering this argument. The Bloc, far beyond being a party in favour of Quebec independence, is seen as defending Quebec's interests against a centralizing Canada that would undermine the autonomy and powers of the National Assembly. It is also seen as a party that defends Quebec's specificity, its language, values, and culture, in the face of the federal government's desire to centralize and standardize.

The Bloc's attacks on Canada's Charter of Rights and Freedoms and its desire to give precedence to the Quebec Charter of Human Rights on Quebec soil should be understood in this light. This protective stance in the face of a threat to Quebec's identity from English Canada appeals to a large segment of the population. In fact, the pool of Quebec nationalist voters far exceeds that of independentist voters. Indeed, while independentists identify themselves more broadly as nationalists, a significant proportion of Quebecers who also identify themselves as nationalists would rather see Quebec gain greater autonomy within Canada. Moreover, for Quebecers, Quebec nationalism remains widely perceived as a positive force.[7]

When Quebecers initiated a referendum process, precipitating votes on their self-determination as a nation, they were posing an existential threat to the Canadian federal system. With the arrival of Donald Trump, who repeated his threats to annex Canada and make it his fifty-first "cherished state," the existential threat was external. For many Quebecers, it was far more serious than the Canadian threat. It was not just a question of identity; it was also a question of their way of life. The reflex of many voters in the face of an existential threat without contemporary precedent was to protect themselves behind the Canadian shield. And this goes beyond the geological analogy.

The US administration's imposition of tariffs on Canada certainly created economic uncertainty at a time when the Canadian economy was just beginning to recover from the inflationary crisis resulting from the pandemic. The Office of the United States Trade Representative (USTR) even raised Quebec's language laws, requiring labelling of products in French, as a trade hindrance it wanted removed.[8] Faced with the throttling of sales to the American market, Quebec entrepreneurs were quick to aim to diversify their business by developing new markets, particularly in Canada and Europe. The various premiers also initiated discussions to facilitate trade and break down internal barriers between their provinces.[9] On the economic front, the Canadian domestic market was also seen as a lifeline for many entrepreneurs. The Quebec sovereigntists' historic openness to free trade with the US and Europe was not based solely on an economic premise of wealth creation. It was also geopolitical, insofar as it reduced the Quebec economy's dependence on the Canadian domestic market. The Americans' new position undermined this argument.

A new phenomenon has appeared since the second swearing-in of Donald Trump. The unprecedented threat that followed encouraged a reassessment of Canadian identity. It was as if people rallied together under the flag, even in Quebec. Thus, for the Bloc Québécois, the threat of annexation of Canada was even more politically challenging than the tariffs. It caused a rise in nationalist sentiment in Canada. And Quebec has not escaped it. Fear of the

United States seems to revive a feeling of attachment to Canada that had waned in recent years. According to a survey by the Leger firm carried out in February 2025, support for Quebec independence had fallen to 29 per cent, the lowest rate ever recorded by this firm.[10]

Following his election, Donald Trump began a series of attacks on Canadian sovereignty. First by attacking Justin Trudeau, demeaning him as only the governor of the great American State of Canada, then by arguing that we "need to be tougher on Canada, because it's supposed to be our 51st state, and many Canadians want Canada to become the 51st state." On Canadian election day itself, he claimed that the border between the two countries was artificial.[11] Donald Trump's rhetoric towards Canada is part of what can best be described as imperialist nationalism. Unlike his rhetoric towards Greenland, Trump's annexationist rhetoric towards Canada incorporates a dimension of identity. It is as if, in his mind, Canadians were or would be happy to be Americans. This is not unlike the rhetoric of Russian leaders towards Ukrainians and Ukrainian sovereignty.[12]

In this context, the threat posed by Canada to Quebec's identity appeared to many Quebecers be much less significant in the short term than that posed by Donald Trump. Canada, as a member of the G7 and a larger entity, can even be seen as a shield to protect Quebec identity in the face of an even greater threat of Quebec assimilation into the United States. And when it comes to confronting Donald Trump, "Je choisis le Québec," the Bloc Québécois' campaign slogan, was not at odds in 2025 with Pierre Poilievre's "Canada First" or Mark Carney's "Canada Strong."

CONFRONTING MARK CARNEY

In a normal election, the Bloc would have had plenty of material to attack the new Liberal leader's positions, even more so since Mark Carney expresses himself in hesitant French. In the early days of his campaign, he misnamed one of his star candidates in Quebec, while at the same time confusing the killings at the École polytechnique with those at Concordia University. On the identity front, not only did the new Liberal leader continue his predecessor's policy of opposing Bill 21 on Quebec secularism in court but also attacked Quebec's language policies. The Act Respecting French as the Official and Common Language of Québec – also known as Bill 96 – is not, for the moment, the subject of a case before the Supreme

Court of Canada. That being said, the Liberal leader put it this way: "We are the party of the Charter [of Rights and Freedoms] and we will intervene at the Supreme Court in cases that [may] come up."[13] This position was quickly denounced by both Conservative and NDP leaders. The leader of the BQ even saw an opportunity to associate the Liberal leader with Donald Trump: "Is Mr Trump's threat becoming a pretext to weaken Quebec identity in the name of a Toronto leader's Canadian multiculturalism?" Blanchet asked. "We need to look at Mark Carney with a more wary eye."[14] Likewise, the Quebec government also made a rare direct intervention in the federal campaign, denouncing the Liberal leader's intentions.

On the economic front, from the very first days of the campaign the Bloc tried to put its Liberal opponent on the defensive, accusing Carney of wanting to trade Quebec's economic interests for those of Ontario, particularly in regard to supply management in agriculture, the cultural industries, and forestry. Blanchet also attacked Carney's centralizing economic vision. Like all the parties in Quebec National Assembly, the leader of the Bloc Québécois rejected the idea of merging the "thirteen economies" of the provinces and territories into a single Canadian economy, as Carney advocated. According to Blanchet: "There are thirteen Canadian economies, each with the right, capacity and jurisdiction to define its own future."[15] He thus positioned himself as a defender of the autonomy of the National Assembly.

This initial critical stance vis-à-vis the Liberals was not working, so the BQ changed to a more cooperative mode. During the French-language leaders' debate, Blanchet criticized the Liberal leader for not collaborating with opposition parties. He even pointed out on camera that he and Carney had never spoken before and that this was the first time they had met. An amusing exchange ensued, with the Liberal leader offering to exchange phone numbers and even to meet for dinner.

A few days later, at an editorial meeting with the team from La Presse, the Bloc leader opened up even more: forget a "Parliament of confrontation." He reached out to the Liberal leader, calling Carney "talkable," and said that he was ready to work with him on a swift resolution of the trade war with the US.[16] And to make it clear that his stance was not an anti-system one, he added: "The message I'm giving, let people understand, it's not to prevent the machine from working that I want the maximum number of seats, it's so that the machine also works in Quebec's interests."[17]

At the same time, in order to retain a portion of the Bloc Québécois electorate who might be tempted to vote Liberal to avoid the election of a Conservative government under Pierre Poilievre, Blanchet took the bold step of acknowledging the Liberal victory in advance. As Larin points out, "If [the voters] are sure that it will be Mark Carney, [Blanchet] expects to rally them behind him 'to protect the Quebec difference.'"[18] This new strategy led veteran analyst Josée Legault to describe the Bloc leader as practicing "the Art of the Possible."[19]

To mobilize another part of the Bloc electorate, this change in rhetoric didn't stop the Bloc leader from making an anti-system statement about Canada a few hours before the vote, saying that for him, sitting in Ottawa is like sitting in a foreign parliament. "We are, whether we like it or not, part of an artificial country with very little meaning, called Canada ... It's a foreign parliament because this nation is not mine ... I don't feel more at ease in the Canadian Parliament than [Alberta premier Danielle] Smith would feel at ease in the National Assembly of Quebec."[20]

Less than twenty-four hours before the vote, he was back at it again. In his words: "It is no insult to observe that the collage that is Canada, if it is built by denying the identity of its regions and of Quebec, can only be an artificial country."[21] Did this fluctuation between confrontational and cooperative messages detract from the overall impact of the campaign? One thing is certain: this clearly illustrates the anti-system and cooperation dilemma and the Bloc leader's desire to try to have it both ways.

Blanchet has never concealed his preference for the federal government to remain a minority in the House. He could thus hope to hold the balance of power.[22] And the 2025 election did indeed result in a minority government. At his first press conference after his election, the new prime minister confirmed that he had reached out to the opposition parties and spoken to the Bloc's leader. At the same time, he also publicly claimed to have won the largest number of seats for the Liberal Party in Quebec since Pierre Elliot Trudeau in 1980. By pointing out that he had more elected representatives than the Bloc Québécois in Quebec, Carney was attempting to undermine Blanchet's authority to speak on behalf of Quebecers.

A STRAINED RELATIONSHIP WITH THE PQ LEADER

The day after the federal election, Parti Québécois leader Paul Saint-Pierre Plamondon accused the Bloc Québécois leader of behaving like a "collaborator" with Mark Carney. The term "collaborator" is historically loaded. In this context, it can be synonymous with treason: collaboration with the enemy. Yet the Bloc Québécois and Parti Québécois are regularly portrayed in the media as sister parties within the Quebec sovereigntist family. While the PQ aims for power in Quebec, the Bloc is supposed to be preparing for independence in the federal parliament. But the reality is far more complex. This is all the truer given that, with the passage of time and the PQ's inability to secure a majority in favor of its fundamental option, the Bloc Québécois has taken refuge behind a discourse defending Quebec's interests.

This dynamic is also symptomatic of a reality within the sovereigntist movement. On the one hand, there is a segment of the movement that is more ideological, more eager to hold a referendum on the future of Quebec which adopts a more anti-system stance. On the other hand, a more pragmatic part integrates a Canadian dimension into the defense of its project, more respectful of institutions. In this vein, we could say that Plamondon, like Jacques Parizeau in the 1990s, embodies the ideological current. Conversely, Blanchet, like René Lévesque in the 1970s, would belong to the pragmatic current.

Since his election as the head of the PQ, Plamondon has promised to hold a referendum on Quebec independence as soon as he and his party gain power. Long before the Quebec election scheduled for 2026, and against all odds, he succeeded in overtaking the Coalition Avenir Québec in the polls. This had the effect of putting the question of Quebec's constitutional future back on the agenda.

In fact, from the very first days of the federal campaign, Blanchet set the table for a new referendum. Addressing a national council of activists to try to persuade them to adopt his election platform, he declared that it was the Bloc's job to "set the table" for a Parti Québécois victory. He continued in a speech warmly applauded by the members: "I want our friends and unequivocal, lifelong allies and partners in the Parti Québécois to arrive in a position of strength in the fall 2026 election campaign to form a majority pro-independence government in Quebec's National Assembly ... It's the same world. It's the same activists. It's the same project. It's the same country."[23]

That said, with part of his electorate slipping away from him, mainly to the Liberals, Blanchet was, as we have seen, quick to suggest that he would adopt a responsible, collaborative approach with the federal government. In short, until things settled down with the US, he would act as a partner with Canada's prime minister. In response, Plamondon chose to publicly attack the Bloc's electoral strategy the day after the election. At a press conference at the Quebec National Assembly, he declared: "This was not the desired result ... We're preparing for what I think is going to be a fairly hostile and/or indifferent government to Quebec's interests."[24]

Plamondon continued in this vein, explaining his relative absence from the Bloc's campaign by insisting on a profound disagreement with its leader: "The strategy adopted by the Bloc, which validates Mark Carney as a collaborator, as someone who is about to collaborate with Quebec, set limits to what the Parti Québécois could do under the circumstances, because that's not what we think."[25] Publicly, the PQ's leader's support for his sister party was very limited indeed. It essentially boiled down to one single post on social media, four days before the vote. Here's an excerpt from that post on X: "You know my opinion: achieving Quebec independence is a matter of linguistic and cultural survival for Quebec. That's what I'm working on and what I'll be working on over the next few years. In the meantime, the only option – albeit a defensive posture that doesn't constitute a long-term plan – is to support the only party that will be loyal only to Quebec. By supporting the Bloc Québécois, we can limit the strength of Mark Carney's mandate and allow the election of a minority government, so that we give the balance of power to a party that will be loyal to us 100 per cent of the time. That's why I'll be voting for the Bloc Québécois next Monday."[26]

In addition to a strategic dispute between the two parties, various media outlets also reported personal tensions between the two leaders and disagreements over the mobilization of resources.[27] A conflict even broke out between the two parties over candidate recruitment.[28] For his part, the Bloc leader tried to play down the differences. Some of the party's candidates also chose to explain this gap in vision by the different posture that a political party must adopt when evolving on the federal scene. On Plamondon's part, it seems that he would have liked to see Blanchet adopt the resolutely pro-independence and anti-system stance previously adopted by Martine Ouellet when she was head of the Bloc Québécois.

However, it should not be forgotten that Ouellet, shortly after her election as head of the Bloc in 2017, faced a mutiny from her caucus and was forced to resign less than a year later by party members. At the time of her resignation, she even criticized sovereigntists for being too timid. As she said, "I thought the Bloc had made its transition, that the Bloc had adopted an unabashed attitude, an assumed attitude, that people, MPs, members had stopped being embarrassed about being independentists."[29] After thanking MPs Xavier Barsalou-Duval and Marilène Gill, who had remained loyal to her, "who stand up for themselves, people who are not afraid, who take responsibility," she then declared: "My main observation is that, at present, the main obstacle to the realization of the Quebec republic comes from within the sovereigntist-independence movement. This is not normal. The movement is sick ... If all the energies that have been deployed in petty, internecine, fratricidal struggles had been deployed to achieve the republic of Quebec, I'm convinced that today it would be a done deal."[30]

The tensions between the different factions of Quebec's sovereigntist movement, as revealed in the 2025 election, are nothing new. But this time, the roles were reversed. The most pro-independence faction runs the Parti Québécois rather than the Bloc Québécois.

JE CHOISIS LE QUÉBEC (OR QUEBEC FIRST)

A closer analysis of the party's electoral platform, "Je choisis le Québec," enables us to better understand its strategic and ideological stance. For the purposes of this chapter, we have chosen to assess the nationalist and anti-system character of its main proposals. By nationalist, we mean positions aimed at promoting or defending the specificity or interests of Quebec. By anti-system, we focus on elements that mark a break with the current political regime or major public policies.

The Bloc Québécois' 2025 election platform clearly reflects the delicate balance between the two strategies of emphasizing Quebec's need for independence while maintaining cooperation within the federation. The following excerpts illustrate the two strategies that paradoxically coexist in the same document. This reveals the party's inability to focus on one objective. So, while the Bloc has held several nationalist and anti-system positions since its inception, it seems to be adapting and tempering its message in this platform. In fact, several of the party's proposals reflect a desire to take advantage of the system of it in order to uphold Quebec's interests rather than to destroy it.

Beyond the party's usual agenda, the Bloc Québécois' 2025 platform was largely set in the geopolitical context of the moment: while highlighting the resilience of the Quebec people over time, the new US presidency was presented as a significant "threat" to Quebec's economy, right from the leader's foreword. Indeed, the first section of the platform was reserved for countering the threat represented by the Trump government. For example, the protection of Quebec's economic nationalism can be seen in proposed measures such as the introduction of local procurement criteria in public tenders, including guarantees of economic spinoffs for Quebec. The effects of Trump's tariffs were also mentioned, particularly in terms of natural, energy and industrial resources, such as aluminum. On the cultural front, the Bloc opposes the cancellation of the tax on digital services demanded by Donald Trump.[31]

The nationalism of the Bloc's platform, however, was not solely dependent on who occupies the White House. On a more general level, the Bloc's nationalism was articulated by repeatedly presenting Quebec as a nation, and Quebecers as a "proud, strong and audacious people." What's more, it called for the consolidation of its relations with other stateless and non-sovereign nations to reiterate the right to self-determination of peoples.[32]

Still, several elements of its platform fell within the Canadian federal framework and aimed to ensure that the system functioned more effectively while respecting Quebec's autonomy. In fact, the Bloc presented several elements working within the system, such as proposing bills to be voted on in the House of Commons. The party pledged to cooperate with the federal government on certain issues, while collaborating transparently with Quebec. It also aimed not to abolish various federal programs, but to simplify them and align them with those of Quebec.[33]

Its slogan was "Choisir le Québec," meaning that choosing Quebec entails, among other things, to work for its prosperity, its businesses, and its workers. Although scarcely present in terms of an economic agenda that could be considered as anti-systemic, the party's platform included such elements as the abolition of the GST for second-hand goods, or for certain services for first-time buyers, such as notaries or building inspectors.[34]

The protection of the French language and Quebec culture also continued to be asserted by the party. This included statements to the effect that the Bloc would oppose any attempt trying to impose harmful policies on Quebec and weakening the protection of the French language. It also mentions that it will work in order to remove Quebec from the application of the Official Languages Act, so that Quebec is the "sole master of its language policy," and that there be French language proficiency demonstration requirements, particularly for federal public servants working in Quebec or judges appointed to the Supreme Court. The party also proposed that Ottawa fund initiatives to support Quebec culture and promote its digital platforms and creators.[35]

Regarding the powers of the National Assembly, the Bloc aimed to transfer all immigration powers to Quebec as well as a single tax form administered by Quebec. The party pledged to amend the Emergency Measures Act so that it cannot be invoked without the explicit consultation and agreement of Quebec and the provinces concerned. It proposed measures such as decentralizing Canada Economic Development by entrusting the sums to regional funds.[36]

The party also called for the federal dental care program to be transferred to Quebec, for the symbolic position of governor general to be remunerated by the symbolic sum of $1, for the expenses of visits to Canada by the multi-billionaire British Crown to be charged for it, and for a fight against federal spending power, resulting in a fiscal imbalance. The Bloc also advocated that Quebec should be able to select the judges from Quebec to be appointed to the Supreme Court.[37]

The party stated that it aimed to amend certain laws, including abolishing the religious exception in the Criminal Code authorizing hate speech, and put forward a proposal excluding Quebec from Canadian multiculturalism, so that Quebec could choose its own model for integrating newcomers.[38]

With regard to the political and constitutional system, the Bloc Québécois opposed certain initiatives, such as the federal challenge to Quebec's Bill 21, and stated its intention to remove from the oath of citizenship any reference to the British monarchy, adding instead a commitment to respect certain fundamental values, notably equality between men and women, the rights of sexual minorities and the secular nature of the state.[39]

The relationship with anti-system characteristics, present in the Bloc's DNA since its beginnings, was less present than nationalism in the 2025 platform. For example, we find a more pronounced desire for minor, rather than major, changes to the system. Nevertheless, if we take a closer look, the goal of achieving Quebec sovereignty was clearly on the agenda, unlike in the 2021 election platform. This time, the party clearly outlined in its manifesto the role it intended to play in preparing for a referendum: "All Bloc Québécois elected officials will present a fair image of Quebec to the international community and the diplomatic corps in Canada and Quebec, thereby preparing them for the eventuality of a future referendum on sovereignty and, if necessary, recognition of Quebec's independence."[40]

However, the eventual nature of the process makes the degree of the party's anti-system character less than if it were to set out, like the Parti Québécois, a precise timetable for achieving sovereignty. Likewise, it is important to note that the party's platform did not include breakaway gestures aimed at disrupting the very workings of the federal system or the House of Commons. At most, the party wanted to replace the daily prayer with a moment of reflection respectful of freedom of conscience and abolish the Senate.[41]

In regard to the relationship with sovereignty, this echoes the results obtained by Duval and Villeneuve-Siconnelly,[42] which indicate a significant fluctuation in the attention paid to this issue, as well as the framing of it around the elections by the Bloc in its press releases. The contextual influence of the 2011 Orange Wave and Martine Ouellet's internal struggles with the leadership are particularly apparent. The authors also found a generally more positive tone towards sovereignty before the election than after. Hence, the generally positive tone associated with sovereignty and the protection of Quebec's interests within the 2025 platform appears consistent, as is the fact that the platform gave considerable space to the prevailing geopolitical context rather than focusing on sovereignty as the primary theme. Therefore, the Bloc Québécois' 2025 position would appear to be less anti-system than that of Plamondon's Parti Québécois.

FROM OFFICIAL OPPOSITION STATUS TO DAMAGE CONTROL

A few months before the election, hopes were high in the Bloc camp. A few months earlier, the party had won a by-election in southwest Montreal, where former justice minister David Lametti had left after being ousted from cabinet by Justin Trudeau. A January 2025

Leger poll commissioned by the Bloc Québécois gave Yves-François Blanchet's party 37 per cent support in Quebec. It was followed by the Conservatives at 26 per cent, the Liberals of outgoing leader Justin Trudeau at 21 per cent, and the NDP at 7 per cent. Among francophones, the Bloc was predicted to win 45 per cent support, which would translate into a sizeable increase in the number of seats in the House of Commons. In short, as summarized by the Canadian Press, the poll showed "that the sovereigntist party does not live in a dream world when it talks about its major electoral ambitions."[43]

But in just a few weeks of campaigning, its hopes of forming the official opposition were quickly dashed. Instead of aiming for gains, it had to fall back on a more defensive strategy to try and hold onto its previous seats. Despite his difficulties in expressing himself clearly in French, Carney's rise in Quebec was as unexpected as it was sudden.

Ultimately, 6.3 per cent of the pan-Canadian official votes gave the BQ the same percentage as the NDP, which ran candidates across the country. In Quebec, the Bloc won 27.7 per cent of the votes cast, translating into twenty-two seats. By comparison, the Liberals won 42.6 per cent of the Quebec vote and forty-four seats in the province. The Conservatives and New Democratic Party won 23.3 per cent and 4.5 per cent respectively. This translated into eleven Conservative seats and a single NDP seat. For comparative purposes, in the previous election of 2021, the Bloc had won 7.6 per cent of the Canadian vote (32.1 per cent in Quebec alone) and thirty-two seats. This was only three seats fewer than Justin Trudeau's Liberals, who took thirty-five Quebec ridings. In just a few weeks of the 2025 campaign the Bloc lost eleven MPs.

But what happened to cause the Bloc to lose more than a third of their MPs? As we saw earlier, Liberal leader Carney embodied the Canadian shield in the face of Trump's threats. Three days before the vote, a Leger survey showed that Carney was, in the opinion of Quebecers, running the best election campaign,[44] swinging some Bloc supporters, even sovereigntists, to the Liberals. What's more, another, more left-leaning segment of the Bloc's electorate was tempted to vote Liberal to prevent Poilievre from becoming prime minister, rightly or wrongly associating the Conservative leader's agenda with that of the American president. This was the polarization dynamic that Blanchet sought to combat by conceding victory to the Liberals a few days before the vote.

On election day, of the seats the BQ lost, almost all went to the Liberals, ten out of eleven. It lost one seat, Montmorency-Charlevoix, to the Conservatives. Although imperfect due to the redrawing of the electoral map, this exercise nevertheless illustrates the Bloc's loss of momentum in certain regions.

To analyze these results, we need to focus on three regions. These are Quebec's national capital, Mauricie, and the suburbs of Montreal. The Mauricie riding of Trois-Rivières had already been hotly contested in 2021: the Bloc won by just a few votes over its Conservative rival, a former mayor of the city. This time, in a three-way race, the surprise came from the Liberals. A candidate parachuted into that riding was elected. Representing the neighbouring riding, the Liberal star candidate Louis-Philippe Champagne's presence in the regional media was undoubtedly a factor in this unexpected victory.

In the case of the Quebec City region, two Bloc ridings were in the Conservative sights. They had previously voted for Conservative MPs. There too, we saw a three-way battle. One, the more urban Beauport-Limoilou, went to the Liberals, while the other, the more rural Montmorency-Charlevoix, went to the Conservatives.

But it was in the 450-area code, which essentially includes ridings in the Montreal suburbs, that the fate of the Bloc Québécois hung in the balance. Six of these BQ ridings went to the Liberals, representing more than half of its losses. There were even concerns that the leader would have difficulty winning re-election in his own riding of Beloeil-Chambly.[45] In La Prairie-Atateken, (located south of Montreal) the party's house leader was defeated. As former MP Alain Terrien said, feeling the fear of Trump on the part of voters as he campaigned door to door: "Seeing people use fear for political purposes, I found it very ordinary, and it's one of the reasons we lost. It's like stopping a wave with your bare hands."[46] After a judicial recount, the riding of Terrebonne on Montreal's North Shore,[47] swung to the Liberal camp by a single vote. The Bloc candidate had not conceded her defeat due to alleged electoral irregularities.[48] In February 2026, the Supreme Court of Canada annulled this result, thereby imposing a new byelection.[49] Even a Bloc stronghold was threatened.

While the Bloc was hoping to make gains, it quickly found itself on the defensive, needing to bolster campaigning in ridings it had taken for granted.[50] Abandoning its hopes of forming the official opposition, it had to revise its strategy to save what could be saved.

It was certainly too late to revise the entire advertising plan for the campaign. From the midpoint of the campaign onwards, this new stance was reflected in adjustments to the leader's tour to support his MPs in difficulty, but also in changing the tone of his attacks during the leaders' debate, while acknowledging Mark Carney's victory several days before the vote.

CONCLUSION

Donald Trump's shadow hung over the 2025 election campaign. The sudden salience of the issue of Canada-US relations among the electorate radically altered the dynamics of the campaign in Quebec as elsewhere. Whereas a few months earlier the Bloc was in offensive mode against Justin Trudeau and could have hoped to make significant gains, the political dynamic quickly changed. In Quebec, this context benefited Carney, mainly at the expense of the Bloc Québécois, so much so that Blanchet had to change strategy and fight to defend ridings he had assumed were safe. As it was, he lost almost a third of his seats in the House of Commons.

Blanchet certainly tried to mobilize issues associated with Quebec identity, as he had done so successfully against Justin Trudeau in both 2019 and 2021. Paradoxically, with a Liberal leader who didn't know Quebec well, nor had mastered the French language, the recipe didn't work. Yet Carney did not change his party's position against Bill 21 on secularism. He even announced his support to a hypothetical challenge to Quebec's language laws. And unlike Conservative leader Poilievre, the Liberal leader didn't even make any specific commitments to Quebec. Quebecers simply saw in him the best person to face Trump because of his economic profile. They saw in him a Canadian shield to protect themselves from the American threat. Will this be the case? Everything suggests that this is the issue on which the Liberal leader will eventually be judged by the Quebec electorate. For his part, in the aftermath of the election the leader of the Bloc reached out to the new prime minister leading a minority government, pledging to make Parliament work. However, he does not hold the balance of power alone as he had hoped.

This election also highlighted the precarious position of the Bloc Québécois. While the Parti Québécois is resolutely committed to initiating a referendum process if elected to power in the next Quebec election, Blanchet chose instead to mute his appetite for independence. In fact, the BQ adopted its traditional stance of defending Quebec's interests.

This divergence of strategy with the leader of the PQ became clear the day after the election. In a rare public attack against a sister party, Plamondon harshly criticized the leader of the Bloc Québécois. Of course, divergences between the different currents of the sovereigntist movement are nothing new. No one knows what the Bloc would have achieved if it had campaigned resolutely on independence, as the PQ leader wanted. Clearly, Blanchet anticipated an even worse result if he had opted for this strategy.

We have to recall that the Bloc Québécois has a parliamentary origin. It was founded by Liberal and Conservative MPs in the wake of the failure of the Meech Lake Accord. From the outset, the Bloc has had to choose between an assertive anti-system stance and a more collaborative tone. Whether Lucien Bouchard, Michel Gauthier, or Gilles Duceppe, these party leaders preferred to collaborate and make the House of Commons work, rather than derail it. Only Martine Ouellet opted for an anti-system strategy. She wanted to address the dysfunctions of Canadian federalism and even provoke them. In doing so, it cost her political career.

This raises the following question for the future: How will the Bloc tie in with the Parti Québécois in the next Quebec election? In a context where the latter intends to bring sovereignty back to the fore, what role will the BQ play? Will Blanchet adopt a more anti-system tone in response to the PQ leader's demand? Or is the Bloc's setback, like a canary in a mine, a harbinger of more difficult times ahead for the Quebec sovereigntist movement? And if Donald Trump's threats are still current in 2026, could the PQ mute its independence objective? So far, Plamondon insists that this will not be the case.

NOTES

1 Michel Saba, "Aux portes de l'opposition officielle, Blanchet prône la modestie," *L'Actualité*, 27 December 2024, https://lactualite.com/actualites/aux-portes-de-lopposition-officielle-blanchet-prone-la-modestie/.

2 For the purposes of this chapter, all quotations from French-language media have been translated into English.

3 Eric Montigny, "The 2019 Election: A Battle For Quebec," in Jon H. Pammett and Christopher Dornan (eds), *The Canadian Federal Election*

of 2019 (Montreal and Kingston: McGill-Queen's University Press, 2020), 101–27.

4 Eric Montigny, "The Bloc Québécois as a Safe Bet," in Jon H. Pammett and Christopher Dornan (eds), *The Canadian Federal Election of 2021* (Montreal and Kingston, McGill-Queen's University Press, 2022), 84–104.

5 Michel David, "La deuxième période," *Le Devoir*, 23 January 2025, https://www.ledevoir.com/opinion/chroniques/835411/chronique-deuxieme-periode.

6 Eric Montigny, "Partis autonomistes et indépendantistes: Paradoxes et influence institutionnelle," *Civitas Europa* 37, no. 2 (2017).

7 Eric Montigny, "Nouvelle phase du nationalisme québécois: un PLQ coincé," *Canadian Journal of Political Science* 55 (2022): 978–88.

8 Rachel Lau, "US Government Classifies Quebec's Bill 96 as 'Foreign Trade Barrier,'" CTV News, 1 April 2025, https://www.ctvnews.ca/montreal/article/quebecs-bill-96-classified-as-foreign-trade-barrier-by-us-government/.

9 La Presse Canadienne, "Les provinces réclament la fin des barrières commerciales," *Les Affaires*, 21 March 2025, https://www.lesaffaires.com/secteurs/politique/mark-carney-rencontre-les-pm-des-provinces-et-des-territoires-vendredi/.

10 Maura Forrest, "Le PQ face à une baisse de popularité de l'indépendance," *Le Charlevoisien*, 23 February 2025, https://www.lecharlevoisien.com/2025/02/23/le-pq-face-a-une-baisse-de-popularite-de-lindependance/.

11 Mark Gollom, "Trump Implies Canadians Vote For Him on Election Day, Poilievre Tells President to Butt Out," CBC News, 28 April 2025, https://www.cbc.ca/news/politics/donald-trump-election-canada-truth-social-1.7520212.

12 Taras Kuzio, "Imperial Nationalism as the Driver behind Russia's Invasion of Ukraine," *Nations and Nationalism* 29, no. 1 (2023): 30–8.

13 Emilie Bergeron, "Mark Carney croit qu'Ottawa devra intervenir si la loi 96 est examinée par la Cour suprême," *La Presse*, 28 March 2025, https://www.lapresse.ca/elections-federales/2025-03-28/mark-carney-croit-qu-ottawa-devra-intervenir-si-la-loi-96-est-examinee-par-la-cour-supreme.php.

14 Borris Proulx, "Québec dénonce 'l'affront direct' de Mark Carney contre sa loi sur le français," *Le Devoir*, 31 March 2025, https://www.ledevoir.com/politique/canada/861460/quebec-denonce-affront-direct-mark-carney-contre-loi-francais.

15 Raphaël Pirro, "Blanchet rejette l'idée de fondre les 'treize économies' des provinces en une

seule économie canadienne," *Journal de Montréal*, 2 April 2025, https://www.journaldemontreal.com/2025/04/02/blanchet-rejette-lidee-de-fondre-les-treize-economies-des-provinces-en-une-seule-economie-canadienne.

16 Gabriel Béland, "Blanchet s'engage à collaborer avec Carney," *La Presse*, 24 April 2025, https://www.lapresse.ca/elections-federales/2025-04-24/blanchet-s-engage-a-collaborer-avec-carney.php.

17 Béland, "Blanchet s'engage à collaborer avec Carney."

18 Vincent Larin, "Blanchet prédit une victoire de Carney," *La Presse*, 18 April 2025, https://www.lapresse.ca/elections-federales/2025-04-18/blanchet-predit-une-victoire-de-carney.php.

19 Josée Legault, "L'art du possible," *Journal de Montréal*, 22 April 2025, https://www.journaldemontreal.com/2025/04/22/yves-francois-blanchet-decouvre-lart-du-possible.

20 Joshua Freeman, "Blanchet Calls Canada 'An Artificial Country with Very Little Meaning," CTV News, 25 April 2025, https://www.ctvnews.ca/federal-election-2025/article/blanchet-calls-canada-an-artificial-country-with-very-little-meaning.

21 Raphaël Pirro, "Le Canada, 'un pays artificiel': Blanchet persiste et signe dans sa déclaration qui choque," *Le Journal de Québec*, 26 April 2025, https://www.journaldequebec.com/2025/04/26/le-canada-un-pays-artificiel-blanchet-persiste-et-signe-dans-sa-declaration-qui-choque.

22 Mylène Crête, "Un parcours ardu pour la balance du pouvoir," *La Presse*, 16 April 2025, https://www.lapresse.ca/elections-federales/2025-04-16/bloc-quebecois/un-parcours-ardu-pour-la-balance-du-pouvoir.php?sharing=true.

23 Raphaël Pirro, "Blanchet veut 'mettre la table' pour les élections québécoises de 2026," TVA Nouvelles, 29 March 2025, https://www.tvanouvelles.ca/2025/03/29/blanchet-veut-mettre-la-table-pour-les-elections-quebecoises-de-2026.

24 Tommy Chouinard and Fannie Arcand, "St-Pierre Plamondon critique la stratégie du Bloc, Blanchet la défend," *La Presse*, 29 April 2025, https://www.lapresse.ca/elections-federales/2025-04-29/st-pierre-plamondon-critique-la-strategie-du-bloc-blanchet-la-defend.php.

25 Chouinard and Arcand, "St-Pierre Plamondon critique la stratégie du Bloc, Blanchet la defend."

26 Paul St-Pierre Plamondon, "Mark Carney pose une menace existentielle pour le Québec," X, 24 April 2025, https://x.com/PaulPlamondon/status/1915493509723013374.

27 Michel Saba, "Tensions Bloc-PQ: 'S'il y a des difficultés, on va les régler,' dit Blanchet," *L'Actualité*, 26 February 2025, https://lactualite.com/

actualites/tensions-bloc-pq-sil-y-a-des-difficultes-on-va-les-regler-dit-blanchet.

28 Nicholas Lachance, "'Manques de respect': la tension monte entre les péquistes et les bloquistes en raison du chevauchement électoral," *Le Journal de Québec*, 14 February 2025, https://www.journaldequebec.com/2025/02/14/manques-de-respect--la-tension-monte-entre-les-pequistes-et-les-bloquistes-en-raison-du-chevauchement-electoral.

29 Lia Lévesque, "Martine Ouellet démissionne et se vide le cœur," Journal Métro, 4 June 2018, https://journalmetro.com/actualites/national/1603601/ouellet-demissione-de-son-poste-de-chef-du-bloc/.

30 Lévesque, "Martine Ouellet démissionne et se vide le cœur."

31 Bloc Québécois, "Choisir le Québec – Plateforme Politique 2025," 6, 7, and 20, https://www.blocquebecois.org/wp-content/uploads/2025/03/blocqcplateforme-2025web.pdf.

32 Bloc Québécois, "Choisir le Québec," 4, 5, 14, and 15.

33 Bloc Québécois, "Choisir le Québec," 7, 8, 9, 14, and 17.

34 Bloc Québécois, "Choisir le Québec," 16, 17, and 32.

35 Bloc Québécois, "Choisir le Québec," 6, 7, 18, 20, and 25.

36 Bloc Québécois, "Choisir le Québec," 8, 9, 13, 22, 24, and 25.

37 Bloc Québécois, "Choisir le Québec," 18, 19, 24, and 25.

38 Bloc Québécois, "Choisir le Québec," 22.

39 Bloc Québécois, "Choisir le Québec," 22.

40 Bloc Québécois, "Choisir le Québec." Authors' translation.

41 Bloc Québécois, "Choisir le Québec," 19 and 22.

42 Dominic Duval and Katryne Villeneuve-Siconnelly, "Le Bloc québécois et la souveraineté: une analyse des communiqués de presse de 2002 à 2021," *Canadian Journal of Political Science* 57, no. 1 (March 2024): 1–14.

43 Michel Saba, "Le Bloc obtiendrait 37 % des intentions de vote au Québec," *La Tribune*, 23 January 2025, https://www.latribune.ca/actualites/politique/2025/01/23/le-bloc-obtiendrait-37-des-intentions-de-vote-au-quebec-YJN3JOWO4ZBDPKXK2EASYZEHKY/.

44 Dominique Plante, "Mark Carney mène la 'meilleure campagne électorale' selon un sondage Léger," *Le Journal de Québec*, 25 April 2025, https://www.journaldequebec.com/2025/04/25/mark-carney-mene-la-meilleure-campagne-electorale-selon-un-sondage-leger.

45 Antoine Robitaille, "Blanchet contre des candidats fantômes dans Belœil-Chambly," *Le Journal de Montréal*, 19 April 2025, https://www.journaldemontreal.com/2025/04/19/blanchet-contre-des-candidats-fantomes-dans-belil-chambly.

46 Agence QMI, "Défait dans La Prairie: 'C'est comme arrêter une vague avec les mains nues,' confie un ancien député bloquiste," *Le Journal de Québec*, 17 May 2025, https://www.journaldequebec.com/2025/05/17/defait-dans-la-praire-cest-comme-arreter-une-vague-avec-les-mains-nues-confie-un-ancien-depute-bloquiste.

47 The last time a Liberal had won there was in 1980.

48 A woman from Terrebonne has since claimed that her postal vote for the Bloc Québécois was not recorded due to an error by Elections Canada and the party has taken legal action to invalidate the result and obtain a rerun of the election.

49 Darren Major, "Supreme Court Nullifies Liberal Single-Vote Election Win in Montreal-Area Riding," CBC, 13 February 2026, https://www.cbc.ca/news/politics/terrebonne-tatiana-auguste-supreme-court-result-9.7088850.

50 Gabriel Béland, "Des milliers de kilomètres en pays bloquiste," *La Presse*, 25 April 2025, https://www.lapresse.ca/elections-federales/2025-04-25/des-milliers-de-kilometres-en-pays-bloquiste.php.

6

Campaigning from the Outside: The Other Parties

Gala Palavicini

On the night of the English-language leaders' debate, Jonathan Pedneault, the Green Party's co-leader, sat alone watching the event on a projector screen. He had been slated to join the other federal leaders on stage, but the day before, just moments ahead of the French debate, the Leaders' Debates Commission abruptly revoked the Green Party's invitation, citing the party's failure to meet two of the three eligibility criteria. The Greens had an incumbent MP, but they had dropped below 4 per cent in the polls and were no longer running candidates in at least 90 per cent of ridings.

What followed was a flurry of frantic and increasingly desperate efforts from inside the party. Co-leader Elizabeth May publicly pleaded for the decision to be reversed. Staff blamed administrative confusion and rushed to correct what they said was a bureaucratic error.[1] Supporters flooded social media. "The Leaders' Debates Commission is making a mockery of our democracy," the party declared.[2] But none of it worked. The debates went on without them. And Pedneault, the co-leader once tasked with being the party's face, was left on the outside, delivering commentary on Instagram Live to a small online audience.

The image was, in a way, both amusing and quietly devastating. Amusing in the way Pedneault played the pundit, offering real-time analysis and sharp, uninterrupted one-liners about the major parties and the leaders on the screen. Devastating in what it signalled. A party that had looked once on the cusp of national relevance, with what seemed like a rising youth base and seats in three provinces, was now relegated to the margins. In a campaign marked by internal contradiction, dwindling visibility, and slipping support, the Green

Party found itself back where it had once fought so hard to escape, alongside "the others," the "minor" parties, those that are rarely seen and rarely heard.

Indeed, while voters tuned in to hear Mark Carney and Pierre Poilievre clash over taxes, Trump, and the future of Canada, a dozen other registered political parties existed largely in the shadows of the major parties. This chapter is about those "other" parties and begins with a simple question: What does it mean to campaign when most people don't even know you're in the race?

THE ELECTORAL LIMBO OF THE "OTHER PARTIES"

As pollsters debated the probabilities of the Liberals or the Conservatives forming government and exactly how many seats they, the NDP, and the Bloc Québécois could expect, a voter would be forgiven for not knowing there were more than just four political parties. Indeed, according to Elections Canada, sixteen political parties registered for the 2025 election. Out of these, twelve were what we often refer to, sometimes even dismissively, as "other parties." These are the parties that exist outside of the mainstream, largely absent from television, barely visible in national coverage, and often known only through the voice of a single candidate or leader.

There is no formal definition for what counts as an "other" or "minor" party in Canadian politics. Elections Canada considers any group that meets basic registration criteria – that is, a party constitution, a financial agent, and at least one endorsed candidate – to be a party. This inclusive threshold was reinforced by the Supreme Court's 2003 *Figueroa* ruling, which struck down the rule requiring parties to run at least fifty candidates to qualify. Since then, even parties with minimal presence, sometimes even just a single candidate, can gain official registration.

But in political shorthand, "minor" typically refers to those that run few candidates, win only a sliver of the national vote (often below 4 per cent), and operate without the visibility or resources of the major players. These parties are sometimes also known as "niche" parties, rather than minor parties, that exist not to cover the full spectrum of public policy but to speak loudly and persistently to one part of it. Indeed, founding a party is appealing. Registration offers official status, access to electoral communications, and the symbolic weight of standing as a "party" rather than just a cause, making it a tempting but often fleeting vehicle for activists and regional movements alike. This includes a wide range of parties.

Some are known for being fringe or protest movements, like the Rhinoceros Party, a satirical party that pokes fun at the political establishment by positioning itself as a parody of the electoral process itself. Some, like the Animal Protection Party or the Christian Heritage Party (CHP), build their identity around a single issue. Some are long-standing parties that endure despite never having won a seat,[3] such as the Communist Party of Canada, founded more than a century ago, which runs fewer than thirty candidates in each election but offers a comprehensive platform. And yet, other minor parties are broader parties that are not only more organized with candidates across most ridings, like the Green Party and the People's Party of Canada (PPC), but campaign on wider platforms that clearly prioritize certain themes – such as climate change or immigration – as defining issues.

Of course, not all of these parties endure; in fact, many disappear from the electoral landscape entirely. De-registration can take many forms, and Canada's list of defunct parties reflects the varied trajectories of fringe and emerging political movements. Some parties, like the Canadian Nationalist Party and the Maverick Party, have been involuntarily de-registered by Elections Canada after failing to meet legal requirements, such as maintaining a minimum number of members or submitting necessary financial documents. Others, such as the United Party of Canada and the National Citizens Alliance of Canada, have chosen to voluntarily de-register, often after leadership changes, dwindling membership, or financial issues. Some parties, including the National Alternative Party of Canada and the Ontario Party of Canada, lost their eligibility to become fully registered. And some eligible parties have withdrawn from the process altogether, such as the Absolutely Absurd Party and Québec Debout. In total, Elections Canada lists thirty-two de-registered political parties, with approximately 80 per cent of them removed involuntarily.

The influence of these minor parties in Canada has historically ebbed and flowed. While most rarely secure seats, they have occasionally shifted the broader political conversation. In the 1980s, the rise of the Reform Party and later the Bloc Québécois, transformed the Canadian party system, even though both began outside the mainstream. The Greens saw their own brief ascent in 2019, electing three MPs and polling in double digits. These moments show that while most minor parties remain on the margins, the boundary between "fringe" and "viable" is not always fixed. On the contrary, voter frustration with major parties, widespread discontent with government, economic issues, charismatic leaders, or sudden political shocks can catapult a small party into the national spotlight, sometimes temporarily, sometimes in a definitive realignment of the system.

For some voters, the other parties offer an appealing alternative. Unlike those in major parties who are highly managed and discipline, candidates in minor parties are often blunt, unfiltered, and unbothered by conventional political etiquette. They speak directly to voters' frustrations and fears, sometimes with sincerity, sometimes with provocation. As a PPC candidate described his own party: "We are more than a political party. We are a kind of a think tank. We are informing and educating the population, and we believe that we have the right ideas."[4] Often without the constraints of the party's headquarters, which lacks the resources to manage campaigns on the ground, candidates can also adapt their campaigns more easily to their riding. This can make them attractive to those disillusioned with party discipline, centralized leadership, or what they see as the transactional nature of politics

Similar reasons motivate candidates, many of whom are political newcomers, driven less by ambition than by conviction. Behind every minor party ballot line is a candidate often campaigning without staff, without funding, and generally without realistic hopes of winning. They knock on doors after work, print flyers with their own money, and send their party leaders to debate in church basements and community halls. Their campaigns are less about vote totals and more about visibility, sometimes getting an idea out there or making sure a debate includes at least one of their main policy issues. Some aspiring candidates may also be attracted to the willingness of some minor parties to break not just with political convention, but with norms around inclusive language or respectful discourse. The PPC, for instance, has faced recurrent criticism for promoting rhetoric regarded as xenophobic or inflammatory.[5] Although not every small party seeks controversy, in the current media environment volume sometimes matters more than nuance and noise can become a strategy.

Regardless of the motives behind candidates or voters, and how passionate these may be, the other parties ultimately inhabit an electoral limbo, away from the media and the national attention, and sometimes away from potential voters themselves. In 2025, together, minor parties received 2.7 per cent of the national vote, with the best performing party, the Greens, receiving 1.2 per cent. In comparison, the Liberal Party alone received 43.7 per cent. Although minor parties rarely expect to poll in double digits or necessarily win a seat, the results are still a significant decrease from 2021, when nearly 8 per cent of voters cast ballots for minor parties, driven largely by the PPC's sudden rise. That momentum did not last and for some parties, including the Maverick Party and the Veterans Coalition, the 2021 election was their last and they were no longer on the ballot.

As voters coalesced around the major parties, in the face of tariffs, threats, and Justin Trudeau's resignation, the 2025 federal election represented the collapse of support for the other parties. The following discussion on these parties draws on a series of in-depth interviews with individuals who ran as federal candidates across Canada with two minor political parties: the People's Party of Canada and the Christian Heritage Party. These interviews were then supplemented with media coverage to enhance interview findings, fact check, and provide context. While all efforts were made to contact candidates from the Green Party, it was not possible to schedule an interview. Participants were identified through political party directories and only individuals whose contact information was already publicly available were contacted. Between May and April, ten interviews were conducted.

ELIZABETH MAY'S PARTY: THE GREENS

If the 2025 election was a disappointment for the PPC, for the Green Party it represented yet another chapter in its long, difficult decline. Once riding a wave of climate consciousness, eco-anxiety, and youth support, the Greens entered the campaign with a new logo, an ambitious platform, and a shared leadership arrangement, but little to no indication that the party had successfully recovered from the implosion of 2021.

Following Annamie Paul's resignation after the previous election, the party attempted to stabilize itself under a new co-leadership model featuring longtime MP Elizabeth May and human rights activist Jonathan Pedneault.[6] The move was part of a larger revamp that attempted to stabilize the party after years of internal division and leadership turnover through collaborative decision-making, a model, they argued, has been used by Green parties across the world. As Elizabeth May claimed in a party statement: "This is a transformational moment for our party and for Canadian politics ... Our members have embraced a model rooted in cooperation, inclusivity, and shared responsibility."[7]

But more importantly, the dual leadership dynamic, a rare sight in Canadian federal politics, also marked a deliberate attempt by the Greens to rebrand themselves as energetic, youthful, and willing to experiment. "We need to maintain at least two per cent of the national vote in order to simply continue to exist as a party. The last thing we want is to simply disappear from the face of the Earth," Pedneault said.[8] In February, for instance, the Greens unveiled a new logo: a minimalist green dot, meant to symbolize the planet, circular economies, and grassroots accessibility. "It's a statement around the things that really matter. Yes, a round dot – the planet ... yes, a circular economy," May explained, while Pedneault added that the design's simplicity made it easy for members to replicate. "The great thing about this logo is that it is easily reproducible ... It is also an emoji, quite frankly."[9]

The Greens also released their 2025 platform, "Change: Vote for It," by far one of the most detailed documents in the election. At 124 pages, the platform was a sweeping vision of climate justice, economic transformation, and democratic renewal, that attempted to position the Green Party as more than a "single-issue" party. As Pedneault tried to frame it, the campaign, he said, was a necessary ideological intervention. "Without the Greens, we wouldn't be talking about climate in these debates. Without us having rung the alarm bells for 40 years ... the status quo parties wouldn't even be close to having a serious discussion about climate." Indeed, the platform attempted to connect environmental policy with economic nationalism, calling for a complete halt to new fossil fuel projects, a guaranteed universal income, major investments in public housing and green infrastructure, and a transition to proportional representation.

But if the platform was bold, it was also largely ignored. On the one hand, climate change fell to the bottom of the priority list for most voters. According to an Abacus Data poll, only 3 per cent of respondents ranked it as the most important issue in the election.[10] Even in safe Green territory like Saanich-Gulf Islands, longtime supporters were more concerned about affordability and US tariffs than pipelines and carbon targets, as headlines suggested May's seat might not be guaranteed.[11] The Greens' attempts to connect climate policy to pocketbook concerns were also largely ineffective in an election defined by strategic voting, and where, similarly to PPC voters, voting for the Green Party became risky. This disconnect – between what the Greens were offering and what voters were prioritizing – was perhaps the most telling theme of the campaign. While the party proposed what it argued were bold reforms, many Canadians remained focused on other issues such as affordability, economic anxiety, and geopolitical uncertainty.

On the other hand, the branding refresh and the bold platform may have made some headlines but did little to shift perceptions. The party's deeper problems, particularly its organizational dysfunction, remained firmly intact. Indeed, the Greens faced immediate logistical setbacks. Though they initially claimed to have candidates in over 90 per cent of ridings, only 232 candidates ultimately appeared on the Elections Canada list, which meant they fell short of the threshold required for inclusion in the national debates. The Greens' exclusion from both French and English debates proved devastating, by depriving them of national exposure while amplifying internal confusion.

While Pedneault told Radio-Canada that the candidate shortfall was a strategic decision to avoid splitting the progressive vote in close ridings, May said the issue was unrelated to strategic voting and far more complicated.[12] Returning officers, she alleged, had delayed paperwork and volunteers had faced harassment while collecting signatures, to the point that she reported these incidents to Privy Council members and the Canadian Security Intelligence Service.[13] These contradictory accounts became a story entirely of their own. The *Toronto Star*, *Globe and Mail*, and *National Post* all published features on the party's unclear messaging and confusing argument, reinforcing a narrative of disorganization that the Greens have long struggled to shake. The moment called to mind earlier leadership tensions and suggested, yet again, that the party was not prepared to function as a united national organization.

The electoral outcome underscored the party's decline. Despite running fewer candidates than the PPC, the Greens earned a higher national vote share (1.2 per cent, or 238,893 votes) but lost two of their three seats. Only Elizabeth May retained hers. Her re-election was not just a personal win; it was the party's sole toehold in federal politics. Her campaign in Saanich-Gulf Islands leaned heavily on her track record, emphasizing that she remained a rare independent voice in a Parliament dominated by party-line discipline. "In this riding, having Elizabeth's voice in Parliament is far more powerful than having another party's candidate who is automatically told to toe the party line," a campaign communiqué read.[14]

Yet May's continued presence is both an asset and a liability. She remains an effective MP among progressives, often capable of commanding attention and building cross-party alliances. But her prominence also makes it harder to reach voters who are not already convinced and for the party to grow beyond her. Not long after the election was over, Pedneault, who came fifth in the Outremont riding, resigned as co-leader of the Green Party. "Twice now, I have failed to convince my fellow citizens to send me to Ottawa," he posted online. "While I remain proud of the program the party built and the values we brought forward during this campaign, I recognize that we were not able to break through in a way that could shift the course of our country – and that is a responsibility I must carry."[15]

Looking forward, the Greens may find more durable traction at the provincial level, where the party has seen modest success, particularly in British Columbia, Prince Edward Island, and New Brunswick. In those contexts, the absence of a strong provincial Liberal brand has created more space for Green organizing, as resources also go further. It may be that the future of the party lies not in building a national machine, but in establishing regional strongholds where climate action and democratic reform can resonate more powerfully.

Whether the federal Greens, however, will survive this downturn and expand or whether they will remain as a single-seat federal party remains to be seen. Without a clear succession plan or charismatic national figure, the Greens risk becoming even more synonymous with one person, a particularly tough challenge for a party trying to present itself as the engine of a broader movement. For now, the party seems increasingly like "Elizabeth May's party," a sentiment that rang truer with every passing week of the campaign and crystallized on election day. Indeed, the Green Party, much like May, remains well-meaning, but increasingly alone.

THIRD TIME IS NOT THE CHARM: THE PEOPLE'S PARTY

The 2025 election marked the third federal campaign for the People's Party of Canada (PPC) and a sharp drop in support in its short but attention-grabbing history. Founded in 2018 by former Conservative minister Maxime Bernier, the PPC had once seemed poised to upend Canadian right-wing ideology. In 2021, it more than tripled its vote share from the previous election, rising to 4.9 per cent and managing to outpoll the Greens nationwide. Bernier was commanding packed rallies, trending on social media, and was widely credited or blamed for splitting the Conservative vote in key ridings, with some reporters referring to the PPC as the new "kingmaker."[16]

The PPC's unexpected rise in 2021 was the product of a very particular political moment. COVID-19 vaccine mandates, lockdown fatigue, and masking requirements polarized the electorate in ways not seen in recent Canadian memory. On the one hand, the pandemic underscored existing electoral issues such as health care, the economy, and the environment, while creating new concerns, including vaccine mandates, government responses to COVID-19, and debates over civil liberties. On the other hand, it created an uncharacteristically divisive election, with frequent confrontational protests against the pandemic health measures and the government. In this context, Bernier positioned himself and the PPC as the only ones standing unequivocally against what it labelled as "draconian" and "fascist" measures, and in doing so tapped into a volatile but energized segment of the public. At least twenty-five PPC candidates in Ontario participated in anti-vaccine protests, many of them aimed at hospitals and politicians.[17]

But by 2025, that moment had passed. The party's signature energy was still present, but Bernier's rallies were smaller, even as he continued to post on social media more than four times a day. Media coverage was also thinner, with no "kingmaker" claims or fear of split votes. In a way, this was a consequence of the party's own success. After its 2021 election loss, the Conservative Party, under Pierre Poilievre, adapted and re-vamped its image, moving to absorb disaffected right-wing voters.[18] Although for some the Conservatives still did not go far enough in their policies and language, Poilievre's interview with Jordan Peterson[19] and speeches targeting the World Economic Forum were likely alluring for many who had voted for the PPC in 2021 against then-CPC-leader Erin O'Toole, whom they found insufficiently conservative.

But it was not only the PPC's previous success that worked against the party. For many voters who might once have supported the People's Party, the stakes of the 2025 election, particularly the prospect of the Liberals maintaining power, were too high to risk a protest vote. Repeatedly on the campaign trail, candidates encountered voters who felt they could not afford to vote PPC. "I think there's a lot of people that voted for Conservatives because they felt they had to. I heard a lot of 'I'd love to vote for the PPC, but we got to get the Liberals out.'"[20] Internally, the party understood the challenge, as PPC members, many founding members themselves, openly announced their intentions to vote Conservative. "This time it is very important to beat the Liberals and they said that they will vote Conservative."[21]

The result, in many ways, was a crushing defeat. The PPC ran candidates in 247 ridings, just under three-quarters of all constituencies, and earned only 136,974 votes, a mere 0.7 per cent of the national share. Compared to its performance in 2021, when it earned almost 5 per cent of the national vote, the PPC lost more than 700,000 votes.[22] When once the PPC had bled support from the Conservatives, now it was the Conservatives who siphoned support from the PPC. Additionally, but equally important, many of the issues that had once galvanized PPC supporters, especially pandemic mandates and immigration, had receded in the public mind.

The party, despite polling that suggested trouble ahead, insisted on staying the course. In 2021, the PPC had cast itself as the political home of those opposing vaccine mandates and lockdowns. By 2025, its platform retained the focus on anti-establishment policies, changing only the angle to emphasize immigration, economic "freedom," and the rejection of the "woke ideology," including the elimination of all diversity, equity, and inclusion (DEI) policies in the public sector. Bernier repeatedly called this a continuation of the movement that started with the pandemic, a mass rejection of what he described as elite control through globalization, censorship, and cultural engineering. "We need to stop [immigration] to preserve our culture, our standard of living, our economy," Bernier said.[23]

Although the People's Party did maintain the course, it is also worth noting that its 2025 platform also signalled a deeper turn toward populist and nationalist ideals. The party's platform focused almost entirely on "anti-globalist" policies, promising to withdraw from the Paris Agreement on climate change, defund the CBC, impose a moratorium on new permanent residents (even those married to Canadians) and end what it called "radical leftist policies" across government, education, and health care. Bernier's language often echoed populist leaders abroad. At a campaign stop in Nova

Scotia, he decried DEI as incompatible with "Western civilization values," and dismissed military diversity quotas and climate targets as ideological overreach.[24] Its 2025 campaign also leaned heavily into conspiratorial language, accusing media outlets of censorship, and suggesting the Conservatives and Liberals were "fake patriots," working together to maintain the elite's grip on Canadians.[25] "Poilievre and his fake conservatives won't do anything, either. The Conservative Party is only conservative in one sense – it conserves everything the Liberals have done."[26]

Undeniably the party shares many of the undertones that have made Donald Trump and the Republican Party the new symbol of anti-establishment, conservative politics. Although the major Canadian parties have traditionally refrained from embracing this style of politics, the PPC is part of a broader global populist trend that connects personal freedom to national purity and institutional distrust. Some candidates, for instance, embraced the comparison with Donald Trump. "We're probably the party in Canada that is most aligned with those things Trump is doing now," said the PPC candidate for Sault Ste Marie-Algoma.[27] Others were more cautious, but nevertheless willing to position the PPC as ideologically adjacent to Trump's messaging. "I don't agree with everything Donald Trump does, but I admire he is doing what he feels best for his country and doesn't care what other countries tell him. I think every country should have leaders who say 'No, we're putting our country first and if you don't like it, too bad.'"[28]

Despite reaching almost 5 per cent of the national vote, the PPC's biggest impact in 2021 was not electoral, but gravitational: helping the Conservative Party move further to the right. In 2025, that gravitational pull disappeared. Third time, as it turns out, was not the charm.

GOD'S PARTY: THE CHP

The Christian Heritage Party (CHP) represents the archetype of a single-issue advocacy party: ideologically uncompromising, electorally marginal, but deeply committed. Despite being one of the longest-standing parties in Canada, it might be one of the least visible political actors in federal politics. Founded in 1987, the CHP has participated in every federal election since and yet has never elected a single member of parliament.[29] It runs few candidates – just thirty-two in 2025 and concentrated primarily in Ontario, Alberta, and British Columbia – and receives little media coverage.

This lack of visibility presents a persistent challenge. While CHP candidates are at times invited to participate in local debates and forums, they are still frequently excluded from major events or dismissed as marginal actors. Federally, the party is practically non-existent. The party's limited resources compound the issue. Most campaigns are run on shoestring budgets, with small teams of volunteers doing everything from designing social media posts to distributing lawn signs. "The local radio station sent me a price list for advertising," an Ontario candidate recalled, "and all I could say was, 'Thank you very much, but I can't even afford that.'"[30]

Adding to these limitations is the issue of institutional memory. Despite being active for over four decades, many CHP candidates are new to politics and unfamiliar with campaigning. With few repeat candidates at the riding level, the party struggles to build organizational continuity. Training and knowledge transfer happen informally, if at all, which is especially hard for new candidates. "I received some support, but I didn't really know what I was getting into. It was kind of just, okay, you're the candidate now. Figure it out."[31] This lack of internal infrastructure leaves the party reliant on personal networks and volunteer teams, rather than institutional strength.

Yet despite these structural challenges, the CHP measures success by a different yardstick. For its candidates, there is little surprise in the electoral outcome and no real expectation of winning a seat. Like many single-issue or advocacy-based parties, their goal is not electoral victory but visibility. "When the majority of our fellow citizens and our elected representatives have abandoned a biblical worldview ... we, in the CHP, have a responsibility to stand in the gap for them. If we were not here – with our prophetic witness – our country would be that much closer to anarchy and judgment," writes party leader, Rod Taylor, in the party's weekly newsletter.[32]

At the heart of the CHP's platform is a desire to root Canadian governance in what it calls "biblical principles," interpreting the preamble of the Charter of Rights and Freedoms – "Canada is founded upon principles that recognize the supremacy of God and the rule of law" – as a mandate for explicit Christian governance. This theological basis, however, is centred on one particular issue that animates the rest of its platform: abortion. While the CHP does offer a more comprehensive platform, its core commitments remain firmly centered on its pro-life stance, opposing abortion and medical assistance in dying (MAiD) in all cases. In other areas, the CHP adopts a mix of populist and social conservative policies, aimed at reverting the damage done by successive Liberal governments "led by a globalist ... piling on debt and censoring free speech are acceptable practices for the Canadian government."[33] The party supports defunding or privatizing the CBC, eliminating funding for the arts unless the content is family-friendly, and promoting requirements for newcomers to adopt "Canada's historic and Christian values."

But whereas for candidates and supporters, this foundation provides both a rationale and a responsibility, for the public and potential voters these positions are problematically presented not as policy stances, but as moral absolutes. This creates a tension within the party. On the one hand it aims to be taken seriously as a national political option. On the other, its explicit religious convictions create boundaries that exclude those who do not share those convictions. Candidates, for instance, regularly emphasize that they "run for all Canadians," not just Christian voters. Yet the party's platform focuses almost exclusively on Christian values and non-Christians are not permitted to run under the CHP banner.[34] The contradiction creates confusion in its public messaging. For the CHP in particular, low name recognition remained a persistent challenge. "It was amazing to me that even in my own church, people didn't know there was a Christian political party."[35] Even in ridings where the CHP has consistently run candidates in nearly all elections, the party struggles to be recognized among voters. "We've run in this riding for 35 years, and there are still people who don't know we exist which baffles me because the name is right on the ballot."[36] Even among their core constituency, CHP candidates face the uphill task of introducing not just their platform, but the very existence of the party.

This tension, however, is at the heart of single-issue advocacy parties. Electorally, they are less viable than major parties that can provide comprehensive platforms, and more importantly that can adapt and re-brand when needed. In the 2025 election, the CHP earned 0.05 per cent of the national vote share. This is equivalent to 10,063 ballots nationwide, which is less than most major parties' candidates earn in a single riding, even when coming in second place. Nonetheless, for parties like the CHP, politics is more about participation. Unlike the Greens, who have sought to rebrand and adapt, or the PPC, which often chases headlines and controversy, the CHP prefers the margins in exchange for ideological clarity. Far from pragmatic, the party and its candidates insist that the central objective remains the same, regardless of the context or the polls or the headlines: to speak truth, as they understand it, into public life. As an Ontario candidate put it, "I'm a realist. My goals for the election were basically for me to glorify God, to do what I think he called me to do, to bring awareness to the party, and to literally declare in the public forum that, I believe in the supremacy of God. It's enough and it's a good thing."[37]

The CHP is unlikely to enter the mainstream in future elections, but it is also unlikely to disappear. As long as there are Canadians who feel unrepresented by the secular consensus, the CHP is likely to continue to find candidates and supporters. Indeed, in certain communities, especially in rural Alberta and Ontario, the party's message still finds a home. In the 2025 election, for instance, the CHP candidate for Oxford, Ontario, earned 1,203 votes, nearly doubling the PPC's showing and more than the Greens.

OUTSIDE LOOKING IN: WHAT HAPPENED IN THE 2025 ELECTION

Elections can be turning points for Canada's major parties. They can produce new leaders, reset policy debates, and sometimes transform the entire political landscape. For smaller parties, however, election campaigns often pass with little change. Their support remains flat or peaks but causes no significant changes. At times, though, elections can even result in a shorter lifespan if disappointment or a complete drain of the available resources collapses minor parties. In 2025, this familiar pattern largely held, but it was shaped by an unusual political context that made the struggle for minor parties even harder.

In 2021, in a context where anger with the establishment and discontent with the major parties lessened these fears, some minor parties experienced unexpected momentum. The PPC surged to 4.9 per cent of the national vote, nearly doubling the Green Party's support, while the Greens, despite leadership turmoil, still entered the campaign with three MPs and a sense of potential. The 2025 election, in contrast, produced one of the most polarized vote splits in recent history. With Justin Trudeau's resignation in the face of what seemed like the Liberals' implosion, followed by the election of Mark

Carney as leader, and the growing anxiety over the economy and tariffs, the campaign took on the character of a two-party contest. Even when Canadians in most ridings encountered far more names on the ballot, the majority of voters zeroed in on one key question: Would the Liberals or the Conservatives form government? What made 2025 especially difficult was the emotional weight of the election itself. With Trump's foreign policy threats and a wide perception that Canadian sovereignty was at stake, many voters chose to play it safe.

PPC candidates, for instance, frequently encountered voters who expressed agreement with their platform but opted to vote Conservative. "Once we actually got a person to look at our policies, they say, 'I love these, but I'm going to have to vote Conservative.' And I would say, 'Okay, I respect that, but would you be able to tell me why?' And they said they just can't afford to have the Liberals stay in for another term."[38] The Christian Heritage Party faced similar obstacles. Their candidates faced constituents, especially among religious voters, who supported the party's policies but with little willingness to back the party at the ballot box. "I know you'd be the best person for the job, but I have to vote Conservative," was the refrain candidates said they heard repeatedly.[39] Even progressive voters who might have leaned Green turned to the Liberals out of fear of a Conservative majority. These experiences point to a key feature of minor party politics in Canada: even when the message resonates, the fear of vote-splitting leads supporters to choose major parties they see as more viable.

"Crisis voting" became the norm, and with it, the margin for minor party engagement narrowed even further, whatever support minor parties may have gathered in previous elections all but vanished in 2025. The result was a dramatic collapse in support for all other parties. To put this in perspective, the Liberals and Conservatives collectively captured over 80 per cent of the national vote, leaving little oxygen for smaller players, including the Greens and the New Democratic Party, let alone the PPC or CHP.

The election also revealed just how difficult it remains for minor parties to gain public visibility and overcome structural and financial barriers. At the national level, minor parties, unlike the major organizations, rely considerably on debate participation and mainstream coverage to validate their campaigns and amplify their message. When criteria shift or invitations are revoked, as it happened in 2025, it can feel like the rules were changed mid-game. "The PPC met the requirements for the national debate and then suddenly the requirements changed," said an Ontario PPC candidate, pointing to Bernier's exclusion as a critical blow to their national outreach.[40] The Greens experienced a similar setback, disinvited from both national debates over candidate thresholds. Without visibility, parties struggle not only to grow but to simply remind voters they exist.

Although this dynamic was especially visible in 2025 it is also not new. It is the recurring pattern of Canadian federal elections under first-past-the-post: a narrowing of viable choices, little media attention, and the structural design of the system. Under Canada's first-past-the-post (FPTP) electoral system, candidates must win a plurality of votes in a riding to gain a seat, with no prizes for second place, and no mechanism to reflect national vote share in parliamentary representation. This disproportionately disadvantages smaller parties whose support is diffuse rather than regionally concentrated. Even if a minor party earns hundreds of thousands of votes nationwide, as the PPC did in 2021, it may not win a single seat unless it finishes first in a riding. Additionally, Canada's political financing rules reimburse a portion of campaign expenses only to parties that receive at least 2 per cent of the national vote. For parties that fall short of this threshold, as the PPC, CHP, and Greens all did in 2025, there is no post-election reimbursement, making it even harder to sustain operations between campaigns.

Running a campaign also demands more than messaging. It requires candidates and volunteers to knock on doors, supporters to post signs, and small donors to cover basic costs. Minor party candidates often found themselves doing it all, with very little access to funding. Limited by this lack of resources, candidates were often unable to canvass their entire ridings or keep up with the pace of the major parties. "I had a hard time. I was only able to raise a small amount of money. And I was only able to deliver flyers to 8,000 houses when in my riding there are 90,000," said an Ontario PPC candidate.[41] Local media coverage was also scarce, and local forums were restricted. "In this election, in some ridings, the CHP was not invited to debates. Candidates were told to leave when they showed up or sit in the audience. I think in some even the People's Party was invited, but Christian Heritage Party wasn't."[42] Local advertising costs were also often prohibitive. "Unless you can buy advertisement or you're a mainstream party, it is almost impossible to hit all the houses in your riding."[43] Moreover, it can be difficult for candidates to have means and resources to support themselves while effectively taking a leave from their jobs to run for office. This, in turn, hinders a party's ability to field candidates.

Not surprisingly, many minor parties favour electoral reform that would level this playing field. The Green Party has long championed proportional representation (PR), arguing that it would produce fairer and more representative outcomes: "Our current voting system isn't fair. A party can win total power with less than half the votes."[44] The Christian Heritage Party likewise supports electoral reform, whether for a PR system or preferential ballots. As one CHP candidate explained, "I think we need electoral reform and I don't know exactly how ... Preferential ballots I think would be a good step in the right direction; at least then you could list your preferences in order, so it would be more likely to get a conservative government without you having to compromise your beliefs."[45] Yet not all parties believe electoral reform is necessary. The PPC, for instance, does not advocate for change. This may reflect the views of its leader, Maxime Bernier, a former Conservative MP and minister, who, like many on the right, is ideologically skeptical of PR, or it may stem from a strategic belief that the PPC can gain seats under the existing system as its support grows.

AFTER THE BALLOTS: WHAT'S NEXT FOR THOSE OUTSIDE THE MAINSTREAM?

By any conventional measure, the 2025 federal election was a failure for Canada's minor parties. No new seats were won. The Greens retained Elizabeth May's seat in Saanich-Gulf Islands but lost their other incumbents. The PPC lost over 700,000 votes compared to its 2021 peak. The CHP remained largely invisible, despite running for the better part of four decades.

For the two most prominent minor parties, the Greens and the People's Party, the consequences of 2025 are different but equally pressing. For the Greens, the latest election was a possible step towards collapse. The party lost two of its three seats, struggled with internal communications, and missed the national debates due to failing to field enough candidates. In a year where climate change was no longer a top voter concern, the Green Party was left trying to reassert its relevance amid economic anxiety and geopolitical tension. That they outperformed the PPC is technically true, but electorally misleading. With just 1.2 per cent of the national vote, the Greens are facing questions not just of momentum, but of long-term viability.

This is particularly troubling given the party's recent history. It was the youth vote that once propelled the Greens toward national prominence, the young Canadians who sought more progressive policies than the Liberals offered and more climate urgency than the NDP delivered. But 2025 confirmed a generational shift: young voters are now more concerned with affordability than environmental policy, and right-wing politics is gaining traction among young men especially. These trends mirror patterns across the world, where conservatism increasingly appeals to younger demographics. For the Greens, this could mark a turning point, or as Dimitri Lascaris, who lost the 2020 party leadership to Annamie Paul, said, it could represent "the verge of extinction."[46] The Green's platform remains ambitious, but it is no longer clear whether a substantial voting bloc is listening.

For the People's Party, the 2025 results revealed the fragility of its earlier breakthrough. In 2021, the PPC surged to nearly 5 per cent of the national vote, outpolling the Greens and dominating media attention as a right-wing populist force. That success, however, was circumstantial, mainly fuelled by public anger over COVID-19 mandates and internal fractures within the Conservative Party. The election of Pierre Poilievre and his embrace of populist messaging effectively pulled the rug from under the PPC, as the Conservatives absorbed much of the PPC's ideological base, leaving the party struggling to differentiate itself. This was most evident in Western Canada, where the PPC had once performed strongly, polling at more than 15 per cent in some ridings like Portage-Lisgar, Manitoba where the PPC received 21.88 per cent of the vote. In 2025, by contrast, the PPC received only 2.1 per cent of the vote in Portage-Lisgar. The election became a two-horse race between the Liberals and Conservatives, and voters with populist leanings prioritized strategy over ideology.

And yet, for the People's Party, all may not be lost. The Conservative coalition is not without its tensions. Newly elected MPs like Jamil Jivani have already sparked internal debate by advancing policies that echo the PPC platform, such as cutting the temporary foreign worker program.[47] Bernier himself remarked on social media, "This outspoken guy is one of the newly elected Conservative MPs. He sounds more like the PPC, doesn't he? Is he Pierre's new immigration critic? No. In fact, Pierre could not find a place for him in his humongous 74-member shadow cabinet. What does that tell you?"[48] Jivani's media profile suggests that the Conservative Party will continue to grapple with these internal ideological divisions that have in the past galvanized PPC voters. If those fractures deepen, and if Poilievre's leadership falters, the People's Party could once again position itself as the uncompromising alternative.

After all, the PPC's rhetorical throughline – from vaccine resistance to immigration control – rests on a deeper narrative: that Canada is under threat from globalist elites, identity politics, and government overreach. This remains appealing for those who share a common disillusionment with politics as usual and prefer to use their votes as protest. For them, the People's Party is less a party than a statement, an affirmation that the system is broken and someone needs to say so. As a PPC candidate put it, "when you don't vote for your values, when you don't vote for what you believe in, you won't have any chances to have what you want. And I believe that these people will come back to us."[49] Among young men, in particular, the party may yet find a pool of possible future supporters.

Still, the party's future depends on factors beyond its "uncompromising" ideology. Financial viability, organizational strength, and Bernier's continued leadership all hang in the balance. A fourth leadership term seems likely, but that alone does not guarantee stability. Members may grow weary of repeated losses or start looking for new strategies that clash with the current party executive. Bernier himself may tire of carrying the party or simply quit politics. In many ways, the fundamental question for the People's Party is the same as it is for the Greens: whether the party can survive beyond its founding leader and long enough to try again in the next election.

However, for the other parties as a whole, the grim results of the 2025 election should be taken in stride. For these parties that operate outside the mainstream, success is not always, or even often, measured in seats and they are unlikely to feel discouraged. This is not to say that minor parties do not face enormous disadvantages after this election. Parties that fail to secure votes or sustain public attention are eventually de-registered or dissolve under financial and organizational strain. Many vanish from the electoral landscape entirely, like the Maverick Party did in 2021, while others re-emerge as new, short-lived political experiments only to collapse again. Even those that endure in name, like the Rhinoceros Party or the Communist Party, sometimes exist only barely and far from fully operational organizations.

Yet, what it means to "win" an election is less clear for these parties. That ambiguity can be a strength. Minor parties like the Christian Heritage Party remain unwavering in their purpose. Despite never electing an MP since its founding, the CHP has not backed away from federal politics. It continues to run candidates, to post almost daily on its website and on streaming sites like Brighteon, and to promote its vision of biblical governance. For candidates such as the CHP's, running is less about winning and more about the belief that someone must stand outside the system and still speak. For them, electoral success may be hard to measure, but even a hundred votes can be an accomplishment.

Regardless of the party or its particular circumstances, for the "other" parties, viability largely rests on their ability to continue providing voters with vehicles for political dissent and dissatisfaction, both of which are rarely in short supply. Voter turnout in Canada has hovered below 70 per cent for over a decade, and for some minor parties that gap represents not apathy, but a constituency waiting to be galvanized. As one PPC candidate put it: "We think we can attract people from the left but also our growth, I hope, can come with non-voters. There's about 36 per cent of the population who didn't vote at the 2025 election, and I believe if they don't vote, it's because they don't believe in these mainstream political parties."[50] This sense of disillusionment, and the desire to give it voice, is what continues to animate many minor parties, even when electoral success remains unlikely.

NOTES

1 Emily Haws and Chen Wang, "Greens Say They Are Being Silenced after Commission Disinvites Them from Leaders' Debates," *Globe and Mail*, 16 April 2025, https://www.theglobeandmail.com/politics/federal-election/article-green-party-removed-from-both-election-debates/.

2 Green Party of Canada, "The Leaders' Debate Commission Is Making a Mockery of Our Democracy," Green Party of Canada, 17 April 2025, https://www.greenparty.ca/en/news/the-leaders-debate-commissionis-making-a-mockery-of-our-democracy.

3 Although in 1940 a Community Party candidate was elected for Parliament, at the time ballots did not have labels. Since ballots were introduced, the party has not had any candidates elected to Parliament.

4 Quebec PPC candidate, video-call interview with the author, 9 May 2025.

5 Zachary Kamel, Martin Patriquin, and Alheli Picazo, "Maxime Bernier's Party Has an Alt-Right Problem," *Toronto Star*, 10 February 2019, A1.

6 David Legree, "Jonathan Pedneault Rejoins Greens as Co-Leader," iPolitics, 27 January 2025, https://www.ipolitics.ca/2025/01/27/jonathan-pedneault-rejoins-greens-as-co-leader/.

7 Green Party of Canada, "Historic Vote: Greens Choose Co-Leadership," Green Party of Canada, 4 February 2025, https://www.greenparty.ca/en/news/historic-vote-greens-choose-co-leadership.

8 Darren Major, "Green Co-Leader Jonathan Pedneault to Be Face of Party's National Campaign," CBC News, 21 March 2025, https://www.cbc.ca/news/politics/jonathan-pedneault-co-leader-green-party-election-campaign-1.7489822.

9 David Thurton, "Green Party Adopts Green Dot Emoji As New Logo," CBC News, 18 February 2025, https://www.cbc.ca/news/politics/green-party-emoji-branding-1.7461800.

10 Benjamin Steven Lopez, "Fewer Canadians Say Climate Change Is Their Top Issue. This Green Candidate's Not Worried," CBC News, 12 April 2025,https://www.cbc.ca/news/politics/fewer-canadians-say-climate-change-is-their-top-issue-this-green-candidate-s-not-worried-1.7508673.

11 Chad Pawson, "How Safe Is BC's Safe Federal Green Party Seat?" CBC News, 8 April 2025, https://www.cbc.ca/news/canada/british-columbia/federal-green-party-saanich-gulf-islands-1.7504183.

12 Haws and Wang, "Greens Say They Are Being Silenced after Commission Disinvites Them from Leaders' Debates."

13 Rahim Mohamed, "Green Party Booted from Leaders' Debates due to Lack of Candidates," *National Post*, 16 April 2025, https://nationalpost.com/news/canada/green-party-booted-from-leaders-debate

14 Pawson, "How Safe Is BC's Safe Federal Green Party Seat?"

15 Peter Zimonjic, "Jonathan Pedneault Resigns as Green Party Co-Leader after Failing to Secure Seat for 2nd Time," CBC News, 30 April 2025, https://www.cbc.ca/news/politics/jonathan-pedneault-resigns-again-1.7522519.

16 Lorrie Goldstein, "PPC Set to Be Kingmaker: Bernier More Than a Footnote in Canadian Politics," *Calgary Sun*, 15 September 2021, A6.

17 Toronto Star, "At Least 20% of Ontario PPC Candidates Have Participated in Hostile Anti-Vaccine Protests," *Toronto Star*, 17 September

2021, https://www.thestar.com/politics/federal-elections/at-least-20-of-ontario-ppc-candidates-have-participated-in-hostile-anti-vaccine-protests-why/article_19419b3f-662c-5b34-a2dc-30a5808e9b59.html.

18 Stuart Thomson, "How Pierre Poilievre's 'Soft Populism' Is Riding a Global Wave of Voter Frustration," *National Post,* 2 December 2023, https://nationalpost.com/news/politics/how-pierre-poilievres-soft-populism-is-riding-a-global-wave-of-voter-frustration

19 Jordan Peterson is a polarizing figure, admired by many conservatives and libertarians for his critiques of "woke" culture, identity politics, and institutional liberalism. He's been criticized by others for promoting ideas that resonate with reactionary and traditionalist worldviews, and conspiracy theories. See Dorian Linskey, "How Dangerous Is Jordan B Peterson, the Rightwing Professor Who 'Hit A Hornets' Nest'?" *Guardian,* 7 February 2018, https://www.theguardian.com/science/2018/feb/07/how-dangerous-is-jordan-b-peterson-the-rightwing-professor-who-hit-a-hornets-nest.

20 Alberta PPC candidate, video-call interview with the author, 13 May 2025.

21 Quebec PPC candidate, video-call interview with the author, 9 May 2025.

22 Jenna Benchetrit, "With Less Than 1% of the Vote, Does the People's Party Of Canada Have a Future?" CBC News, 2 May 2025, https://www.cbc.ca/news/politics/peoples-party-of-canada-ppc-maxime-bernier-election-2025-1.7523653.

23 Holly Cabrera, "Maxime Bernier Says PPC Would Cut Foreign Aid to Shrink Government Spending," CBC News, 24 March 2025, https://www.cbc.ca/news/politics/maxime-bernier-ppc-campaign-launch-1.7492181.

24 Taryn Grant, "Maxime Bernier Decries 'Woke Ideology' Campaign Stop in Dartmouth," CBC News, 31 March 2025, https://www.cbc.ca/news/canada/nova-scotia/maxime-bernier-people-s-party-dartmouth-nova-scotia-1.7498371.

25 National Post, "Mark Carney and Pierre Poilievre Are 'Fake Patriots,' Maxime Bernier Tells Tucker Carlson," *National Post*, 17 April 2025, https://nationalpost.com/news/canada/maxime-bernier-tucker-carlson.

26 Noah Brennan, "'Fake Conservatives': Bernier Slams Poilievre, Leading Federal Parties during Calgary Stop," *Calgary Herald*, 15 April 2025, https://calgaryherald.com/news/national/federal_election/maxime-bernier-peoples-party-canada-calgary-campaign-stop.

27 Maggie Kirk, "PPC Candidate for Sault Ste Marie-Algoma Says Party Most Aligned with Trump," *Sault Star*, 31 March 2025, https://www.

saultstar.com/news/ppc-candidate-for-sault-ste-marie-algoma-says-party-most-aligned-with-trump.

28 Alberta PPC candidate, video-call interview with the author, 13 May 2025.

29 Christian Heritage Party, "Introducing The Christian Heritage Party Of Canda," Christian Heritage Party, https://www.chp.ca/media/post/introducing-the-christian-heritage-party-of-canada.

30 Ontario CHP candidate, video-call interview with the author, 20 May 2025.

31 Ontario CHP candidate, video-call interview with the author, 15 May 2025.

32 Rod Taylor, "Standing in The Gap in 2025!" *CHP Commentary,* 13 May 2025. https://www.chp.ca/commentary/standing-in-the-gap-in-2025.

33 Taylor, "Standing in the Gap in 2025!"

34 Christian Heritage Party, "Constitution (Amended 2024)," Christian Heritage Party, https://www.chp.ca/images/uploads/CHP_Constitution_2024.pdf.

35 Ontario CHP candidate, video-call interview with the author, 12 May 2025

36 Ontario CHP candidate, video-call interview with the author, 15 May 2025

37 Ontario CHP candidate, video-call interview with the author, 12 May 2025

38 Ontario PPC candidate, video-call interview with the author, 15 May 2025

39 Ontario CHP candidate, video-call interview with the author, 12 May 2025

40 Ontario PPC candidate, video-call interview with the author, 15 May 2025.

41 Ontario PPC candidate, video-call interview with the author, 15 May 2025

42 Ontario CHP candidate, video-call interview with the author, 15 May 2025

43 Alberta PPC candidate, video-call interview with the author, 13 May 2025.

44 Green Party of Canada, "Strong Democracy," Green Party of Canada, https://www.greenparty.ca/en/our-plans/strongdemocracy.

45 Ontario CHP candidate, video-call interview with the author, 20 May 2025.

46 Marco Chown Oved, "Green Party Struggles as Voters Focus on Donald Trump Instead of Climate Change," *Toronto Star*, 19 April 2025, https://www.thestar.com/politics/federal-elections/green-party-struggles-as-voters-focus-on-donald-trump-instead-of-climate-change/article_d913d580-1872-4fef-823b-db5ba9e4644b.html.

47 Canadian Press, "Jamil Jivani Launches Petition to End Temporary Foreign Worker Program," CTV News, 22 May 2025, https://www.ctvnews.ca/politics/article/conservative-mp-launches-petition-to-end-temporary-foreign-worker-program/.

48 Maxime Bernier, "This Outspoken Guy Is One of the Newly Elected Conservative MPs. He Sounds More Like the PPC, Doesn't He? Is He Pierre's New Immigration Critic? No. In Fact, Pierre Could Not Find a Place for Him in His Humongous 74-Member Shadow Cabinet. What Does That Tell You?" X, 23 May 2025, https://x.com/MaximeBernier/status/1925970083593007285.

49 Quebec PPC candidate, video-call interview with the author, 9 May 2025.

50 Quebec PPC candidate, video-call interview with the author, 9 May 2025.

7

Electoral Legislation 2015–25: The Conventional Wisdom Returns

Louis Massicotte

The unexpected majority victory of the Justin Trudeau Liberals in 2015 was followed by their attempts to implement some of the promises of electoral reform they had made during the campaign. They had proposed to change the electoral system, to do away with the first-past-the-post system. Second, they wanted to undo most of the changes implemented in the Harper government's Fair Elections Act. Under Stephen Harper, electoral rules reform reached unusual salience in the political arena, and the tone of the discussion was most of the time highly partisan and acrimonious, with the government's controversial Bill C-23, the 2014 Fair Elections Act, typifying the era. The bitterness of the debates that then took place stemmed from the conflict between the conventional wisdom that had prevailed in the wake of the charter and of the Lortie Report, which emphasized the facilitation of the vote in order to dampen the erosion of voter turnout, and the unwavering conviction, especially among Conservatives, that election fraud was rampant, to the point of hampering the integrity of the voting process, and that tighter controls were necessary. This chapter is the fourth of a series that started in 1997 and summarizes the changes in electoral legislation during the Trudeau years.[1]

THE ELECTORAL SYSTEM REFORM FLOP

In 2015, the Liberal platform under Justin Trudeau had included an unusual, and apparently categorical, commitment to eliminate the first-past-the-post system for the 2019 election. Having won the 2015 election, Trudeau declared that it would be the last to be fought under the system. Yet, at the end of what journalist Aaron

Wherry called a "calamitous reform adventure,"[2] the existing system was kept intact. Why?

There is no doubt that Trudeau's preferred substitute was the so-called ranking ballot (hereafter referred to as RB) system, commonly known outside America as the alternative vote, that has been a distinctive feature of Australian elections for a century. Voting would still be conducted in single-member constituencies; however, instead of supporting a single candidate by marking the ballot paper accordingly, voters would express ordinal preferences for candidates. Their preferred candidate would be indicated by marking 1 besides the name of the candidate instead of an X, but in addition other candidates would be granted successive preference votes (2, 3, 4, etc.). On election night, any candidate securing a majority (more than 50 per cent) of first preferences would be declared elected. Whenever no candidate reached a majority of first preferences, the candidate obtaining the smallest number of first-preference votes would be eliminated, and the second preferences expressed in their ballot papers would be transferred to the remaining candidates. The process would go on until the transfers produced a majority for a candidate.

No electoral system is completely neutral, yet in the political context of these days, RB would likely have been an asset for either the Liberal or the New Democratic parties, whichever was leading in a specific constituency. Both parties were left of the center, in contrast with the Conservatives, and it was reasonable to expect that wherever the Conservative candidate was short of a majority of first-preference votes, the second preferences of the supporters of the two other parties could put one of them on top. Simulations conducted on the basis of earlier federal elections suggested that this expectation was quite plausible.[3]

On the other hand, such a move might backfire. As the Conservatives (in contrast with the Liberals) had no ally to rely on, it was easy to dismiss RB as a scheme designed to keep the Conservatives out of office no matter what, and that therefore would be perceived as illegitimate by many. Moreover, British Columbia's experience with that system in the early 1950s served as a warning that the actual behaviour of voters confronted with RB could not be predicted with certainty and might disappoint those who had introduced it.[4]

Despite his known preference for RB, Trudeau made the issue thornier by including a study of proportional representation in the

Liberal platform. This was a far more sweeping reform, which had been proposed earlier for provincial elections in Ontario, Quebec, British Columbia, New Brunswick, and Prince Edward Island. In all settings, the idea had failed to secure the support of the ruling party, or the support of voters at a referendum, especially when the threshold for success had been raised to 60 per cent. It was popular within the New Democratic Party, and gospel to smaller parties like the Greens.

After the Liberals secured their 2015 majority, more than seven months elapsed before the topic of electoral reform was referred to a special committee of the House of Commons. In contrast with standard practice for striking parliamentary committees, the Liberals agreed, under pressure, not to have a majority on this committee. The committee heard at length from expert witnesses, both Canadian and foreign, as well as the interested public. The Conservatives were adamantly opposed to the two formulas under consideration, and the Bloc Québécois had no strong interest in either. The NDP and the Greens supported proportional representation. Liberal MPs were careful in expressing no position throughout the proceedings. Little support was expressed for RB.

In the end, in December 2016, all opposition parties united against the Liberals and produced a majority report that, while rejecting both first-past-the-post and RB, advocated holding a nationwide referendum offering two options: first-past-the-post, and "a proportional system."[5] However, they refrained from being specific, and instead invited the government to devise its own formula, subject to two provisos: it should not be a system where all members would be selected on the basis of party lists (which they said would damage the relationship between MPs and their constituents); and the distortions between the votes cast for the parties and the seats they won, as measured by the Gallagher index, would not exceed five.[6] In other words, the opposition parties offered no formula on which they could agree.

Predictably, Liberal members dissented, and the government reacted by opposing the report. In February 2017, Trudeau concluded publicly that a clear preference for a new electoral system, let alone a consensus, had not emerged, and that without a clear preference or a clear question, a referendum "would not be in Canada's interest."[7]

There is no evidence that the Liberals lost much public support by reneging on their election commitment. Ironically, on the very day in 2025 when Justin Trudeau announced his resignation, at a time when the Conservatives held a twenty-point lead in the polls, he felt compelled to repeat that his chief regret was having buried the idea of imposing RB during his first term, when he had a majority.[8] With the benefit of hindsight, it can now be suggested that many New Democratic Party and Bloc Québécois supporters provided something quite close to what RB might have produced, by simply switching to the Liberals in the 2025 election.

Since then, subsequent developments in the provinces have done little to shatter the widely shared view (right or wrong) that any electoral system reform change is bound to fail in Canada, and that debates on this topic amount to a waste of time. In Quebec, Premier Legault reached office in 2018 with a categorical commitment to adopt the mixed member proportional representation system, only to embrace the status quo three years later, while referendums on PR in British Columbia (2018) and Prince Edward Island (2019) were negative. Further, the Conservatives have continued to oppose change even if, twice in a row (2019 and 2021), they did not obtain a plurality of seats in the House while they were leading in the popular vote.[9] Nevertheless, on 7 February 2024, an NDP motion calling for a citizens' assembly on electoral reform secured the support of 101 MPs, while 230 voted against.[10]

In recent years, proponents of electoral system reform have tried to re-ignite the debate on the issue through an unusual tactic. The appropriately named Longest Ballot Committee managed to sponsor scores of "independent" candidates to run in specific districts, all committed to proportional representation. The rationale was to catch public attention through unusually lengthy ballot papers, which had the effect of delaying the proclamation of the winning candidate. This was facilitated by an Alberta court ruling that had the effect of abolishing the $1,000 deposit requirement (see below) for candidates.[11]

The long-ballot tactic was tested for the first time during the 2021 general election in the riding of St Boniface-St Vital (Manitoba) but did not attract much public attention. It was more successful in ensuing by-elections held in Mississauga-Lakeshore (2022), Winnipeg South Centre (2023), Toronto-St Paul's (June 2024), and LaSalle-Émard-Verdun (September 2024). In St Paul's, a meter-long ballot paper was needed for all eighty-four candidates to be listed, and the outcome of the election – the Liberals lost a seat they had held since

1993 to the Conservatives – was not known until 4:30 a.m. the next day. One of the "fake" candidates standing in St Paul's likely created another record in electoral history by obtaining zero votes. Together, all these candidates secured 4 per cent of the vote.

In the 2025 general election, ninety-one candidates stood for election in the electoral district of Carleton (Ontario), the home riding of Conservative leader Pierre Poilievre. The same person acted as official agent for eighty-five of them. As a consequence, the ballot paper was 93 cm (3 feet) long, but the cause of reform arguably moved forward by less than an inch. In the end, the eighty-five candidates obtained between zero and fifty-five votes each, or an aggregate 922 votes out of a total of 86,371, amounting to an inglorious 1.07 per cent of the valid votes, which hardly suggested that electoral system reform mattered much for the voters.

In the by-election held in August 2025 in the Alberta riding of Battle River-Crowfoot, the Longest Ballot Committee broke its own record by sponsoring no less than 201 independent candidates, bringing the total to 214. They secured between zero and eleven votes each, for a total of 282, being 0.55 per cent of the vote. However, this time Elections Canada ruled that the ballot paper to be used would be a "write-in" (voters expressed their choice by writing on a blank ballot paper the name of the candidate they supported). This eliminated the necessity of printing a ballot paper listing all candidates. Concerns about the possibility that this unusual voting procedure would confuse many voters were groundless. Compared with the previous election, the percentage of rejected ballots actually went down from 0.60 to 0.41.

BILL C-50 ON POLITICAL FINANCING (JUNE 2018)

This short measure was advertised as an attempt "to create an unprecedented level of openness and transparency for political fundraising events," and virtually no attention was paid to it by the media.[12] It did not re-institute the state subsidies to political parties that had been abolished by the Harper government, and left intact the basics of the regulation of political finance in Canada: contributions can be made only by Canadian citizens and permanent residents, and their size is limited to $1,550 to a party and an aggregate $1,550 to all the riding associations, candidates, or nomination contestants of a party. The identity and postal code of donors is disclosed for contributions exceeding $200 and public disclosure of the event itself is required.

The bill secured the approval of the Liberals and the New Democratic Party, while being opposed by the Conservatives and the Bloc Québécois. It was pointed out that although so-called "cash for access" or "pay to play" activities (where donors paid a certain amount of money in order to meet a cabinet minister) would henceforth be advertised, and so be more transparent, such practices would still be allowed. Numerous examples of pay to play practices were offered during the debate.[13]

THE ELECTIONS MODERNIZATION ACT, 2018

The unusually high degree of controversy generated by the adoption of Pierre Poilievre's Fair Elections Act in 2014 suggested that later governments would undo some of those features they had not agreed with while they sat on the opposition benches. Indeed, both the Liberals and the NDP had indicated that they would do so. However, action was delayed by changes at the top of Elections Canada. On 6 June 2016, Chief Electoral Officer Marc Mayrand informed the speaker of the House of Commons that he would step down on 28 December 2016. He said he wanted to allow his successor the necessary time to assume the responsibility and guide the future direction of Elections Canada. Meanwhile, he issued his post-election "retrospective" report in September 2016.[14] The Liberal government introduced a bill (C-33) amending the Elections Act, in November 2016.[15] However, no further action was taken on that measure. Finding a successor to Mayrand proved thornier than usual. Stéphane Perrault was appointed acting chief electoral officer but had to wait eighteen months before being confirmed on a permanent basis on 8 June 2018.[16]

Bill C-76, the Elections Modernization Act, was introduced in April 2018, and was assented to in December.[17] The sponsor of the bill left no doubt as to the resentment the Liberals still felt about the Bill C-23 episode.

> In 2014, the previous government passed the Fair Elections Act. This was a regressive piece of legislation that former chief electoral officer Marc Mayrand said contained measures that would "undermine [its] stated purpose and won't serve Canadians

> well." One hundred and sixty academics signed a *National Post* editorial stating that the Fair Elections Act would 'damage the institution at the heart of our country's democracy: voting in federal elections.' The *Globe and Mail* ran five editorial board pieces, pleading with the Conservatives to reconsider that legislation.
>
> The Harper Conservatives did not listen to reason. They did not pay attention to evidence, and Canadians paid the price. After the passage of the so-called Fair Elections Act, we saw the disenfranchisement of more than 170,000 Canadian voters who lacked sufficient identification.[18] That is according to Statistics Canada. We saw it become more difficult for Canadians to get information about where, when, and how to vote. We saw it became easier for elections lawbreakers to actually evade punishment.[19]

Needless to say, the new bill did not secure the approval of Conservative MPs.[20]

In sharp contrast with the elaboration of Bill C-23, the minister claimed that 85 per cent of Elections Canada's recommendations had found their way into the current bill. The ability of one elector to vouch for another, and the voter information cards were restored as a form of proof of address. The five-year deadline for expatriate voting was eliminated, and expatriates no longer needed to state their intention to return to Canada. The limitations on public education and information activities conducted by the chief electoral officer were removed. The commissioner of Canada elections was relocated within the office of the chief electoral officer, was empowered to lay charges, and was to be appointed by the chief electoral officer, after consultation with the director of public prosecutions, for a non-renewable term of ten years. The duration of campaigns was limited to a maximum of fifty days. Advance polls would still be open on four days, but voting hours were extended from 9 a.m. to 9 p.m. (previously 12 noon to 8:00 p.m.).[21] Counting ballots from advance polls one hour before the regular polls close was allowed. In order to prevent non-citizens from voting, the minister of citizenship and immigration was authorized to provide the chief electoral officer with information about permanent residents and foreign nationals for the purpose of updating the register of electors.

The bill also included some innovative features. A register of future electors was created in which Canadian citizens fourteen to seventeen years of age could consent to be included. A financial incentive was also created for registered parties and candidates to take steps to accommodate persons with a disability during an election period. In order to increase transparency regarding the participation of third parties in the electoral process, political parties and third parties were obliged to identify themselves in partisan advertising during the defined period before the election period. Oaths were replaced with a solemn declaration. Vacancies occurring during the last nine months (previously, six) of the normal life of a parliament would no longer be filled. The reimbursement rate for candidate expenses related to caring for a family member was increased to 90 per cent, with those expenses being exempted from the campaign spending limit.

Amendments to the bill were brought by both sides during its consideration in committee. Liberal MPs came with a complete ban on foreign money spent at any time, not just during the writ or pre-writ periods, for third parties; a new obligation on social media platforms to create a registry of all digital advertising published and paid for by third parties, political parties and candidates during the pre-writ and writ period; and allowing employees of long-term care facilities to vouch for residents. Other amendments sponsored by opposition MPs were agreed on. They included more protection for information contained in the register of future voters; creating a better definition for third party activities in Canada; and expanding vouching so that any voter on the list in the same polling station can vouch for another voter.[22]

JUDICIAL DECISIONS

a) Five-Year Limit on Expatriate Voting

Voting by citizens living out of the country has a long pedigree in Canadian history. The first steps in that direction were taken during both world wars, when soldiers fighting overseas were enfranchised for the duration of both conflicts. In 1948, as some soldiers were now stationed in foreign countries, this privilege became permanent. It was extended in 1955 to the dependents of soldiers, and in 1970 to federal civilian employees working in foreign countries. Expatriate voting was then limited to military and civilian federal employees and their dependents, on the widely accepted rationale that Canadians who were obliged by their government to live overseas should not be deprived of the right to vote. The numbers were not very high, and the identity of these voters could easily be controlled.

Extending this privilege to other expatriate Canadians proved thornier. Many questioned how connected with their country Canadian citizens really were after having lived overseas for, say, ten years, or indeed whether they were strongly interested in participating in the election of the government of a country they had left a long time ago. Just before the 1993 election all parties agreed on a compromise whereby the right to vote was extended to expatriates, provided they had been absent for less than five years. The five-year deadline was struck down as unconstitutional by an Ontario judge in May 2014. The government announced it would appeal the decision, but lost when it tried to have the decision suspended before the appeal was decided.[23] The government reacted by introducing legislation that would have scrapped the register of Canadian electors overseas and obliged Canadians living abroad to register again once the election had been called.[24] Ultimately, this proved unnecessary, as the Ontario Court of Appeal, in July 2015, overturned the earlier decision.[25] The issue reached the Supreme Court of Canada in January 2019, and the five-year deadline was struck down as unconstitutional.[26] Parliament had made clear its own view on the issue by removing the deadline a few months earlier.

Official reports by Elections Canada indicate a significant surge in the number of electors abroad who took advantage of their right to vote. The number of registered electors abroad to whom special ballots were issued rose from 16,000 in 2015 (when the deadline was in force) to 55,000 in both 2019 and 2021, and 102,000 in 2025. Similarly, the number of ballots received and counted increased from 11,001 in 2015 to 34,144 in 2019, 27,035 in 2021, and twice as much (57,440) in 2025. The latter figure amounted to about an average of 167 per riding, and to 0.29 per cent of all ballots counted countrywide.[27]

(b) Candidate Deposit

Since 1874, would-be candidates had been obliged to pay an amount of money for having their name on the ballot paper. The amount was increased from $50 to $200 in 1882 and was forfeited for a candidate who obtained less than one-half of the votes cast for the winning candidate in their riding. The Lortie commission recommended that the amount be increased to $1,000, to be forfeited only for candidates who failed to submit a report on their election expenses. Parliament opted in 1993 for a compromise. While an increase to $1,000 was accepted, only half of the amount would be reimbursed to candidates who filed their election expense report, the other half being reimbursed only to candidates who had obtained 15 per cent of the vote in their riding. From 2000, it was enough for candidates to recover their deposits if they had submitted their election expense report.

On 25 October 2017, the Court of Queen's Bench of Alberta invalidated the obligation for candidates to deposit a sum of $1,000 together with their nomination papers. The federal government did not appeal that decision.[28] This ruling had the unforeseen effect of facilitating the subsequent multiplication of "fake" candidacies by supporters of proportional representation, as described above.

(c) Election Misinformation

At stake in this case was one of the changes made by Bill C-76, which attempted to curb misinformation during election campaigns. Prior to 2018, section 91 of the Canada Elections Act read: "No person shall, with the intention of affecting the results of an election, knowingly make or publish any false statement of fact in relation to the personal character or conduct of a candidate or prospective candidate."

As amended, the new section omitted the word "knowingly," and now read:

> 91 (1) No person or entity shall, with the intention of affecting the results of an election, make or publish, during the election period,
> (a) a false statement that a candidate, a prospective candidate, the leader of a political party or a public figure associated with a political party has committed an offence under an Act of Parliament or a regulation made under such an Act – or under an Act of the legislature of a province or a regulation made under such an Act – or has been charged with or is under investigation for such an offence; or
> (b) a false statement about the citizenship, place of birth, education, professional qualifications or membership in a group or

association of a candidate, a prospective candidate, the leader of a political party or a public figure associated with a political party.

The Canadian Constitutional Foundation, a self-described "non-partisan Canadian legal charity that fights for fundamental freedoms in Canada," challenged the new provision in the Ontario Superior Court of Justice. On 19 February 2021, the court struck down the provision as an unconstitutional limit on freedom of expression and declined the request of the attorney general to suspend the declaration of invalidity for twelve months.[29] The decision rested on the fact that the new section, in contrast with the previous one, omitted the word "knowingly."

The government did not appeal that decision.[30] Law professor Pierre Trudel later agreed that removing the word "knowingly" from the act had been a bit clumsy.[31]

THE REDISTRIBUTION OF 2023

The Trudeau government had no intention of tinkering with the redistribution formula passed under Harper in 2011. So the complex operation whereby, following each decennial census, seats in the House of Commons are redistributed among provinces, and the boundaries of electoral districts are re-adjusted in order to reflect demographic changes, was kicked off on 15 October 2021, when the chief electoral officer disclosed how many seats each province would obtain under the existing redistribution rules, on the basis of Statistics Canada's population projections. Six provinces kept the same number of seats, as their representation is protected by the constitution. Both Ontario and British Columbia gained one seat (bringing their respective totals to 122 and 43), while Alberta got three new seats (37). Quebec, however, was scheduled to lose one seat (77 instead of 78).

This allocation immediately ignited protest. Residents from Ontario, BC, and Alberta could take offence from the fact that their population entitled them to many more seats. Their aggregate proportion of all seats (including the three territorial seats) was 59.1 per cent, while their share of the total population was 64.0 per cent. This resulted from the protections granted by the redistribution formula to provinces with declining populations. In other words, they had more seats than before, but full compliance with the ideal of representation by population would have given them even more seats. This point was made in the media but did not gain traction.[32]

In Quebec, on the other hand, the loss of one seat, in a House enlarged to 342, was bitterly resented. This resulted from a major change made in 2011, whereby Quebec was no longer treated as one of the seven declining provinces, all protected by legislation, but as a special case governed by the so-called "representation rule," which provided that the representation of the province would be in strict proportion to its population, but which no longer guaranteed that it would not lose any seat.[33] The National Assembly unanimously demanded that its representation stay the same and this position found wide support in the media. The Bloc Québécois, meanwhile, held to its traditional stand that Quebec's representation should be set at 25 per cent of the total, as proposed by the Charlottetown Accord of 1992.

For months, observers speculated about a possible change to the redistribution formula, but when the Quebec boundary commission started to work in February 2022, it had no choice but, under the law as it was, to delimit seventy-seven districts. However, a Bloc Québécois motion pertaining to the issue was put to a vote on 2 March. It held that "any scenario for redrawing the federal electoral map that would result in Quebec losing one or more electoral districts or that would reduce Quebec's political weight in the House of Commons must be rejected," and called on the government to act accordingly. The motion was carried 266 to 62, thanks to the massive support from all parties but the Conservatives, who split against it 65 to 50. Three weeks later, the Liberal government introduced a measure that amended the formula so that Quebec's contingent would remain at seventy-eight.

Ten independent boundary commissions had been appointed in November 2021 and started to work once the final census figures were available.[34] By August 2022, all had tabled their respective proposals, and public hearings were held. Then, the commissions tabled their final decisions, and Elections Canada drafted a representation order, which was duly passed on 27 September 2023.[35] Any election called before 22 April 2024, would have been held under the then-existing boundaries. Fortunately, none was called before 23 March 2025.[36]

While all boundary commissions were bound to obey the same constitutional and legal criteria, some provinces ended up with districts that varied more widely from the provincial quota. This was notably the case in Newfoundland and Labrador, Nova Scotia, and Saskatchewan. Deviations from the quota were lower in PEI and in most western provinces, with Ontario and Quebec standing in the middle.

Only forty-eight of the existing 338 ridings survived unaltered. But the impact of boundary changes on party standings was less important than at the previous redistribution, largely because this time only five seats were added, compared with thirty in 2013. A transposition of the votes cast at the 2021 election into the boundaries of the new districts was later published by Elections Canada.[37] Assuming that electors would have voted for the same party within the new boundaries, 157 Liberals would have been elected instead of 160, 126 Conservatives instead of 119, thirty-four Bloc Québécois instead of thirty-two, twenty-four NDP instead of twenty-five. The Greens remained unchanged at two.

At the initiative of the Quebec boundary commission, Indigenous names were added to the names of existing ridings in that province, on the rationale that every one of the eleven Indigenous nations officially recognized in the province should have a name of its own somewhere on the electoral map. This initiative was well received by the public, even if it had the side effect of lengthening constituency names.[38] MPs reacted favourably to changes affecting the name of their ridings, some even suggesting other names on their own which were ultimately accepted. Other commissions did not go as far, but in Ontario, for example, the Toronto riding of Parkdale-High Park was renamed Taiaiako'n-Parkdale-High Park. As Parliament's agenda was clogged during the months that preceded Trudeau's resignation, MPs did not find time to alter the names chosen by the boundary commissions before Parliament was dissolved.

LEADERS' DEBATES

Leaders' debates proved to be the most controversial feature of the election machinery in 2025. Creating an "arm's-length body" to organize future leaders' debates had been promised by the Liberal 2015 platform. Hitherto, all leaders' debates had been organized by a consortium of broadcasting organizations, and such events were outside government regulation.[39] This came to an end in 2018 when the Trudeau government adopted an order in council creating the Leaders' Debates Commission.[40]

This new body was tasked with organizing two leaders' debates during federal general elections (one in each official language) and reporting to Parliament following the debates, outlining findings, lessons learned, and recommendations. Former governor general David Johnson was appointed debates commissioner by the government in October 2018 and re-appointed in November 2020. He was assisted by a seven-member advisory board including former Liberal, Conservative, and New Democratic MPs. The position was not filled after Johnston's resignation in 2023, and the next year, it was decided that the debates commissioner would be the director of the Leaders' Debates Commission.

The most crucial feature of leaders' debates is obviously which leaders will be entitled to be invited. During the campaign, sixteen parties were registered with Elections Canada, but many would doubt that the presence of the Animal Protection Party of Canada was indispensable in an event focused on who would become prime minister of Canada, while excluding parties like the Bloc Québécois, the Greens, and the People's Party, would be more controversial, even if they had little chance of forming a government.

Initially, the order in council opted for the following compromise. Leaders of political parties that met two of the following three criteria would be included: if they had an MP at the time the election was called; or intended to run candidates in at least 90 per cent of electoral districts; or if they had either obtained 4 per cent of the vote in a previous election or had a "legitimate" chance to win seats in the upcoming election.[41] The commission was later granted greater flexibility. In both 2021 and 2025, a panel of seven expert political scientists was consulted in order to ascertain which polls would be considered for determining the support each party recently had.[42]

Liberal, Conservative, New Democratic, and Bloc Québécois leaders have been invited to participate in each of the debates held in 2019, 2021, and 2025, while People's Party leader Maxime Bernier was invited in 2019 only. However, in 2025 the commission encountered unusual difficulties that necessitated last-minute amendments to its decisions.

Green Party co-leader Jonathan Pedneault was initially invited to participate, on the understanding that his party would endorse candidates in 90 per cent of the ridings, as it had promised. However, on nomination day, the Greens actually ran in only 232 ridings, about two-thirds of the total. Bloc Québécois leader Blanchet then objected to the inclusion of the Green leader, and editorials in the *Globe and Mail* and the *National Post* concurred.[43] Pedneault arguably damaged his own case by publicly revealing that the party had made a "strategic decision" not to run candidates in about fifteen ridings where they thought Conservatives would likely win,[44] and explained that by nomination day many other would-be candidates had not been able to satisfy the requirements of the act.[45]

On early morning, 16 April, the very day that the French-language debate was to be held, the commission withdrew its invitation to the Green Party leader. The decision was based on the number of nominated candidates. The relevant criterion demanded that "28 days before the date of the general election, the party has endorsed candidates in at least 90 per cent of federal ridings."

It was also realized that the very moment the French-language debate was scheduled to start (8 p.m.) unfortunately conflicted with the broadcasting of a hockey game that would determine whether les Canadiens de Montréal would make the playoffs for the Stanley Cup (they ultimately did). Both NDP and Bloc Québécois leaders asked for the debate to be rescheduled.[46] On 15 April, the commission obliged by determining that the French-language debate would start two hours earlier, at 6 p.m. None of the parties objected.

Following the debates, party leaders typically answer questions from the media. At the 2025 French language debate, Rebel News activists were allowed to participate in the news conference on the same footing as mainstream media professionals, to the dismay of the latter. The head of Canada's Leaders' Debates Commission later admitted he "wasn't aware" that organizations linked to Rebel News had registered as a third-party advocacy group with Elections Canada before allowing its employees to take part in the post-debate news conferences.[47] The next night, following the English-language debate, the commission solved the dispute by cancelling the event on safety concerns.

Of course, other leaders' debates can still be, and have been, organized by the privately-owned media. In 2021, the Quebec TV network TVA organised a debate. In 2025, the same network intended to do so again, but the new Liberal leader refused to participate on the ground that the Green leader had not been invited, and so the debate was cancelled.[48]

MEASURES ADOPTED FOR A PANDEMIC ELECTION, 2021

Canada was struck by COVID-19 in March 2020. Preparations for the possibility of delivering a pandemic election started within Elections Canada in spring 2020. In his report, the chief electoral officer stated that "the agency's overarching priority was to ensure that Canadians would feel safe participating in the election, whatever their role."[49] A General Election Pandemic Intelligence (GEPI) task force was created within the agency and Elections Canada submitted a report to the speaker of the House of Commons on 5 October 2020.[50] In December 2020, the government tabled a measure to adapt the electoral machinery in order to facilitate voting in this context. The measure was supported by all parties at second reading in May 2021, and its consideration in committee was completed in June;[51] however, it died on the order paper when Parliament was dissolved on 15 August. In his report, the chief electoral officer noted that "although Bill C-19 was not enacted, parliamentary debates, including those conducted at PROC, were useful in that they confirmed the agency's approach and inspired the addition of new measures."[52]

Voting by mail was suggested as the best way for minimizing the risks of viral exposure at polling stations. The number of electors voting by mail from inside their electoral district went from 4,980 in 2019 to 375,093 in 2021. This was lower than expected. The vast majority of electors (94 per cent) voted in person at advance or regular polling stations. In each polling station, the duties of deputy returning officers (DROs) and clerks were fulfilled by a single person operating behind a transparent screen.

After the election, Elections Canada commissioned a survey of public opinion[53] which found that 78 per cent of the general public had confidence in Elections Canada, a figure that exceeded the level of trust in the alternatives offered, which were the police, the provincial government, the "mainstream media," the federal government and "Big business/corporations." A strong majority (87 per cent) also believed that Elections Canada conducted fair elections. Three-quarters of respondents thought that the voting system in Canada was safe and reliable. However, concerns were expressed by respondents about the spread of false information, voter fraud, and especially voting by mail.

TRUST IN THE ACCURACY OF THE RESULTS

Defeated party leaders refrained from challenging the outcome of the 2025 vote, but a post-election poll by Leger found that just under 65 per cent of respondents trusted that the election results were accurate; 16 per cent said they trusted the results only "a little" and 13 per cent said they didn't trust them "at all." Trust was highest in Quebec at 77 per cent, compared to 70 per cent in British Columbia, 62 per cent in Ontario, and 53 per cent in Alberta. Trust tended to increase with age and varied considerably depending on party support. Only 44 per cent of Conservatives trusted the results, compared with 74 per cent of NDP voters and 96 per cent of Liberals.[54]

Following polling day, Elections Canada felt the need to apologize for problems that arose in the northern riding of Abitibi-Baie-James-Nunavik-Eeyou.[55] It was discovered that 822 ballots cast under the special voting rules and coming from seventy-four different ridings had remained in the office of the returning officer from Coquitlam-Port Coquitlam instead of being sent to the central counting station.

More serious errors relating to special ballots occurred in the riding of Terrebonne, and as a result the election was contested. The outcome was extremely tight. On election night, out of 61,000 votes cast, the Liberal candidate was leading by thirty-five votes, later modified to a forty-four-vote lead for the Bloc Québécois candidate. Following an automatic judicial recount, the Liberal candidate was declared elected by a single vote, bringing the total number of Liberals elected to 170, two seats short of a majority. Then, coup de théâtre, an elector, having received the unopened envelope containing her ballot paper four days after polling day, revealed that she had voted by special ballot for the Bloc Québécois candidate, but that her vote had not been counted because the outer envelope, to be returned to the returning officer, bore an address where the last three characters of the postal code were incorrect, an error seemingly attributable to the district level that was later acknowledged by Elections Canada.[56] The Bloc Québécois announced on 15 May that they would contest the election.[57] On 14 July 2025, Quebec's Superior Court refused to cancel the election. However, this was overturned by the Supreme Court of Canada in February 2026: the seat of Terrebonne was declared vacant, and a by-election will be held during the Fall.

CONCLUSION

The 2025 election will be remembered for the astounding recovery the Liberals, after three terms, were able to accomplish within two months under a promising but untested new leader. Looking at the debates on electoral reform and the bitterness they reveal among politicians, one may get the impression that institutional details matter immensely. The election machinery had very little to do with this seismic change. The Harper government tried to impose new rules, some of them self-serving, yet in the end the Conservatives lost the 2015 election, and most of the new rules were later abolished.

Once in office, the Liberals briefly toyed with changes of unprecedented magnitude like imposing a new electoral system implicitly biased against the Conservatives, before backing off. Those, including Justin Trudeau himself, who despaired of their party's chances under first-past-the-post, were ultimately proven wrong. Horrified by the prospect of their country becoming the fifty-first state of the American Union, many Canadians, including even some Quebec nationalists, simply switched their votes to the larger party that stood unequivocally against that idea, thus ensuring the kind of outcome that a ranked ballot system would likely have produced. Turnout in 2025 was the highest since 1993, an achievement that had much more to do with the fact that this was in many ways an "existential" election, where for many the very survival of Canada as a sovereign country was at stake.

It is telling that the only part of the 2025 Conservative platform, drafted under the former sponsor of Bill C-23, merely advocated the closing of Elections Act loopholes to stop third parties from hiding funding sources that can allow for foreign financing of third parties engaging in regulated electoral activities. Such a proposal squared perfectly with the conventional wisdom that had prevailed since the 1980s, except under Harper, and could have been endorsed by all other major parties.

The immediate outcome of the election was that Carney government was in a minority position, three seats short of a majority. The Liberal platform was mute on election law issues. Interestingly, for the first time since 2003 (except for the years 2019 to 2024), as of May 2025 the government no longer includes a minister specifically responsible for the reform of democratic institutions. It is to be expected, however, that the government will have to focus in the future on the organization of leaders' debates.

NOTES

1 Earlier chapters by this author: "Electoral Reform in the Charter Era," in Alan Frizzell and Jon H. Pammett (eds), *The Canadian General Election of 1997* (Toronto: Dundurn Press, 1997): 167–91; "Electoral Legislation Since 1997: Parliament Regains the Initiative," in Jon H. Pammett and Christopher Dornan (eds), *The Canadian Federal Election of 2006* (Toronto: Dundurn Press, 2006): 196–219; and "Roll Back! The Conservatives Rewrite Election Laws, 2006–15," in Jon H. Pammett and Christopher Dornan (eds), *The Canadian Federal Election of 2015* (Toronto: Dundurn Press, 2016): 163–94.

2 Aaron Wherry, "Will Trudeau End Up Regretting His Decision to Walk away from Electoral Reform?" CBC News, 2 February 2024, https://www.cbc.ca/news/politics/trudeau-electoral-reform-1.7101929.

3 Antoine Bilodeau, "L'impact mécanique du vote alternatif au Canada: une simulation des élections de 1997," *Canadian Journal of Political Science* 32, no. 4 (1999): 745–61.

4 See Louis Massicotte, "Réforme électorale. De la futilité des calculs partisans," *Policy Options*, 30 June 2016, https://policyoptions.irpp.org/fr/magazines/juin-2016/la-reforme-electorale-de-la-futilite-des-calculs-partisans/.

5 Special Committee on Electoral Reform, *Strengthening Democracy in Canada: Principles, Process and Public Engagement for Electoral Reform* (Ottawa: House of Commons, 2016), https://www.ourcommons.ca/Content/Committee/421/ERRE/Reports/RP8655791/errerp03/errerp03-e.pdf.

6 The index was devised by Irish political scientist Michael Gallagher and measures party distortions generated by electoral systems. For a summary, see the appendix in Michael Gallagher and Paul Mitchell (eds), *The Politics of Electoral Systems* (Oxford: Oxford University Press, 2005): 602.

7 Interested readers are referred to the following webpage for a list of contributions on electoral reform: https://policyoptions.irpp.org/magazines/june-2016/electoral-reform/.

8 Darren Major, "Trudeau Says Abandoning Electoral Reform Is His Biggest Regret," CBC News, 9 January 2025, https://www.cbc.ca/news/politics/trudeau-electoral-reform-biggest-regret-1.7426407.

9 This disjuncture occurred due to the combined effect of two different factors. In 2021, the ridings won by the Conservatives tended to be more populous (84,000 electors on average, against 78,000 for the Liberals). A

probably more decisive factor was the enormous pluralities won by the Conservatives. Votes wasted in pluralities were an average 15,000 in Conservative ridings, against 10,600 in Liberal ridings. Gargantuan pluralities, defined as anything over 40 per cent of the vote, were won by 27 Conservatives, but only 8 Liberals. Whenever the gap between the two major parties is thin, in this case 1.2 per cent of the vote nationwide, such factors can be decisive.

10 House of Commons, "Vote No. 634," 44th Parliament, 1st Session, 7 February 2024, https://www.ourcommons.ca/Members/en/votes/44/1/634?view=party. Among those who supported the motion were 39 Liberals, 3 Conservatives, 30 Bloc Québécois, 24 NDP, 2 Greens and 3 independents. However, in the 2025 election, only the NDP and the Greens had platforms expressing support for proportional representation. The Liberal leader was non-committal on the issue.

11 The plaintiff in the Alberta case later became a member of the National Board of Fair Vote Canada, an organization that supports proportional representation, and acted as the official agent for scores of candidates committed to electoral system reform who ran in by-elections. See Sami Parvez, "Kieran Szuchewycz: The Fight to Make Running for Office Affordable and Fair," Substack, 31 August 2024, https://samiparvez.substack.com/p/kien-szuchewycz-the-fight-to make?utm_campaign=post&utm_medium=web.

12 *Statutes of Canada, 2018*, SC 2018, c. 20, [*Statutes of Canada, 2018*].

13 House of Commons, "*Debates*,", no. 12366 (8 June 2017), online: https://www.ourcommons.ca/Content/House/421/Debates/190/HAN190-E.PDF.

14 Marc Mayrand, *Retrospective Report on the 42nd General Election of October 19, 2015* (Gatineau: Office of the Chief Electoral Officer of Canada, 2016).

15 Bill C-33, *An Act to Amend the Canada Elections Act and to Make Consequential Amendments to Other Acts,* first reading, 24 November 2016.

16 There was no debate in the House on the issue, but for the first time since the position was created almost a century ago, the motion that appointed the chief electoral officer was adopted on division. See House of Commons, "*Debates*,", no. 20552 (8 June 2018), online: https://www.ourcommons.ca/Content/House/421/Debates/311/HAN311-E.PDF. Such a motion does not require any supermajority for being carried.

17 *Statutes of Canada, 2018*, c. 31.

18 Policy and Research Group, "Turnout and Reasons for Not Voting during the 42nd General Election: Results from the Labour Force Survey,"

Elections Canada, 5 May 2016, 3, https://www.elections.ca/res/rec/eval/pes2015/lfs/lfs_e.pdf. See also Statistics Canada, "Reasons for Not Voting in the Federal Election, October 19, 2015," 22 February 2016, https://www150.statcan.gc.ca/n1/daily-quotidien/160222/dq160222a-eng.pdf .

19 House of Commons, "*Debates*," no. 19352 (10 May 2018), online: https://www.ourcommons.ca/Content/House/421/Debates/296/HAN296-E.PDF.

20 At votes on second and third reading of the measure, the bill was opposed by all Conservative and Bloc Québécois MPs.

21 Voting in advance has become increasingly popular with the electorate in recent election, as exemplified by the percentage of the voters who took advantage of this procedure: 14 per cent in 2011, 20.7 per cent in 2015, 26.6 per cent in 2019, 34.2 per cent in 2021, and 37.9 per cent in 2025. The number of voters who voted in advance polling stations went from 2.1 million in 2011, to 5.8 million in 2021, and to 7.5 million in 2025.

22 House of Commons, "*Debates*," no. 22991 (30 October 2018), online: https://www.ourcommons.ca/Content/House/421/Debates/345/HAN345-E.PDF.

23 *Frank* v. *Canada (AG)*, 2014 ONCA 485, available online at http://www.ontariocourts.on.ca/decisions/2014/2014ONCA0485.pdf.

24 Bill C-50, *Citizen Voting Act*. The bill was given second reading and sent to committee but was never passed.

25 *Frank v. Canada (AG)*, 2015 ONCA 536.

26 *Frank v. Canada (AG)*, 2019 SCC 1, [2019] 1 S.C.R. 3.

27 Data from Stéphane Perrault, *Report on the 45th General Election of April 28, 2025* (Gatineau: Office of the Chief Electoral Officer of Canada, 2025), 20.

28 *Szuchewycz v. Canada (AG)*, 2017 ABQB 645.

29 *Canadian Constitution Foundation v. Canada (AG)*, 2021 ONSC 1224.

30 The *Budget Implementation Act, 2021, No.1* (SC 2021 c. 23) later re-introduced the word "knowingly" in the wording of the penalties inflicted under s. 91(1). It is exceedingly rare for the *Elections Act* to be amended through omnibus legislation.

31 Mathieu Gobeil, "Punir ceux qui relaient des faussetés, est-ce le moyen de lutter contre la désinformation?" Radio-Canada, 21 March 2021, https://ici.radio-canada.ca/nouvelle/1778463/desinformation-loi-electorale-federale-fausses-declarations-reseaux-sociaux-trudel.

32 See however Andrew Coyne, "Your Vote Is Not Worth the Same as that of a Voter in Another Riding or Province. And It's Getting Worse," *Globe and Mail*, 26 January 2024, https://www.theglobeandmail.com/opinion/

article-your-vote-is-not-worth-the-same-as-that-of-a-voter-in-another-riding/.

33 With a thirty-seat increase in the size of the House, the reform increased Quebec's share by three seats, which then hid the fact that Quebec would no longer be spared seat losses in the future.

34 This author served as a member of the boundary commission for Quebec.

35 For purely technical reasons, there were two representation orders, one for Quebec and one for all other districts. However, both were enacted through a single proclamation. See *Canada Gazette, Part II* vol. 157, no. 2 (27 September 2023).

36 Two court challenges were later launched against decisions by Quebec and Nova Scotia. Both were rejected by the Federal Court of Canada in November 2024 and February 2025, respectively.

37 Elections Canada, "Transposition of Votes from the 44th General Election to the 2023 Representation Orders," Elections Canada, 8 April 2024,

38 For example, Montmagny-L'Islet-Kamouraska-Rivière-du-Loup became Côte-du-Sud-Rivière-du-Loup-Kataskomiq-Témiscouata, and Pontiac will henceforth be known as Pontiac-Kitigan Zibi.

39 Standing Committee on Procedure and House Affairs, *The Creation of an Independent Commissioner Responsible for Leaders' Debates* (Ottawa: House of Commons, 2018), https://www.ourcommons.ca/document-viewer/en/42-1/PROC/report-55/page-5. Conservative MPs dissented from the committee's report.

40 The legal basis for the commission is found not in an act of parliament, but in regulations passed by cabinet: Order in Council PC 2018-1322, 29 October 2018, later amended by Order in Council PC 2020-0871, 5 November 2020, and by Order in Council PC 2024-0598, 24 April 2024.

41 Kristy Kirkup, "David Johnston Tapped to Plan Federal Leaders' Debates in 2019 Election," Global News, 30 October 2018, https://globalnews.ca/news/4611809/david-johnston-federal-leaders-debates-2019/.

42 Leaders' Debates Commission, "Participation Criteria for the Next Leaders' Debates," Leaders' Debates Commission, 6 February 2025, https://www.debates-debats.ca/en/45/participation-criteria/participation-criteria-next-leaders-debate/.

43 Summing up this episode, a subsequent *Globe and Mail* editorial later concluded: "In excluding the Greens, the commission did the right thing for the wrong reasons in the wrong way at the wrong time." See Editorial Board, "There's No Question: Debates Should Be for Voters, Not the Parties," *Globe and Mail*, 20 April 2025, https://www.theglobeandmail.

com/opinion/editorials/article-theres-no-question-debates-should-be-for-voters-not-the-parties/.

44 Darren Major, "Greens Held Back Some Candidates Despite Giving Full Slate to Debates Commission," CBC News, 15 April 2025, https://www.cbc.ca/news/politics/green-party-list-of-candidates-debates-1.7510915.

45 The Conservative candidate in Québec-Centre also encountered obstacles of that nature, and her nomination papers were rejected, so in the end the party stood in only 342 ridings.

46 Isaac Olson, "Time Changed for French-Language Leaders' Debate due to Montreal Canadiens Game," CBC News, 15 April 2025, https://www.cbc.ca/news/canada/montreal/french-language-debate-quebec-1.7510909 . A similar decision had been made by the networks in 2011.

47 Darren Major, "Debates Commission Unaware Rebel News Registered as Advocacy Group, Official Says," CBC News, 17 April 2025, https://www.cbc.ca/news/politics/rebel-news-rightwing-media-press-conferences-debates-1.7512714.

48 Ian Bailey, "Federal Leaders' Debate Set for April 16 and 17 but TVA Cancels Third Debate because Carney Will Not Participate," *Globe and Mail*, 24 March 2025.

49 Perrault, *Report on the 44th General Election on September 20, 2021*, 7.

50 Stéphane Perrault, *Special Report of the Chief Electoral Officer: Administering an Election during the COVID-19 Pandemic* (Gatineau: Office of the Chief Electoral Officer of Canada, 2020).

51 Bill C-19, *An Act to Amend the Canada Elections Act (COVID-19 Response)*, 2nd.session, 43rd parliament, 2020–21, online: https://www.parl.ca/LegisInfo/en/bill/43-2/c-19.

52 Perrault, *Report on the 44th General Election on September 20, 2021*, 11.

53 Leger Marketing Inc, *Public Opinion Research Study on Electoral Matters, Wave 1* (Gatineau: Elections Canada, 2021), https://www.elections.ca/res/rec/reg/porsem/porsem_trackingSurvey_e.pdf.

54 Catherine Morrison, "Three Quarters of Canadians Say Misinformation Affected the Federal Election: Poll," *Moose Jaw Today*, 3 May 2025, https://www.moosejawtoday.com/national-news/three-quarters-of-canadians-say-misinformation-affected-the-federal-election-poll-10609465.

55 For details, see Samuel Wat, "Elections Canada Apologizes to Nunavik Voters Left out of Vote," CBC News, 30 April 2025, https://www.cbc.ca/news/canada/north/elections-canada-apologizes-nunavik-voters-1.7523310.

56 Isaac Olson, "Liberals Won Terrebonne, Que., Riding by One Vote – but This Woman's Bloc Ballot Wasn't Counted," CBC News, 12 May 2025,

https://www.cbc.ca/news/canada/montreal/elections-canada-investigating-terrebonne-1.7533228.

57 Ian Bailey, "Bloc to Ask Court to Overturn Election Outcome in Riding that Liberals Won by Single Vote," *Globe and Mail*, 15 May 2025, https://www.theglobeandmail.com/politics/article-bloc-to-ask-court-to-overturn-electionoutcome-in-riding-that-liberals/.

8

The Pragmatist and the Disruptor: The Unexpected Role of Leadership in the Election

Jonathan Malloy

Leaders always matter profoundly in elections. But arguably no Canadian election in history has been less about policies and more about "leadership" than the 2025 federal race. That election presented an unprecedented situation in which one leader, Mark Carney, though heading a longstanding governing party seeking re-election, was brand new to formal electoral politics (though a participant in public life and Liberal Party activities). Conservative leader Pierre Poilievre positioned himself as a populist leader for the twenty-first century, channelling public frustrations against elites and "gatekeepers," especially Justin Trudeau. But the chaos precipitated by Donald Trump dislodged Trudeau and created an opportunity for the very different leadership style of Carney. Carney's limited ties to the previous government allowed him to abandon key policies, most notably the carbon tax, and present himself as a fresh new individual unattached to a governing record. Carney then successfully made the election revolve around the question of which leader was best suited to deal with Trump. This chapter examines the contrasting leadership styles of Poilievre and Carney, how they fit into past archetypes of political leadership in Canada, and how context and timing allowed Carney's style to prevail.

THE TRICKY CONCEPT OF LEADERSHIP

The concept of "leadership" is tricky. It can evoke stereotypes and narrow simplifications, especially gendered and others, with white men taken as the baseline comparison. And while there is a vast literature on the subject, both scholarly and popular, it can be vague and contradictory. As a social science concept, leadership is best approached with caution.

However, understandings of leadership are moving away from a conception of a fixed set of skills and qualities (e.g. "decisive") and more toward the importance of context and timing; knowing when to apply which skills in a specific moment ("to read the room").[1] Leadership literature increasingly recognizes that leadership depends on the situation; a person may be a successful leader in one context and moment, but unsuccessful in others, because the context and timing require a different type of leader. The most successful leaders are able to fine-tune their leadership style according to context, drawing on different skills appropriate to the moment. Leadership also encompasses a broader conception of values – what matters most and motivates a leader. Values can be especially important in projecting forward; to anticipate how a leader will approach a future situation. But context and timing will often shape how these values play out. For example, before running for the Liberal leadership Carney championed environmental causes; but the circumstances of 2025 – the context of the moment – led him to downplay those values in favour of economic and trade priorities.

The importance of timing and context are seen in the decline of Justin Trudeau's popularity. Trudeau's style of leadership envisioned leading an activist state that moved Canada toward a more egalitarian society, with an emphasis on gender and racial diversity. It was also based on a strong inner confidence; both John Ivison and Stephen Maher suggest Trudeau has a rhinoceros hide – impervious to criticism regardless of its validity.[2] Ivison also suggests Trudeau had "an almost adolescent need to be adored."[3] This style and vision excited voters in 2015, and Trudeau's personal popularity was key to the Liberal comeback in 2015 that saw the party win a majority government; but a decade later Trudeau's unpopularity and mixed governing record was weighing the party down. While no longer in favour, Trudeau's personal leadership style, based on strong self-confidence and an activist agenda, was largely unchanged; it was the context, and the perceptions of that style, that had changed. His inspiring charisma and progressive outlook were now seen by many as aloof and disconnected from ordinary Canadians.

In mass politics, evaluations of leadership are built primarily on imagery and impressions, since few voters will have even fleeting personal encounters with leaders, much less interact with them substantially. Instead, voters examine leaders' public images for cues of their values and abilities. This makes communication skills among the most important leadership traits in politics, typically as part of an overall package of messages and imagery designed to convey the leader's skills and values – or at least the skills and values that they and their party want to convey. To some extent this again invokes context and timing: successful leaders will emphasize qualities appropriate to the moment, often through specific symbolic words or actions. Famous Canadian examples include Pierre Trudeau's "just watch me" quip during the October 1970 crisis, which communicated decisiveness and resolve; or Brian Mulroney's "you had an option, sir" in the 1984 election debates, which conveyed integrity and character. The reality behind both leaders was considerably more complex and sometimes quite different than these fleeting lines, but the statements were very well-timed for the context, and shaped impressions of their overall leadership style.

The importance of imagery and impressions is perhaps even more important in negative perceptions of a leader. History also abounds with examples of leaders who have struggled to overcome minor but highly visible mishaps that then shape subsequent impressions of their leadership skills, such as 1970s Conservative leader Joe Clark losing his luggage on an official trip, symbolizing amateurism and a lack of gravitas. Increasingly these negative impressions are purposefully shaped by political opponents. For example, the Conservative Party was highly effective at negative advertisements that shaped early impressions of Liberal leaders Stéphane Dion ("Not a Leader") and Michael Ignatieff ("He Didn't Come Back for You"), and attempted to do the same with Justin Trudeau ("Just Not Ready").

To what extent can voters discern discrepancies behind leadership images? Can they detect leaders pretending to be something they are not? At the highest and most scrutinized levels of politics, inconsistencies are more likely to be detected, especially the longer a leader is in office. On the other hand, evidence suggests that once voters form an impression of a leader, either positive or negative, many will continue to embrace that image even in the face of contrary evidence.

Women leaders, Indigenous Peoples, and racialized politicians can face greater obstacles in conveying positive impressions as leaders because of pre-existing expectations, stereotypes, and divergences from white men as the standardized norm. The overwhelming preponderance of white men at the top ranks allows other white males to either present themselves as following that norm ("a regular guy") or to differentiate themselves subtly from that standard through images and cues, for example as a leader who "really listens" or "doesn't suffer fools." Women and persons of colour rarely enjoy the same baseline set of expectations and assumptions (at least positive ones) on which they can anchor their own leadership style and so must work harder to convey a more individualized positive image.

Political scientists have long known that leaders act as key cues in voting; that is, the images that leaders project of themselves resonate more than specific policy positions or even their political party labels. Clarke et al. suggest: "For many voters the leader personifies the party."[4] As suggested above, voters are guided by their perceptions of leaders in both positive and negative ways; electors may even vote primarily against the image of one leader, rather than primarily for one that they favour. Somewhat more contested is whether leaders have become more important over time to voting decisions. Amanda Bittner suggests there has been little change over time in recent decades, with leaders always important to voters.[5] However, going back further to the mid-twentieth century, it may be that television contributed to the acceleration of the importance of communication skills and specifically visual imagery as critical in shaping voters' impressions. More recently, social media is a critical tool for leaders to build and shape their image, though it allows ordinary MPs and candidates to also cultivate their personal images apart from the party and leader. Regardless, few would disagree that leaders are critically important to voting decisions.

However, the type of leader that voters respond to can vary over time, especially for certain groups of voters, along with the reasons why voters may respond or recoil. The most obvious example is Donald Trump, whose undisciplined style and often outrageous and inconsistent statements would have been bizarrely unacceptable for any previous American president, but have been repeatedly rewarded by many American voters. More broadly, Trump is part of a wave of populist leaders around the globe who implicitly or explicitly position themselves as disruptors against existing models and expectations of leadership. "Populism" is also a tricky and contested concept. However, from a leadership dimension, its key characteristic is to portray other leaders as self-interested elites, while the populist leader instead represents "the people" and channels popular power.

The 2025 election gives us an unusual case to examine the role and impact of leadership as an independent variable on political success, mediated by context and timing. In 2024, the Liberals under Justin Trudeau were lagging badly in the polls behind Pierre Poilievre's Conservatives. Yet the Liberals won a respectable victory in 2025, despite being mostly the same team, the crucial differences being a completely new leader, Mark Carney, and a change in context, namely the threat of the Trump administration. Leadership, mediated through context and timing, made the difference. And the contrast between Carney and Poilievre taps into more longstanding models of Canadian political leadership: pragmatists and disruptors.

TWO ARCHETYPES: PRAGMATISTS AND DISRUPTORS

The categories of pragmatists and disruptors are broad archetypes, not precise classifications. But Canadian political leadership at the national level has historically tended toward pragmatic figures able to balance trade-offs in the regional and linguistically complex country, along with a few more clearly disruptive figures challenging establishment consensus. John A. Macdonald and Wilfrid Laurier were both longstanding and pragmatic "nation-builders" able to straddle the growth of new provinces while managing trade-offs between French-speaking and English-speaking Canada. The longest-serving prime minister, William Lyon Mackenzie King, is primarily known for an evasive and opaque style that often deferred decisions and sought muddled compromises. Other leaders like Louis St Laurent, Lester Pearson, and Jean Chrétien, though overseeing significant policy changes, also cultivated images of pragmatic adaptation and incrementalism rather than visionary drama. Most recently Stephen Harper, though at times a polarizing figure, oversaw a government characterized more by incrementalism than disruption. While there are many differences between them, all these leaders ultimately governed and presented themselves more as pragmatists rather than disruptors, even if they oversaw significant policy changes.

The one clearly disruptive prime minister was John Diefenbaker, who cast himself as an outsider and challenger to the elite and central Canadian status quo. Even though his government was not dramatically different from others, he actively presented himself in that style. Brian Mulroney also aspired to be seen as a bold and dramatic leader, though his actual record was more mixed; Paul Martin also did not live up his stated aspirations for great change. Joe Clark, a pragmatic incrementalist at heart, felt the need to look more disruptive, a discrepancy that was widely detected at his expense.

One reason pragmatist prime ministers are more common is the imperative of brokering different regions of the country together, which requires trade-offs and compromise. Disruptors are more evident at the provincial level and in opposition, such as William Aberhart, Réne Lévesque (though in retrospect more pragmatic than seen at the time), Preston Manning, Lucien Bouchard, and others, all of whom openly challenged the national consensus and status quo from a regional perspective. Most recently, Ontario premier Doug Ford has cultivated a disruptive style, though his governing record is relatively pragmatic. Alberta premier Danielle Smith has more clearly presented herself in both style and action as a disruptor, following a long Alberta tradition of challenging central Canadian economic and political dominance.

The two prime ministers not clearly fitting either archetype are the Trudeaus, father and son. Both stand apart as compelling but also polarizing personalities that simultaneously attracted and repelled large swaths of the electorate. The 1968 "Trudeaumania" election as well as the 2015 race were to some extent personal mandates for each Trudeau, elected amid great popular appeal and enthusiasm. Yet at the same time the leadership style of both evoked a particular personal loathing, especially in western Canada. Their records are uneven as they took risks but also often settled for compromise; Pierre Trudeau's greatest achievement, the 1982 patriation of the constitution, left great holes in the country. And both had low ratings when they resigned the office.

It is important not to overstate things here; these are archetypes, rather than measurable classifications. And they depend significantly on how the leader presents themselves to voters: the cues they give to their values and skills and leadership style. Whether or not Diefenbaker and Pearson governed all that differently behind closed doors is less important than the contrasting images and styles they presented to the electorate in their four elections against each other. And it is the contrast between the two styles that makes the 2025 election so interesting.

THE DISRUPTOR: PIERRE POILIEVRE

In late 2024, Poilievre appeared to be at the crest of a wave of new populist leadership in Canada, mirroring trends around the world and especially the United States. His Conservatives held a strong polling lead, and, more than his Conservative predecessors, Poilievre presented himself as a populist disruptor willing to challenge elites and the status quo. His pledge in the 2022 leadership race to fire the governor of the Bank of Canada[6] or his 2024 attack on Bell CEO Mirko Bibic as "overpaid"[7] are examples of his willingness to confront elites on a personal basis.

Stephen Harper was a polarizing figure as prime minister, and at times positioned himself against what is sometimes called the "Laurentian Elite" of central Canada. But he was not a populist in the conventional understanding. Harper did not rail broadly against elites and institutions generally, nor did he claim to have a special connection with "the people" in an abstract sense, both key characteristics of populism. While an important figure in the semi-populist Reform Party of the 1990s, Harper oversaw the merger of its Canadian Alliance successor with the centrist Progressive Conservative Party and sought coalitions with Ontario and Quebec centrists. And though he acquired a reputation for an overly controlling internal leadership style and indifference to non-Conservative voters, his public persona was soft-spoken (though some found it cold and humourless) and by all accounts he was a highly competent and pragmatic administrator.

Harper's successor Andrew Scheer had limited time to make a clear impression but generally was seen as a more amiable version of Harper – as one critic put it, "Stephen Harper with a human face."[8] After only holding Justin Trudeau to a minority in the 2019 election, Scheer lost his leadership for largely internal and still somewhat unclear reasons. However, at least one reason was a feeling that Scheer did not display the sufficiently tough and combative leadership image needed as an opposition leader; nor did he electrify supporters with a populist style. (It is worth remembering that Scheer won his leadership narrowly over Maxime Bernier, who in the 2017 race portrayed himself more as a small-state free-market libertarian than the xenophobic populist who soon left the Conservatives to found the People's Party of Canada.)

The subsequent 2020 Conservative leadership race had four entrants. The two minor candidates, Leslyn Lewis and Derek Sloan, both positioned themselves as populists and disruptors, especially Sloan, a strong opponent of COVID-19 mitigation measures. In contrast the presumed frontrunner, veteran cabinet minister Peter MacKay, was a pragmatist, drawing from his many years in politics including as a cabinet minister and final leader of the Progressive Conservative Party. However, the eventual winning candidate was Erin O'Toole. Also a former Harper minister, O'Toole presented himself as a "True Blue Conservative," implying a fidelity to right-wing principles held by the core party membership, and a rejection of excessive pragmatic adaptability, and his campaign was scrappy and confrontational, successfully portraying himself as an outsider against elites like MacKay. All these are characteristics of populism. Yet as leader O'Toole displayed a more flexible and inclusive style, though it was insufficient to win the 2021 election that returned another Trudeau minority.

The "trucker convoy" of early 2022 was a pivotal moment in Conservative leadership history. Spurred by skepticism of COVID-19 vaccines and the infringement on personal liberty that came with vaccine mandates and prohibitions on public congregation, protestors occupied the streets of downtown Ottawa for weeks and blocked border crossings in Ontario and Alberta. This was a classic populist action, expressing broad anger against establishment elites, though without coherent leadership, inarticulate disruptive tactics such as incessant honking, and a ubiquitous obscene message of "F*** Trudeau" that limited their appeal. While many Conservative MPs supported the protestors, leader O'Toole was more equivocal and distanced himself. This hesitation led to a caucus vote overthrowing him as leader.

The subsequent race was a stark matchup between, in addition to several minor candidates, another established pragmatist, former Quebec premier and federal Progressive Conservative leader Jean Charest, and Pierre Poilievre, who had spent his entire life building an image of scrappy confrontation. In the 1990s as a teen in Calgary he was active in the upstart Reform Party, later working as a party staffer before winning an Ottawa-area riding in 2004. As an MP, Poilievre was an aggressive partisan, serving briefly in junior ministerial posts in the final years of the Harper government. However, it is difficult to call the Poilievre of this era a populist.

He conducted himself consistently through a sharp and disciplined partisan lens that defended his party and excoriated opponents, but with limited invoking of popular power and certainly no open criticism of elites within his own party or sweeping attacks against "gatekeepers" in the public service, the judiciary, or corporate Canada.

However, the end of the Conservative government in 2015 allowed Poilievre to speak more freely against those in power, and new prime minister Justin Trudeau presented an easy and obvious target. The rise of Donald Trump in the United States further normalized disruptive and populist rhetoric. While he did not run in the 2017 or 2020 leadership races, Poilievre increased his prominence and popularity within the party with his aggressive approach against Trudeau and implicitly, and sometimes explicitly, other elites. This populist and disruptive turn accelerated with the COVID-19 pandemic. For example, in November 2020 Poilievre posted a petition on his website protesting against discussion of a post-pandemic "reset" which he attributed to "global financial elites" who "have called for the same 'Great Reset,' which would re-engineer economies and societies to empower the elites at the expense of the people, Canadians must fight back against global elites preying on the fears and desperation of people to impose their power grab."[9] And when the trucker convoy occupied Ottawa, Poilievre embraced it, though distancing himself from isolated cases of Nazi flags and other extremist symbols. Using classic populist language, he said the convoy represented "people who want to stand and speak for their freedoms" and "all those that our government and our media have insulted and left behind."[10] In Poilievre's 2022 leadership campaign he regularly criticized "gatekeepers," as in his pledge to fire the governor of the Bank of Canada, Tiff Macklem.[11] While this was roundly criticized by many outside the party, Poilievre won an overwhelming victory against pragmatist Charest.

However, while cultivating a disruptive anti-elite style, Poilievre was and is a highly disciplined politician, quite unlike the chaotic Donald Trump. He did not repeat his pledge to fire the governor of the Bank of Canada after winning the leadership. He sometimes declined to take clear positions on issues where a populist anti-elite reaction might seem obvious, such as whether government employees should be compelled to return to the office or be allowed to continue working remotely.[12] He spoke in clear complete sentences, never musing or thinking out loud and almost never issuing retractions or clarifications either himself or through his staff.

The party under Poilievre put forward few concrete policy proposals. Instead, Poilievre's messaging focused on the failings of the Liberal government. He relied repeatedly on a set of slogans: "Axe the Tax, Build the Homes, Fix the Budget, Stop the Crime." Yet beyond the elimination of the carbon tax, Poilievre offered few details on how the remaining three would be accomplished. In a 2024 op-ed, Poilievre roundly criticized business lobbyists for "sucking up to anti-resource, high-tax, big-government politicians" and said businesses "will get nothing from me unless they convince the people first."[13] And while occasionally lapsing into anti-elite rhetoric, Poilievre avoided extremist statements and conspiracy theories, though he did not necessarily distance himself from those whose rhetoric was more heated than his.

Given his disciplined messaging, it is ultimately unclear whether Poilievre was and is truly a populist disruptor, or whether he selected a populist leadership style that fit the circumstances. As mentioned earlier, leadership depends heavily on timing and context. Trudeau's "sunny ways" style of enlightened progressivism was very popular in 2015. But by the 2020s, much of the country had grown cynical and disillusioned, certainly toward Trudeau. Poilievre's style of channelling popular anger presented a very different model that seemed to better suit concerns held by many Canadians about the cost of living and housing.

What is clear, in retrospect, is that Poilievre overlty contrasted himself and his leadership qualities with one person and one other leadership style: Justin Trudeau. Building on the longstanding anti-Trudeau resentment among the Conservative base, he targeted Trudeau's leadership style of confidence in his activist and progressive vision of Canada as evidence of being out of touch with ordinary Canadians. Similar to Stephen Harper, Poilievre emphasized his own modest roots and tastes as evidence of being representative and in touch with ordinary Canadians. But, more than Harper, he presented an aggressive and confrontational style that was focused overwhelmingly on the specific leadership figure of Justin Trudeau. As his own leadership style had been calibrated against that of Trudeau, this caused Poilievre difficulties when he was abruptly faced by the very different leadership style of Mark Carney.

THE PRAGMATIST: MARK CARNEY

Carney presents a unique case for Canada of a federal party leader and prime minister running to re-elect a government that he himself had not been part of, and who had never even won a seat in the House of Commons. Canada has seen other relative newcomers ascend to the highest political office. Brian Mulroney won the 1983 Progressive Conservative leadership despite never serving in Parliament, but he assumed the leadership of a party in opposition. John Turner became Liberal leader and prime minister without a seat in 1984, but he had been a cabinet minister in the governments of both Lester Pearson and Pierre Trudeau before leaving federal politics in 1976, and he lost the prime ministership two months after winning the leadership of the Liberal Party. A third relative novice is Pierre Trudeau, who was recruited to run as a Liberal candidate in 1965, and only three years later was sworn in as prime minister. But none of these compared to Carney's assumption of the prime ministership as an entry level position upon winning the Liberal leadership in March 2025 and winning the general election six weeks later.

While new to politics, Carney was not new to public life. After an early career in the private sector, and a short stint as a senior public servant, Carney became a national figure when he was named governor of the Bank of Canada in late 2007. He then moved to heading the Bank of England from 2013 to 2020, steering it through the UK withdrawal from the European Union ("Brexit"). Returning to Canada, Carney combined private sector commitments with continuing public policy activities and growing involvement with the Liberal Party of Canada.

Carney's position as a two-time central banker allowed him to cultivate a leadership image of technical competence and independent thinking while avoiding overt politicization. The position of a central banker is much more high profile than a regular public service position, requiring public and media visibility, and is traditionally and explicitly insulated from direct political pressure (hence the controversy when Poilievre vowed that he would fire the governor of the Bank of Canada because he disagreed with the bank's monetary policy). On the other hand, its complex and technical nature means it is not a traditional springboard for public office – none of Carney's predecessors or successors, at least in Canada, has ever appeared interested in entering electoral politics. And though central bankers are well-known to political, financial, and media elites, they attract less notice among the general public; when they do, it is often for negative reasons such as high interest rates. A "technocrat" image is not often a popular image. Indeed, only two Canadian prime ministers have come from any kind of extended public service background, and not recently, namely King and Pearson.

However, Carney made the most of the opportunity. His relative youth (forty-two when he was appointed Bank of Canada head) and crisp appearance gave a sense of energy and vitality – again, an example of how white men are able to subtly differentiate themselves from the baseline norm. He was a clear communicator, able to master media sound bites, and demonstrate wit and clarity. Most of all, his handling of major crises on his watch – the global financial crisis in 2008 and Brexit – allowed him to present an image as a problem-solver above ordinary politics and partisan and ideological debates: that is, a pragmatist of the highest order, able to perform under pressure. By all accounts Carney performed well in his roles – while in the 2025 election Stephen Harper dismissed Carney's work in 2008 as minor, no such criticism arose before Carney's entry into Liberal politics.

Nevertheless, after returning to Canada in 2020, Carney was reluctant to act on his obvious interest in public office. He did not run in the 2021 election, nor did he join cabinet and run in a by-election, a common way for a high-profile individual to directly enter cabinet. One reason is presumably the sagging fortunes of the Liberal government under Justin Trudeau: it would have been risky to join a sinking ship. But a second likely reason is the limited likelihood of Carney's pragmatic, technocratic image to propel him to the prime ministership. While obviously qualified for cabinet, Carney appears to have been uninterested in settling for that level, roughly equivalent to his previous central bank positions, and presumably aspired only to the top job. But his lack of deep roots in the party or an exciting public image hampered him compared to other aspirants; in fact, his deep ties to the global financial establishment and his own comfortable circumstances made him seem particularly out of step in a time of anxiety over affordability and cost of living. Until close to the end of 2024, the idea of Mark Carney as prime minister seemed unlikely, because his leadership image of competent pragmatism did not fit the context of the moment.

CONTEXT AND TIMING

It is no exaggeration to say that Canadian politics was upended by the re-election of Donald Trump, and specifically Trump's 25 November pledge to impose heavy new tariffs on Canada and Mexico. This shock was then compounded by Trump's musings that Canada should become the fifty-first state, along with his regular denigration of the prime minister as "Governor Trudeau." This threw the Trudeau government into panic mode, leading to Trudeau's still somewhat unclear plan to bring Carney into cabinet, and Chrystia Freeland's abrupt 16 December resignation in response. Chaos continued until 6 January when Justin Trudeau announced his intention to resign. There was now both a new crisis facing Canadian politics, and a vacancy at the top of the Liberal Party. The context had changed, drastically.

While finally an opportunity for Carney, it remained a risk. It is worth remembering how unpopular the Liberal Party was in early 2025, with no guarantee that Trudeau's resignation would make a difference. While Carney immediately expressed interest in running for leader, along with Freeland, other leading ministers such as Dominic LeBlanc, Melanie Joly, Francois-Philippe Champagne, and Anita Anand all declined, citing the need to stay in their portfolios to deal with the threat posed by the Trump administration. That situation resembled 1993, when Brian Mulroney's unpopularity left Kim Campbell and Jean Charest as the sole major figures interested in succeeding him, and to a lesser extent 1984, when John Turner succeeded the unpopular Pierre Trudeau. In both cases, Campbell and Turner were unable to revive their parties and took them to crushing defeats. Given the low polling for the Liberals at the end of the Justin Trudeau era, these precedents did not bode well for Carney or any other new leader's prospects.

On the other hand, neither 1984 nor 1993 saw a sharp, massive change in the political context. Trump's tariff war and his menacing statements about subjugating Canada triggered fear and even paranoia among many Canadians. For those voters, Carney's leadership style of pragmatism under pressure, seemingly irrelevant a few months earlier, suddenly became highly appealing and appropriate to deal with the Trump threat. Carney himself captured the moment when he said, "If it's not a crisis, you wouldn't be seeing me. I'm most useful in a crisis. I'm not that good in peacetime."[14] Carney presented not only a strong record of relevant experience, but a sense of cool-headed competence that the menace of Trump demanded.

While the Liberals changed direction under their new leader, the Conservatives under Poilievre stayed largely on course, emphasizing Poilievre's established leadership image of scrappy confrontation and implicit populism. The Conservatives attacked the Liberal record while shifting aim from Trudeau to Carney, with slogans such as "Carbon Tax Carney" that attempted to frame the new Liberal leader just as they had the old one. However, the clear differences between Trudeau's fading progressive style and Carney's manner of cool pragmatism made this shift difficult, since the two presented such contrasting leadership images, despite heading the same party.

Timing also became highly relevant, in two intersecting ways. Trump's aggressive pace created a sense of urgency that further created an opening for Carney's perceived skill set of crisis leadership, while diminishing concerns about his lack of actual political experience, his knowledge or interest in non-economic issues, and most of all his willingness to abandon or downplay many of his past environmental priorities, including discarding the carbon tax that he had previously endorsed. Actions that might have seemed hypocritical or opportunistic a few months earlier could now be excused as pragmatic and justified in the name of urgent crisis.

The second timing factor is due to the Conservatives, namely their pledge to bring down the government at the earliest opportunity. Under Trudeau, the Liberals had narrowly survived repeated non-confidence votes initiated by the Conservatives, saved primarily by the NDP and sometimes the Bloc Québécois. However, in the late December chaos after Freeland's resignation, the NDP pledged to no longer support the government. While Parliament was prorogued until late March at Trudeau's request after he announced his resignation, the likelihood of an immediate government defeat further accelerated a sense of exigency that accommodated Carney's style of leadership. Normally several months in duration, the Liberal leadership race was compressed into less than two, and Carney was able to swiftly take office and call an election. While the election call was also prompted by his own lack of a House of Commons seat and the Conservatives' criticisms of his unelected status, it intersected with the sense of urgency and need for immediate action precipitated by the Trump crisis. The timing seemed right for Carney's leadership style.

Over the course of the federal election campaign both Carney and Poilievre further leaned into their leadership styles. The questions that will long be debated are whether the Conservatives sufficiently shifted their strategy to fit the new Liberal leader, and whether Poilievre should or could have adjusted his own leadership image, particularly to distance himself more sharply from Trump's style. While Poilievre did repeatedly state his disagreement with Trump on tariffs and annexation, Trump's rapid acceleration to a far more disruptive agenda than his first term created uncertainty about Poilievre's own plans for governing.

The first – whether the Conservatives should have adjusted their strategy – is difficult to answer. Carney was new but headed a decade-old government with a mixed record, and the Conservatives repeatedly tried to make that record a focus of the election. But the threat of Trump had so disrupted and changed the conversation, creating a sense of urgency and crisis, that Carney was able to make dealing with Trump the pivotal election question, and to make himself the answer. The context had changed so rapidly that it is unclear whether the Conservatives could have changed the conversation back under any circumstances.

The second question – if Poilievre should, or could, have changed his style – is also complicated. It is worth noting that the election was primarily decided by shifts among non-Conservative voters, especially traditional NDP supporters. Conservative support itself did not significantly drop. Voters who were attracted to Poilievre's leadership style in 2024 largely remained with him in 2025; Angus Reid Institute reports[15] that favourable views of Poilievre barely shifted on a monthly basis between 36 per cent in September 2024 to 34 per cent in April during the election. However, negative ratings increased somewhat, concurrent with Trump's rise, from 52 per cent in September to 60 per cent in April. The election result suggests that many of those who held a negative view of Poilievre, especially NDP and to a lesser extent Bloc and Green supporters, were driven to vote for the Liberals under Carney, after having previously been reluctant to turn to the Liberals under Trudeau. Would a softened Poilievre leadership image, more clearly differentiated from Trump's style beyond tariffs, have made a difference by reducing his negative numbers and being less likely to drive opponents to huddle under Carney? Would a softened Poilievre image have dismayed those Conservative supporters who were drawn precisely to his uncompromising, combative persona? Would a softened Poilievre image have been possible, or simply seen by supporters and opponents alike as false, and therefore a betrayal? We do not know the answers.

CONCLUSION

Leadership matters in elections, but in unpredictable ways. As with all leadership, context and timing make the difference. Carney won both the Liberal leadership and the general election by convincing party members and voters that he was the right person at the right time, something that would have been much more difficult a year earlier. Similarly, Poilievre was on track to win an election against Justin Trudeau, and probably most other plausible Liberal leaders, with his quasi-populist style. But the return of Trump, with his aggressive stance against Canada and overall disruptive style, created an unflattering contrast that drove non-Liberal voters toward Carney's style. "Leadership," almost completely divorced from actual policies and governing records, made all the difference.

NOTES

1 See for example Richard N. Osborn, James G. Hunt, and Lawrence R. Jauch, "Toward A Contextual Theory Of Leadership," *The Leadership Quarterly* 13, no. 6 (2002): 797–837; and, Elizabeth A. Castillo and Mai P. Trinh, "In Search Of Missing Time: A Review of the Study of Time in Leadership Research," *The Leadership Quarterly* 29, no. 1 (2018): 165–78.

2 John Ivison, *Trudeau: The Education of a Prime Minister* (Toronto: McClelland and Stewart, 2019), 3; Stephen Maher, *The Prince: The Turbulent Reign of Justin Trudeau* (Toronto: Simon & Schuster Canada, 2024), 16.

3 Ivison, *Trudeau: The Education of a Prime Minister*, 4.

4 Harold D. Clarke et al., *Absent Mandate: Strategies and Choices in Canadian Elections* (Toronto: University of Toronto Press, 2019), 97. See also Harold D. Clarke et al., *Political Choice in Canada* (Toronto: McGraw-Hill Ryerson, 1979), especially chapter 7, "Images of Party Leaders."

5 Amanda Bittner, "Leaders Always Mattered: The Persistence of Personality in Canadian Elections," *Electoral Studies* 54 (2018): 297–302.

6 Brian Platt, "Pierre Poilievre Says He Would Fire the Bank Of Canada Governor if Elected Prime Minister," *Financial Post*, 12 May 2022, https://financialpost.com/news/economy/trudeaus-tory-rival-says-hed-fire-bank-of-canada-governor.

7 John Paul Tasker, "Poilievre Lashes Out at Bell Canada after CTV Airs Altered Clip," CBC News, 24 September 2024, https://www.cbc.ca/news/politics/poilievre-lashes-out-ctv-1.7332571.

8 David J. Climenhaga, "Corporate Media Have Reached Consensus about Andrew Scheer: He's Stephen Harper with a Human Face!" rabble.ca, 29 May 2017, https://rabble.ca/politics/canadian-politics/corporate-media-have-reached-consensus-about-andrew-scheer-hes/.

9 Alex Boutilier, "A Conservative MP Warns that Justin Trudeau Wants a 'Great Reset.' Conspiracy Theorists Are Worried, Too," *Toronto Star*, 20 November 2020, https://www.thestar.com/politics/federal/a-conservative-mp-warns-that-justin-trudeau-wants-a-great-reset-conspiracy-theorists-are-worried/article_618fe48b-f9d5-5bb2-a6ce-f4fed5fd15a5.html.

10 Aaron Wherry, "Conservatives Hitch Their Wagons to the Convoy Protest without Knowing Where It's Going," CBC News, 1 February 2022, https://www.cbc.ca/news/politics/poilievre-conservative-otoole-convoy-vaccine-mandate-1.6335286.

11 Platt, "Pierre Poilievre Says He Would Fire the Bank of Canada Governor if Elected Prime Minister."

12 Catherine Morrison, "Pierre Poilievre's Failure to Take Stance on Remote Work 'Surprising,' Expert Says," *Ottawa Citizen*, 24 May 2024, https://ottawacitizen.com/news/pierre-polievres-failure-to-take-a-stance-on-remote-work-is-surprising-says-expert.

13 Pierre Poilievre, "Pierre Poilievre: Memo to Corporate Canada – Fire Your Lobbyist. Ignore Politicians. Go to the People," *National Post*, 3 May 2024,https://nationalpost.com/opinion/pierre-poilievre-corporate-lobbyists-keep-sucking-up-to-high-tax-anti-resource-liberals.

14 Robert Hurst, "The Liberals Reach the Finish Line, with an Eye on the Bigger Fight," *Globe and Mail*, 8 March 2025, https://www.theglobeandmail.com/politics/article-carney-poised-to-win-liberal-leadership-race-sunday-setting-the-stage/.

15 Angus Reid Institute, "Views of Conservative Leader Pierre Poilievre," Angus Reid Institute, https://angusreid.org/poilievre-monitor/.

9

Foreign Interference and the 2025 General Election

Lori Turnbull

Foreign interference in democratic institutions is a serious concern for Canada and for democracies around the world. We cannot take for granted that hostile foreign entities and their proxies will not dedicate resources towards undermining our democratic processes, including elections, nominations and leadership contests, and political debate more broadly. To the contrary, we must assume they will. The countries that are most often identified as problematic with respect to foreign interference are China, India, Russia, and Iran. We live in an era in which the broad accessibility and availability of digital communications and social media make it relatively cheap and easy for malicious actors to insert themselves in the democratic ecosystems of other countries. Foreign interference is a threat to democracy because it undermines the capacity of the citizens of a country to choose their representatives freely and in an informed manner.

As is discussed more fully later in the chapter, foreign interest and involvement in Canadian elections can take many forms and not all of these are a cause for worry. For example, it is not unusual to hear other world leaders and social influencers outside of Canada express their views about the outcome of a Canadian election. US president Donald Trump has a lot to say about Canada and takes pride in his capacity to affect public discourse north of the border. At the same time, many of us in Canada opine openly about our preferences regarding the outcome of other elections, particularly those in the United States. Let's face it: most of us talk more about the implications of the Trump presidency than we do about our own politics. But this is not foreign interference. It is not problematic because it is not clandestine or manipulative. It does not affect our ability to vote based on information and free choice.

The types of interference we do have to worry about are things like disinformation campaigns, threats and intimidation directed at communities of voters, cyberattacks that weaken the infrastructure of democracy, illegal funding of political campaigns, and transnational repression. These measures undermine the integrity of democracy by applying undue pressure on voters to make inauthentic choices at the ballot box, by breaking campaign finance laws, and by using lies to discredit candidates and confuse voters.

The good news is that Canada's system of electoral administration, though not immune to foreign interference, is robust, rigorous, and trustworthy. The public inquiry into foreign interference, which issued its final report in January of 2025, found that foreign threats did not affect the overall outcome and results of the 2019 and 2021 elections. Commissioner Marie-Josee Hogue wrote: "Although there are a very small number of isolated cases where foreign interference may have had some impact on the outcome of a nomination contest or the result of an election in a given riding, there is no evidence to suggest that our institutions have been seriously affected by such interference or that parliamentarians owe their successful election to foreign entities."[1] Although a report of the National Security and Intelligence Committee of Parliamentarians (NSICOP) released in 2024 suggested that some parliamentarians had colluded with foreign states, the commissioner found that evidence has not borne out suggestions of divided loyalties among our elected officials.

Now for some bad news: foreign interference is a normal part of Canadian electoral democracy and has been for a while.[2] The 2025 election was no exception. For example, the Security and Intelligence Threats to Elections (SITE) Task Force picked up on a disinformation campaign aimed at prime minister and Liberal leader Mark Carney before and during the campaign. The SITE Task Force observed "coordinated inauthentic behaviour" about Carney on the WeChat platform via an account linked to the People's Republic of China (PRC) Chinese Communist Party's (CCP) Central Political and Legal Affairs Commission.[3] Further, while elections themselves are resilient to some types of foreign interference in that votes are conducted by secret ballot and presided over by Elections Canada, there have been complaints that nomination contests and leadership races are more vulnerable to foreign actors with nefarious intent.

We can trust in the integrity of our electoral institutions, but we need to be vigilant about the very real and persistent threat of foreign interference. Further, public worry about threats of foreign interference can undermine trust in our democratic institutions even if election results are not skewed.

This chapter starts by giving some background information on how the issue of foreign interference in Canadian democracy penetrated the public consciousness. Second, the chapter distinguishes between different types and methods of foreign interference. Third, there is a discussion of the various institutions that play a role in safeguarding Canada's democracy against foreign interference, including Elections Canada, the Security and Intelligence Threat to Elections Task Force (SITE), and the Critical Election Incident Public Protocol Panel. Fourth, the chapter addresses the specific threats that surfaced during the 2025 election. It concludes with suggestions for how to manage threats of foreign interference going forward. We cannot remove the desire for foreign actors to interfere with our democratic health and processes, but we can do more to fortify ourselves against these threats so that our democratic integrity remains intact.

BACKGROUND

As of the fall of 2022, it looked as though foreign interference was going to be a defining issue of the next federal election campaign. The *Globe and Mail* and Global News were publishing stories and reports alleging foreign interference in Canadian democracy by China and other countries. Their reports were based on leaks of classified intelligence.[4] Questions were raised about the quality of the intelligence and about what then prime minister Justin Trudeau knew of these allegations and when. Opposition parties mused about whether the Liberal government had chosen not to tell the public about instances of foreign interference to protect their partisan interests because they did not want to be seen as lax on foreign meddling. For months, the Trudeau government struggled to get its arms around the issue. The key for any government trying to manage the politics of foreign interference is to show they are taking it seriously (and not pretending it doesn't exist) but, at the same time, stopping short of causing the public to panic and doubt the health of democracy and the integrity of election results. Finding the right balance in this regard has proven an evergreen challenge for democratic governments around the world. There is no perfect response.

Two standing committees of the House of Commons – Procedure and House Affairs and Access to Information, Privacy and Ethics – launched studies into the government's response to foreign interference in the fall of 2022. They heard from various officials, politicians, and subject matter experts but neither committee had access to classified information. Much of the witness testimony painted a picture of a troubled and broken flow of communication within and between government entities with respect to security and intelligence. It was not clear whether critical information from security and intelligence services was getting to the prime minister's office (PMO) at all, let alone in enough time to do anything with it, and it was not clear whether the information and intelligence that did reach them was being read and absorbed by the right people.

In March of 2023, there was a flurry of activity. Prime Minister Trudeau asked the National Security and Intelligence Review Agency (NSIRA) to conduct a study of how national security agencies shared information with decision makers during the 2019 and 2021 elections. He also appointed former governor general David Johnston to act as a special rapporteur on the issue, file an initial report, and make a recommendation to the government about whether there should be a public inquiry into foreign interference (which the opposition parties were calling for). Prime Minister Trudeau also asked the National Security and Intelligence Committee of Parliamentarians (NSICOP) to conduct a review to "assess the state of foreign interference in federal election processes" in the 2019 and 2021 elections.[5] On 17 March an unnamed security official published an article in the *Globe and Mail* to alert the public of their concern that while threats and instances of foreign interference grew, "serious action remained unforthcoming." Further, they wrote that "evidence of senior public officials ignoring interference was beginning to mount."

Meanwhile, Liberal member of parliament Han Dong abruptly left the Liberal caucus that month to sit as an independent member amid allegations published in the *Globe and Mail* and by Global News, based on leaked intelligence, that he counselled the Chinese consul general in Toronto against the release of Michael Kovrig and Michael Spavor, two Canadians detained in Beijing for over one thousand days on politically motivated charges. In a report released in May of 2023, David Johnston concluded that there were "irregularities" in Han Dong's nomination process and that these issues were suspected to be tied to the People's Republic of China consulate in Toronto, though he did not find evidence that Dong was aware of these irregularities.[6] Dong denied wrongdoing and launched a defamation suit against Global News, which was settled in 2025. Justice Hogue's final report corroborated Dong's statement that he did not counsel the Chinese government against the release of the "two Michaels."

In a particularly impactful development that seemed to resonate with members of the public, we learned that family members of Conservative member of parliament Michael Chong who live in Hong Kong were targeted by a Chinese diplomat named Zhao Wei, who was trying to obtain information on them after Chong referred to Beijing's actions in the Xinjiang region as genocide.[7] Canada expelled Zhao Wai in May of 2023.

Commissioner Hogue's mandate was to "examine and assess the interference by China, Russia and other foreign states or non-state actors."[8] All states engage with others in some way and make attempts at affecting each other's behaviour on the global stage, but some states engage in activities that go beyond what can be described as legitimate diplomacy. When states act in clandestine or threatening ways that undermine democratic processes in other states, such as through transnational suppression, we call that foreign interference. Not all states do this. China, Russia, India, Iran, and Pakistan were recognized by the commission as being particularly active in foreign interference, with the PRC spending more resources on these efforts than other countries. States that engage in foreign interference typically do so to protect themselves and further their interests by seeking alignment with their goals and perspectives. For example, India is known to have taken an increasing interest in Canada's South Asian communities out of concern that the spread of "anti-India" sentiment could undermine national stability and security in India.[9]

Though David Johnston had argued against it in his report, the government decided to create a public inquiry into foreign interference in September of that year. The report of the inquiry was released in January of 2025, just two months prior to the election call. The conclusions of commissioner Justice Marie-Josee Hogue that foreign interference is present but not impactful gave assurance to Canadians that they could trust the results of the 2025 vote.

FOREIGN INTERFERENCE: DEFINITIONS AND METHODS

In her final report, Commissioner Hogue explained that "foreign interference" means different things in different contexts.[10] She defined the term as including acts that are "clandestine, deceptive or threatening" by a foreign entity or its proxy that are detrimental to the interests of Canada. This chapter embraces this definition for the purposes of its analysis.

Foreign interference aims to disrupt the election processes and undermine democratic institutions in another country through intimidation, coercion, grooming, disinformation, manipulation, or illegal funding. Ultimately, these are power moves aimed at advancing the interests of a foreign state or non-state actor.

Specific acts of foreign interference include but are not limited to the following:

Disinformation: Commissioner Hogue identified the spread of misinformation and disinformation through social media and other networks as the "single biggest risk" to Canadian democracy. She wrote that information manipulation, whether from a foreign or a domestic source, is an "existential threat" and, if not addressed, has the capacity to "distort our discourse, change our views and shape our society."[11] Foreign interference via disinformation tends to take the form of false or misleading information aimed at political actors in attempt to discourage voters from supporting them.

Cyberattacks: attacks on secure data systems aimed at undermining the infrastructure of democracy, including hacks on the personal data of voters.

Espionage, including economic espionage: the use of spies to obtain illegal access to classified or private information.

Elicitation: drawing out sensitive or classified information through casual conversation or subtly over time. For example, foreign actors or their proxies could attempt to create relationships with cabinet ministers, members of parliament, senators, and their staff so that, over time, they build trust with these officials are more able to extract information from them.

Intimidation or bribery of officials: foreign agents or their proxies could threaten, intimidate, or bribe politicians, their staff, or public officials to achieve a desired policy goal.

Illegal funding: making illegal donations, whether via cash or in-kind contributions, from foreign entities in attempt to influence the result of an election. In Canada, only citizens and permanent residents are legally eligible to contribute to election contests, including leadership and nomination contests.

Transnational repression: repression by a foreign state "generally targeting political dissidents or members of diaspora communities living in Canada."[12] This can include silencing, harassing, coercing, or harming people. Diaspora communities can be targeted by foreign actors who want to pressure them into voting for their preferred candidates (or against others).

Foreign interference tactics can be used in attempts to sway the results of elections as well as other democratic and electoral processes, including candidate nomination contests and leadership competitions. As noted in Johnston's report and in the Hogue Commission's final report, Canada has intelligence to suggest that the Liberal nomination process in the Don Valley North riding in 2019 experienced "irregularities" tied to the PRC.

A 2024 report released by the National Security and Intelligence Committee of Parliamentarians (NSICOP) flagged nomination and leadership contests as being "particularly vulnerable" to foreign interference. The NSICOP report points to several reasons for this, including: nomination contests in "safe seats" for political parties are highly consequential because whoever wins the nomination is very likely to win the election; also, parties have different rules for nomination and leadership processes, including around membership and eligibility to vote, and Elections Canada is not involved in monitoring the voting process. Fraudulent practices would be easier to carry out in relation to these processes as compared to general elections.[13]

Though all forms of foreign interference are threatening to democracy, it is worth echoing Commissioner Hogue's comments regarding the unique dangers posed by disinformation campaigns. Both Elections Canada and NSICOP have also acknowledged the prevalence of disinformation campaigns in foreign interference. Hostile actors rely on both social media and mainstream media to reach large audiences in their attempts to manipulate voters, undermine candidates, and push false narratives. At the same time, the rise of social media has allowed these actors to target specific audiences or communities with sophisticated disinformation campaigns. Such targeted operations are smaller and therefore often harder to detect. The use of generative AI is particularly concerning given the capacity to create large amounts of false content including impersonations of political actors.[14]

FOREIGN INTERFERENCE AND CANADA'S ELECTORAL ECOSYSTEM

As mentioned earlier, the public inquiry into foreign interference report was delivered roughly two months before the writ period began on 23 March 2025. This left insufficient time for any of Commissioner Hogue's fifty-one recommendations to be acted upon in time for the election. Furthermore, since Parliament was prorogued from January 2025 until it was dissolved in March, there was no way for parliamentarians to take any sort of formal consideration of the recommendations.

Nevertheless, Canada's electoral infrastructure includes several institutions that play key roles in monitoring the electoral landscape for evidence of foreign interference, informing Canadians about instances of foreign interference when appropriate, and protecting Canada's democratic institutions against threats of foreign interference. The key institutional players and their roles are described below.

Elections Canada

Elections Canada is an independent, non-partisan agency with a mandate to conduct elections, by-elections, and referenda. It administers campaign finance laws and election laws more broadly. The organization also has a mandate to educate the public on matters related to voting, which includes communications on the risk of foreign interference. Elections Canada has held briefings and has communicated with the public via their website in efforts to define the threat of foreign interference in elections and help Canadians to be more aware of it. Chief Electoral Officer Stephane Perreault has made recommendations to Parliament to amend the Canada Elections Act to address concerns related to foreign interference. For example, Perreault suggests that Elections Canada play a heavier scrutiny role in leadership and nomination contests to protect them against the threat of foreign interference.[15]

The Commissioner of Canada Elections, which is a separate office within Elections Canada, is responsible for enforcing compliance with election law. This office carries out reviews and investigations connected to violations and complaints regarding election law.

The Canada Elections Act contains provisions that specifically prohibit foreign interference in Canada's electoral democracy, but they focus on the role of money in elections. Foreign actors are banned from making political contributions and from registering as third parties, and third parties are not permitted to use funds from foreign sources towards their election activities. The legislation also prohibits foreign actors from unduly influencing the voting behaviour of Canadian citizens.[16]

Security and Intelligence Threat to Elections Task Force (SITE)

SITE was created in 2019 as part of the federal government's "Plan to Protect Canadian Democracy" initiative. It is the principal mechanism for monitoring threats to Canadian elections from foreign interference. This task force is a "whole of government" working group that consists of experts from the Canadian Security Intelligence Service (CSIS), Communications Security Establishment Canada (CSE), Global Affairs Canada (GAC), and the Royal Canadian Mounted Police (RCMP). SITE's role is to protect Canadian elections from foreign interference by coordinating collection and analysis efforts regarding threats to elections; providing a point of engagement and contact between the security and intelligence community and other government partners working on elections; reviewing and focusing intelligence collection, assessment, and open-source analysis related to foreign interference; and providing situational awareness for government partners. SITE's mandate extends to by-elections and to federal leadership contests.[17]

Critical Election Incident Public Protocol Panel (the Panel)

The Panel was established also in 2019 via cabinet directive as part of the government's effort to "safeguard the integrity of Canadian elections."[18] The protocol lays out when and how to communicate to the public about an occurrence that threatens the integrity of an election during the writ period (and do not fall within the mandate of Elections Canada.) The threshold that would trigger such a communication with the public is limited to "exceptional circumstances."[19] During elections, the Panel receives regular intelligence briefings from the SITE Task Force and, based on the intelligence passed on in those briefings, decides whether and when to inform the public that a threat has reached this threshold. The public may still be informed about threats that, while present, do not affect the integrity of the election. This was the case during the election campaign in 2025.

The Panel's membership consists of the clerk of the privy council; the national security and intelligence adviser to the prime minister; the deputy minister of justice and deputy attorney general; the deputy minister of public safety; and the deputy minister of foreign affairs.

THE FORTY-FIFTH GENERAL ELECTION

On 25 June 2025, the commissioner of Canada Elections, Caroline Simard, announced that she had no evidence to suggest that the 2025 election was affected by foreign interference, disinformation, or voter intimidation. Her office received more than sixteen thousand complaints about the election campaign in total – seven times the number received in the previous two elections – but the number of complaints related to foreign interference, disinformation, and voter intimidation was lower than her office had expected.[20]

Foreign interference was still present during the campaign in several forms, just not at the level that would compromise the integrity of the results or the ability of citizens to vote in an informed manner. Representatives from the Privy Council Office (PCO), Global Affairs Canada, Canadian Centre for Cybersecurity, and the SITE Task Force gave briefings throughout the campaign on matters related to foreign interference based on intelligence gathering by the SITE Task Force as it was communicated to the Panel. The briefings were led by the assistant secretary for communications at PCO. The instances of foreign interference that were detected during the 2025 campaign, which ran from 23 March until 28 April, are described below.

On 24 March, these officials briefed the public on the "information landscape" and on the measures that would be taken throughout the campaign to monitor for foreign interference. On 31 March, due to the intensification of threats of violence directed at Canadian public figures, the government introduced the Candidate Security Program for candidates who felt intimidated or threatened.[21] Throughout the campaign, unarmed, private security was provided to twenty-two candidates. It is not clear to what extent these circumstances arose from threats from foreign agents.

On 7 April, officials briefed the public on a disinformation campaign that was directed at Prime Minister Carney, who was the Liberal candidate in the riding of Nepean. The operation was executed on WeChat and was launched by Youli-Youmian, the platform's most popular news account that, according to intelligence, is linked to the PRC Chinese Communist Party's Central Political and Legal Affairs Commission. The SITE Task Force observed "large spikes of coordinated inauthentic behaviour" beginning on 10 March which was almost two weeks before the campaign started and was the day after Carney became leader of the Liberal Party. The operation included both positive and negative narratives about Carney and focused on his credentials and his stance on the United States.[22] Ostensibly, the point was to manipulate and confuse voters. No doubt, whoever won that leadership race was to become a target of foreign actors with the goal of disrupting Canadian democracy. SITE concluded that the levels of engagement with the content were not at a level that would undermine or affect the results of the election but warned voters to be cautious about the information they were consuming and to be vigilant about evaluating the "information landscape" with a critical eye and an awareness of the prevalence of disinformation.[23]

On 21 April, it was reported that SITE had detected a transnational repression operation on social media platforms that have a high participation rate from Chinese-speaking users in Canada, including Facebook, WeChat, TikTok, RedNote, and Douyin. The content of the operation, consisting of disparaging comments and a "wanted" poster, were meant to undermine the candidacy of Conservative Joe Tay in the riding of Don Valley North. Tay has been vocal in his opposition to PRC laws and practices with respect to Hong Kong. The levels of engagement with the content of the operation were generally low but they spiked several times throughout the campaign. The SITE Task Force expressed concern that such operations would send a broader message to the targeted community, "who are well aware of malign actors' methods of transnational repression, and may avoid supporting their preferred candidate as a result (having signs on their property, providing donations, etc.)." SITE made the Conservative Party and the social media platforms aware of what was happening and reminded the public that all votes are "secret and secure."[24]

Though it occurred outside the writ period, it is important to note the salience of foreign interference in the Liberal leadership race that selected Mark Carney. Justin Trudeau announced on 6 January that he was intending to leave politics once the Liberals found a new leader. The party was eager to select a new leader expeditiously because the election was scheduled for the fall. From the beginning, the Liberal Party was clearly cognizant of the threat of foreign interference and took measures to protect themselves and the process. To fortify against voter fraud, the party changed its rules so that only Canadian citizens and permanent residents could vote in the leadership selection process. To cast a ballot, members were required to verify their address and identity via the Canada Post app or in person at a Canada Post location. Though these measures would help to protect the race against disruption through foreign interference, there were reports towards the end of the race that the app was difficult to work with. Many Liberals voiced their frustration on social media.[25] The SITE Task Force monitored the Liberal leadership race in its entirety.

As mentioned earlier, leadership races are particularly vulnerable to foreign interference for several reasons. First, the stakes are big. Political leaders are very powerful and influential, and so the processes to select them are likely to attract the attention of foreign actors who have preferences about who takes on these positions. In the case of the Liberal leadership race in 2025, the winner would become prime minister almost immediately. The stakes could not have been higher.

Second, leadership contests are run by the parties themselves rather than by Elections Canada. The party sets the rules around candidate eligibility, membership, timing, entry fees, and candidate disqualifications. The only role that Elections Canada plays is to monitor the flow of money in the form of donations to candidates. Further, the rules that parties make are just rules. They are not laws. There is no legal punishment or sanction if they are broken.

Third, voting in leadership races tends to be open to all party members and parties have become much more inclusive in their approach to membership. Political parties have adopted new voting rules for leadership contests in recent decades largely due to a push for more grassroots involvement. Instead of having a select number of the party faithful gather in a delegates' convention to choose leaders, parties now extend the right to vote to every person who is registered as a member of the party (some conditions apply, but not many). The "democratization" of leadership selection processes occurs as our political culture becomes more focused on leaders and their brands, personalities, and values rather than on the parties themselves. Poguntke and Webb refer to this as a "presidentialization" of party politics in Westminster systems like Canada's.[26]

Ostensibly, this shift was meant to make leadership selection processes more democratic, less elitist, and more meaningful and empowering to the party membership. However, there have been unintended consequences, some of which have undermined the influence of devoted party members and increased vulnerability to foreign interference. Under the "one member, one vote" model, the person who wins the modern leadership contest is almost guaranteed to be the person who signs up the most members. Some of these members will be loyal to the goals and vision of the party but, for others, the commitment to the party may be fragile. The "one member, one vote" system is highly vulnerable to entryism, which is a political strategy whereby the members of an organization or group are encouraged to sign up as members of another organization with intent to "take it over" and redirect its goals and plans. It comes down to leveraging the power in numbers.

Political parties' leadership contests are vulnerable to this approach because they are permissive about who can become a member and, again, due to the power that they could wield in politics and government, they are an attractive target. Agents of disruption, including foreign actors, could find opportunities in the openness of the leadership selection process, the ease of acquiring party memberships, and the frequent lack of rigour in the verification process with respect to a political party's list of members. For example, candidates are always permitted to do their own verification process to scrutinize the validity of the full membership list – including members signed up by other candidates. However, the process is often severely lacking. In the Conservative Party leadership selection process in 2022, candidates signed up a record number of new members (over 600,000) but candidates and their teams had only ninety-six hours to verify the identities of the people on the full members' list. This is not enough time for fraud detection.

Arguably, delegated conventions were more resistant to the efforts of disrupters, whether foreign or domestic. Those who participated in delegated conventions tended to be committed members of the party (or else they would not have devoted the time and resources to attend the convention in the first place) and the choice for the new leader was made on the convention floor. Delegates showed their credentials at the door to gain access to the meeting. Failed candidates become kingmakers and deals between various factions within the party were made in real time. Candidates were incentivized to make appeals to those who were committed party members rather than to sell as many memberships as possible. This process was less inclusive of the full party membership but also more resilient to potential sources of entryism and foreign interference.

Chandra Arya, the member of parliament for Nepean at the time, was the first person to throw his hat in the ring for the Liberal leadership after Trudeau announced his intent to step aside. In late January, the Liberals announced that he was disqualified from being a candidate but did not give clear reasons for their decision. Two months later, the *Globe and Mail* ran a story about how Arya was banned from running over allegations of foreign interference, specifically with respect to his ties to the government of India. In the summer of 2024, he had taken a trip to India and met with Prime Minister Narendra Modi. He did not tell the government that he was taking the trip, even though diplomatic relationships between the two countries were severely strained at that time. A confidential source from the Liberal Party who was tasked with monitoring for foreign interference told the *Globe and Mail* that there were "troubling inconsistencies" in a questionnaire filled out by Arya.[27]

In February, the Liberals decided to bar another candidate, Ruby Dhalla, from the race due to concerns over foreign interference. Dhalla, a former Liberal MP turned businessperson, was accused of, among other things, failing to disclose the involvement of a non-Canadian in her campaign, which the party said would amount to foreign interference if it happened during an election.[28]

DISCUSSION AND CONCLUSION

Political parties are increasingly aware of the prevalence of foreign interference and take their own measures to monitor the information landscape and protect themselves, their candidates, and their processes. These can include helping elected officials, political staff, and candidates to become more literate in recognizing the signs of foreign interference, practicing good data hygiene to protect privacy, and developing sound internal communications and data practices within the party. During campaign periods, parties receive information about foreign interference threats from the SITE Task Force when it is deemed appropriate. Also, political parties work with CSIS and CSE on an ongoing basis to maintain an understanding of the existence of foreign threats to Canada's democratic institutions.

Nevertheless, there is reason to be concerned that political parties do not do enough about foreign interference. In the case of the Liberal leadership race for example, when two candidates were disqualified due to allegations related to foreign interference, it was notable how little evidence and explanation was provided to the public about what happened. It is difficult for the public to know whether political parties truly take foreign interference seriously. Parties could do more to protect themselves and, by extension, voters, and democratic processes, and as public institutions they have an important role to play in safeguarding democracy. But political parties are also private clubs that make their own rules and decide what to prioritize and how to allocate their scarce resources. When they are fighting election campaigns at break-neck speed, and never have enough volunteers or money, they might not put the fight against foreign interference at the top of their to-do lists.

There are measures that political parties could take against foreign interference but have largely chosen not to. For example, though the Liberals tightened up the rules around who was eligible to vote in their leadership race, they did not impose a membership fee, which would have been an extra step in dissuading foreign actors from buying up memberships to sway the results. As Ryan Alford points out, it is not that the money would be a deterrent to a state like China. It is that the payment would leave a financial trail that could lead to detection.[29]

Nomination contests have long been considered a vulnerable point in the system when it comes to foreign interference. As Justice Hogue wrote in her final report, "the eligibility for voting in nomination contests does not seem very stringent, and the control measures in place do not seem very robust." The media reports of the irregularities in the Don Valley North Liberal nomination process in 2019, combined with the related testimony before the public inquiry into foreign interference from Han Dong and high-ranking political staffers, drew the public's attention to the problems in nominations processes. An editorial in the *Globe and Mail* in 2024 referred to nomination contests as "unregulated affairs" with each party setting its own rules that could vary in practice from riding to riding.[30] But despite all of this attention, the election of 2025 came and went with no evidence that political parties changed their approach to nominations in any way whatsoever so as to guard against the effects of foreign interference.

There is no way that the rules governing leadership races and nomination contests will tighten if party leaders do not make it a priority. There is little reason for optimism about this. In fact, Conservative leader Pierre Poilievre seems to want to avoid the topic altogether. He refused to get top security clearance like the other party leaders in order to be eligible for security briefings related to foreign interference. When then prime minister Justin Trudeau asked CSIS to find a way to brief Poilievre even though he didn't have the proper clearance, he still refused.[31] Other leaders and members of the media questioned why he was ducking clearance, with some suggesting he must have something to hide.

There is no way to truly prevent foreign interference, because foreign actors will continue trying to disrupt other democracies for their own ends. All we can do is become better at protecting ourselves against its effects. This means taking measures like adopting tighter rules around nomination and leadership processes, protecting ourselves and our information online, and practicing good civic self-defence when syphoning through online content. This won't be easy, particularly as artificial intelligence becomes more sophisticated and hostile states use it in efforts to manipulate voters.

Given that political leaders are not clamouring to take up the fight against foreign interference, this leaves a daunting responsibility to the public and the media. It is important that we continue to build on the best practices that Canada has adopted since the Plan to Protect Canadian Democracy initiative began in 2019. Regular briefings during elections on the nature and scope of foreign interference, intelligence sharing between institutions and partners, and public education campaigns to build awareness and civic literacy are key steps in fortifying ourselves against foreign interference. Anything further will depend on political will.

NOTES

1 Marie-Josée Hogue, *Public Inquiry into Foreign Interference in Federal Electoral Processes and Democratic Institutions. Final Report. Volume 1: Report Summary* (Ottawa: Foreign Interference Commission, 2025).

2 Hogue, *Public Inquiry into Foreign Interference.*
3 Privy Council Office, "Update on Canada's Actions to Protect General Election 45," Government of Canada, 7 April 2025, https://www.canada.ca/en/privy-council/news/2025/04/update-on-canadas-actions-to-protect-general-election-45.html.
4 David Johnston, *First Report The Right Honourable David Johnston Independent Special Rapporteur on Foreign Interference* (Ottawa: Independent Special Rapporteur on Foreign Interference, 2023).
5 National Security and Intelligence Committee of Parliamentarians, *Special Report on Foreign Interference in Canada's Democratic Processes and Institutions* (Ottawa: NSICOP, 2024).
6 Peter Zimonjic, "Han Dong Tells Foreign Interference Inquiry He Tried to Help Spavor and Kovrig, Wants to Be a Liberal Again," CBC News, 2 April 2024, https://www.cbc.ca/news/politics/han-dong-party-officials-foreign-interference-1.7160866.
7 Darren Major, "Canada Expelling Diplomat Accused of Targeting MP Michael Chong's Family," CBC News, 8 May 2023, https://www.cbc.ca/news/politics/canada-expelling-chinese-diplomat-1.6836336.
8 Foreign Interference Commission, "Commission Mandate," *Public Inquiry into Foreign Interference in Federal Electoral Processes and Democratic Institutions*, https://foreigninterferencecommission.ca/about/commission-mandate.
9 Foreign Interference Commission, "Country Summaries," *Public Inquiry into Foreign Interference in Federal Electoral Processes and Democratic Institutions*, https://foreigninterferencecommission.ca/fileadmin/foreign_interference_commission/Documents/Exhibits_and_Presentations/Exhibits/CAN.SUM.000030.pdf.
10 Hogue, *Public Inquiry into Foreign Interference*, 21.
11 Peter Zimonjic, "5 Things We Learned from the Final Report on Foreign Interference," CBC News, 28 January 2025, https://www.cbc.ca/news/politics/final-report-public-inquiry-foregin-interference-1.7443597.
12 Marie-Josée Hogue, "Chapter 19: Recommendations to Better Protect Against Foreign Interference in Canada's Democratic Institutions and Processes," in *Public Inquiry into Foreign Interference in Federal Electoral Processes and Democratic Institutions. Final Report, Volume 5* (Ottawa: Foreign Interference Commission, 2025), 47.
13 Catherine Tunney, "Nomination Races Are a 'Gateway' for Foreign Interference – Is Anyone Doing Anything about It?" CBC News, 19 June 2024, https://www.cbc.ca/news/politics/foreign-interference-nominations-nsicop-hogue-1.7238450.

14 Elections Canada, "The Information Ecosystem," Elections Canada, 4 November 2024, https://www.elections.ca/content.aspx?section=res&dir=rep/oth/prthr/rpt&document=p3&lang=e.

15 Elections Canada, "Foreign Interference," Elections Canada, 21 March 2025, https://www.elections.ca/content.aspx?section=abo&dir=comp/nov2124&document=p8&lang=e.

16 Elections Canada, "Understanding Foreign Interference," Elections Canada, 25 March 2025, https://www.elections.ca/content.aspx?section=vot&dir=ing&document=index&lang=e.

17 Government of Canada, "Security And Intelligence Threats To Elections (SITE) Task Force," Government of Canada, 21 February 2025, https://www.canada.ca/en/democratic-institutions/services/protecting-democracy/security-task-force.html#toco.

18 Government of Canada, "Critical Election Incident Public Protocol," Government of Canada, 2 July 2025, https://www.canada.ca/en/democratic-institutions/services/protecting-democracy/critical-election-incident-public-protocol.html#toc1.

19 Canada, "Critical Election Incident Public Protocol."

20 Nick Murray, "No Evidence Federal Election Was Affected by Foreign Interference, Commissioner Says," *Canadian Press*, 25 June 2025, https://nationalnewswatch.com/2025/06/25/no-evidence-federal-election-was-affected-by-foreign-interference-commissioner-says.

21 CPAC, "Security Task Force Provides Update On Upcoming Election – March 31, 2025," *YouTube*, 31 March 2025, https://www.youtube.com/watch?v=oU3d9WIEcxo.

22 Jim Bronskill, "Security Officials Report a Beijing-Linked Online Operation Focused on Carney," CBC News, 7 April 2025, https://www.cbc.ca/news/politics/carney-wechat-china-1.7503711.

23 Privy Council Office, "Update on Canada's Actions to Protect General Election 45," 7 April 2025.

24 Privy Council Office, "Update on Canada's Actions to Protect General Election 45," Government of Canada, 21 April 2025, https://www.canada.ca/en/privy-council/news/2025/04/update-on-canadas-actions-to-protect-general-election-450.html.

25 Peter Zimonjic, "Registered Liberals Say Online Leadership Voting Is Rife with Problems," CBC News, 28 February 2025, https://www.cbc.ca/news/politics/liberal-leadership-voting-problems-1.7471740.

26 William Cross and Andre Blais, "Who Selects the Party Leader?" *Canadian Political Science Association*, 2009, https://www.cpsa-acsp.ca/papers-2009/Cross.pdf.

27 Robert Fife and Stephen Chase, "Ousted Liberal MP Chandra Arya Barred From Running Under Party's Banner over Alleged Ties to India," *Globe and Mail*, 26 March 2025, https://www.theglobeandmail.com/politics/article-liberal-mp-chandra-arya-ousted-alleged-foreign-interference-india/.

28 Catharine Tunney and David Cochrane, "Ruby Dhalla Kicked out of Liberal Leadership Race after 'Extremely Serious Violations': Party," CBC News, 21 February 2025, https://www.cbc.ca/news/politics/ruby-dhalla-liberal-leadership-1.7465430.

29 Ryan Alford, "Liberals' New Election Rules Are Not Enough to Prevent Foreign Interference," *National Post*, 20 January 2025, https://macdonaldlaurier.ca/liberals-new-election-rules-arent-enough-to-prevent-foreign-interference-ryan-alford-in-the-national-post/.

30 The editorial board, "Political Parties Need to Step up and Fight Foreign Interference," *Globe and Mail*, 14 June 2024, https://www.theglobeandmail.com/opinion/editorials/article-political-parties-need-to-step-up-and-fight-foreign-interference/.

31 Darren Major, "Poilievre Rejects Terms of CSIS Foreign Interference Briefing," CBC News, 28 January 2025, https://www.cbc.ca/news/politics/poilievre-csis-briefing-1.7444082.

10

The Media Narratives that Defined the Mainstream Election Coverage

Brett Popplewell, Adrian Harewood, and Patrick White

As has been increasingly the case in recent Canadian elections, the stories that defined the 2025 federal campaign did not simply reach the Canadian public through the traditional mainstream media of print and broadcast news. Online echo chambers, social media influencers, and a plethora of Canadian alternative independent media outlets played important roles in creating the stories that defined this election for many Canadians. Trust in the mainstream media was a partisan issue before the election began and became a campaign topic, spurred on by promises from party leaders to either fund or defund the Canadian Broadcasting Corporation. Conservative leader Pierre Poilievre's continuous rhetoric around bias within the media's coverage of Canadian politics was one of the campaign's inescapable narratives, buoyed by Leger polls indicating that Conservative voters no longer trust the mainstream media's political coverage.[1]

Unlike in the 2021 election, which mainstream outlets across the media spectrum cynically branded as unnecessary, the 2025 campaign was widely presented as the most important Canadian election in decades, one that would determine the fate and existence of the nation itself.

The 2025 contest featured a heightened complexity of disinformation and factual distortions that spread far and wide online, largely via social media. While these issues were also prevalent in previous elections, the sophistication seen during the 2025 campaign was unprecedented. As was the case in the 2019 and 2021 elections, there was much concern that the mainstream national media and Canadian voters themselves might be overwhelmed by malicious disinformation spread via bots and trolls. These fears proved justified as deep fakes and networked attacks of "bot-like" social media accounts became a concern to election officials who could not contain or limit the audience manipulation permeating online. As was the case during the 2021 election, angry protestors continued to disrupt campaign stops and berate politicians and reporters alike. Unlike 2021, however, some of the most contentious moments in this campaign came not from random protestors, but from accredited journalists employed by outlets that operate outside the traditional mainstream.

This chapter chronicles the major narratives in media coverage of the campaign, first examining the media in English Canada before turning to the French language media in Quebec. Coverage has been arranged chronologically in order to capture the prevailing narratives that dominated different periods of the election itself.[2]

The news outlets monitored in this study often view the political landscape in Canada through different ideological lenses. While each outlet claims that its coverage is true to fact and events, they present Canadians with competing, and often incompatible, versions of the same story. In the case of the 2025 election, Canadians received starkly different readings of the election based on their media consumption. Analyzing all the coverage of each of these outlets is an impossible task. Here, we have focused on exploring differences within the prevailing narratives as presented by the traditional mainstream media (in the case of the nationally focused newspapers, this included monitoring coverage from the traditionally right-leaning *National Post* and *Toronto Sun* to the traditionally left-leaning *Toronto Star*) in order to understand what the journalists covering the campaign themselves considered important enough to transmit to their audiences. Coverage by the country's major broadcast networks has also been incorporated as has reporting from the Canadian Press, the wire service that provides coverage to media outlets across the country.

HOW IT STARTED

News coverage throughout the last few months of 2024 often told a similar story of an unpopular prime minister slumping in the polls and poised to lead his party to electoral defeat. By mid-November 2024, many news outlets had published articles predicting a decimation of the Liberal caucus in a forthcoming election. Pundits and columnists across the board predicted the Conservative Party of Canada under Poilievre would win an easy majority. By the second week of October 2024 the main narrative coming out of the Parliamentary Press Gallery focused on growing dissent within the Liberal caucus especially after Liberal MPs began holding meetings to quietly and publicly urge Trudeau to step down. As the 5 November 2024, US election drew near, pundits began predicting that nothing short of a return of Donald Trump could possibly reverse the prime minister's fortunes. Upon Trump's re-election, former Liberal strategist Warren Kinsella predicted, in a headline published across the Postmedia chain, that "Trump's win will bring boost to floundering Justin Trudeau."[3]

By 11 December, the Logic was reporting that a poll conducted for them by Abacus Data showed that the predicted boost had failed to materialize: there was no "Trump bump" for Trudeau.[4] The prevailing political narrative across the board remained one of imminent doom facing the Liberals especially after news began trickling out that Trump had mused with Trudeau during a late November dinner at the president-elect's Florida estate that Canada should become the fifty-first US state. Talk of a potential US-Canada tariff war had yet to consume the mainstream news agenda when Trump took to NBC News and referred to the prime minister as "Governor Justin Trudeau of the Great State of Canada" and reiterated his own push for the country to give up its sovereignty and join the United States.[5] Trump's quips were still being digested by journalists across the Canadian mediascape when news broke that Trudeau was facing further unrest within his own cabinet. Then came Finance Minister Chrystia Freeland's resignation on 16 December 2024. Coverage of Freeland's resignation predicted Trudeau had no choice but to resign his position as Liberal leader. As politicians and journalists broke for the Christmas holidays, the question repeated in most political coverage was whether the prime minister would officially step down.

Insistent that the traditional media were unflaggingly hostile to conservatism generally and the Conservative Party in particular, Poilievre had made a point of ignoring legacy media journalists when he could and responding sharply when subjected to what he saw as their belligerent questioning. However, he sat down to a two-hour interview with the like-minded Jordan Peterson, the former University of Toronto psychology professor and right-wing social media influencer, which was released on 2 January 2025, and which presented Poilievre to viewers as "Canada's next Prime Minister."[6]

On 6 January, Trudeau held a press conference to announce his pending resignation. Coverage of that announcement within the three largest national newspapers captured the tone of the narrative circulating at the time. The lead op-ed in the *National Post* was headlined "Justin Trudeau resigns a failure,"[7] while at the *Globe and Mail*, current affairs columnist Robyn Urback took a similar swing with her column headlined: "Justin Trudeau resigned too late. There is no salvaging the Liberal Party now."[8] Even the traditionally liberal-minded editorial board of the *Toronto Star* judged that "Justin Trudeau finally made the right decision."[9]

Much of the preliminary coverage across the mainstream platforms predicted that whomever the Liberals selected as their leader would face certain defeat once the election was called. In the days immediately following, the usual speculative stories circulated over who might replace Trudeau. Freeland and former Bank of Canada governor Mark Carney were the perceived frontrunners. Early coverage of Carney's candidacy told of a political neophyte with an unrivalled résumé but limited face and name recognition among voters. That narrative changed quickly during the leadership campaign, as fresh polls began to show a wave of support for a Carney-led Liberal Party. Freeland was generally presented in reports as having been tarnished by her affiliation with the Trudeau era. By 9 March, when Carney won the party leadership, the Conservatives had already seen a more than twenty-point lead in the polls evaporate. Coverage in the mainstream media focused on whether the Liberal Party was simply experiencing a "Carney bump" or if the momentum had shifted. Pundits and columnists began trying to predict when the new prime minister might ask the governor general to dissolve Parliament and trigger an election. All seemed to agree it would be ill-advised for Carney to attempt to govern. On 23 March, Carney made the anticipated visit to Rideau Hall to dissolve Parliament. Robert Fife of the *Globe and Mail* captured the mood of the mainstream media that day when he wrote of the pending "supercharged election."

"The political parties have their planes and buses ready, star candidates picked and war rooms up and running for what could be the most monumental election in Canada's history. Economic uncertainty triggered by US president Donald Trump's global trade war and rhetoric about making Canada the fifty-first state are top of mind for voters."[10]

The next five weeks would see many sub-narratives emerge, but the economic uncertainty and the perceived existential threat emanating from Washington would remain the main storyline throughout the campaign.

WEEK ONE: 23 MARCH–29 MARCH

On the day after the writ was dropped, the CBC's flagship news podcast Front Burner prefaced the pending contest as "an election in a polluted media environment." In that episode, host Jayme Poisson spoke with Taylor Owen, director of the Centre for Media, Technology and Democracy at McGill University, about how the very role of Canadian journalism in the 2025 election had changed drastically from its role during the 2019 or even 2021 election. The shift, Owen explained, was due in large part to what he called a "cratering" of trust in traditional news outlets and a precipitous decline in consumption of Canadian journalism amongst the public. According to Owen, this had been amplified since the 2019 election by multiple factors including the Meta ban on Canadian news and the steady rise of social media influencers as replacement sources of "news" for a large swath of Canadians.

"We're becoming more polarized," Owen said. "There is more toxic and hostile and manipulative information in our ecosystem, and all of that. But trust levels in 2019, for the major media outlets, like the *Toronto Star*, the *Globe and Mail*, the CBC, Global, the *National Post*, were really high all the way across the political spectrum. So, it wasn't an ideological thing. It was pretty consistent. Those have all cratered ... And we're just moving to different kinds of information consumption. We're not going to the traditional journalism outlets anymore for our news. And those two things have made a major difference. But the other huge thing that's changed is that Meta turned off news." The unclear role of online influencers in the election, and notably US-based podcasters and social media icons with large followings among Canadian male voters aged 18–35, would become a consistent sub-narrative throughout the election, especially as polling data began to show significant support for Poilievre's Conservatives among what many pundits and writers have labelled "the manosphere."[11]

While podcasters and social media influencers waxed online to an ever-growing audience, spreading an array of partisan information and misinformation, the main narrative percolating on most news sites from day one of the election was a question of how Trump's constant talk of economic annexation of Canada would impact the election outcome.

The day after the Owen interview aired, Front Burner released an episode exploring "Pierre Poilievre's Donald Trump problem." Poisson and CBC colleague J.P. Tasker spoke at length about how Liberal and NDP attempts to brand Poilievre as a Trump-like candidate appeared to have impacted Canadian perceptions of the Conservative leader. "In a country where the majority of people have negative views of Trump, this start to the campaign likely wasn't an ideal one for Poilievre and his team."[12]

Meanwhile, over at the *Toronto Star*, Andrew Phillips of that newspaper's editorial board had a different take on the role Trump might ultimately play in the election when he questioned whether Mark Carney would ultimately have a bigger Trump problem since a Trump endorsement would likely not be embraced by Canadian voters. "As the campaign buses rev up for a federal election call this weekend, Donald Trump handed Pierre Poilievre a nice gift," Philips wrote. "Trump dissed the Conservative leader hard, and publicly. Even better for Poilievre, he seemed to be favouring Mark Carney, though that wasn't nearly as clear as Conservatives are claiming." Philips branded Trump "the Dark Lord" of the campaign, "looming over all, his malevolent presence setting the tone for all other players in the drama. His slightest utterance can change the mood: his merest twitch forces lesser characters to react. So, when Trump told Fox News that 'I would rather deal with a liberal than a conservative' because it would be 'easier' for him to have a liberal running Canada, you could feel the glee in the Conservative camp. Even better for Poilievre, Trump added: 'The conservative that's running is, stupidly, no friend of mine. I don't know him but he said negative things.'"[13]

Another sub-narrative that gathered traction across multiple outlets during the first week of the election was the electorate's apparent appetite for discussions on national defence. The CBC's Murray Brewster reported on 24 March that "The economy, health care, social programs and the environment were the tried-and-true, bread-and-butter issues politicians took to the stump for decades. The established political wisdom was that there are no votes in defence, especially defence procurement. That long-established paradigm has been thoroughly and completely upended by US president Donald Trump's trade war and repeated threats to annex this country."[14] The *National Post* published multiple stories in the first week of the election focused on the Canadian military and speculation that the country might cancel its planned purchase of American warplanes. By the end of the week, the *Globe and Mail* had commissioned a Nanos research survey which found that 62 per cent of Canadians supported, or somewhat supported, scrapping a federal government deal to buy 88 F-35 Lightning planes from US defence contractor Lockheed Martin.[15]

As the first week of the election came to a close, the *National Post* released an investigation into Mark Carney's 1995 Oxford University doctoral thesis. The newspaper reported that after analysing the thesis, it had found "10 instances of apparent plagiarism, according to the judgment of three university academics who reviewed the material for the Post."[16] *Canadaland*'s Jesse Brown would later note with interest that the plagiarism story did not gain much traction beyond the *National Post*'s coverage.

Foreign interference allegations remained a topic of conversation across many media outlets. There were multiple stories after Alberta premier Danielle Smith asked Donald Trump to pause tariffs until the election was over. That narrative was soon overtaken by a *Globe and Mail* report alleging that agents of India and their proxies raised money and organized for Poilievre during the Conservative leadership contest, which reignited a longstanding debate among journalists and pundits over why the Conservative leader had refused to submit to the checks necessary to obtain security clearance during the previous parliamentary sitting of Parliament.

WEEK TWO: 30 MARCH–5 APRIL

The mainstream media's coverage during week two of the campaign centred largely on three interconnected narratives: infighting within the Conservative ranks, early hints of an NDP collapse, and growing Liberal momentum.

Reports of festering Conservative dissent began with remarks made at an Empire Club of Canada luncheon by Ontario premier Doug Ford's campaign manager, Kory Teneycke, on 26 March, during which Teneycke warned that Poilievre was on track to lose the federal election. "He looks too much like Trump," Teneycke said of Poilievre. "He sounds too much like Trump. He uses the lexicon of Trump."[17] Teneycke's critique of the Conservative leader became a focal point of mainstream media coverage for days. The story grew well beyond Teneycke's comments when the *Globe and Mail* reported that the newspaper "spoke to 17 Conservatives, who are close to the campaign, and they describe a dysfunctional operation with tensions rising as public-opinion polls show the Liberals now ahead of the Poilievre-led party."[18] The *Globe and Mail* further reported that Poilievre's campaign manager, Jenni Byrne, "has belittled campaign workers; given top staff positions to people who work for her consulting company; and discounted advice from party stalwarts, including onetime cabinet ministers, premiers and top advisers to former prime minister Stephen Harper." The reports of infighting within the Conservative campaign grew from there as the CBC, *Toronto Star*, *National Post*, and other outlets matched the story. Several outlets soon began referring to "civil war" within the party after the CBC's Catherine Cullen reported that "one Conservative suggested the tension – not only between Teneycke and Byrne but also between the Ontario and federal Conservative leaders – amounts to a civil war within the Conservative movement."[19]

By the start of the second week of the campaign the narrative of Conservative dissent had become as central as any other surrounding Poilievre's campaign. Canadian Press prefaced their election round up going into the week with the headline: "Second week of campaign underway amid criticism, leaks within Conservative ranks."[20] That report by the Canadian Press's Jim Bronskill also made mention of a significant leak that had irritated Poilievre's campaign and added to further fuel to the narrative of civil war within the Conservative establishment. Internal Ontario Tory polling, which is typically not released but which Teneycke provided to the *Toronto Star*, showed the Conservatives fifteen points behind the Liberals in Ontario. Amanda Galbraith, a Conservative strategist, said the repeated leaks and anonymous insiders publicly complaining were "unhelpful, irritating and unnecessary." Bronskill's report highlighted, however, that while the Conservatives' lead had shrunk significantly the party was still polling at higher numbers than in previous elections.

Other media attention to the Conservative campaign during week two focused on the notable size of the crowds attending Poilievre's rallies and on Poilievre's own campaign messaging. When Poilievre announced that a Conservative government would hand down life sentences for gun, human and fentanyl traffickers, the report filed by Rahim Mohamed to the *National Post* framed the announcement as an attempt to shift the focus to Poilievre's preferred terrain of law and order. Mohamed's report concluded that: "Poilievre's unwillingness to pivot from his pre-planned campaign messaging is a source of frustration for some of his fellow conservatives."[21]

Week two also saw a wave of new polls adding to a growing collection of stories highlighting significant demographic shifts in voter allegiances, with young male voters leaning more Conservative than in elections past and voters aged older than sixty-five indicating stronger support for the Liberals than anticipated. Several pundits took to the airwaves throughout the week to discuss both phenomena while countless journalists and pollsters tried also to explain what was happening. They found themselves adding to a prevailing narrative that indicated the Liberals had secured a reliable voter base through older voters while the Conservatives were now relying on a younger male demographic that did not traditionally have the strongest voter turnout come election day. As a result, anyone following the mainstream media's news coverage during week two would have been subjected to reports indicating that the Liberals seemed to be winning the election. Seeded within those reports and backed up by polling was another sub-narrative that had been present since week one of the election[22] but which was gathering increasing traction as the election wore on, especially after it became apparent in poll after poll that the NDP's vote had collapsed. Canadians would have been hard pressed to find positive reporting surrounding the NDP campaign in any of the major mainstream news outlets during the first two weeks of the election.

WEEK THREE: 6 APRIL–10 APRIL

Campaign interference became an important narrative as the federal election moved into week three. Several outlets began reporting on the growing influence of bots. On 7 April, the Logic alerted its subscribers that "A network of X accounts is 'artificially' amplifying misinformation about Canada's economy and leadership." That report was based on information shared with the Logic by a digital threat research group called Reset Tech. "A coordinated campaign from these accounts spread false stories about businesses decamping for the US as a result of Canada's alleged economic decline, as well as Canadian support for Donald Trump's goal to annex the country." Martin Patriquin provided a lengthy report into how Facebook was being flooded with deepfake news reports about Mark Carney. "The posts are widespread on the Meta-owned platform, with 25 per cent of Canadians saying they've seen content on Facebook mimicking legitimate news in the last month ... Nearly 57 per cent of Canadians continue to rely on Facebook as a news and current affairs source despite the block of news content on the site."[23]

On 7 April, the *Globe and Mail*'s Steven Chase reported that the federal election-interference watchdog, the Security and Intelligence Threats to Elections (SITE) Task Force, had uncovered an information operation from China "aimed at shaping public opinion among Chinese Canadians about Liberal Leader Mark Carney." SITE identified messaging that "was laudatory toward Mr Carney with a social-media post carrying a headline saying 'the United States is facing a tough prime minister from Canada.'" This influencing effort is happening "on the Chinese-language social-media platform WeChat and through Youli-Youmian, WeChat's most popular news account." The task force added that their intelligence reporting "links the Youli-Youmian account to the Chinese Communist Party's Central Political and Legal Affairs Commission."[24] The *Globe and Mail*'s Robert Fife then published a story on 10 April linking a Carney-selected Liberal candidate, Peter Yuen, to "a Beijing-friendly lobby organization."[25] Yuen had himself succeeded a former candidate who'd withdrawn from the race after he'd said his Conservative rival, a human rights activist, should be kidnapped and sent to China.

During the campaign's third week "crowd size" became a major talking point. Pierre Poilievre had an awkward exchange in a media scrum with the *Globe and Mail*'s Laura Stone in which he cheekily asked her rhetorical questions about the size of his crowds. Crowd size had seemingly become for some political observers, like Poilievre himself, a credible barometer of the level of enthusiasm for party leaders. Despite a range of polls indicating a clear lead for Carney's Liberals, supporters of Poilievre's Conservatives now raised doubts about the veracity of polling data. They argued that the polls didn't correspond with the overwhelming number of people flocking to the Conservative leader's campaign rallies in cities and towns across the country. The *National Post* insinuated that the large crowds showing up for Poilievre's events suggested it was he who was, in fact, gaining momentum and that the relatively modest number of supporters turning up for Carney's "functions" was a sign of the political debutante's lackluster performance on the hustings: a sure sign his campaign was flagging. And so, while the right-leaning *Post* acknowledged that the Liberals were ahead in the polls, it was also asserting that with a little over two weeks to go until election day, the Tories had the proverbial wind in their sails.[26]

MIDPOINT

For the media, the halfway point of any election campaign is a time to take stock of the race, assess the strengths and weaknesses of the parties, identify possible trends or emerging themes, and forecast what may occur in the election's closing weeks. On 10 April, the midpoint of the thirty-six-day election campaign, the *Toronto Star*'s Robert Benzie reported that the Liberals had opened up a lead of nearly 5 per cent over the Conservatives.[27] These results were in keeping with polling conducted by five other Canadian pollsters (EKOS, Angus Reid, Leger, Mainstreet & Abacus Data).

At the outset of the federal election campaign on 23 March, one could scarcely have imagined a scenario in which Jordan Peterson would become a full-throated advocate for a generational political upheaval mounted by Generation Z and Generation Y (millennials). According to a Nanos poll, only 33 per cent of Canadians aged 18 to 34 supported the Liberals, while 43 per cent approved of the Conservatives. So, in the 11 April edition of the *National Post*, right-wing firebrand Peterson appealed to baby boomers and Gen. Xers (whom he considered were either "selfish or blind") to switch their vote to the Tories. "Unlike you – because they have much more to lose – your children and grandchildren see Carney as he is: not as the warm-milk and grandfatherly-advice 1950s Jimmy Stewart banker who will stand up to the mad Yankee mob and Make Canada Sensible Again but as The Man at the vanguard of anti-growth economic collapse and authoritarian financial control."[28]

About ten days later, Peterson was a guest on the US-based the *Joe Rogan Experience*, one of the most popular podcasts in the world. During his 190-minute appearance, Peterson tried to account for the generational political divide in Canada. "The boomers aren't radical. They are simply pining for the Old Canada. And who better than three-piece-suited, pro-capitalist, free-market-but-not-too-harshly, 'I'll set things right, you bet, Mark J [Carney]?'"[29]

With eighteen days to go until e-day, the New Democratic Party was languishing at around 8 per cent in the polls. A consensus had emerged among media commentators that the 2025 election was already over for the NDP: the risk of political extinction was now real. In a 10 April piece, the *Toronto Star*'s Richard Warnica echoed the sentiments of most pundits about the future of NDP leader, Jagmeet Singh. "I do believe these are the final weeks of Singh's federal career. If that's true he will be remembered as a talent who never quite panned out, the prospect who became the boss far too soon." Warnica's column read like a requiem for a man once touted as a political wunderkind cast in the mould of NDP phoenix Jack Layton. "The Singh who limped through Toronto on Monday looked deflated, a political blimp without any air."[30] He had become, paradoxically, both a permanent political neophyte and yesterday's man.

In the 12 April edition of the *Globe and Mail*, the Anishinaabe journalist Tanya Talaga framed the election as pitting "a straitlaced central banker [Mark Carney] whose father [Robert Carney] was the principal of a residential school" against Pierre Poilievre, "a Conservative career politician whose idol is Sir John A. Macdonald and who voted against the United Nations Declaration on the Rights of Indigenous Peoples." She noted that nearly three weeks into the five-week-long campaign, the political leaders had only talked about Indigenous issues in rather narrow transactional terms, primarily in relation to "critical mineral extraction, investments and consultations."[31]

The day before, on the 11 April episode of the left-leaning the *Breach Show* podcast, Toronto Metropolitan University Mi'kmaw academic and broadcaster Pam Palmater had spoken about the controversy swirling around Mark Carney following the revelation about his father's principalship of the Joseph Burr Tyrell (Residential) School in Fort Smith, Northwest Territories in the 1960s, and his description, in a March 1965 CBC Radio interview, of certain Indigenous students as being "culturally retarded." Palmater absolved the Liberal leader Mark Carney of responsibility for the "sins" of his father. "You can't do anything about what your family's done, but you need to speak to it, and you need to say, yeah, I'm in line with that or I'm not."[32]

Palmater also addressed federal Conservative attempts during the campaign to engage in "economic reconciliation" through initiatives like the proposed Canadian Indigenous Opportunities Corporation, which would offer loan guarantees for Indigenous-led resource projects. She argued that in the proposal "you don't see a high emphasis on revenue sharing or environmental protection or letting Indigenous people decide what happens on their lands … which is ignoring the fact that the federal government passed Bill C-15, the United Nations Declaration on the Rights of Indigenous People."

Palmater also mentioned that "residential school denialist" Aaron Gunn was running for the Conservatives in the Vancouver Island riding of North Island Powell River. Gunn had tweeted in 2022 that "there was no [Indigenous] genocide [in residential schools in Canada]. Stop lying to people and read a book. The Holocaust was a genocide. Get off Twitter and learn more about the world." Tanya Talaga noted in her 12 April *Globe and Mail* article that, when asked about Gunn's suitability as a Conservative candidate, Pierre Poilievre stood by the embattled Gunn, saying that "Mr Gunn denying the consequences of residential schools is 'just misinformation'" and that "Mr Gunn wants to continue to condemn the residential schools." On CBC News Grand Chief Stewart Phillip, of the Union of British Columbia Indian Chiefs (UBCIC), called Gunn's posts "absolutely reprehensible and repugnant and completely devoid of any sense of compassion for Indigenous Peoples who suffered enormously through the residential school experience. I don't think this man is fit for public office."[33]

Brian Giesbrecht in the right-wing Western Standard was one of the few media commentators who came to Gunn's defence, claiming that the Chiefs who had criticized him "should not be so quick to condemn Aaron Gunn for speaking the truth. Instead, they should remember the words of the chiefs of yesterday who requested residential schools for the education they knew that their children needed in order to succeed."[34]

WEEK FOUR: 13 APRIL–19 APRIL

During week four, the week of the two crucial debates, the release dates of the federal parties' election platforms became a story with staying power. Sonia Aslam wrote on the City News platform that, "with the Canadian federal election just over a week-and-a-half away, the clock is ticking for the parties to unveil their full costed platforms. None of the major parties have released them yet." The

Globe and Mail's Campbell Clark insisted that, "it's time for the leading contenders to show how election promises add up: Poilievre and Carney have to tell us what they'll cut, or how much debt they will bear."[35]

Week four also saw Mark Carney face his first political scandal. The Liberal leader was forced to apologize "unreservedly" after CBC reporter Kate McKenna uncovered a "dirty tricks" operation by Liberal staffers who admitted planting "Stop the Steal" buttons at a national gathering of Conservatives in Ottawa called the Canada Strong and Free Network Conference. The pro-Trump conspiratorial slogan on the button was meant to discredit the Tories by tying them to the US MAGA movement. The story was widely reported. In a 15 April opinion piece for the *Toronto Star*, Luke Lebrun, editor of the left-leaning PressProgress, wrote that the Liberals did not need to "fake evidence showing a segment of Poilievre's base is sympathetic to Trump. That's well documented." He added that "such deceptive tactics can do real and lasting damage by emboldening conspiratorial thinking and eroding trust in our democracy."[36] Carney insisted he was unaware of the plot and that the workers had been reassigned.

Going into the debates of 16 and 17 April, the pundits wondered whether Carney's competence in French would be up to the challenge of the French debate. How might he handle the political heat and manage his tendency to become prickly when challenged? Was Poilievre capable of showing humanity and gravitas? How might he appeal to voters beyond his base? Could he best Carney in the debating ring?

On the 16 April edition of the right-leaning the *Hub* podcast, panelist Amanda Galbraith, provided her forecast of the debates. Since winning the Liberal leadership Carney had earned plaudits from pundits for his "unflappable" manner. However, at times he'd revealed weaknesses that Galbraith felt could be exploited by his debate opponents. "We've seen stuff get under his skin. Anywhere he feels really personally affronted, he goes hot. So, I think they're going to try to expose that." Galbraith offered debate advice for the Conservative leader. "Poilievre's job is to keep a level head. He's really got to speak to women voters [and] older voters ... He's got to take a run at Carney, but he can't be so pugilistic that it puts people off."[37]

The French and English leaders debates were supposed to be "the story" during the fourth week of the campaign. However, both debates were somewhat overshadowed by the ham-handedness of the "impartial and independent" public agency responsible for organizing them. Sean Speer of the *Hub* podcast was not alone in lambasting the Leadership Debate Commission for "just a shambolic effort to host debates [in what] is a high stakes election. The bureaucratic mishandling is just such a letdown, such a failure of state capacity."[38] On 16 April the commission threw the opening French debate into disarray when mere hours before it was to begin, it rescinded its invitation to Green Party co-leader Jonathan Pedneault, citing the Greens' failure to reach certain election campaign thresholds. And then on the night of the English debate, on 17 April, the commission abruptly cancelled the media scrum that typically follows election debates. The dubious explanation offered by the Leaders' Debate Commission's executive director, Michel Cormier, was that "We don't feel that we can actually guarantee a proper environment for this activity." Traditional journalists had been outraged that media outlets were limited to one journalist at the post-debate scrums, except for the right-wing website Rebel News which somehow secured five spots – a disproportionate number. The *Toronto Star* reported that the decision to allow so many Rebel News journalists "was likely the result of Rebel News owner Ezra Levant threatening a lawsuit."[39]

As to the debates themselves, the consensus among the major media outlets was that despite his language deficiencies Carney had survived the first French election debate. The debate was a missed opportunity for Pierre Poilievre who, according to Althia Raj of the *Toronto Star*, "couldn't land a knockout blow" against his Liberal rival.[40] The English debate, held on 17 April, was judged by most pundits to be a more intense affair. On the 18 April edition of the CBC podcast *Front Burner*, CBC reporter Aaron Wherry said, "I mean it's pretty clear that at least the other party leaders think Mark Carney is the front runner given the amount of attention they focused on him and the attacks they focused on him ... I don't know if the Liberals would have come out of this debate thinking that their guy suffered any kind of grievous blows."[41]

WEEK 5: 20 APRIL–26 APRIL

In the campaign's last week, Abacus polling confirmed renewed public concerns about the cost of living and bolstering the economy. The Trump threat had receded as a top priority. Poilievre and the

Tories were closing the gap with the Liberals. The *National Post*'s Antoine Trepanier noted that Yves- François Blanchet and the Bloc Québécois were making a late surge in Quebec that could deny the Liberals a majority.[42] Mainstream media coverage focused on the party leaders gearing up for the final sprint to election day. Reports stressed that this was now a two-party race and that the beleaguered NDP were careening toward an electoral apocalypse.

Meanwhile, Carney's recently released costed Liberal platform, which called for $130 billion in new spending over four years, adding $225 billion to federal debt, was described by some pundits as Trudeauesque, and thus an opening for the Tories in the last week of the campaign. To the *National Post*'s John Ivison, "the platform has created an opportunity for a Conservative counter-offensive – a chance to win back Liberal switchers worried about passing on too much debt to the future generations."[43]

With just days to go before the election, multiple media outlets reported that Conservative leader Pierre Poilievre was in trouble in his local riding, that the Liberal candidate was poised to earn an upset victory, and that Conservative Party headquarters was scrambling to avert political disaster by "funneling resources into Poilievre's faltering campaign."[44]

Julia Simone Rogers, writing on 18 April for the Narwhal, noted that while climate change was largely ignored during the campaign, and an Abacus poll had indicated it was less of a priority for Canadians, it did not mean Canadians had stopped caring about the environment. Rather, according to Abacus Data vice-president Eddie Sheppard, "climate change is just being outshouted by louder and more immediate concerns housing affordability and taxes."[45]

During the election campaign Canadian mainstream media outlets carried little analysis of Israel's ongoing attacks on Palestinian civilians and the worsening humanitarian situation in the occupied Palestinian territory. On 25 April Mark Carney condemned Israel's food blockade saying, "the World Food Program must be allowed to work in Gaza." He wrote on X: "The UN World Food Programme just announced that its food stocks in Gaza have run out because of the Israeli Government's blockade – food cannot be used as a political tool," Carney added "Palestinian civilians must not bear the consequences of Hamas' terrorist crimes. The World Food Programme must be allowed to resume its lifesaving work."[46]

WEEK 6: 27 APRIL AND 28 APRIL (ELECTION DAY)

A deadly car-ramming attack in Vancouver that killed eleven people on 26 April stopped the election campaign in its tracks. The massacre at the Lapu-Lapu festival cast a pall over the final day of the campaign and election day itself. Mainstream media outlets carried the statements made by all federal party leaders expressing solidarity with the victims and their families. Liberal leader Mark Carney cancelled large rallies planned for Calgary and Richmond BC.

On election day media outlets provided basic information so that people could vote. They answered questions about identification requirements, voting locations, and what they should do if they hadn't received their voter information.

THE NEWS MEDIA COVERAGE IN QUEBEC

The news coverage of the 2025 federal election campaign by French-speaking media in Quebec was quite different because of the financial crisis faced by media in the province, a consequence of their eroding revenue bases. It was also the first ever campaign with generative AI content, which had been creating a buzz since the launch of ChatGPT 3 in the fall of 2022. And news influencers were now starting to be more visible than in past campaigns.

One of the authors of this chapter (Patrick White) teamed with Quebec media monitoring firm Influence Communication, which conducted a thorough content analysis of the Quebec and English Canadian election coverage, including online, press, TV, and radio. The data collected by Influence Communication showed that the media coverage of the federal election campaign in Quebec from 24 March to 27 April represented 9.19 per cent of the overall news content during the period versus 11.92 per cent in Canada across the board. We can state that the media coverage was high and sustained. Only the death of Pope Francis and the beginning of the NHL playoffs competed with the election coverage at any point during those thirty-seven days.

"This result is tremendous and clearly demonstrates the enthusiasm generated in the media," wrote Jean-Francois Dumas, head of Influence Communication, in his final report about the campaign. He said that the extensive coverage given to the campaign in the country's media was all the more surprising considering that the winner was announced even before the hostilities began.[47]

In these five weeks, the US-Canada relationship (i.e. trade war) was the number one theme covered by Quebec news organizations in French, followed by the economy and taxes, language and culture, health, and housing. The other top issues were immigration, education, environment, the military, and finally foreign interference.

The portrait was similar in English Canada, with the trade war being in the top spot and with heavier coverage than in Quebec. The US-Canada relationship theme was followed by economy and taxes, health, housing, and education. The other top issues were the environment, immigration, the military, culture and languages, and foreign interference.

Both top issues (trade war and the economy) were the same in Quebec compared to the rest of Canada. Unsurprisingly, the themes of culture and French language and immigration were prominent in Quebec. In English Canada, the issue of foreign interference and of several Conservative candidates sidelined received more news coverage, though a federal report issued in late June 2025 showed that foreign interference did not have an impact on the outcome of the federal elections. (See chapter 7.)[48]

The trade war between the US and Canada was the top news during the first three weeks of the campaign, in Quebec and in the rest of Canada (ROC). The leaders' TV debates in French dominated in week four and the financial frameworks of parties in week five was also another top news topic.

"We can say that Yves-François Blanchet ... succeeded in bringing attention to certain issues, especially starting in the third week. Unlike previous federal campaigns, the CAQ (the ruling party in the Quebec National Assembly) government had little influence on the topics discussed in Quebec. Bill 96 on the status of the French language and the appointment of judges were the only two topics associated with the provincial government," Influence Communication found in its report conducted solely for this book chapter.[49]

Note as well that the TVA network tried to compel the federal parties to pay for its French TV debate in April 2025, a first in Canadian politics. Mark Carney's Liberal Party refused and that ended the controversial initiative. However, this illustrated how bad the budget crunch in the Quebec media industry was in 2025. And this does not bode well for future campaigns. Who will be able to organize

Table 10.1 | Content of election coverage of party leaders in Quebec and English Canadian media, 24 March to 27 April 2025

Canada	*Percentage of coverage*
Mark Carney	44
Pierre Poilievre	31
Jagmeet Singh	16
Yves-François Blanchet	6
Jonathan Pedneault	2
Elizabeth May	2
Total	100
Quebec	*Percentage of coverage*
Mark Carney	39
Pierre Poilievre	26
Jagmeet Singh	15
Yves-François Blanchet	17
Jonathan Pedneault	3
Elizabeth May	1
Total	100

Source: Influence Communication, https://www.influencecommunication.com/.

large TV debates in French besides Radio-Canada and the Leaders' Debate Commission, plagued by controversy in this election following the fiasco of the media scrums after the debates?

Table 10.1, from Influence Communication, shows how much coverage English Canadian and Quebec media accorded to the leaders of the five main parties.

Surprisingly, Bloc Québécois leader Yves-François Blanchet only captured 16.8 per cent of the Quebec campaign media coverage, even though the Bloc had the largest number of province's members of parliament when the election was called. By comparison, Liberal leader Mark Carney was the subject of 39 per cent of the coverage and Conservative chief Pierre Poilievre captured 26 per cent. NDP leader Jagmeet Singh received 14.6 per cent of Quebec media coverage, almost the same level as the Bloc Québécois leader, despite the NDP having only one Quebec MP going into the election. Those numbers tell a story: Quebec media have become bored with the separatist Bloc, which has been around since 1990, and their main focus went to Carney because of his lead in opinion polls (also see chapter 5). Poilievre's hostility toward the news media seems to have significantly reduced his media power of attraction while Quebec media largely ignored the Green Party, as did those in the rest of Canada.

Data for the rest of Canada show that the Bloc Québécois was considered once again as almost irrelevant (capturing only 6 per cent of total coverage). The two solitudes of Canada stand here: the Quebec angle is not considered sexy anymore and a huge fatigue about this topic has taken over Canadian media news organizations in the past decades. Nonetheless, Quebec is a province with close to 23 per cent of Canada's population. The focus on the province has vacillated from one extreme to the other in thirty-five years.

Table 10.1 shows that Canadian media news organizations outside Quebec mainly focused on Carney (44 versus 31 per cent for Poilievre and 16 per cent for Singh). That the polls favoured Carney and the trade war with Trump enticed the country's media ecosystem to double down on Carney, who was also prime minister during the campaign.

Something that became vividly evident in this campaign is that the wall-to-wall, in-the-field coverage of the party leaders that was a feature of previous elections is now a thing of the past, because of prohibitive costs. Covering an election in a country as large as Canada is burdensomely expensive. The consequence? Radio-Canada and RDI, the French arms of the CBC, and La Presse Canadienne (PC), the French service of Canadian Press (CP) news agency, were the only French media outlets (except the TV pool) covering Bloc leader Blanchet and Liberal leader Carney during the entire campaign.

In past elections, it was expected that correspondents for the major media would join the party leaders on their campaign planes and cover their activities almost hour by hour. In 2025, news media focused more than ever on news analysis and commentary and left the dogged day-to-day coverage in Quebec to La Presse Canadienne or all-news channels RDI (Radio-Canada) and LCN (TVA Nouvelles, owned by Quebecor Media). It was much the same for the English-language media.

With scrums and press conferences now carried live on television, there does not seem to be enough added value to having full-time reporters with each party leader on their campaign buses and planes. Taking into account hotel rooms, per diem, overtime and the costs charged by the parties to media organizations for seats on the leader's plane or bus, it no longer made sense financially to have these boots on the ground merely to report the politicians' daily talking points. Only big media players could now afford to accompany the party leaders from coast to coast, and even they scaled back their on-the-bus coverage from what had been the norm in past elections.

Another major hurdle was the decision by the Conservatives to prohibit reporters from travelling with the party leader, including camera operators and technicians. This led to a logistical nightmare for most national news organizations, including Radio-Canada and RDI and the Canadian Press and La Presse Canadienne, to try to follow Poilievre via local bureaux or national correspondents in some cases. The lack of access and transparency, as well as attempts to control reporters and camera people, did not play well with media organizations, which cut back on Poilievre's coverage overall.

OPINION VS NEWS

A distinguishing feature of the campaign coverage was the continued emphasis on commentary over news reporting, especially on all-news TV channels RDI and LCN in Quebec. For instance, RDI announced in January 2025[50] that its news morning show would start at 6 a.m. instead of 5 a.m. RDI used the trade war with the US as a pretext to also extend several of its programs, but filled them with panels and pundits rather than field reporting. La Presse reported in January 2025 that the Quebec journalists' union was quite concerned[51] about a possible takeover of news commentary at the expense of daily news reporting, and this is indeed what we saw during the campaign on RDI. They featured wall-to-wall commentary from analysts, former politicians, lobbyists, former public relations officers, former political advisers, with less and less actual reporting from its national network of correspondents across Canada. LCN, owned by Quebecor, did the same.

Quebecor-owned dailies *Le Journal de Montréal* and *Le Journal de Québec* also have dozens of columnists now, which gives them an opinion focus. On Quebecor's radio network, QUB Radio, all shows focus on hard-hitting opinion from well-known commentators such as Richard Martineau, Sophie Durocher, Mathieu

Bock-Côté, Benoit Dutrizac, and Isabelle Maréchal. Does too much commentary kill the news? It is an open question, but these panels, often filled by the same guests every day or so, gave the impression that all-news channels fill the airwaves with talking heads, just as CNN, Fox, and MSNBC have been doing in the US for years. Observers are concerned about future election campaign coverage, which may feature more and more commentary and less and less actual news reporting.

NEW MEDIA AND SOCIAL

A trend researchers observed during the 2025 elections was the use of newer social networks such as Bluesky and TikTok by politicians and voters. The transformation of X (formerly Twitter) into a far-right propaganda engine following its takeover by billionaire Elon Musk pushed many citizens, researchers, scientists, politicians, and journalists towards other social networks. "It's one of the most notable shifts in this election," Aengus Bridgman of McGill University told the Canadian Press in an interview.[52] He said that "there was slightly more engagement with conservatives than Liberals on X and Instagram, while almost all political engagement on Bluesky goes to Liberal candidates." He said his researchers analyzed close to five thousand accounts on all social networks' platforms in the campaign.

Major inroads were also made by newer digital media covering federal politics, including InfoBref, La Converse, and Pivot in Quebec, as well as several outlets in English Canada, such as the Narwhal, Canada's National Observer, Rebel News, Juno News, Ricochet, the *Hill Times*, and PressProgress. These outlets, as well as Quebec news influencers like Alexane Drolet, Helene Buzzetti, Rachel Gilmore, Paul Wells, Farnell Morisset, and P.J. Fournier, were major players during the campaign with their blogs or their own platforms. Podcasts are also becoming more credible than ever with citizens, according to the Reuters 2025 digital news report.[53] In Quebec, podcast platforms include Ohdio (by Radio-Canada), Spotify, and YouTube. Patrick White had his own weekly election podcast on InfoBref Quebec during the campaign to engage with citizens and voters.

This shows a trend sure to become the norm: specialized sites or personal brands that cover various issues including federal politics have considerable influence, making some of those influencers media brands themselves.

Quebec digital media like La Converse and Pivot provided in-depth coverage of the federal elections, including streaming the two leaders' debates in both official languages with live blogs and videos. This enlarges the spectrum of news coverage that in the past had been provided by big media players only.

AI FIRST

The 2025 campaign was the first ever to be conducted since the arrival of generative AI, ChatGPT having made its debut in November 2022. That alarmed federal authorities, which created the Security and Intelligence Threats to Elections (SITE) Task Force to track election disinformation (see chapter 7). This committee briefed journalists on a weekly basis and would seem to be a first step to take disinformation seriously during campaigns.

According to Canadian Press,[54] AI-generated content about the election flooded the online news void[55] created by Meta's decision in August 2023 to prohibit Canadian news on Facebook and Instagram. Meta's action was a response to the Online News Act, which compelled web giants that traffic in Canadian news to pay compensation to the media companies that generate the news. But "a large amount of sophisticated and false online content has seemingly had a low impact on Canadian electors," CP reported, quoting Aengus Bridgman from McGill University's Media Ecosystem Observatory. The content mentioned included memes and deepfake videos of federal politicians on YouTube, Facebook, Instagram, TikTok, Bluesky and Telegram. One of the viral memes during the campaign in Quebec and across Canada showed Liberal leader Carney in a doctored photo with pedophile Jeffrey Epstein.

"We don't have any evidence yet that Canadians are being manipulated or were convinced of things that are not true," Bridgman told CP on 25 April just a few days before the end of the campaign. His report, "Social Media Platforms Host and Profit from Scams Using AI and Fake News Websites during Canada's 2025 Federal Election"[56] showed that "Fake news websites are increasingly sharing political content to deceive and scam Canadians: since the start of the election campaign, we have identified over 40 Facebook pages sharing (AI-generated) ads masquerading as legitimate news sources and linked to cryptocurrency scams."

The report also stated that almost a quarter of Canadians (24 per cent) indicated they had encountered "a social media post or webpage that falsely presented itself as a legitimate news source (e.g., CBC, *Toronto Sun*, La Presse Canadienne) by imitating names, logos, or design" during the campaign. A Leger poll released in April 2025 indicated that most Conservative voters did not trust media coverage of the federal campaign[57] versus 27 per cent of Liberals who did not trust the coverage and 45 per cent of Bloc Québécois voters.

The increasing prominence of opinion polls during Canadian election campaigns has impacts on media coverage. Many believe that the over-reliance on polls analysis and poll projections in media coverage led the media to undermine their own role in democracy (i.e. challenge politicians and leaders in society, double check everything, etc.) and abdicate their role as gatekeepers. Leading Quebec journalist Pierre Sormany, former editor in chief of Radio-Canada news coverage, wrote in May 2025 that the prominence of polls in the public sphere is now a threat to the media themselves.[58] "The problem is that polls never give us the details," Sormany wrote in the Quebec independent outlet L'autjournal. "As a result, many people are tempted to answer based on what they've read in the newspapers, lacking the means to truly weigh the issues."

WHAT FUTURE?

Only the remaining big media players can still afford to be on the planes and buses with federal party leaders and that has become a major issue of accessibility. Canadian Press is a private sector news service and can only provide robust coverage as long as it has clients willing and able to pay for the product. What if La Presse Canadienne, CP's French service, were to disappear, for example? That would be a disaster.

Should we now turn our back on the traditional news coverage of campaigns since most public events are now broadcast on CPAC, LCN, RDI, CTV News Channel and CBC News Channel? Who will ask questions on the ground to represent the concerns of citizens? At what costs to the media organizations? And at what price to democracy and the integrity of the vote if there are not conscientious journalists to bear honest witness on behalf of the public to how an election unfolds?

Civic media education will be essential in the next twenty-five years in Canada in order to equip citizens with a better understanding of the media's role and functioning. Otherwise, voters will be vulnerable to manipulation by partisan interests and malicious actors with unparalleled tools of public persuasion at their disposal.

NOTES

1 Canadian Press, "Most Conservative Voters Say They Don't Trust Media Reports on Party Leaders: Poll," CHCH-TV, 23 April 2025, https://www.chch.com/chch-news/most-conservative-voters-say-they-dont-trust-media-reports-on-party-leaders-poll/.

2 Specific attention has been paid to the coverage of several Canadian English-language members of the Parliamentary Press Gallery (CTV, Global TV, the *Globe and Mail*, POLITICO, the Narwhal, *Toronto Star*, CBC News, the Canadian Press, CPAC, APTN [Aboriginal Peoples Television Network], *National Observer*, the *Hill Times*, OMNI Television, *National Post*, iPolitics, Citytv, Politics Today, Policy Options, Rabble.ca, *Toronto Sun*, the Logic and *Ottawa Citizen*).To canvas a fuller range of English media coverage, attention has also been paid to several international news outlets including Agence France Presse, Bloomberg News, Reuters, CNN, the *Economist*, and *Wall Street Journal* (all members of the Parliamentary Press Gallery) as well as the *New York Times* and the *Guardian*. Coverage from a selection of independent outlets such as the *Herle Burly Podcast*, the Breach, the Maple, Rebel News, the Western Standard and True North News were also monitored in an attempt to capture a wider picture of the narratives that defined the election from different ideological standpoints.

3 Warren Kinsella, "KINSELLA: Trump's Win Will Bring Boost to Floundering Justin Trudeau," *Toronto Sun*, 6 November 2024, https://torontosun.com/opinion/columnists/kinsella-trumps-win-will-bring-boost-to-floundering-justin-trudeau.

4 David Reevely, "No 'Trump Bump' for Trudeau, New Poll Finds," Logic, 11 December 2024, https://thelogic.co/news/trump-trudeau-abacus-poll/.

5 Rebecca Shabad, "Trump Mocks Prime Minister Justin Trudeau as the 'Governor' of the 'Great State Of Canada,'" NBC News, 10 December 2024,https://www.nbcnews.com/politics/donald-trump/trump-mocks-prime-minister-justin-trudeau-governor-great-state-canada-rcna183570.

6 Jordan B. Peterson, "Canada's Next Prime Minister, Pierre Poilievre, ep. 511," *The Dr Jordan B. Peterson Podcast*, 2 January 2025, https://www.youtube.com/watch?v=Dck8eZCpglc.

7 Jamie Sarkonak "Jamie Sarkonak: Justin Trudeau Resigns a Failure," *National Post*, 6 January 2025, https://nationalpost.com/opinion/jamie-sarkonak-justin-trudeau-resigns-a-failure.
8 Robyn Urback, "Justin Trudeau Resigned Too Late. There Is No Salvaging the Liberal Party Now," *Globe and Mail*, 7 January 2025, https://www.theglobeandmail.com/opinion/article-justin-trudeau-resigned-too-late-there-is-no-salvaging-the-liberal/.
9 Star editorial board, "Justin Trudeau Finally Made the Right Decision," *Toronto Star*, 6 January 2025, https://www.thestar.com/opinion/editorials/justin-trudeau-finally-made-the-right-decision/article_96faf398-cc6f-11ef-80f5-3b34d59d6ba7.html.
10 Robert Fife, "Economic Uncertainty Top of Mind for Voters as Parties Gear up for Monumental Federal Election," *Globe and Mail*, 23 March 2025,https://www.theglobeandmail.com/politics/article-economic-uncertainty-top-of-mind-for-voters-as-parties-gear-up-for/.
11 Front Burner with Jayme Poisson, "An Election in a Polluted Media Environment," CBC *Listen*, 24 March 2025, https://www.cbc.ca/listen/cbc-podcasts/209-front-burner/episode/16135703-an-election-in-a-polluted-media-environment.
12 Front Burner with Jayme Poisson, "Pierre Poilievre's Donald Trump Problem," CBC *Listen*, 25 March 2025, https://www.cbc.ca/listen/cbc-podcasts/209-front-burner/episode/16135932-pierre-poilievres-donald-trump-problem.
13 Andrew Phillips, "Trump, the Dark Lord of Canada's Looming Election, Hands Poilievre an Apparent Gift," *Toronto Star*, 21 March 2025, https://www.thestar.com/opinion/star-columnists/trump-the-dark-lord-of-canadas-looming-election-hands-poilievre-an-apparent-gift/article_03780100-6431-48b9-a57b-dc7342dacc9c.html.
14 Murray Brewster, "National Defence Is Often an Afterthought in Canadian Elections. Not this Time," CBC News, 24 March 2025, https://www.cbc.ca/news/politics/national-defence-canada-election-1.7490509.
15 Steven Chase and Mike Hager, "Majority of Poll Respondents Support Ottawa Cancelling Contract For US Warplanes, Nanos Finds," *Globe and Mail*, 1 April 2025, https://www.theglobeandmail.com/politics/federal-election/article-majority-surveyed-want-poilievre-to-get-security-clearance-carney-to/.
16 Catherine Lévesque, "EXCLUSIVE: Mark Carney Faces Plagiarism Accusations for 1995 Oxford Doctoral Thesis," *National Post*, 28 March 2025, https://nationalpost.com/news/mark-carney-plagiarism-accusations.

17 Aaron Wherry, "Is Pierre Poilievre Too 'In Sync' with Donald Trump?," CBC *News*, 29 March 2025, https://www.cbc.ca/news/politics/poilievre-trump-smith-analysis-1.7496125.

18 Robert Fife and Stephanie Levitz, "Pressure Mounts on Poilievre to Refocus Conservative Campaign on Donald Trump," *Globe and Mail*, 28 March 2025, https://www.theglobeandmail.com/politics/article-pressure-mounts-on-poilievre-to-refocus-conservative-campaign-on/.

19 Catherine Cullen, Kate McKenna, and John Paul Tasker, "Conservatives Fear 'Dysfunctional' Campaign and 'Civil War' in the Party: Sources," CBC News, 29 March 2025, https://www.cbc.ca/news/politics/conservatives-campaign-civil-war-party-1.7497029.

20 Jim Bronskill, "Second Week of Campaign Underway as Poilievre Faces Criticism, Leaks within Conservative Ranks," CityNews, 31 March 2025, https://toronto.citynews.ca/2025/03/30/second-week-of-campaign-underway-amid-criticism-leaks-within-conservative-ranks/.

21 Rahim Mohamed, "Life Sentences for Gun, Human, Fentanyl Trafficking, Poilievre Pledges," *National Post*, 28 March 2025, https://nationalpost.com/news/politics/life-sentences-for-gun-human-fentanyl-trafficking-poilievre-pledges.

22 Marina von Stackelberg and David Thurton, "This Election, the NDP Could Be Fighting for Its Own Survival," CBC News, 21 March 2025, https://www.cbc.ca/news/politics/ndp-polling-election-2025-1.7489648.

23 Martin Patriquin, "A Network of X Accounts Is Targeting Canada Ahead of the Election," Logic, 7 April 2025, https://thelogic.co/news/canada-election-x-misinformation/.

24 Steven Chase, "Election Interference Watchdog Detects Beijing Effort to Influence Chinese Canadians on Carney," *Globe and Mail*, 7 April 2025, https://www.theglobeandmail.com/politics/article-election-watchdog-china-influence-opinion-mark-carney/.

25 Robert Fife and Steven Chase, "Liberal Candidate Peter Yuen, Chosen to Replace Paul Chiang, Linked to Pro-Beijing Groups, Events," *Globe and Mail*, 10 April 2025, https://www.theglobeandmail.com/politics/article-liberal-candidate-peter-yuen-chosen-to-replace-paul-chiang-linked-to/.

26 National Post , "NP View: What Pierre Poilievre's Massive Rallies Tell Us about the Election," *National Post*, 12 April 2025, https://nationalpost.com/opinion/np-view-what-pierre-poilievres-massive-rallies-tell-us-about-the-election.

27 Robert Benzie, "Mark Carney's liberals Open up a Larger Lead over Pierre Poilievre's Conservatives, Poll Analysis Suggests," *Toronto Star*, 10 April 2025, https://www.thestar.com/politics/federal/mark-carneys-liberals-

open-up-a-larger-lead-over-pierre-poilievres-conservatives-poll-analysis-suggests/article_71a708df-534f-4787-a86d-99b2e68f99c0.html.

28 Jordan Peterson, "Jordan Peterson: Are Older Liberal-Voting Canadians Selfish – or Blind?" *National Post*, 11 April 2025, https://nationalpost.com/opinion/jordan-peterson-are-older-liberal-voting-canadians-selfish-or-blind.

29 Joe Rogan, "Joe Rogan Experience #2308 – Jordan Peterson," *Joe Rogan Experience*, 22 April 2025, https://www.jrepodcast.com/episode/joe-rogan-experience-2308-jordan-peterson/.

30 Richard Warnica, "There's Only One Thing Left for Jagmeet Singh to Do," *Toronto Star*, 28 April 2025, https://www.thestar.com/opinion/star-columnists/there-s-only-one-thing-left-for-jagmeet-singh-to-do/article_42b30213-0021-4a94-98b6-0840e07945a7.html.

31 Tanya Talaga, "Carney and Poilievre Are Both Falling Short on Indigenous Issues," *Globe and Mail*, 12 April 2025, https://www.theglobeandmail.com/opinion/article-carney-and-poilievre-are-both-falling-short-on-indigenous-issues/.

32 Breach Show, "The End of the Reconciliation Era?," *Breach Show*, 11 April 2025, https://breachmedia.ca/reconciliation-era-federal-election-canada-indigenous-peoples/.

33 Brenna Owen, "Poilievre Stands by BC Candidate Called out for Residential School Posts," CBC News, 5 April 2025, https://www.cbc.ca/news/canada/british-columbia/pierre-poilievre-aaron-gunn-1.7503105.

34 Brian Giesbrecht, "GIESBRECHT: Gunn Sticks to His Gun," Western Standard, 14 April 2025, https://www.westernstandard.news/opinion/giesbrecht-gunn-sticks-to-his-gun/64005.

35 Campbell Clark, "It's Time for the Leading Contenders to Tell Us How Election Promises Add Up," *Globe and Mail*, 14 April 2025, https://www.theglobeandmail.com/politics/opinion/article-time-to-tell-us-how-election-promises-add-up/.

36 Luke LeBrun, "The Liberal 'Button' Scheme Was a Colossal Self-Own. That's Not the Worst Part of It," *Toronto Star*, 15 April 2025, https://www.thestar.com/opinion/contributors/the-liberal-button-scheme-was-a-colossal-self-own-thats-not-the-worst-part-of/article_db5b38c2-bfdf-4206-8c62-c3f1d37e2547.html.

37 Hub, "'The First Time We'll See Carney and Poilievre up against Each Other': Amanda Galbraith on What to Expect from the Upcoming Leaders' Debates," *Hub Podcasts*, 16 April 2025, https://thehub.ca/podcast/video/the-first-time-well-see-carney-and-poilievre-up-against-

each-other-amanda-galbraith-on-what-to-expect-from-the-upcoming-leaders-debates/.

38 ChatPods, "Election 2025: Day 24, Tightening Polls and the 'Shambolic' Government-Funded Debate Commission," *ChatPods*, 16 April 2025, https://www.chatpods.com/search/episode/TLM2P5YBCJdBo5SOyoOm/transcript/.

39 Justin Ling, "Rebel News Wins Fight to Send Five Reporters to Post-Debate Scrums as Other Outlets Limited to One," *Toronto Star*, 17 April 2025, https://www.thestar.com/politics/federal/french-federal-debate-live-blog/article_092932c1-453c-497a-84f8-b829f829e063.html#688bc861-cec5-4760-8913-fceb0ee74f25.

40 Althia Raj, "Mark Carney Needed to Escape this Debate Unbloodied – and Even with a Smile, Pierre Poilievre Couldn't Land a Knockout Blow," *Toronto Star*, 22 April 2025, https://www.thestar.com/politics/political-opinion/mark-carney-needed-to-escape-this-debate-unbloodied-and-even-with-a-smile-pierre-poilievre/article_3ad7d4fa-bba2-41fc-a39e-8f75e05a9915.html.

41 Front Burner with Jayme Poisson, "Recapping the High-Stakes Leaders' Debate – Transcript," CBC News, 22 April 2025, https://www.cbc.ca/lite/story/1.7515657.

42 Antoine Trépanier, "As Polls Tighten in Quebec, the Bloc Sees an Opportunity to Play 'Offence,'" *National Post*, 23 April 2025, https://nationalpost.com/news/canada/as-polls-tighten-in-quebec-the-bloc-sees-an-opportunity-to-play-offence.

43 John Ivison, "John Ivison: Conservative Hopes Are Resurrected by Carney's Eye-Watering Spending Plan," *National Post*, 21 April 2025, https://www.msn.com/en-ca/news/canada/john-ivison-conservative-hopes-are-resurrected-by-carney-s-eye-watering-spending-plan/ar-AA1DjOpQ.

44 Raisa Patel et al., "Conservatives Pour Resources into Pierre Poilievre's Riding Amid Fears of a Tight Race," *Toronto Star*, 24 April 2025, https://www.thestar.com/politics/federal-elections/conservatives-pour-resources-into-pierre-poilievres-riding-amid-fears-of-a-tight-race/article_557b4a9f-6538-4fe9-920a-de3147ee19a6.html.

45 Julia-Simone Rutgers, "Canadian Voters Ranked Climate Change as a Top Issue – Even during a Pandemic. Has the US Trade War Changed That?" Narwhal, 18 April 2025, https://thenarwhal.ca/climate-voters-canada-federal-election-2025/.

46 Thompson Reuters, "Carney Condemns Israeli Blockade on Food to Gaza," CBC News, 25 April 2025, https://www.cbc.ca/news/politics/mark-carney-gaza-blockade-1.7519408.

47 Influence Communication, "Analyse de la couverture médiatique de la campagne électorale 2025 du 24 mars au 27 avril 2025," Influence Communication, 1 May 2025.

48 Nick Murray, "L'ingérence étrangère n'aurait pas influencé les élections, selon la commissaire," *Le Devoir*, 25 June 2025, https://www.ledevoir.com/politique/canada/894685/ingerence-etrangere-aurait-pas-influence-elections-selon-commissaire.

49 Influence Communication, "Analyse de la couverture médiatique de la campagne électorale."

50 Radio-Canada, "Dès le 20 janvier, ICI RDI adapte sa programmation au contexte politique et économique," Radio-Canada, 13 January 2025, https://presse.radio-canada.ca/television/13662/des-le-20-janvier-ici-rdi-adapte-sa-programmation-au-contexte-politique-et-economique/.

51 Étienne Paré, "Inquiétudes autour du changement de grille," *La Presse*, 15 January 2025, https://www.lapresse.ca/arts/2025-01-15/ici-rdi/inquietudes-autour-du-changement-de-grille.php.

52 Canadian Press, "'It Feels Dystopian:' AI-Generated Content about Election Flooded Online News Void." CTV News, 25 April 2025, https://www.ctvnews.ca/federal-election-2025/article/it-feels-dystopian-ai-generated-content-about-election-flooded-online-news-void/.

53 Bruno Guglielminetti, "Le balado s'impose comme une source d'information credible," *Mon Carnet*, 17 June 2025, https://moncarnet.com/2025/06/17/le-balado-simpose-comme-une-source-dinformation-credible-chez-les-canadiens/.

54 Canadian Press, "'It Feels Dystopian:' AI-Generated Content About Election Flooded Online News Void."

55 Matina Stevis-Gridneff and Stuart A. Thompson, "News Is Blocked on Meta's Feeds in Canada. Here's What Fills the Void," *New York Times*, 28 April 2025, https://www.nytimes.com/2025/04/21/technology/canada-election-facebook-instagram-meta.html.

56 Mathieu Lavigne et al., "Social Media Platforms Host and Profit from Scams Using AI and Fake News Websites during Canada's 2025 Federal Election," Canadian Digital Media Research Network, 25 April 2025, https://www.cdmrn.ca/publications/scam-ai-fake-news.

57 La Presse Canadienne, "Élections fédérales: faites-vous confiance aux médias?," Les Affaires, 23 April 2025, https://www.lesaffaires.com/secteurs/politique/elections-federales-faites-vous-confiance-aux-medias/.

58 Pierre Sormany, "La dépendance aux sondages," *L'aut'journal*, 21 March 2025, https://www.lautjournal.info/20250321/la-dependance-aux-sondages.

11

Polling's Ups and Downs

Christopher Adams

During each federal election Canadians are now exposed daily to the "horserace" of who is winning and who is losing. Due to the first-past-the-post system for choosing who wins in each riding, voters can only choose one party's candidate. And because one's preferred party may not have a chance of winning at the national level, polling can assist Canadians to vote "strategically" in order to avoid wasting their vote. For those leaning to the left, historically this has benefitted the Liberal Party of Canada (LPC) to the detriment of the New Democratic Party (NDP).[1] To those leaning to the right, this has benefited the Conservative Party of Canada (CPC), to the detriment of such minor parties as the People's Party of Canada (PPC) and the Christian Heritage Party (CHP). As will be shown in this chapter, the NDP paid dearly for this in 2025, as voters were pushed towards choosing between the LPC and the CPC on the following major questions: Who is the best leader? Is it time for a change in government after ten years of Liberal government? And who is best suited to handle Donald Trump's threats to the Canadian economy and sovereignty?

Years ago, the *Los Angeles Times* pollster John Brennan remarked that, like the airline industry, "people only remember the crashes."[2] In the 2016 US presidential election many predicted a Hillary Clinton victory over Donald Trump, and in 2024, the polls erroneously predicted Kamala Harris would outdo Trump in the popular vote. Such problems have also occurred in Canada. In the 2013 BC provincial election, every single poll predicted the NDP in the lead while in the end the Liberals won with a four-point lead.[3] On the eve of the 2024 Saskatchewan provincial election, polls were showing a surge in NDP support, with CTV calling it a close race.[4] In the end, the NDP lost to the governing Saskatchewan Party, which amassed a twelve-point lead in the actual vote.[5] Despite this, polling remains the most reliable means by which we can measure the way the electoral winds are blowing. It remains superior to measuring the size of party rallies, studying media coverage and editorials, monitoring radio call-in shows, and talking to barbers and taxi drivers. Polling continues to be what George Gallup and Saul Rae in their classic 1940 work on the topic refer to as "the pulse of democracy."[6]

To illustrate the increasing prevalence of polls, only twelve national polls were released to the media during the 1984 Canadian federal election.[7] In the 2000 federal election this number had increased to twenty-seven. Both the 2021 and 2025 federal elections lasted a mere thirty-seven days. Despite their brevity, the first of the two produced a total of 151 national polls in the media, and the second produced 167.[8] A total of fifteen firms produced the national polling in 2025. Not included in this count are firms producing regional, provincial, or locally specific polls. When averaged out across the 2025 campaign, 4.5 national polls appeared in the media each day. Along with increased polling, there has been an increased propensity to produce seat count projections for each based on the polls and other election-related data. As will be discussed, while most of the seat counts were not radically wrong, the projections in 2025 erroneously predicted a high likelihood that the Liberals would win a majority victory.

Connected with the increased use of polling is a shift away from live telephone interviewing and towards interactive voice response (IVR) surveying systems and online polling. IVR polling involves fully automated (i.e. non-human) outbound calling with respondents using their keypads to answer questions. EKOS was the first to use IVR for federal polling in 2008. Others followed, including Mainstreet Research and Forum Research which regularly conduct national polls using IVR with interviews exceeding one thousand in a single day. By eliminating the need for live interviewers located in large field centres, the cost of interviewing has dropped considerably. One downside of IVR surveys is that they must be short as few respondents are willing to spend more than a minute or two punching numbers on their phone. This effectively restricts IVR pollsters from exploring important and nuanced election issues.

Regarding online polling, 90 per cent of Canadians are reported to have access to the internet[9] making them eligible for recruitment to online sample databases, otherwise known as "panels."[10] As evidence that most pollsters have moved to either IVR or online methodologies, in both the 2021 and 2025 federal elections only one firm, Nanos Research, exclusively deployed live telephone interviewing for its national surveys, with all others using either IVR or online methodologies.[11] The only other firm to employ live telephone interviewers was Ipsos. However, it did so by blending its telephone samples with online surveys.

As in previous elections, many of the major media providers partnered with a polling firm as part of its election coverage. Nanos provided polling for the *Globe and Mail* and CTV while Ipsos provided polling for Global News. Leger provided its numbers to the *National Post* and the *Journal de Montréal*. As in recent years, rather than rely on a specific pollster, CBC again turned to the poll aggregator Éric Grenier of the *Writ* podcast to operate the CBC News Poll Ttracker. As discussed later in this chapter, there was some backlash within the Conservative Party to the ongoing media attention on the Liberals' surge in the polls and likely re-election as the campaign was underway. At one rally CPC supporters were spotted waving banners calling the polls wrong.

THE NEW YEAR AND THE POLLS

The 2025 year began with pollster Nick Nanos reporting (on 3 January) that the Conservatives were holding a twenty-two-point lead over Justin Trudeau's Liberal Party. The CPC was at 45 per cent versus the Liberals at 23 per cent, with the NDP trailing at 16 per cent.[12] A week after Trudeau's announcement that he would be stepping down as party leader, on 13 January a Leger poll had the CPC with an even larger lead: by 26 points, with 47 per cent for the CPC compared to the Liberals at 21 per cent, and the NDP trailing at 17 per cent.[13] Regardless of what the Liberals might or might not do, the Conservatives appeared to be cruising to a majority win in the next election.

What a difference a few weeks can make! In mid-February, Danielle Groen of the *Globe and Mail* captured the radically shifting political landscape: but you know what happened next. Justin Trudeau said he would step down as prime minister. Bold-faced names emerged to take his place. And newly inaugurated US president Donald Trump went on an absolute tear, threatening to impose hefty tariffs on Canadian imports or maybe just make Canada the fifty-first state.[14]

On 14 March, Nanos was reporting the CPC and LPC at a statistical tie, with just one point separating the two main parties: the CPC were at 35.3 per cent and the Liberals at 34.1 per cent.[15] Just days after winning the Liberal Party leadership, on 23 March newly minted prime minister Mark Carney asked Governor General Mary Simon to dissolve Parliament, and the polling industry went into high gear.

THE PRE-WRIT PERIOD

A review of aggregated national polling results from Éric Grenier's poll tracker for the CBC released after the 2021 election and up to the 2025 election shows three phases. The first started just after September 2021 with the Liberals and Conservatives at roughly equal levels of support. This lasted until the Spring of 2023. The second phase was marked by a precipitous and steady decline for the LPC, moving from just under 30 per cent as of 10 July 2023 to 20 per cent on 6 January 2025, while the CPC had climbed above the 40 per cent mark. Support for the Liberals had dropped so low that less than one point separated them from the NDP, which was at just over 19 per cent. The third phase, the last before the writ was dropped, commenced with Trudeau's 6 January 2025 announcement that he was stepping down as party leader.[16]

Shortly after Trudeau's announcement, the Liberals began inching up in the polls, with EKOS on 22 January the first to show them emerging above the 30 per cent mark (at 31.7), yet with the CPC still in the lead at 38.5 per cent.[17] Things improved further for the Liberals when leadership contender Mark Carney borrowed a main plank from Pierre Poilievre's "Axe the Tax" policy by announcing his own intention to cancel the federal government's consumer carbon tax. If voters wanted a change in government policies, Carney could offer this. Indeed, on 11 February, Leger released numbers showing that many Canadians liked what they saw in Carney, and if Carney won the leadership race, the LPC and CPC would hypothetically be tied at 37 per cent, with the NDP dropping even further behind at 12 per cent.[18] At the time, and on

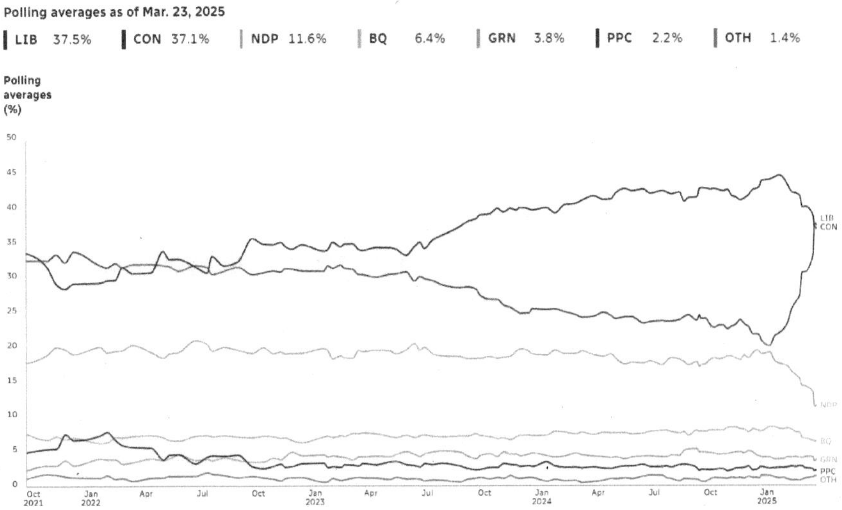

Figure 11.1 | Aggregated polls from 21 September 2021 to 23 March 2025
Source: Éric Grenier, CBC News: Poll Tracker. Used with permission.

their popular political podcast, the *Numbers*, on 14 February Éric Grenier and Philippe J. Fournier posed the question: "Have we entered an entirely new federal race?"[19]

On 25 February, both EKOS and Ipsos released polls showing the Liberals with a very slight lead over the CPC.[20] Except for a single poll released by Nanos on 1 September 2023 pegging the main parties at a statistical tie,[21] one had to go as far back as March of 2023 to find any polls not showing the Conservatives in the lead. Then, just over a week later, on 6 March 2025, Frank Graves of EKOS declared he was seeing "a profound transformation of the political landscape" with the LPC at 41.7 per cent and the CPC at 35.5 per cent.[22] A six-point Liberal lead? No one else was showing such numbers. EKOS was out alone for a week, yet others would soon follow.

Carney won the Liberal leadership on 9 March and was sworn in as prime minister on 14 March. Shortly afterwards, on 23 March, the PM asked the governor general to dissolve parliament. It was during this third pre-writ phase of choosing a new leader and before sending Canada to the polls that the LPC moved from the gloom of certain defeat to the tantalizing prospect for their supporters of re-election and perhaps even a Carney majority government. For the previous twelve months and up until 17 February, the CBC News Poll Ttracker had been projecting a 99 per cent probability that the Conservatives would win a federal election if held at that time; by 21 March, their probability of winning the election had dropped to 23 per cent.[23]

In much of Canada the Liberals' surge was largely coming at the NDP's expense. In the 2021 federal election, the NDP received 17 per cent of the national vote, yet by 19 March 2025, the aggregated polling numbers were showing NDP support at only 10 per cent across Canada. At the same time, the surge in LPC support in Quebec was coming at the expense of the Bloc Québécois (BQ). On 29 March, Eric Andrew-Gee of the *Globe and Mail* reported that Quebec polling was showing the LPC at 40 per cent, and "leading the Bloc and Conservatives by double digits."[24] Apparently, separatism was less palatable to Quebec voters with a bellicose American president musing about annexing Canada. A Leger poll conducted in mid-March revealed that 51 per cent of Quebecers cited tariffs and American aggression as their biggest concerns.[25] Furthermore, inside Montreal the Angus Reid Institute showed Liberal support had moved from a paltry 34 per cent in its 30 December 2024 poll to 64 per cent on 24 March 2025, while BQ support declined from 32 per cent to 16 per cent.[26]

POLLING IN THE CAMPAIGN PERIOD

The campaign began on 23 March and lasted for thirty-seven days. By the end of the first full day of the campaign, four firms had finished fielding a national survey: Research Co., Liaison Strategies, Mainstreet Research, and the Angus Reid Institute were all showing the Liberals in the lead by at least five points. As the campaign proceeded, of the thirty-two polls released after the writ was dropped and to the end of March, except for two (Abacus and Innovative Research), all the polls showed the Liberals leading. By month's end, Philippe J. Fournier on his 338Canada.com website was projecting a 90 per cent likelihood of a Liberal majority victory.[27]

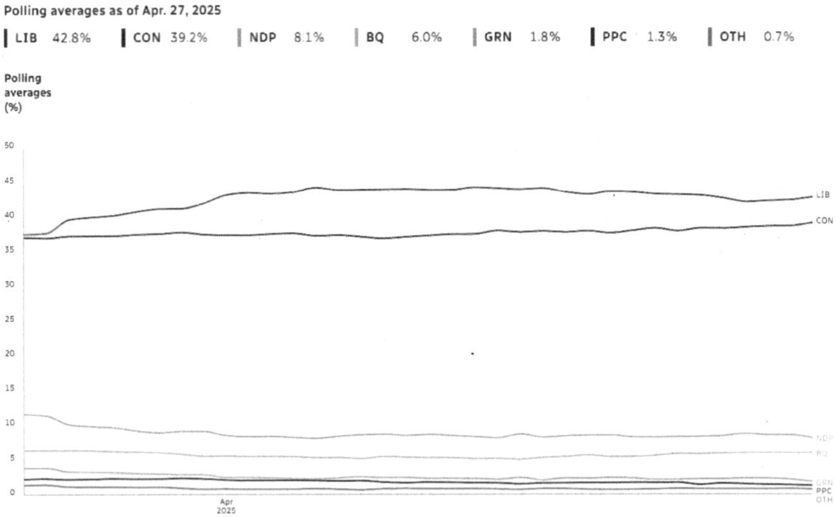

Figure 11.2 | Aggregated campaign polls from 23 March to 27 April, 2025
Source: Éric Grenier, CBC News: Poll Tracker. Used with permission.

THE CONSERVATIVE LEAD EVAPORATES

In early January, before Donald Trump's inauguration, Canadians were asked by Nanos in an open-ended manner to identify which single national issue was causing them the most concern. The top three were typical for most other Canadian federal and provincial elections: jobs and the economy (with 18.8 per cent mentioning this as their single biggest issue), inflation (12.0 per cent) and health care (8.1 per cent).[28] After Trump's inauguration, and following a relatively calm four years with Joe Biden in the White House, things changed markedly in the minds of Canadians. On 24 March, the Angus Reid Institute noted that "concern over the cost of living and US relations have both risen, largely at the expense of health care ... In many ways, cost of living and US relations are related issues as tariffs have increased the price for many goods."[29] A few days later, Nanos reported to his CTV and *Globe and Mail* clients: "In a world disrupted by Trump-era politics, Canadians are laser-focused on who will steer the nation through these turbulent times. The stakes are high, and the campaign is just starting to unfold."[30]

Of course, many were shocked by the dramatic change in fortunes for the Conservatives in such a short period of time. David Herle, a longtime campaign director and adviser to various provincial and federal Liberal leaders, and host of the popular podcast the *Curse of Politics*, remarked: "The combination of Trudeau's departure and Trump's arrival has caused Canadians to take a serious look at Poilievre. A lot of people who intended to vote for him six months ago ... are no longer convinced he is the right person for this moment. Not because he has changed but the moment has changed."[31]

Dan Arnold of the polling firm Pollara, and a past director of the federal LPC's campaign research operations, echoed Herle's remarks: "with Trudeau leaving, it has put the spotlight a bit more on Poilievre than was there before. Before, he [Poilievre] was just not Trudeau. And that was enough."[32] Such comments are supported by the Angus Reid Institute's numbers. Earlier, the CPC's high polling numbers were masking Poilievre's low popularity. On 20 December 2024, while the ARI was reporting that Trudeau was rated unfavourably by 68 per cent of Canadians, 55 per cent also gave unfavourable ratings for Poilievre.[33] Nor did things improve as the election proceeded; on 25 April ARI reported that 60 per cent reported being unfavourable towards the CPC leader.[34]

Political parties only reveal their internal private polling data when it is to their advantage. Yet due to what was increasingly evident bad blood between the Ontario Progressive Conservatives (PC) and Poilievre's campaign team, most notably national campaign director Jenni Byrne,[35] on 26 March, Kory Teneycke, Doug Ford's campaign director for the 2025 provincial election, released the provincial party's internal federal polling data to the *Toronto Star* (see chapter 3). The poll revealed that for Ontario, the LPC was at 48 per cent, the CPC at 33 per cent, and the NDP and Greens respectively at 11 and 4 per cent.[36] The *Toronto Star* reported: "In an Empire Club of Canada panel ... Teneycke expressed grave concern at the direction of Poilievre's campaign, which remains fixated on tax cuts while Carney is focused on the threat of US president Donald Trump's 25 per cent tariffs on Canadian goods. 'For the Conservatives ... in the campaign cockpit, every buzzer and alarm is going off and the plane is like going 'bzzzzz' and it's like, 'Pull up, pull up, pull up,'" he told the two hundred attendees at the event.'"[37]

Teneycke starkly claimed on the *Curse of Politics* that the total evaporation of the CPC's lead, and surge in LPC support, amounted to "campaign malpractice" on the part of Jenni Byrne.[38] Teneycke explained that he released the poll to deliver a "shock to the system" and get the federal party to take corrective action. In response to the resulting furor, both in the media and among CPC supporters, Ontario premier Ford simply responded: "Sometimes the truth hurts."[39]

In response to the press coverage on the polls and the CPC's decline, at a Poilievre rally held in Brampton, Ontario, supporters unfurled a banner asking, "Do You Believe the Polls?" Those holding the banner were sporting matching hoodies with the same text. This led to questions regarding whether the party was fomenting conspiracy theories about the election, and whether Poilievre would respect the outcome. Others felt it was simply meant to bolster the spirits of CPC supporters. In response to whether Poilievre was questioning the election's validity by attacking both the polls and possible vote count on election day, as did Trump after the 2020 US election, the CPC leader unequivocally stated he would respect the election results, regardless of whether he won or not.[40]

THE NATIONAL DEBATES

The French and English language debates occurred respectively on 16 April and 17 April. As a veteran politician with strong debating credentials, Poilievre needed a clear win over Carney. He performed well, but so too did Carney. Shortly after there were signs of a possible post-debate improvement for the CPC. On 18 April Mainstreet Research conducted an IVR poll with results showing the CPC two points ahead of the LPC (43 vs 41 per cent), and again with results from the following evening with the CPC at 43 per cent and the LPC at 39 per cent.[41] Along with Mainstreet, two other firms revealed a possible strengthening of the CPC. One was from the lesser-known Ontario-based firm, Kolosowski Strategies, with data showing the CPC and LPC tied, and Innovative Research with two polls: the first from 21 April showing the CPC with a five-point lead, and then on 23 April with the parties tied. However, these were the exception rather than the norm, as no other pollster had the Liberals losing their lead up to the eve of the election.

ADVANCE VOTING

One of the many interesting features of the 2025 election was the high turnout in the advance polls. These were open from 18 to 21 April. This was in addition to the earlier advance polls that were open across Canada on many university and college campuses.[42] In total, 7.3 million Canadians voted in this pre-electoral period, up from 5.8 million in 2021.[43] Polling data from the Angus Reid Institute revealed that the LPC benefited from this early turnout. Among those who voted in the advance polls, 46 per cent supported the LPC while 34 per cent supported the CPC, and 6 per cent supported the NDP. At the same time, and in the same ARI poll, among those who had yet to vote, the LPC and CPC were tied with each receiving 38 per cent of the support.[44] One possible reason for the Liberal advantage among advance voters was that for many the ballot question was most likely about which leader could best handle Trump, rather than whether it was time for a change. As one Grimsby Ontario voter told a Global News reporter: "First time in my life I have ever waited in line this long to vote ... Not a problem. We are voting for every Canadian's future."[45] According to David Coletto's regression analysis of his own firm's polling at Abacus, and a week prior to the advance polls opening, the "most consistent and powerful predictor of a Liberal vote is a sense that Mark Carney is the better choice to manage the economy and deal with Donald Trump"[46] (see chapter 12).

THE NDP COLLAPSE

Throughout the campaign the NDP fared poorly, with the LPC taking the wind from its sails. According to an end-of-campaign survey by Abacus, of those who reported having voted NDP in the 2021 federal election, 41 per cent reported they were now supporting the Liberals. Only 47 per cent of those who reported voting NDP in 2021 said they were staying with the party in 2025. In contrast to this, the Conservatives were holding 85 per cent of their 2021 supporters, and the Liberals were holding 79 per cent of their 2021 supporters.[47]

A major problem for the NDP was how unfavourably Canadians held its leader, Jagmeet Singh. According to Abacus's poll at the end of the campaign, Singh had a negative nine rating (31 per cent positive vs 40 per cent negative). In the meantime Carney enjoyed a positive twelve-point favourability rating (46 per cent positive minus 34 per cent negative) while Poilievre had a negative three-point rating (41 per cent positive vs 44 per cent negative).[48] Furthermore, the NDP's usual "bread and butter" social and labour issues, including employment and income security, became increasingly irrelevant in the face of the more prominent ballot question of who was the best to lead the country in the face of Donald Trump. As noted in chapter 4, the repercussions for the NDP were severe. In the end they would win only seven seats, thereby losing party status in the House of Commons, with Singh losing his own seat and stepping down as leader.[49]

WERE THE POLLS ACCURATE?

To what extent were the polls accurate? The day following the election, the Canadian Research Insights Council (CRIC), the organization representing the public opinion research industry, issued a media release stating: "The final published polls from CRIC members were, once again, all within a few percentage points of the actual voting results."[50] Not all of the polls that appeared in the media were conducted by firms that are members of CRIC;[51] however, as table 11.1 shows, the polls were very accurate in measuring the popular vote.

Shown here in table 11.1 are the differences between each firm's results in the final days of the campaign for each party and the actual votes (in terms of percentages) that each party received. Of the fourteen firms listed here, every firm was able to predict LPC's support within three points of the actual results, ranging from 0.1 for EKOS to 2.7 for Abacus, Pollara, and Innovative Research. There was more variability when examining the differences between the polling and the CPC's actual outcome, with some firms more accurate than others. Mainstreet and Liaison Strategies missed the mark by only 0.3 while Innovative Research was out by 4.3 percentage points. Overall, for all the parties in total, Mainstreet's final poll proved to be the closest of all, with a total error across all parties of only 2.7 points, followed by the Angus Reid Institute with 3.1 and Liaison Research with 3.5 points.[52]

Sometimes national polls can mask inaccuracies at the regional level. To what extent were the pollsters accurate within the battlegrounds of the seat-rich provinces of Ontario (122 seats), Quebec

Table 11.1 | Accuracy of final polls in the 2025 election

Polling firm	Field dates	Sample	Mode	LPC	CPC	NDP	BQ	PPC	GPC	Other	Total error
Mainstreet Research	25–27 April	2,000	IVR	0.3	0.3	0.3	0.3	0.3	0.2	1	2.7
Angus Reid	23–26 April	2,820	Online	0.3	1.3	0.7	0.3	0.3	0.2	0	3.1
Liaison Strategies	27 April	1,000	IVR	0.7	0.3	0.7	0.3	0.3	0.2	1	3.5
Nanos Research	26–27 April	1,707	Online and telephone	1.1	1.4	1.5	0.1	0.4	0.7	0	5.2
Research Co.	26–27 April	1,050	Online	0.3	2.3	0.7	0.3	0.3	0.8	1	5.7
Pallas Data	26 April	1,294	IVR	0.7	2.3	0.7	0.3	0.3	0.8	1	6.1
Forum Research	27 April	1,153	IVR	0.7	2.3	1.7	0.3	0.3	0.8	1	7.1
Leger	21–25 April	1,502	Online	0.7	2.3	1.7	0.3	0.3	0.8	1	7.1
Ipsos	22–26 April	2,500	Online and telephone	1.7	3.3	2.7	0.3	0.3	0.8	1	10.1
MQO Research	23–26 April	2,236	Online	0.3	3.3	3.7	1.3	0.7	1.8	0	11.1
Abacus Data	24–27 April	2,500	Online	2.7	2.3	3.7	0.3	2.3	0.2	0	11.5
Ekos	24–26 April	1,124	IVR	0.1	3.8	2.9	1.9	1.3	0.8	1	11.8
Pollara	22–24 April	2,382	Online, telephone, and IVR	2.7	3.3	3.7	0.3	1.3	0.8	1	13.1
Innovative	24–26 April	1,587	Online	2.7	4.3	4.7	0.3	1.3	1.8	0	15.1

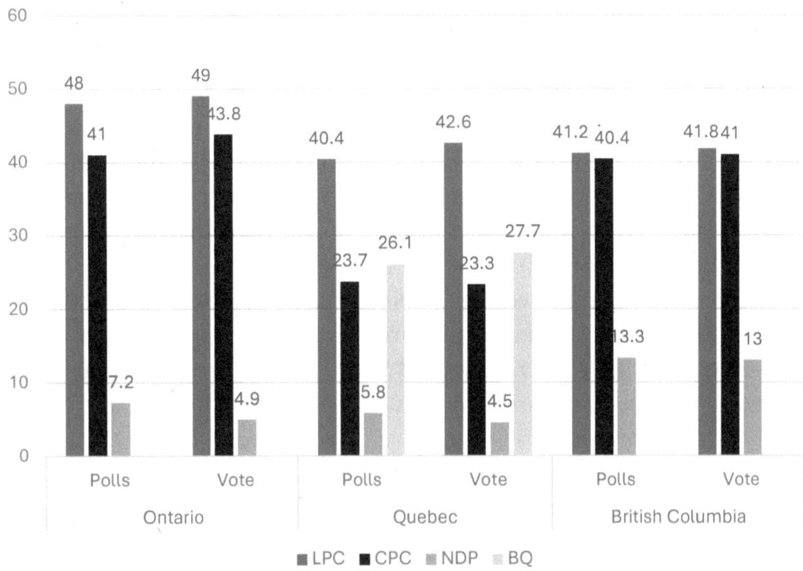

Figure 11.3 | Regional accuracy of polling, 2025

Data Source: Based on CBC Poll Tracker aggregated polling posted 27 April 2025. The actualresults are derived from Elections Canada.

(78 seats), and British Columbia (43 seats)? Provided in figure 11.3 are the polling numbers as aggregated by Grenier's poll tracker for the CBC. As can be seen for Ontario, the polls were collectively only off by one point for the Liberals (48 per cent in the polls vs 49 per cent of the vote), but 2.8 points for the CPC (41 per cent vs 43.8 per cent), and 2.3 for the NDP (7.2 per cent vs 4.9 per cent). In Quebec, the polls had the Liberals' support at 40.4 per cent whereas they took 42.6 per cent of the vote, making a difference of 2.2. The polls for the BQ showed 26.1 per cent support, with the actual vote at 27.7 per cent, a difference of 1.6 points. The CPC polling numbers in Quebec were only off by 0.4 points. Meanwhile in BC, the polls were very accurate with the LPC polling percentages being off by only 0.6 (41.2 per cent vs 41.8 per cent), the CPC by 0.6 (40.4 per cent vs 41 per cent), and the NDP by 0.3 (13.3 per cent vs 13 per cent). These figures are comparable to those from the 2021 election in which the CBC News Poll Tracker showed the aggregated polls numbers were only off by a range of 0 to 3 points for each of the main parties within all three of these battleground provinces.[53]

BEYOND THE POLLS: SEAT PROJECTIONS

While the end-of-campaign polls provided an accurate picture of the national popular support for the parties, the seat projections were less than perfect. Table 11.2 provides both the seat projections and predicted overall outcome put forward by a select number of prominent polling firms and aggregators. All seven of the organizations shown here predicted that the Liberals were likely to win a majority when, in the end, they won only 169 seats, a minority victory. Many offered their projections in the form of ranges. For example, YouGov suggested that the LPC would "win between 170 seats and 204 seats, with a central estimate of 185."[54] Grenier in his CBC News Poll Ttracker provided a range of 141 to 217 seats for the LPC, with 189 seats the main projection.[55]

Just as Nate Silver did for predicting the outcomes of previous US elections (he gave Hillary Clinton a 71 per cent likelihood of beating Donald Trump on the eve of the 2016 election[56]) and following the approach put forward by the economist Philip Tetlock in his *Super Forecasting*,[57] in which good predictors put forward their forecasts in the form of probabilities rather than hard outcomes, those offering Canadian electoral projections in 2025 usually expressed their expected numbers in the form of probabilities. Fournier in his 338Canada.com said the LPC had a 66 per cent chance of winning a majority victory, and a 22 per cent likelihood of being limited to a minority, while Grenier gave the LPC a 70 per cent chance of winning a majority and 19 per cent of winning a minority, and Mainstreet Research gave the LPC only a 55.2 per cent chance of winning a majority and 26.8 per cent of winning a minority.[58]

Projecting seat counts has been problematic in the past. In part this is because the statistical modelling is dependent on many things, but primarily the accuracy of polling data at the regional level as well as the extent to which previous electoral patterns prevail. Furthermore, with over three hundred ridings in play across Canada's many regions, and with multiple parties competing in a first-past-the-post system, precisely predicting the outcome in terms of seat counts for each party is a near impossibility. For the 2011 federal election, the projections failed to predict Stephen Harper's Conservative majority victory.[59] In 2015 Justin Trudeau's Liberals won a majority, yet with the exception of Forum Research all the projectors predicted a Liberal minority and averaged thirty-five fewer

Table 11.2 | Seat projections by pollsters and aggregators, 2025

Organization	LPC	CPC	NDP	BQ	Green / Other	Outcome
Actual Outcome	169	144	7	22	1	LPC minority
338Canada.com	187	125	7	23	1	LPC majority
CBC Poll Tracker	189	125	5	23	1	LPC majority
Canada Projections	176	134	11	20	2	LPC majority
Forum Research	186	122	6	29	0	LPC majority
Mainstreet Research	177	135	5	24	2	LPC majority
YouGov	185	136	3	18	2	LPC majority

Sources in the order shown: Elections Canada, https://enr.elections.ca/National.aspx?lang=e; 338Canada, Federal Elections, https://338canada.com/federal.htm; CBC Poll Tracker https://newsinteractives.cbc.ca/elections/poll-tracker/canada/; Canada Projections, "Cdn Projections Federal Electoral Model," last updated 15 March 2026, https://cdnprojections.ca/canada.html; Forum Research, https://poll.forumresearch.com/post/3181/liberals-within-reach-of-majority-government/; Mainstreet Research, "2025 Canadian Federal Election," last updated 27 April 2025, https://www.mainstreetresearch.ca/dashboard/canada; YouGov, "Final YouGov MRP for the 2025 Canadian Federal Election: Liberals Likely to Win a Majority," 25 April 2025, https://yougov.co.uk/politics/articles/52070-final-yougov-mrp-for-2025-canadian-federal-election-liberals-likely-to-win-majority-poll .

seats for the party.[60] In 2019, while correctly predicting a Liberal minority, the projections on average under-projected the Liberals by seventeen seats, and over-projected the NDP by eleven.[61] However, in the 2021 federal election Grenier for the CBC poll tracker and his subscriber service the Writ was very close to the actual result with an under-projection for the Liberals of only five seats.[62] Overall, media commentators and political scientists now need to realize that projections have been challenging in the past, and will likely be so for future elections.

CONCLUSION

The 2025 campaign brought the Liberals back to power with a new leader who convinced voters he was the best person to handle Donald Trump's tariffs and ongoing threats to Canada's sovereignty, bumping many other election issues off the ballot. At the same time, Poilievre's CPC defied the projections by winning 42 per cent of the vote and holding the Liberals to a minority. With the two-way battle for victory, the smaller parties paid the price, most notably the NDP which lost its official party status in the House of Commons.

The 2025 federal election produced more publicly released national polls than any other election in Canadian history. At a count of 167, this represented sixteen polls more than 2021, which Grenier had labelled "the most (publicly at least) polled election in Canadian history."[63] As noted at the beginning of this chapter, the availability of affordable and easily accessible methodologies in the form of IVR and online surveys continues to have an impact on the polling industry. Polls no longer take many days to field, nor is the national polling industry the preserve of those able to operate field centres with phone banks staffed by live interviewers. Gone are the days of having a handful of polling firms controlling the market and producing results on a sporadic basis during a federal election.

NOTES

The author thanks the editors of this volume, the anonymous peer reviewers, and Scott MacKay for their many suggestions regarding earlier versions of this chapter.

1 Alan Whitehorn, "The NDP and the Enigma of Strategic Voting," in Jon H. Pammett and Christopher Dornan (eds), *The Canadian Federal Election of 2006* (Toronto: Dundurn Press, 2006), 96–8.

2 David Moore, *The Super Pollsters: How They Measure and Manipulate Public Opinion in America* (New York: Four Walls Eight Windows, 1992), 313.

3 Éric Grenier, *Tapping into the Pulse: Public Opinion Polling in Canada, 2013* (IndieBookLauncher.com, 2014), 40.

4 Cole Davenport, "Saskatchewan NDP Gaining Momentum among Decided Voters, New Poll Says," CTV News, 22 October 2024, https://www.ctvnews.ca/regina/article/saskatchewan-ndp-gaining-momentum-among-decided-voters-new-poll-says/.

5 Elections Saskatchewan, "2024 General Election Official Results," Elections Saskatchewan, 9 November, 2024, https://results.elections.sk.ca/.

6 George Gallup and Saul Rae, *The Pulse of Democracy: The Public Opinion Poll and How it Works* (New York: Simon and Schuster, 1940).

7 Alan Frizzell and Anthony Westell, *The Canadian General Election of 1984: Politicians, Parties, Press and Polls* (Ottawa: Carleton University Press, 1985), 75.

8 These numbers are derived from counting the postings for all national polls listed in Wikipedia for both the 2021 and 2025 elections. For 2025, included are polls for which the last date of polling occurred on 24 March. Excluded are polls for which the last date of polling was 23 March. I do the same for 2021 by excluding the polls that finished fielding on the day the election was called. "Opinion Polling For The 2021 Canadian Federal Election," Wikipedia, https://en.wikipedia.org/wiki/Opinion_polling_for_the_2021_Canadian_federal_election; "Opinion Polling for the 2025 Canadian Federal Election," Wikipedia, https://en.wikipedia.org/wiki/Opinion_polling_for_the_2025_Canadian_federal_election.

9 David Wavrock, Grant Schellenberg, and Christoph Schimmele, "Internet-Use Typology of Canadians: Online Activities and Digital Skills," Statistics Canada, 9 November 2021, https://www150.statcan.gc.ca/n1/pub/11f0019m/11f0019m2021008-eng.htm.

10 On the changing methodologies in Canadian survey research, see Christopher Adams, "The Campaign: Elections and Polling in Twenty-First Century," in Tamara A. Small and Royce Koop (eds), *Elections in Canada: People, Players, and Processes* (Toronto: University of Toronto Press, 2025), 176–8.

11 This is based on my own counts for the 2025 election. For the 2021 election see Éric Grenier, "Polling in the 2021 Federal Election," in Jon H. Pammett and Christopher Dornan (eds), *The Canadian Federal Election of 2021* (Montreal and Kingston: McGill-Queen's University Press, 2022), 129.

12 Nic Nanos, "Nanos Weekly Tracking, Ending January 3, 2025," *Nanos Research*, 7 January 2025, https://nanos.co/wp-content/uploads/2025/01/Political-Package-2025-01-03-FOR-RELEASE.pdf.

13 Leger, "Leadership Perspectives For The Liberal Party Of Canada," Leger, 13 January 2025, https://leger360.com/wp-content/uploads/2025/01/

Leger-Trudeaus-Leadership-1.pdf. As noted in the introduction to this volume, Abacus Data had the CPC with a 27-point lead just after Trudeau's announcement.

14 Danielle Groen, "Morning Update: Poilievre's Reversal of Polling Fortune," *Globe and Mail*, 18 February 2025, https://www.theglobeandmail.com/canada/article-morning-update-poilievres-reversal-of-polling-fortune/.

15 Nic Nanos, "Concern About Trump/US Relations Rockets Upward. Conservatives 35, Liberals 34, NDP 16," Nanos Research, 18 March 2025, https://nanos.co/wp-content/uploads/2025/03/Political-Package-2025-03-14-FOR-RELEASE.pdf.

16 These numbers are from data compiled by Éric Grenier, "Poll Tracker," CBC News, 27 April 2025, https://newsinteractives.cbc.ca/elections/poll-tracker/canada/.

17 EKOS Politics, "Liberals Break 30 Points Following Trump Inauguration," EKOS Politics, 22 January 2025, https://www.ekospolitics.com/index.php/2025/01/liberals-break-30-points-following-trump-inauguration/.

18 Leger, "Canadian Politics: Survey of Canadians," Leger, 11 February 2025, https://leger360.com/wp-content/uploads/2025/02/Leger-x-Canadian-Press-Federal-Politics_VF.pdf.

19 Éric Grenier and Philippe Fournier, "The Numbers: Is It a Whole New Race?" Writ, 14 February 2025, https://www.thewrit.ca/p/the-numbers-is-it-a-whole-new-race.

20 EKOS Politics, "Liberals Hold Statistically Insignificant Lead," EKOS Politics, 25 February 2025, https://www.ekospolitics.com/index.php/2025/02/liberals-hold-statistically-insignificant-lead/; Darrell Bricker, "Liberals Take Lead for First Time Since 2021," Ipsos, 25 February 2025, https://www.ipsos.com/en-ca/liberals-take-lead-first-time-since-2021.

21 Polling Canada, "Federal Polling: CPC: 32% (-2) LPC: 32% (-1) NDP: 21% (+3) BQ: 7% (-1) GPC: 6% (+4) PPC: 3% (-2) Nanos Research, September 1, 2023, n=1000, MOE 3.1%, Telephone (% change with 2021 Federal Election). Check out federal details on @338Canada at: http://338canada.com," X, 5 September 2023, https://x.com/CanadianPolling/status/1699163360120496391.

22 EKOS Politics, "Rising Nationalism, Desire for Economic Sovereignty Propels Liberals to Five-Year High," EKOS Politics, 6 March 2025, https://www.ekospolitics.com/index.php/2025/03/rising-nationalism-desire-for-economic-sovereignty-propels-liberals-to-five-year-high/.

23 Grenier, "Poll Tracker."

24 Eric Andrew-Gee, "Quebec Seems Ready to Cut Carney Some Slack," *Globe and Mail*, 29 March 2025: A17.

25 Catherine Morrison, "Canadians Alarmed by US Aggression, Poll Says," *Winnipeg Free Press*, 21 March 2025: A3.

26 Angus Reid Institute, "Liberal Lead over CPC Increases to Eight Points, but Is Carney's House of Dreams Built on Concrete or Sand?," Angus Reid Institute, 24 March 2025, https://angusreid.org/canadian-election-carney-poilievre-trump-liberals-conservatives-ndp-bloc-polling/.

27 Philippe J. Fournier, "338canada Federal Projection," 338Canada, https://338canada.com/federal.htm.

28 Nic Nanos, "Nanos Weekly Tracking, Ending January 3, 2025," Nanos Research, 7 January 2025, https://nanos.co/wp-content/uploads/2025/01/Political-Package-2025-01-03-FOR-RELEASE.pdf.

29 Angus Reid Institute, "Liberal Lead over CPC Increases to Eight Points, but Is Carney's House of Dreams Built on Concrete or Sand?".

30 Nic Nanos, "LPC 41.9, CPC 37.0, NDP 10.6, BQ 5.3, GP 2.6, PPC 1.9 (Tracking Ending March 29, 2025)," Nanos Research, 30 March 2025, https://nanos.co/wp-content/uploads/2025/03/2025-2783-ELXN-FED-2025-03-29-Field-Ended.pdf.

31 David Herle et al., "Prime Minister-Designate Carney," *Curse of Politics*, 10 March 2025, https://open.spotify.com/episode/1ZwF8ogh1sYuGN8qTDeGdF.

32 Éric Grenier, "Ep. #139: The Polls Say It's a Race," *The Writ Podcast*, 19 March 2025, https://www.thewrit.ca/p/ep-139-the-polls-say-its-a-race.

33 Angus Reid Institute, "End of Year Review: While Trudeau's Future Is Unclear, All Three Major Federal Leaders Failing to Connect with Canadians," Angus Reid Institute, 20 December 2024, https://angusreid.org/approval-favourability-trudeau-poilievre-singh-2024-polling/.

34 Angus Reid Institute, "Views of Conservative Leader Pierre Poilievre," Angus Reid Institute, accessed 10 May 2025, https://angusreid.org/poilievre-monitor/.

35 For background on the Ontario PC-federal CPC relations, see Christian Noel, "Pressure Mounting on Poilievre to Fire Jenni Byrne: Sources," CBC News, 22 May 2025, https://www.cbc.ca/news/politics/poilievre-byrne-conservative-caucus-1.7540215.

36 Robert Benzie, "Doug Ford's Internal Polling Paints Grim Election Prospects for Pierre Poilievre in Ontario," *Toronto Star*, 27 March 2025, https://www.thestar.com/politics/doug-ford-s-internal-polling-paints-grim-election-prospects-for-pierre-poilievre-in-ontario/article_11f8b5cc-3

dec-42f6-9d4d-c342d67bee9d.html. See also Éric Grenier, "Election Writ 3/28: Are the Conservatives in Trouble in Ontario?" Writ, 28 March 2025, *https://www.thewrit.ca/p/election-writ-328-are-the-conservatives.* The Ontario poll was conducted by Campaign Research and released under the title: "Federal Election Study – Ontario Advance Analytics: Federal and Provincial Ballot Tests," 26 March 2025, https://qc125.com/proj/2025-03-26-campaign.pdf?utm_source=substack&utm_medium=email.

37 Benzie, "Ford's Internal Polling Looks Grim for Poilievre in Ontario."

38 Vassy Kapelos, "'We Blew a 25-Point Lead': Kory Tenycke Calls out the Conservatives for 'Campaign Malpractice,'" CTV News, 10 April 2025, https://www.ctvnews.ca/video/politics/2025/04/10/we-blew-a-25-point-lead-kory-tenycke-calls-out-the-conservatives-for-campaign-malpractice/.

39 Codi Wilson, "Sometimes the Truth Hurts': Ford Defends Campaign Manager Who Criticized Poilievre," CTV News, 14 April 2025, https://www.ctvnews.ca/toronto/article/sometimes-the-truth-hurts-ford-defends-campaign-manager-who-criticized-poilievre/.

40 Olivia Stefanovich, "Some Conservative Supporters Question Whether the Polls Can Be Trusted," CBC News, 10 April 2025, https://www.cbc.ca/news/politics/do-you-believe-the-polls-poilievre-supporters-ask-1.750 7437.

41 Untitled media releases, Mainstreet Research, 19 April and 20 April 2025, https://cdn.prod.website-files.com/66c8dfb086a015b3b519e988/6802c 6cf087bc55f9a3c5c48_2025-04-19_CAN_Daily_Tracker_Public.pdf; https://cdn.prod.website-files.com/66c8dfb086a015b3b519e988/68046 0edd39bd0623ff968be_2025-04-20_CAN_Daily_Tracker_Public.pdf.

42 Elections Canada, "Vote On Campus," Elections Canada, accessed 25 May 2025, https://www.elections.ca/content2.aspx?section=stu&document=votcamp&lang=e.

43 Catharine Tunney and Darren Major, "Record 7.3 Million Canadians Voted during Advance Polls: Elections Canada," CBC News, 22 April 2025, https://www.cbc.ca/news/politics/elections-canada-record-advanced-polls-1.7515477.

44 Angus Reid Institute, "All Down To E-Day: Liberal Voters Dominate Early Voting But Election Day Support Splits Evenly Between CPC, LPC," Angus Reid Institute, 26 April 2025, https://angusreid.org/all-down-to-e-day-carney-poilievre/.

45 David Akin, "Analysis: Voters Surge to Advance Polls for a Most 'Consequential' Election," Global News, 20 April 2025, https://global-

news.ca/news/11140712/analysis-voters-surge-to-advance-polls-for-a-most-consequential-election/.

46 David Coletto, "Advantage Liberal: What Advanced Modelling Tells Us about Why the Liberals Are Winning," Abacus Data, 11 April 2025, https://abacusdata.ca/2025-federal-election-why-mark-carney-can-win/.

47 David Coletto, "Abacus Data: Our Final Poll of the Campaign," Abacus Data, 27 April 2025, https://abacusdata.ca/2025-federal-election-final-poll-of-campaign/.

48 David Coletto, "Abacus Data: Our Final Poll of the Campaign."

49 A political scientist who specializes on the NDP and its history, David McGrane, speaks about the NDP's current situation, and its future. See Saroja Coelho, "The Future of the NDP," *CBC Listen*, 3 May 2025, https://www.cbc.ca/listen/live-radio/1-1424-just-asking/clip/16143994-the-future-ndp.

50 Canadian Research Insights Council, "Congratulations to Public Opinion Researchers for Accurate and Transparent Polling," Canadian Research Insights Council, 29 April 2025, https://www.canadianresearchinsightscouncil.ca/congratulations-to-public-opinion-researchers-for-accurate-and-transparent-polling/.

51 The list of those who are members of CRIC is provided at the following: "Members Directory," Canadian Research Insights Council, https://www.canadianresearchinsightscouncil.ca/member-directory/.

52 The table is drawn by examining each of the press releases via the links posted on Wikipedia: https://en.wikipedia.org/wiki/Opinion_polling_for_the_2025_Canadian_federal_election#cite_ref-21. For the EKOS results, I chose the results for the firm's three-day rolling sample.

53 Éric Grenier, "How the Polls Did in the 2021 Election," Writ, 29 September 2021, https://www.thewrit.ca/p/pollster-accuracy-2021-election.

54 Patrick English, "Final Yougov MRP for the 2025 Canadian Federal Election: Liberals Likely to Win a Majority," YouGov, 25 April 2025, https://yougov.co.uk/politics/articles/52070-final-yougov-mrp-for-2025-canadian-federal-election-liberals-likely-to-win-majority-poll.

55 Grenier, "Poll Tracker."

56 Nate Silver, "Final Election Update: There's a Wide Range of Outcomes, and Most of Them Come up Clinton," FiveThirtyEight, 8 November 2016,https://fivethirtyeight.com/features/final-election-update-theres-a-wide-range-of-outcomes-and-most-of-them-come-up-clinton/.

57 Philip E. Tetlock and Dan Gardner, *Super Forecasting: The Art and Science of Prediction* (New York: Crown Publishing, 2015).

58 Sources are the same as those for table 11.2.

59 André Turcotte, "Polls: Seeing through the Glass Darkly," in Jon H. Pammett and Christopher Dornan (eds), *The Canadian Federal Election of 2011* (Toronto: Dundurn Press, 2011), 210.

60 David Coletto, "Polling and the 2015 Federal Election," in Jon H. Pammett and Christopher Dornan (eds), *The Canadian Federal Election of 2015* (Toronto: Dundurn Press, 2016), 311.

61 Éric Grenier, "A Close Race from Start to Finish: Polling in the 2019 Federal Elections," in Jon H. Pammett and Christopher Dornan (eds), *The Canadian Federal Election of 2019* (Montreal and Kingston: McGill-Queen's University Press, 2020), 166.

62 Grenier, "How the Polls Did in the 2021 Election."

63 Éric Grenier, "Polling in the 2021 Federal Election," in Jon H. Pammett and Christopher Dornan (eds), *The Canadian Federal Election of 2021* (Montreal and Kingston: McGill-Queen's University Press, 2022), 144.

12

Competence Versus Change: The Role of Valence Politics in the Election

David Coletto and Richard Jenkins

The outcome of the 2025 federal election was surprising from the perspective of the horserace polls throughout 2024. The Conservative Party looked as if it was poised to win a majority driven by voter dissatisfaction, particularly around the issues of the economy and affordability. As 2025 dawned after a decade of Liberal rule, public appetite for change was widespread and the main Liberal protagonist, Justin Trudeau, was all but forced to resign after almost ten years as prime minister in favour of Mark Carney, who had no previous experience in electoral politics. Carney was able to distance himself from the previous government while projecting a sense of competence, especially on the one issue that disadvantaged the Conservative Party: Donald Trump.

The Liberals under Mark Carney were seeking an historic fourth consecutive mandate as no party has won four or more federal elections since the Liberal Party won five in a row between 1935 and 1953. They did so by framing the election around competent leadership and international steadiness in the face of US president Donald Trump's threats. Pierre Poilievre's Conservatives pressed the case for domestic renewal and change. The contest became defined by two competing frames: competence versus change. Ultimately, voters' evaluations of the party leaders, their emotional responses to events, and strategic considerations in a high-stakes environment produced an outcome few anticipated just months earlier.

The election results were striking. Carney led the Liberals to victory, cementing a fourth-straight term in government – a rare feat in Canadian political history. The Liberals captured 169 seats (44 per cent of the popular vote), narrowly short of a majority in the expanded 343-seat House of Commons. Poilievre's Conservatives, while defeated, registered their strongest popular vote result in decades with 41 per cent of the vote that translated into 144 seats (the most seats since 2011).

With the collapse of the New Democratic Party (6 per cent of the vote and just seven seats) and the Bloc Québécois seat count reduced from thirty-two to twenty-two seats, the outcome left Canada essentially a two-party country for the first time in modern memory. Over 80 per cent of votes went to the two front-runners, the highest such share in nearly seventy years.

In late 2024, this outcome seemed unimaginable. An Abacus Data poll in early December showed the Conservative Party with a twenty-three-point lead.[1] This chapter analyzes the dynamics behind the vote, drawing on post-election survey data[2] and campaign narratives. We focus on four themes: leadership and competence, the impact of Donald Trump's re-election, the demand for domestic change, and socio-demographic patterns of support. Throughout, we highlight how leadership evaluations, issue salience, and emotional responses shaped voter behaviour in 2025.

The 2025 Canadian federal election presents a remarkable test of valence politics theory – the idea that elections turn on judgments of competence, leadership, and broadly shared goals rather than what parties stand for. A party's platform is not so much about demonstrating that its policies align with voters as it is about demonstrating competence and a plan. Valence issues are issues for which most people agree on the goals (e.g., a strong economy) but disagree on whose plan is best able to deliver it. Valence theories can be contrasted with spatial theories of voting,[3] where voters cast votes for the party that most aligns with their own views about enduring divisive issues (e.g., role of government). While spatial theories offer insights into the underlying structure of the party competition, previous studies of voting behaviour in Canada have shown that a valence politics model has strong explanatory power for accounting for the election outcome.[4] In this chapter, we explore the dimensions of the vote and its determinants.

THE ECONOMY, CHANGE, AND DONALD TRUMP

Normally, a Canadian government entering its tenth year would face an uphill battle against voter fatigue and demands for change – and indeed, late 2024 polling showed the Liberals in dire shape. Donald

Trump's re-election as US president in November 2024 became an unexpected boon for the incumbent Liberals and a severe complication for the Conservatives.

A powerful undercurrent driving the 2025 election was a widespread demand for domestic political change. Well before Trump's return to the White House, the Trudeau government had been beset by intense public dissatisfaction. High inflation, a housing affordability crisis, and fatigue with scandal and lockdowns in the early 2020s had left Canadians anxious about their economic security. Inflation and housing, which both advantaged the Conservates, are both the kinds of valence issues that could frame the election.

Abacus Data analysis described Canadians in 2023–24 as locked in a "scarcity mindset," feeling that basic necessities were increasingly out of reach. This fostered "fierce anti-incumbent sentiment," part of a global trend in 2024 that saw voters sour on sitting governments. Indeed, by late 2024 only 12 per cent of Canadians believed the Liberal government deserved re-election. When deputy prime minister and minister of finance Chrystia Freeland resigned in December 2024 amid internal party strife, it was the final pressure point on Trudeau's leadership. At that low point, polls put the Liberals a staggering twenty-seven points behind Poilievre's Conservatives (47 per cent to 20 per cent) – the largest margin ever recorded by Abacus in its polling history.[5] In other words, heading into 2025 the default outcome appeared to be a Conservative landslide driven by Canadians' desire to throw out the long-standing Liberal government.

The state of the economy has always been considered a key indicator for incumbent governments. A poor economy, or at least the perception of a poor economy, provides a compelling reason to vote a party out of office.[6] On this score, the challenge for Carney and the Liberal Party was clear. Two thirds of voters evaluated the economy negatively. Negative perceptions had outweighed positive ones at the time of the 2021 election as well, but the difference was not as stark (figure 12.1).

The poor perception of the state of the economy was part of a broader public anger and frustration that was directed at the incumbent Liberals. As one analysis noted, the public mood in 2024 was one of anger ("scarcity-driven anger") which later turned into caution ("precarity-tinged caution") once Trump loomed large. Many Canadians were genuinely anxious about their financial future – a

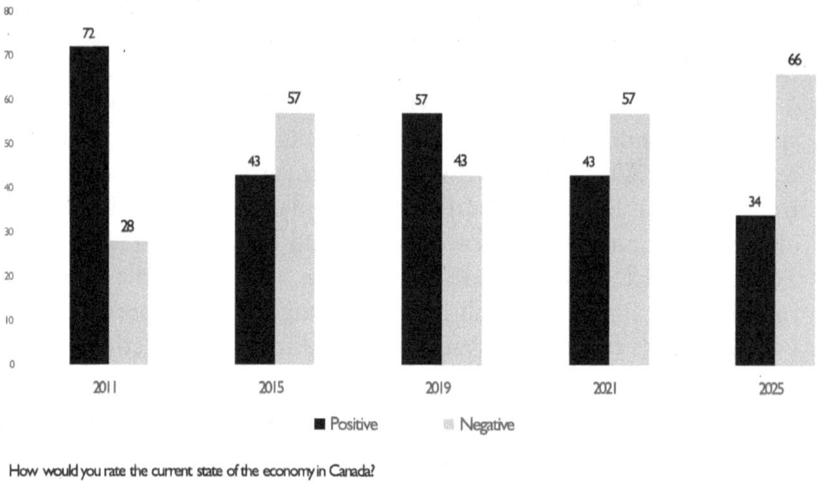

Figure 12.1 | Perceptions of the state of the Canadian economy

valence concern if ever there was one – and such anxiety often translated into anger at those in charge. Poilievre's oft-repeated lines about Canadians "scarcely getting by" and needing to "take back control" resonated emotionally with these voters.

In elections, issues are the substance of campaign platform and promises that provide the context in which the political discourse takes place. Not all issues are equally important, and each campaign tends to be defined by what valence issues become central. In 2021, COVID-19 and the economy were central.[7] In 2025, the economy again loomed large with dealing with and responding to Donald's Trump's actions also important.

In our post-election survey, we asked Canadians to identify the most important issue and the top three most important issues facing the country (figure 12.2). The answer was clear: economic concerns – both macro and micro – and dealing with Trump were the most important priorities for voters. Three in ten viewed the cost of living and inflation as their number one priority and six in ten included it in their top three. Donald Trump and his administration was the number one priority for 21 per cent and 40 per cent included it in their top three. Other notable second tier issue priorities were: health care (a perennial valence issue in Canada) and immigration.

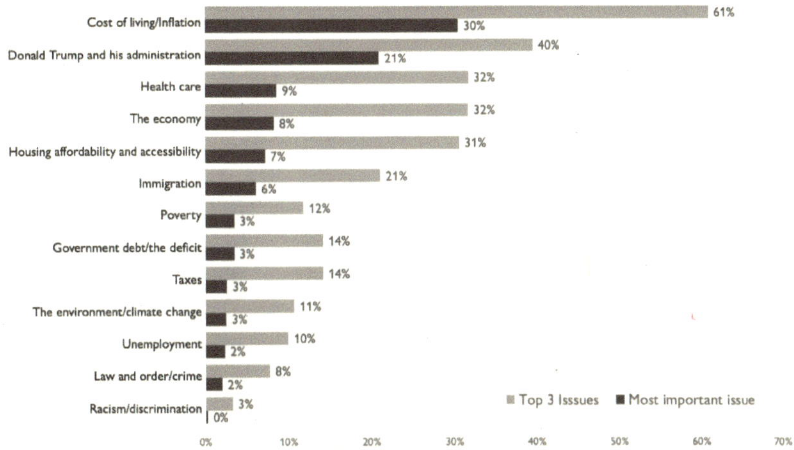

As far as you are concerned, what are the THREE most important issues facing the country at the present time? Please select THREE issues. And what do you think is the single most important issue?

Figure 12.2 | Top three issues and single most important issue

Trump's return to the White House – and his provocative actions toward Canada – dramatically reshaped the election's narrative, making international competence and national unity top-of-mind for many voters. Trump wasted little time in sparking crises that spilled into Canada's political arena. He made inflammatory statements on social media and in the news suggesting Canada should become the "51st state" of the US and even mused about annexation. He also imposed stiff tariffs on Canadian exports early in 2025, rekindling fears of a trade war.

These actions were direct threats to Canada's sovereignty and economic security, and the Canadian public reacted with a wave of outrage and anxiety. According to news reports at the time, many Canadians cancelled vacations to the US and boycotted American goods in protest. Trump's "truculence" deeply infuriated Canadians across the political spectrum. In the words of one historian, "Trump talking is not good for the Conservatives" – meaning that Trump's belligerence was galvanizing anti-Trump sentiment that would benefit the Liberals. Prime Minister Carney hammered this point in his messaging, warning that "President Trump is trying to break us so America can own us," and casting himself as the defender of Canadian sovereignty.

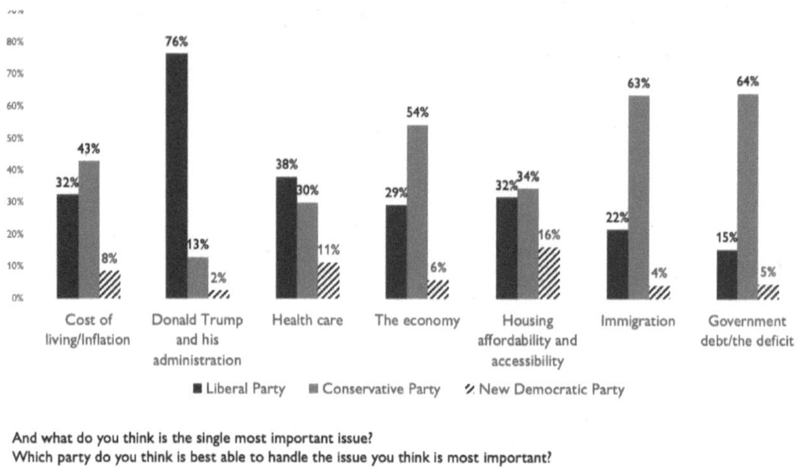

Figure 12.3 | Party best able to handle most important issue

The key theoretical point is that valence politics can cut both ways for an incumbent: if voters see the incumbents as failing to competently manage important issues, valence considerations drive them toward the opposition. And voters often think some parties perform better on specific issues, so the election can turn on which parties have the advantage on the issues that matter most.

On the top priority, the cost of living and inflation, the Conservative Party has an advantage which reflected its broader perception of competence on the economy more broadly. The Conservative Party was also clearly seen as best able to handle immigration and government debt and deficits, but these issues were not the most central ones for the campaign.

The Liberal advantage was confined to one area: dealing with Trump and his administration. As long as the campaign revolved around Trump, the Liberal Party had an advantage. One of the ways Trump benefitted the Liberals was due to the fact that his comments directly impacted Canada's political and economic sovereignty. Since the Liberals were seen as the best party to deal with Trump, they could blunt the negative impact of the domestic economic performance that so advantaged the Conservatives.

The NDP had no clear performance advantage or strength. In fact, the only issue that the NDP was seen as best on was handing racism and discrimination which is one of the lowest public priorities.

Pierre Poilievre's campaign was adept at harnessing the public's desire for change. Since being chosen leader, he hammered on "pocketbook" issues at every opportunity. Reducing the cost of living was the Conservatives' mantra. Poilievre tapped into anger over soaring grocery and gas prices, rising rents and mortgages, and general economic insecurity. He positioned himself as the champion of the "little guy" against a Liberal government he painted as elitist and out of touch. It was fertile ground – so much so that at the start of 2025, many believed a Conservative victory looked certain.

By late 2024, the Liberals' image on the domestic front was abysmal – they were blamed for economic woes and declining affordability. In valence terms, the Liberals had lost their perceived competence on the economy, and Poilievre's Conservatives gained an advantage as the party of potential improvement.

Over the course of the campaign, there was a tug-of-war between the "continuity vs change" narrative and the "stability vs disruption" narrative. Early in 2025, Poilievre successfully framed the choice as simply continuity (another Liberal term) versus change (a new Conservative government). A majority of Canadians did crave change: by election day, 55 per cent of voters said that wanting a change in government was their primary voting motive. This was up significantly from earlier in the campaign which indicates that as the initial shock of Trump's actions faded somewhat, the underlying appetite for change reasserted itself during the campaign.

However, polling captured the tension between change and fear. It can be summarized as: "a majority still longs for change, yet a plurality doubts that the riskier option will deliver it." This encapsulates the psychological battle: desire for change versus fear of uncertainty. The Conservatives had to convince people that change would be positive and not chaotic; the Liberals had to convince them that stability under Carney would be safer and still responsive to their needs, particularly regarding the economy.

LEADERSHIP AND COMPETENCE: CARNEY VERSUS POILIEVRE

Elections often are framed in terms of the competition between party leaders, as leader evaluations are a helpful shortcut for voters and drive the narrative of the campaign for the media and pundits.

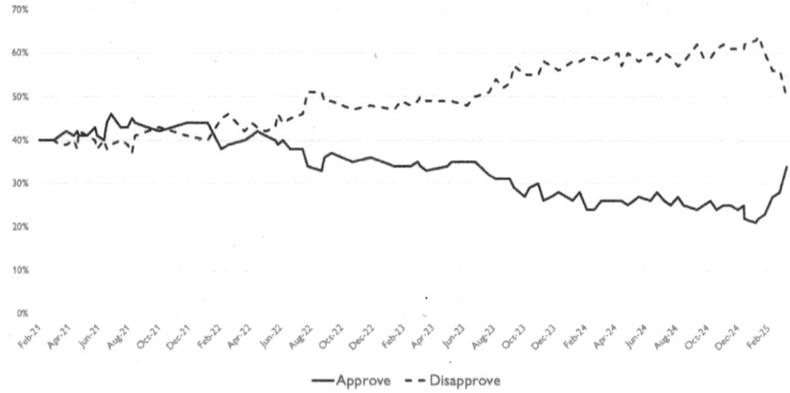

Overall, do you approve or disapprove of the job the federal government led by (Justin Trudeau/Mark Carney) is doing?

Figure 12.4 | Federal government approval 2021 to 2025

Election studies since the 1960s have consistently demonstrated the impact that leader images have on vote choice.[8]

When he announced his resignation in early January 2025 that would take place when a new leader was selected, Justin Trudeau and the government he led were deeply unpopular. Disapproval began to grow shortly after the 2021 election and increased further in the summer of 2023 as voter frustration with affordability grew, particularly around housing, inflation, and rising interest rates. Leaders often own the problems of their government and voters' frustrations with the government for not being focused on the problems of everyday Canadians was evident. Trudeau, who came from a privileged background, took expensive trips, and was found to have violated ethics guidelines, saw his personal image falter. In the fall of 2023, an Abacus poll showed that 94 per cent of Canadians viewed Trudeau as inauthentic and phony.[9]

Carney's selection as Liberal leader in early 2025 marked a turning point and paved the way for a hard reset of the Liberal brand even as Canadians remained pessimistic about the state of the economy and overall affordability.

Carney entered politics with credentials in economic management and an aura of technocratic competence. A former governor of the Bank of Canada and Bank of England, Carney was a novice in electoral politics yet widely respected for his steady-handed leadership

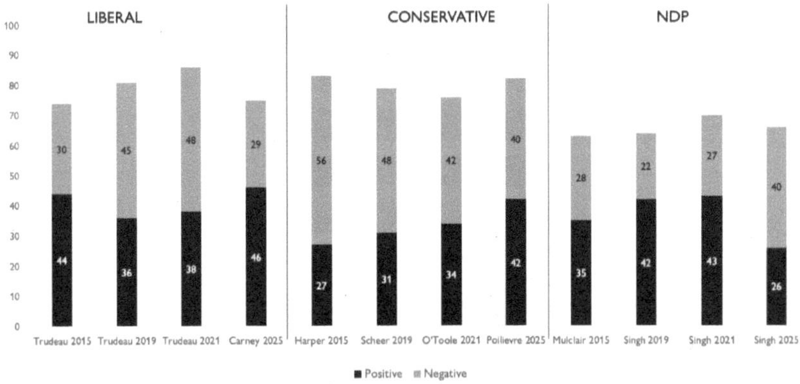

Do you have a positive or negative impression of the following people?

Figure 12.5 | Leader impressions, 2015 to 2025

during past financial crises (see chapter 2). Poilievre, by contrast, was a career politician and firebrand populist who built his brand railing against Liberal "mismanagement" and championing ordinary Canadians' frustrations (see chapter 3). Voters were thus presented with a stark choice of leadership styles: Carney's promise of stability and expertise versus Poilievre's promise of bold change and "common-sense" populism.

Government approval surged immediately after Carney became prime minister, reflecting a clean break from Trudeau's polarizing legacy. Carney's assumption of office in March 2025 boosted Liberal vote intention share from 27 per cent up to 43 per cent within weeks, underscoring how a fresh leader perceived as highly competent can dramatically improve a government's appeal.

By campaign's end, both major party leaders achieved net positive personal ratings – a rare occurrence in such a polarized climate – but Carney enjoyed a commanding +17 net approval (approval minus disapproval) compared to Poilievre's modest +2. In other words, while many Canadians respected Poilievre's energy and advocacy for change, even more were reassured by Carney's calm expertise and trustworthiness.

Figure 12.5 compares the leadership evaluations at the end of the campaign for the past four elections. Three things are worth noting. First, Carney was viewed as positively as Trudeau had been in 2015,

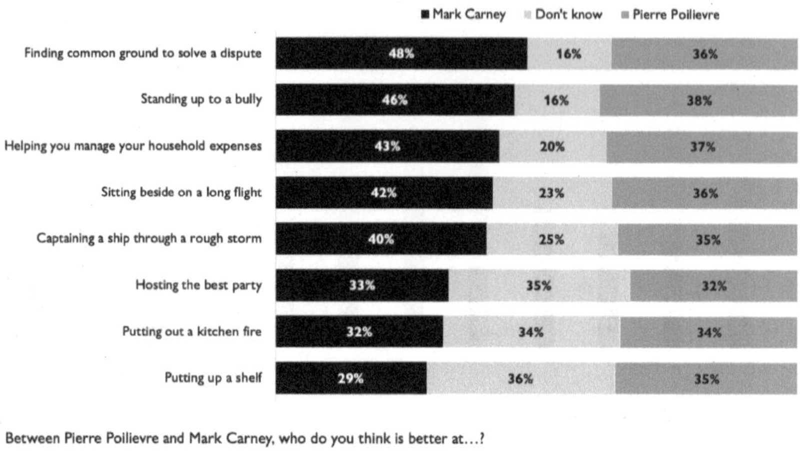

Figure 12.6 | Perceived leadership traits during final week of the campaign

demonstrating that he immediately buoyed Liberal fortunes. Second, Poilievre was the most liked Conservative leader over the past four elections. The Liberal Party had a potentially formidable opponent. Finally, Jagmeet Singh, the leader of the NDP, was unable to maintain the positive image he held previously. Given Singh's unpopularity, the NDP was unlikely to replicate Jack Layton's success in the 2011 election when the NDP surged to official opposition status.

The 2025 election campaign became highly "presidentialized" – centered on the two main leaders – which is a hallmark of valence-driven elections. During the last week of the campaign, Abacus Data[10] found that Canadians rated Carney significantly higher than Poilievre on key image traits (figure 12.6). For instance, on the question of "standing up to a bully" – a proxy for defending Canada's interests given Trump's interventions – 46 per cent picked Carney versus 38 per cent for Poilievre. Likewise, 40 per cent said Carney was better at "captaining a ship through a bad storm" (a metaphor for crisis leadership) versus 35 per cent for Poilievre. Carney's edge on these competence-related metrics reflected his image as a steady hand on the helm, a particularly valued trait in the context of the tumultuous events that defined this campaign.

Poilievre, for his part, was not without appeal. Voters gave him credit for focusing on economic and social grievances felt by many.

However, Poilievre's overall image profile was eclipsed by Carney's "aura of expertise and stability." In essence, Carney successfully distanced himself from the negatives of the long Liberal incumbency while leveraging his technocratic reputation, whereas Poilievre struggled to reassure enough voters that he was a safe or seasoned alternative.

With the spotlight on leadership competence, many previous partisan or ideological considerations took a back seat. Long-term Liberal partisanship and policy differences mattered less than whether Canadians trusted Carney or Poilievre to deliver on broadly shared goals (protecting the country, restoring prosperity). This dynamic mirrors findings from past elections that leader images, party performance, and issue handling often form a triumvirate of forces driving vote choice. In 2025, leader image arguably trumped all: the ballot question became, "who is best suited to lead Canada through crisis and change?"

THE TRUMP FACTOR: INTERNATIONAL CRISIS AND VOTER PERCEPTIONS

It is difficult to overstate how much Donald Trump's re-election as US president reframed the Canadian ballot question. Abacus Data found that as the campaign got underway, one distinct set of voters prioritized "handling the Trump threat" above all else, and among those voters an overwhelming 76 per cent believed the Liberals were the party best able to handle US-Canada relations, versus only 13 per cent who chose the Conservatives. This sixty-three-point Liberal advantage on the Trump issue is a stark indicator of how the Liberals successfully claimed the valence high ground on international competence. Carney, with his background in global finance and diplomacy, was seen as far more credible to stand up to an unpredictable US president than Poilievre, whose foreign policy experience was minimal.

Poilievre, in fact, found himself on the defensive regarding Trump. The Conservative leader had earlier cultivated a populist "Canada First" image not entirely dissimilar to Trump's rhetoric. He advocated policies like tighter borders, smaller government, and an end to "wokeness," and he used slogans echoing neo-conservative themes. While these positions resonated with some voters in normal times, they became a liability once Trump turned openly hostile toward Canada. The Liberals were quick to draw parallels between

Poilievre and Trump. Media coverage noted that many of Poilievre's positions and much of his rhetoric mirrored Trump – albeit on a more moderate level, and that this association ultimately ended up hurting him badly. For swing voters concerned about Trump, the prospect of a Trump-friendly Conservative government was worrying. One Toronto voter was quoted as saying he voted Liberal because Poilievre "sounds like mini-Trump to me" and Trump's tariffs were a serious concern. This sentiment typified how Trump's shadow over the campaign caused some voters who might otherwise lean Conservative to stick with (or switch to) the Liberals as the safer pair of hands internationally and a rejection of "Trump-like" politics.[11] As we show below, about 7 per cent of those who voted Conservative in 2021 voted Liberal this time. Most Liberal voters from 2021 did not defect as would have been predicted based on their own evaluations of the government's performance and the polls from 2024.

Emotionally, Trump's influence injected fear, nationalism, and anger into the Canadian electorate. Fear and anxiety, as pollsters Coletto and Sheppard dubbed a sense of "precarity" surged as Canadians suddenly questioned the stability of the continental order and their economic security.[12] This likely boosted voter turnout and engagement (see chapter 13). A record 7.3 million Canadians cast ballots in advance polls, suggesting heightened mobilization. National pride and nationalist sentiment were also heightened; Carney's framing of the election as "Canada versus Trump" tapped into a rally-'round-the-flag effect. At the same time, anger at Trump energized progressive voters to go to the polls to rebuke his perceived meddling. Indeed, even Donald Trump noted the influence he had on the election, telling the *Atlantic*, "You know, until I came along, remember that the Conservative was leading by 25 points." In sum, Trump served as a polarizing external actor who became a central issue in the Canadian election. His re-election initially helped Poilievre by spotlighting conservative themes, but as Trump's behaviour grew more extreme, it backfired and reframed the election for many Canadians.

By reframing the race around competent crisis management, Trump's intervention allowed the Liberals to transcend some of their incumbency disadvantages. However, Trump did not erase those domestic grievances entirely. As the immediate shock of his actions settled, many voters refocused on the pressing issues at home that had made Poilievre so popular to begin with. The campaign thus evolved, and the salience of Trump versus change shifted over time – a dynamic we explore in the next section.

A TWO-PARTY COMPETITION: THE EROSION OF SUPPORT FOR THE NDP AND BLOC

One of the most dramatic aspects of the 2025 election was the decline of Canada's two prominent third parties, the New Democratic Party, and the Bloc Québécois. Both suffered severe losses in vote share and seats, underscoring how a valence-driven, high-stakes campaign can squeeze out smaller parties. Voters gravitated toward the parties they saw as having the competence and relevance to address their primary concerns, and in 2025 that meant the Liberals or Conservatives.

The Conservatives gained significantly in popular support (up to 41 per cent from 33 per cent in 2021) and made inroads with key demographics, as we detail later. Nevertheless, there is considerable individual continuity from election to election as voters often remain loyal to the same party. Table 12.1 compares the reported vote in 2025 in the survey with the recalled vote from the previous election.

One of the potential areas for change is among those who did not vote in the previous election. These new electors, who did not or were not eligible to vote in 2021, were split almost equally between the Conservative Party and Liberal Party. Among new voters, who were casting a ballot for the first time, the Conservatives outdid the Liberals (54 per cent vs 35 per cent).

Two things are striking about the flow of the vote between 2021 and 2025. First, the Liberal Party was able to retain most of its 2021 vote (78 per cent). The demand for change among Liberal voters did not drive them to abandon their 2021 preference in favour of another party. Second, those who voted NDP in 2021 did not stay loyal to the party. Only 32 per cent of its 2021 voters cast a vote for the NDP in 2025. While about one third of the defectors voted Conservative, two-thirds voted Liberal.

Table 12.1B also compares voting in 2021 and 2025 as percentages of all those who voted in the 2025 election. Almost six in ten voters cast a vote for the same party in both elections and 18 per cent voted in 2025 but not in 2021. Of these 27 per cent of the electorate cast a Liberal vote and 24 per cent cast a vote for the Conservative Party

Table 12.1 | Vote flow from 2021 to 2025

A. How 2021 voters voted in 2025 (column percentages)

	2021 Vote						
2025 Vote	Non-voters	CPC	LPC	NDP	GPC	BQ	PPP
CPC	43	89	16	21	14	13	68
LPC	44	7	78	42	48	15	24
NDP	6	2	3	32	6	2	0
BQ	4	2	3	4	0	71	0
GPC	3	0	0	0	31	0	2
PPP	0	0	1	1	0	0	5

B. Combinations of voting in 2021 and 2025 (percentages of everyone voting in 2025)

	2021 Vote						
2025 Vote	Non-voters	CPC	LPC	NDP	GPC	BQ	PPP
CPC	7	24	5	2	0	1	1
LPC	8	2	27	4	1	1	0
NDP	1	1	1	3	0	0	0
BQ	1	1	1	0	0	3	0
GPC	1	0	0	0	1	0	0
PPP	0	0	0	0	0	0	0

in both elections. Notably only 3 per cent of voters cast an NDP vote in each election, and a higher percentage of the party's 2025 voters (4 per cent) switched to the Liberals.

As mentioned, 55 per cent of voters said that they voted for change in direction and policy rather than the party best able to handle the impact of Trump's decisions on Canada. Overall, these "change voters" broke heavily for the Conservatives – 57 per cent of voters who prioritized change ended up voting Conservative, compared to 30 per cent for Liberals. This demonstrates how Poilievre's message

Table 12.2 | Flow of the vote, 2021–25, among voters who voted for change (column percentages)

	2021 Vote						
2025 Vote	Non-voters	CPC	LPC	NDP	GPC	BQ	PPP
CPC	57	95	24	29	22	12	71
LPC	30	3	70	37	8	14	22
NDP	3	2	4	30	16	1	0
BQ	5	0	1	2	0	72	0
GPC	5	0	0	1	54	0	0
PPP	1	0	1	1	0	0	6

retained potent appeal and how important the election frame was for the outcome.

Under Carney, the Liberals managed to split the change vote to an unusual degree for an incumbent party. Three in ten self-identified change-focused voters chose the Liberals. Table 12.2 shows the flow of the vote for those who wanted change. Despite voting for change, 70 per cent of 2021 Liberal voters cast a Liberal vote in 2025. Only 30 per cent of 2021 Liberal voters who wanted change defected to one of the other parties. And the Liberals were able to benefit more than the Conservatives from 2021 NDP voters who were voting for change.

The change in Liberal leadership was critical. Carney was new and ran on a platform of "Liberal reset." He tacitly acknowledged public fatigue with the Trudeau era and promised a rejuvenated agenda (including some new policies on housing and fiscal responsibility) to signal that a Liberal government under him would not simply be "more of the same." Essentially, Carney blurred the line between continuity and change, allowing some voters to conclude that installing Carney was a form of change – or at least a safer change than electing the opposition amid international instability.

Abacus Data findings underline this point: without Trudeau's resignation, a hypothetical poll indicated the Liberals would have been trounced (28 per cent vs 46 per cent Conservative). Carney's leadership narrowed that gap substantially. In valence terms, Carney helped the Liberals regain some competence credibility on domestic issues (particularly economic management), or at least mitigate the sense of Liberal failure, thus reclaiming some voters who otherwise would have defected for change's sake.

At the same time, those who voted for the best party to handle the impact of Trump's decisions on Canada clearly broke in favour of the Liberal Party. Of those motivated by dealing with Trump, 61 per cent voted for the Liberal Party and only 23 per cent for the Conservative Party. In the absence of the Trump impact, the change vote might have been enough to alter the outcome in favour of the Conservative Party.

The result vindicated the valence politics model: voters weighed the parties' perceived performance on what mattered to them (be it confronting Trump or fixing the cost of living) and many opted for the party they deemed superior on the issue most salient to them. For a large segment, the immediate security of the nation took precedence, boosting the Liberals; for another large segment, domestic stagnation was paramount, boosting the Conservatives. In effect, 2025 became a referendum on two questions simultaneously – national leadership in crisis vs domestic renewal – with different voters answering one or the other as their priority.

THE NEW DEMOCRATIC PARTY

In 2025, the NDP was unable to take advantage of voter disenchantment with the Liberal Party. Hypothetically, progressive Liberal voters who were unwilling to vote Conservative as an expression of their unhappiness could at least express their dissatisfaction with the Liberal Party by voting NDP (see chapter 4). As we demonstrated, the Liberals managed to hold onto many of their own voters and even gained change-oriented voters from the NDP.

During the campaign, Singh struggled to appear relevant. He had performed well personally in the 2019 and 2021 debates and was popular among young progressives. As figure 12.5 shows, in 2021 Singh was viewed more favourably than either Trudeau or Erin O'Toole. By 2025, Singh was much less liked. The low personal favourability likely made it hard for the NDP to offer an alternative to the Liberal Party on the social, progressive dimensions of politics.

The NDP's platform, while progressive, was also seen as lacking relevance to the immediate anxieties of 2025. In a campaign dominated by national security and economic stability concerns, the

NDP's promises (e.g. expanded social programs, wealth tax) did not address the top valence issues on voters' minds. Voters, as demonstrated earlier, did not view the NDP as the best party to handle the top issues facing Canadians. In times of high salience valence issues, smaller parties without a record of delivering on those issues tend to be deserted by voters. The NDP was hence squeezed to the margins, experiencing a collapse comparable only to its 1993 nadir.

THE BLOC QUÉBÉCOIS

The Bloc Québécois also suffered losses, though not as cataclysmic as the NDP's. The number of Bloc seats fell from thirty-two to twenty-two, and its vote share in Quebec declined as well (though the Bloc still placed a strong third in many Quebec ridings). The Bloc's setback can be attributed to Quebec voters' strategic calculus and shifting issue salience (see chapter 5).

Normally, Bloc support is driven by the appeal of Quebec-first representation and Quebec nationalist or sovereignty sentiment. In 2025 Quebecers were the most likely region in the country to vote based on the external threat from Trump. Bloc Leader Yves-François Blanchet found himself in an unusual position: he could denounce Trump's threats, but as the leader of a separatist party, he could hardly present himself as the one to defend Canada against Trump.

Instead, both Liberal Carney and even Conservative Poilievre vied to convince Quebecers that they would best protect Quebec's interests in the federation during the crisis. Carney's message evidently carried more weight, given Liberal gains in Quebec. The Bloc was seen by some soft-nationalist voters as simply not relevant to the immediate challenge.

Another factor was that Trump's antagonism undercut the Bloc's core argument. The Bloc Québécois, which champions Quebec sovereignty, initially might have expected to benefit from any turmoil in federal leadership. Instead, Trump's threats to Canada made many Quebecers rally with English Canada rather than apart from it. In a crisis where national unity and strength were paramount, the Bloc's message was sidelined; voters judged that a regional protest party was not relevant or competent to deal with an aggressive US superpower. Trump's hostility was directed at Canada as a whole – Quebec included – and this arguably fostered a sense of Canadian unity in Quebec, at least temporarily. The idea of Quebec separating is a harder sell when an external bully is menacing the entire country; many Quebecers likely felt stronger solidarity with fellow Canadians and opted for a federalist party that could stand up for Quebec on the world stage.

The election results suggest this was effective: the Bloc fell from thirty-two seats to twenty-two, ceding many seats around Montreal and in soft-nationalist areas to the Liberals. In Quebec and beyond, Trump's re-election elevated a valence issue – defending national interests – that cut across typical partisan or regional lines, disadvantaging parties (like the Bloc or NDP) not seen as capable of rising to that challenge.

As evidence, the Bloc's support "collapsed" in areas where it had made gains in 2019 and 2021. The Bloc still finished third in the seat count, but its influence waned. Like the NDP, the Bloc was a victim of voters' strategic choice for parties perceived as able to govern. And in a valence contest about competence, the Bloc (which by design cannot form a federal government) was always going to be a secondary player. Its comparative advantage – advocating for Quebec's autonomy – simply wasn't a priority issue this time, and on valence dimensions like leadership strength, Blanchet could not compete with Carney or even Poilievre in voters' minds.

In summary, the fates of the NDP and Bloc Québécois in 2025 highlight how perceptions of relevance and competence drive strategic voting in a valence-oriented election. When voters saw the election as a high-stakes choice about Canada's future direction and security, votes for third parties were viewed by many as a luxury they could not afford. Unless a third party could demonstrate it was as credible on the dominant issues (which neither the NDP nor Bloc could, given neither was seen as likely to govern or handle Trump), its support was vulnerable. The result was a collapse of the NDP's support to levels unseen in a generation and a notable weakening of the Bloc's presence in Ottawa. These outcomes not only shaped the 2025 result but may have long-term implications for Canada's party system if two-party dynamics persist.

DETERMINANTS OF VOTE CHOICE

To assess the determinants of vote choice in the 2025 Canadian federal election, we estimate logistic regression models predicting the likelihood of voting for the Liberal and Conservative parties. Using data from the Abacus Data post-election survey, the models include a set of variables widely considered likely to influence electoral behaviour. These include voters' identification of the most important issue, party competence evaluations on that issue, leadership favourability scores, party identification, retrospective economic assessments, views on immigration, and whether respondents reported a general desire for change. We also incorporate controls for demographic, regional, and socio-economic characteristics. Together, these predictors allow us to isolate the factors most strongly associated with support for the two dominant parties in the 2025 contest, and to test the extent to which valence-based considerations structured voter decision-making.

THE LIBERAL VOTE

The results of the logistic regression model predicting support for the Liberal Party underscore the importance of leadership evaluations, strategic behaviour, and perceived competence in driving vote choice (results summarized in table 12.3). Among the strongest predictors of a Liberal vote is a favourable impression of Prime Minister Carney. All else being equal, those with a positive view of Carney were almost twenty-eight percentage points more likely to vote Liberal than those who did not hold that view. This confirms that Carney's personal brand was central to the party's recovery after Trudeau's resignation and that valence-based leadership attributes – such as competence, trustworthiness, and likability – were critical in the 2025 outcome.

In addition to leadership, strategic voting also played a significant role. Voters who reported voting strategically – for a candidate or party that was not their first choice – were sixteen percentage points more likely to vote Liberal. This dynamic highlights the persistence of anti-Conservative sentiment among portions of the electorate and possibly the desire to return a stronger government to respond to Trump. The model also reveals that negative evaluations of Donald Trump had a mobilizing effect: those who expressed a very negative impression of Trump were twelve points more likely to vote Liberal. This aligns with qualitative and media narratives suggesting that the perceived threat of a second Trump presidency in the US pushed many Canadian voters to opt for the stability and perceived competence at handling the US president which Carney projected.

Conversely, negative assessments of the economy significantly reduced the likelihood of supporting the Liberals, with voters rating the economy as "poor" being 8.5 points less likely to vote for the party. This suggests that despite Carney's economic credentials, concerns about affordability and financial insecurity continued to weigh heavily on voter decisions. Perhaps most striking, however, are the penalties associated with believing that the Conservatives – or, more extremely, the People's Party of Canada – were best able to handle the top national issue. These voters were thirty-nine and ninety-five percentage points less likely, respectively, to vote Liberal, reinforcing the extent to which perceived issue competence shaped partisan preferences in 2025.

It's also worth noting that none of the demographic, regional, or socio-economic variables were statistically significant predictors of Liberal voting controlling for all the other factors. Nor were feelings towards Poilievre or any specific issue priority. These findings reinforce the valence model of voting: rather than ideology alone, Canadians appeared to reward competence, punish perceived risk, and act strategically in a complex and high-stakes electoral environment.

THE CONSERVATIVE VOTE

The logistic regression model for Conservative Party support in 2025 also reveals a clear pattern consistent with valence politics. Positive impressions of Poilievre were among the most powerful predictors of Conservative support, increasing the likelihood of voting Conservative by over twenty-eight percentage points. This reinforces Poilievre's status as the defining figure of the Conservative campaign, whose personal image was central to the party's appeal. Conversely, a positive impression of Carney decreased the probability of a Conservative vote by sixteen points, illustrating the polarized nature of leadership evaluations in the 2025 campaign and Carney's ability to transcend partisanship to attract voters who hadn't voted Liberal in the previous few elections.

Issue competence also played a key role. Voters who believed the Conservatives were best able to handle the most important issue were twenty-six percentage points more likely to support the party, while those who thought the Liberals were better on the same issue were 22.5 points less likely to do so. These findings underscore the importance of party reputation on priority issues in shaping vote

Table 12.3 | Changes in probability for Liberal and Conservative parties associated with changes in statistically significant predictors

Predictor variable	Liberal	Conservative
Positive impression of party / leaders		
Carney	.276	-.162
Poilievre		.282
Singh		
Blanchet		
May		
Trump: Very positive		
Trump: Very negative	.12	
Inflation top issue		
Trump top issue		
Health care top issue		
Housing top issue		-18.5
Economy top issue		
Party best able to handle top issue		
LPC		-.225
CPC	-.386	.282
NDP		
BQ		
Green		
PPC	-.947	
Strategic voting	.164	
Canada should welcome fewer immigrants		
Change voter		.241

... continued

Table 12.3 | ... *continued*

Predictor variable	Liberal	Conservative
Poor economic evaluation	-.085	
Atlantic		
Quebec		
Ontario		
Prairies		
BC		
Female		
Age		
HS or less		
College		
Bachelor		
Post-graduate		
McKelvey R-square	.62	.73
Per cent correctly predicted	90%	94%

choice particularly in a context where affordability, dealing with the Trump administration, health care, and housing dominated public concern. Notably, those who identified housing as their top issue were significantly less likely to vote Conservative, suggesting the party struggled to reassure these voters despite its broader lead on economic management.

Finally, the strongest valence cue of all – a general desire for change – was highly predictive of Conservative support. Change voters were twenty-four points more likely to vote for the Conservatives than those who did not express such a desire, all else being equal. This aligns with other evidence from the campaign suggesting that the 2025 election, like many before it, was shaped as much by a rejection of the status quo as by active enthusiasm for an alternative. The

Conservatives were best positioned to absorb this anti-incumbent energy, translating it into one of the most cohesive and committed voting coalitions of the campaign and allowing it to achieve a vote share a national Conservative Party had not achieved since 1988.

CONCLUSION: COMPETENCE BEATS OUT CHANGE

The 2025 federal election vividly demonstrated the power of valence politics in shaping electoral outcomes. Competing frames of leadership competence in dealing with the Trump administration versus domestic change duelled for primacy in voters' minds. Carney's Liberals successfully made the election about who could "safeguard Canada and provide steady leadership" in a time of peril for enough voters, while Poilievre's Conservatives pushed Canadians to ask whether it was "time for a new government" after years of economic and social strain. Both questions were legitimate, and indeed both found resonance, which is why the race ended up so close. In the end, a slight plurality of Canadians gave greater weight to the competence and stability frame, allowing the Liberals to edge out a victory, but the strength of the change sentiment made it a hard-fought and polarized contest.

The theoretical lens of valence politics helps explain why voters behaved as they did. Voters in 2025 largely sorted based on performance-based judgments: Which leader and party do I trust to handle the issues I care most about? For those most alarmed by Trump's presidency and its fallout, the answer was clearly Carney and the Liberals. For those most fed up with inflation, declining affordability, and a sense of domestic stagnation, the answer was Poilievre and the Conservatives. The election became defined by two distinct ballot questions, which divided the electorate nearly down the middle. But both were valence issues, where virtually all voters wanted Canadian sovereignty and a strong economy.

Data from the Abacus post-election survey underscore that issue salience was crucial. When Trump's threats were front-page news, security and stability concerns spiked, boosting Liberal support. As the campaign progressed and those fears slightly waned, the perennial desire for change and focus on cost-of-living reasserted itself, boosting Conservative support. Voters' emotional responses – fear of Trump, anger at the Liberals, hope for change, or fear of the unknown – interacted with these issue frames, moving different segments of the electorate in different directions. The outcome was a kind of equilibrium: neither frame completely overwhelmed the other, resulting in a minority government rather than a landslide.

The 2025 result was, in a sense, a validation of Carney's "competence" appeal and a repudiation of Trump-influenced populism – but also a warning signal. The Liberals extended their "decade of rule," an unusual accomplishment, yet they did so by the slimmest of margins and thanks to extraordinary circumstances. The Conservatives, despite losing, showed they could mobilize a huge base of discontent; their strongest popular vote in years suggests that absent the Trump factor, they were well-positioned to win. The determinants of the vote point to an increasingly polarized electorate, divided by values, priorities, and perceptions of competence rather than by demographics, region, or socio-economic attributes of voters. The collapse of the NDP and erosion in Bloc support in this election further emphasizes how, when voters converge on valence judgments, smaller parties can be marginalized. Whether the NDP and Bloc can recover may depend on a lower-stakes context in future elections, or electoral reforms; otherwise, Canadian federal politics could be dominated by two major parties moving forward.

The 2025 Canadian federal election serves as a case study in valence politics at work. Voters were called to evaluate who could better deliver good governance: the emphasis was on leadership, competence, trust, and performance rather than specific policy positions. It was an election where frames and perceptions fractured traditional partisan loyalty – as seen by large-scale strategic voting and partisan switching. For scholars and observers, 2025 reinforces the idea that Canadian elections (especially in turbulent times) are decided by who owns the narrative of being best able to govern. Carney's Liberals won that narrative by a narrow margin, thanks in no small part to an assist from events abroad and an effective campaign. Poilievre's Conservatives came up short, but their focus on change nearly succeeded. The outcome, a re-elected Liberal minority, reflected a divided electorate – one split between craving stability and craving renewal. As Canada moves beyond 2025, the challenge for the governing Liberals will be to deliver on both fronts: providing competent, steady leadership and addressing the demand for domestic renewal. Failing that, the strong currents of change evident in 2025 may well surge again, perhaps more forcefully, in the next campaign.

NOTES

1 David Coletto, "Abacus Data Poll: No 'GST Tax Holiday' or 'Trump' Bump as Conservatives Hold 23-Point Lead over the Liberals," Abacus Data, 8 December 2024, https://abacusdata.ca/canadian-politics-abacus-data-december/.

2 The survey was conducted online with 1,500 adult Canadians over the age of 18 from 29 April to 2 May 2025. It was paid for by Abacus Data.

3 Anthony Downs, *An Economic Theory of Democracy* (New York: Harper & Row, 1957); Richard Johnston, Patrick Fournier, and Richard Jenkins, "Party Location and Party Support: Unpacking Competing Models," *Journal of Politics* 62, no. 4 (2000): 1,145–60.

4 Harold D. Clarke, Thomas J. Scotto, and Allan Kornberg, "Valence Politics and Economic Crisis: Electoral Choice in Canada 2008," *Electoral Studies* 30, no. 3 (2011): 438–49.

5 David Coletto, "Abacus Data Poll: Post-Trudeau Resignation, Conservative Lead Grows to 27. Freeland and Carney Well Ahead of Others on Recognizability, Familiarity, and Net Favourable Impression," Abacus Data, 9 January 2025, https://abacusdata.ca/canadian-politics-abacus-data-post-trudeau-resignation/.

6 Jean-François Daoust and Ruth Dassonneville, "Beyond Nationalism and Regionalism: The Stability of Economic Voting in Canada," *Canadian Journal of Political Science* 51, no. 3 (2018): 553–71.

7 Harold D. Clarke, Thomas J. Scotto, and Marianne C. Stewart, "Canada Votes in a COVID Election" in Jon H. Pammett and Christopher Dornan (eds), *The Canadian Federal Election of 2021* (Montreal and Kingston: McGill-Queen's University Press, 2022), 295–321.

8 Amanda Bittner, "Leaders Always Mattered: The Persistence of Personality in Canadian Elections," *Electoral Studies* 54 (2018): 297–302; Harold D. Clarke et al., *Absent Mandate: Strategies and Choices in Canadian Elections* (Toronto: University of Toronto Press, 2019).

9 David Coletto, "Poilievre's Conservatives Lead by 13 over Liberals. A Deep Dive on Why More than Half of Canadians Have a Negative Impression of Justin Trudeau," Abacus Data, 6 November 2023, https://abacusdata.ca/poilievres-conservatives-lead-by-13-over-liberals-a-deep-dive-on-why-more-than-half-of-canadians-have-a-negative-impression-of-justin-trudeau/.

10 The online survey was conducted with 2,500 adult Canadians over the age of 18 from 24 April to 27 April 2025.

11 Meg Kinnard and Mike Householder, "What Canadian Voters Had to Say bbout Their Election and Donald Trump," *Independent*, 29 April 2025, https://www.independent.co.uk/news/world/americas/canada-election-results-trump-mark-carney-b2741307.html.

12 David Coletto and Eddie Sheppard, "How an Emerging Precarity Mindset Is Impacting Public Opinion and the Canadian Election," Abacus Data, 28 March 2025, https://abacusdata.ca/2025-election-precarity-mindset/.

13

The Future of Minority Government in Canada

Jon H. Pammett and Lawrence LeDuc

The 2025 Canadian federal election confounded virtually all attempts to predict its outcome. A year earlier, even six months earlier, the ultimate winner looked certain to lose badly. A Conservative landslide was predicted. Then, following a series of dramatic developments, predictions changed to a Liberal victory. The result, yet another minority government, continued a trend of minority governments established this century. Since 2000, six of the nine Canadian federal elections have resulted in a minority government.

The result was certainly a surprise to the political parties, given the way the campaign had evolved. The Liberals, initially hopeful that they would have a four-year window to enact an agenda of economic adjustment which might require painful decisions and sacrifices, were forced by the minority outcome to reevaluate their plans. The Conservatives, who not long before had expected to form the government, were forced to abandon longer term plans for repositioning, and to bring forward a short-term opposition strategy in the midst of leadership uncertainty. Both the NDP and the Bloc, having resigned themselves to yet another period of self-reflection and challenge for relevance, were suddenly able to hope that they might play a balance of power role similar to the one they had played in the previous Parliament.

Recent Canadian electoral history has shown that the conditions are often ripe for the production of a minority government. The 2000 majority victory of the Chrétien Liberals came amidst disarray in the party system. The Reform Party, itself relatively new, had gone through an awkward metamorphosis into the Canadian Alliance, chosen Stockwell Day as its new leader instead of Preston Manning, the founder of Reform, and was staking its hopes on a breakthrough in Ontario which failed to materialize.[1] Other opposition parties maintained their vote shares, but none made a breakthrough, and the Liberals prevailed. However, the period of Liberal infighting which ensued between the faction supporting Chrétien and the faction championing Paul Martin, who eventually replaced Chrétien, sparked a series of minority governments, first under Martin in 2004, and two minority governments under Stephen Harper, which lasted until 2011.

The three federal elections (2004, 2006, 2008) which produced minority governments during this decade shared a number of characteristics. Most crucially, the runner up party (the Conservatives in 2004 and the Liberals in 2006 and 2008) received 30 per cent of the vote or less (26 per cent in 2008). Together with reasonably strong showings by the NDP and the Bloc Québécois, this tripartite opposition prevented the winning party from achieving a majority of the seats in Parliament. It was only with the collapse of the Liberal Party in 2011 (down to 19 per cent support) and the rise of support for the NDP that the Conservatives were able to achieve their majority. The other element in the Conservative victory in 2011 was the modest increase in their own vote, up to 40 per cent from 38 per cent in 2008.

The Liberal majority under Justin Trudeau in 2015 was also achieved with 40 per cent of the vote, and a weakened opposition. The Conservatives dropped to 32 per cent, the NDP was down from 30 to 20 per cent, and the Bloc was reduced to under 20 per cent in Quebec, with many of the seat gains going to the Liberals in that province. Then, as the Liberal vote started to decline, the goal of majority government status eluded them in the elections of 2019 and 2021.

The conditions for majority governments to be achieved in Canadian federal elections, then, appear to be twofold. The winning party needs to achieve 40 per cent of the vote or so. But they also need support for the opposition parties to be substantially lower and preferably divided. The problem for a majority in 2025 was that the victorious Liberals were not alone in achieving a high vote percentage. Despite their vote total of 43.7 per cent (a height not achieved since the Mulroney sweep of 1984), the Conservative vote total was also high (41.3 per cent). The condition of the collapse of the smaller parties was certainly present in 2025, but the close two-party race between the major parties, together with the twenty-two seats won by the Bloc in Quebec, prevented the majority.

But what is it that generates all the volatility we have seen in Canadian electoral outcomes in the first place? For example, a Conservative majority government in 2011 was followed by a Liberal one in 2015. We have seen the NDP go from 9 per cent in 2000 to 18 per cent in 2008, then an historic 31 per cent in 2011, 18 per cent in 2021, and fall to 6 per cent in 2025. Do we have lots of NDPers in Canada or not so many? And how could the Bloc vary from 19 per cent of the Quebec vote in 2015 to 32 per cent in 2019 and 2021, and then go down to 27 per cent in 2025? And how could the polls prior to the 2025 election go from forecasting a Conservative majority to a Liberal majority to no majority in less than a year? The answer to those questions lies in the flexibility of partisanship in Canada.

FLEXIBLE PARTISANSHIP

From the first Canadian election studies in the 1960s, it has been clear that explanations of Canadian federal election outcomes had to account for substantial movement of voters from one party to another between pairs of elections. Any model postulating that most voters feel strongly about "their party" and support it through good times and bad is not in accord with the findings of these studies. In reality, partisanship, or "party identification" as it is sometimes called, is not strongly held by many Canadians, and is often changeable depending on the context of any given election. It is also not strongly related to social characteristics of voters. In previous work, we have referred to most Canadians' ties to political parties as "flexible."[2]

Of course, the generalization that most Canadians are flexible in their partisan ties does not apply to everybody. We all know people who are committed strongly to their party and who support it at the polls no matter what. But research has shown that only about a third of the electorate falls into this category. Most voters have either changed their designation of which party they feel closest to over the years or at least have only weak feelings of attachment to a party. Either way, they see themselves as free of past psychological commitments to a party and able to make up their minds which party to support (or indeed whether to vote at all) depending on the issues and politicians on offer on any given occasion.

The flexibility of Canadian partisanship has gone along with (whether cause or effect, or both, can be debated) considerable change in the Canadian federal party system. The Liberal Party has been relatively consistent throughout the 150 plus years of its existence, but the conservative side of the spectrum has seen the Liberal-Conservative Party, the Conservative Party, the Progressive Conservative Party, the Reform Party, the Canadian Alliance, the Democratic Reform caucus, and the Conservative Party of Canada over the same period. We have also seen the rise and fall of the Progressives, the Social Credit Party, the Créditistes, the Bloc Populaire and others. The CCF became the New Democratic Party in 1961. Since 1993, there has been an ebb and flow of support for the Bloc Québécois such that it has been the official opposition party in Parliament, as well as the subject of predictions of its imminent demise. Canadian voters have moved toward, and away from, all of these parties depending on the issues of the day, the leaders and other politicians associated with them, their record, and actions in and out of government.

Curiously, perhaps, one consistent theme in Canadian elections has been party promises of change, a theme which almost always resonates with a receptive audience. The Liberals, and other parties farther to the left, want change to improve services and redistribution of benefits and wealth. When in opposition, their message is clear – more needs to be done. The Conservatives, and parties of the right, also want change, and also agree more needs to be done, sometimes, and that things at times need to change in the other direction, to undo the unwise policies put in place by their opponents, and furthermore to change the financial plan to avoid spending too much or running a deficit. Opposition parties, and incumbent governments seeking reelection, are united in their messages that change of some type is needed.

The "change" theme is clearly indicated by the 2025 election. The Conservatives under Pierre Poilievre made their demands for change their sole message for years. The country needed change from the Liberals and particularly from leader Justin Trudeau, change from the policy of carbon taxation, change from having too much inflation, change from not having enough housing, change from spending too much money, change from whatever you wanted change from (see chapter 3). The NDP wanted change from not having enough health care programs and from having an inadequate health care system in general (see chapter 4). The Bloc wanted change from having too little money spent on Quebec (see chapter 5). The Greens wanted change from degrading the environment (see chapter 6). The Peoples' Party (see chapter 6) wanted change in ... where to start? And the governing Liberals were also offering change – change in the leader with a new prime minister, change in the carbon tax policy by removing it, change in the attitudes and policies towards the United States (one of the few areas where the Conservatives were not seen as proposing sufficient change), and, as it turned, out, a key area for change (see chapter 2). The electoral arena is where a flexible electorate has opportunity to exercise their flexibility.

Furthermore, the flexible electorate is willing to engage in strategic voting. Rather than making a voting choice based on some dimension such as ideological affinity or leader preference, strategic voting involves a wider set of factors related to the overall political situation. For the strategic voter, the top priority might be keeping some political party or leader out of power or choosing the best alternative to deal with the larger world situation and could mean casting a vote for someone other than their first choice. Strategic assessments of the most meaningful vote choice can take place at a number of levels: the country, province, or the constituency. If one's first choice is not competitive in one's riding, for example, one might well opt for a second choice in order to ensure that a lower choice does not win. Under the current single member plurality electoral system, temptations to make such strategic choices bedevil small party supporters in all areas of the country. With larger parties, there are still regions where they are uncompetitive, and where strategic second choices are made.

A certain amount of strategic voting takes place in every election. In the 2025 election, however, strategic voting seemed to exist at a level unprecedented in recent years. Many of the smaller parties lost substantial portions of their vote: support for the Green Party fell from 2.3 to 1.2 per cent; for the Peoples' Party from 4.9 to 0.7 per cent; and, most dramatically, support for the NDP dropped from 17.8 to 6.3 per cent. Strategic choices were being made between the Liberals and Conservatives for all the reasons the analyses in the chapters of this book make clear. The flexible partisan ties of Canadians allowed these choices to be made.

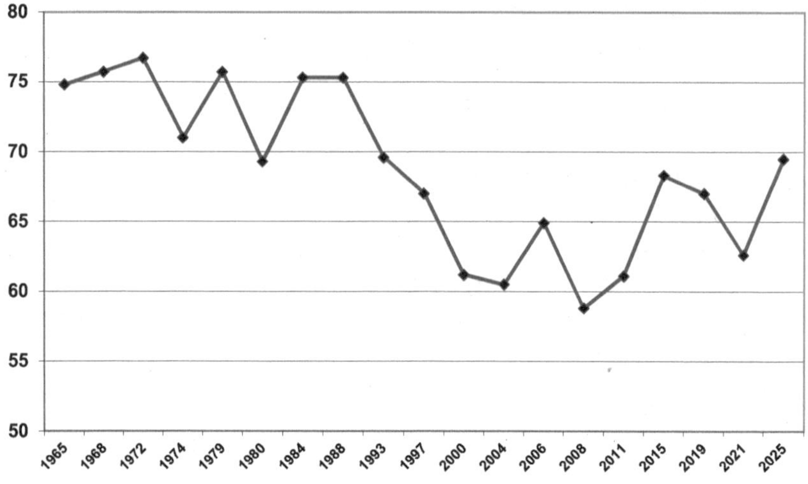

Figure 13.1 | Turnout in Canadian federal elections, 1965–2025
Source: Elections Canada: www.elections.ca.

AN INCREASE IN VOTER TURNOUT

Canada has been experiencing a long-term decline in turnout in federal elections, punctuated by occasional short-term increases in particular elections where the circumstances heighten public interest and desire to participate.[3] Younger voters, cohorts entering the electorate at each of the federal elections since 1993, have tended to vote at lower rates. Older voters are more likely to be imbued with a sense of civic duty whereby voting is a basic element of democratic citizenship. As they leave the electorate, they are replaced by those for whom the vote is more of a choice to be determined by the nature of the factors of importance in the individual election taking place. In 2025, there was a sharp increase in the voting turnout, from 63 per cent in 2021 to 69 per cent.

Figure 13.1 shows the turnout levels in federal elections since 1965. We have extended the data back that far to show the previous turnout levels considered normal in the earlier period; with a couple of exceptions about three-quarters of the eligible voters could be counted on to vote at any given election. Of course, this was not necessarily the same 75 per cent, as some people, whom we have

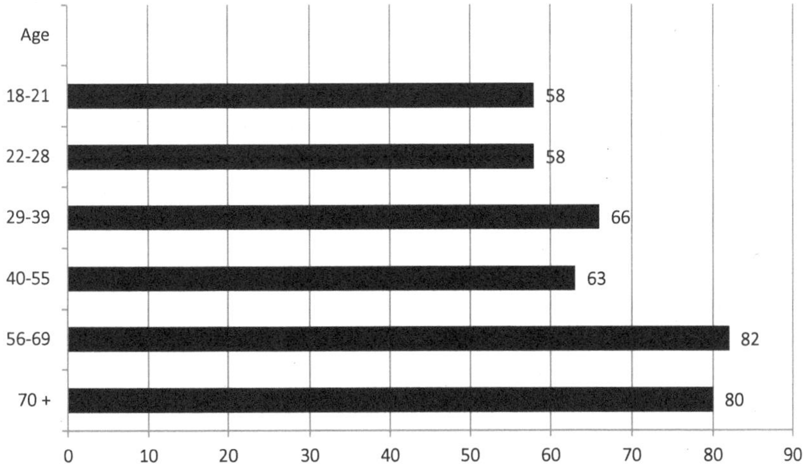

Figure 13.2 | Estimated voting by age groups, 2025 federal election

Source: Abacus post-election survey. Data weighted by actual voting percentage. N=1500.

referred to as "transient voters," moved in and out of the active electorate.[4] But in the period before the 1993 election that level was taken for granted; in fact some consideration was given to ways in which the turnout might be boosted a little higher.[5]

The turnout decline which began in 1993 reached its nadir in the federal election of 2008, when turnout dipped below the 60 per cent mark. It has since rebounded to a new normal level somewhere in the middle of the 60–70 per cent range depending on the circumstances. As can be seen in figure 13.1, there were rises in turnout in the elections of 2006 and 2015, both associated with changes in government, bringing the Stephen Harper Conservatives and the Justin Trudeau Liberals to power, respectively. Once the initial rise takes place, however, the decline starts again, as the 2006 rise was followed by lower rates in 2008 and 2011, and the 2015 rise by declines in 2019 and 2021. The turnout rise in 2025 has taken us back to more or less where we were ten years earlier, after the 2015 election.

The long-term downward trend in turnout is concerning, but in the short-term interpretation of the 2025 election, the relatively higher turnout meant that there were a considerable number of voters moving into the active electorate who were not there four years earlier. These were of two types: new voters and returning voters. If these two groups had gone disproportionately in one direction, they could well have tilted the outcome toward one of the parties. If, on the other hand, they had split relatively equally between the Liberals and Conservatives, that would have simply accentuated the two-party race which seemed to develop during the campaign. While we are not yet ready to predict that the long-term turnout decline is coming to an end, the increase in turnout in the 2025 election to levels approaching 70 per cent suggests that possibility. But we also know that the high level of interest generated by the events surrounding this election certainly contributed to that higher turnout and may not be replicated in future.

The higher rates of voting in this election were particularly noticeable in both the youngest and oldest age groups (figure 13.2). Among those coming of voting age in 2025, the estimated rate of turnout (58 per cent) was much higher than we have found for a comparable group in previous studies.[6] It was equally high among the group which reached voting age in the 2019 or 2021 elections. And the higher rate among the group that had been old enough to vote in the 2015 election, an election that also saw an increase in voter participation, suggests that this cohort may continue to participate in future elections, having developed a "habit of voting." However, the younger and middle-aged cohorts still vote at rates below the overall rate (69.45 per cent). It is the oldest cohorts, who continue to participate at high rates in elections, who are responsible for the voting rate to be as high as it is. Administrative changes such as the greater use of advance polls and mail-in ballots will continue to support high rates of participation among this group, but as they leave the electorate and are replaced by less participative groups, the overall turnout rate may return to its downward trajectory.

THE RE-EMERGENCE OF NATIONAL UNITY ISSUES

As we outlined in our book *Dynasties and Interludes*, although a wide diversity of specific issues occurs in Canadian federal elections, there have been only a few general types. From the beginning, the economy, the prosperity of the country, has been prominent in the campaign programs of all the parties.[7] Since the Great Depression and Second World War periods, social welfare issues, including health care, have joined economic issues in prominence. Both economic and social issues were prominent in the 2025 election (see chapter 12).

It is the third type of issue, those dealing with national unity, which set the 2025 election apart from recent ones by pushing themselves to the fore. National unity issues have often taken the form of accommodating regional interests. With some regions of the country, like the Atlantic, these have been ones of economic support. With Quebec, they have involved linguistic and cultural recognition as well. With the West, though economically based, national unity policy discussion has involved, not only support for the specific resource-based economies of the region, but also accommodation of ideologically based positions such as deficit reduction and social conservatism. Assuring national unity by accommodating Quebec has been a traditional pillar of Liberal support, while the Conservatives have emphasized the importance of the interests of the West.

There were indeed some aspects of the 2025 election which involved the particular economic and cultural interests of the regions. These were subsumed, however, into one major national unity issue which overwhelmed much of the discussion leading up to and throughout the campaign – relations with the United States. The re-election of Donald Trump as president of the United States in November of 2024 was in itself an anxiety-inducing development for Canadians, given the uneasy relationship between the two countries which characterized Trump's first administration from 2016–20. Concern reached new heights, however, with Trump's threats to Canada's economy and national sovereignty in the run-up to this election. The chapters in this book have described the American plans to diminish the Canadian economy as a way to absorb the country. The tables of important issues in the 2025 election reflected the threat to Canadian sovereignty and economic well-being they contained. All parties reacted with condemnation and policy counter-measure proposals.

The 2025 Canadian election was not the first where relations with the United States were an issue. The 1988 election was dominated by discussion of the newly negotiated free trade agreement with the US. Most recently, dealing with the first Trump administration and re-negotiating NAFTA featured as issues in both the 2019 and 2021 elections. The Trudeau Liberals claimed success at securing Canada's interests with the new economic treaty, whereas the other parties pointed to its deficiencies. Looking farther back, we can point to such events as the dispute over whether to accept US Bomarc nuclear missiles in 1963, and the Liberal finance minister Walter Gordon's proposal of a Foreign Investment Review Board to slow American business takeovers in 1965. In general, however, these issues ended up being of relatively minor importance in determining the results of these elections.

Perhaps the most telling, if imperfect, comparative case for the 2025 election can be found if we look back to the 1940 election. A critical external threat had become apparent for Canada's political leadership, but the overall dimensions were not yet clear. The Liberals were in power, and had been since 1935, when a Conservative government had become extremely unpopular. Prime Minister Mackenzie King proclaimed that the Liberals had the experience to run the government in uncertain times, and the Conservatives could not be trusted to do so. The voters returned a Liberal government.

ATTITUDES TO MINORITY GOVERNMENT

Minority government was the context of the 2025 election, both before and afterwards. With the minority outcome of the 2021 election, Prime Minister Trudeau moved quickly to stabilize the situation by signing an agreement with the NDP in which the NDP agreed to support the government on supply and confidence votes in return for progress on policies and issues that it prioritized. The agreement lasted until September 2024, when Jagmeet Singh withdrew his support, but it had allowed the minority Liberal government to survive for most of its term without risking defeat in Parliament and an early election. Canada has been in a minority government situation in the federal Parliament for approximately two-thirds of the period since the turn of the century (2004–11 and 2019–25). But this collective outcome was not necessarily the desired one for individual Canadians. Are voters happy with minority outcomes, or do they perhaps despair at the lack of stability that comes with a parliament in which the government might fall at any moment? And if minority governments continue in future will people be upset, content, or just resigned? The Liberal-NDP agreement had removed the sense of instability sometimes associated with minority governments, but did people see it as delivering better outcomes for Canadians as a result?

Table 13.1 | Preferred outcomes of the last three federal elections (%)

Preferred election outcome	2019 Election	2021 Election	2025 Election
Liberal majority	21	19	31
Conservative majority	25	23	29
NDP majority	13	17	6
TOTAL MAJORITY	(59)	(57)	(69)
Liberal minority	15	12	11
Conservative minority	9	8	10
NDP minority	5	5	3
Other government	4	4	3
Don't know	10	13	8

Note: 2019 CES (n=5142); 2021 CES (n=4065); 2025 Abacus (n=2273)

It is difficult to give definitive answers to these questions, but survey data can provide some tentative answers. First, we can look at the preferred outcomes of recent elections through the opinions of survey responses after the last three federal elections, including 2025 (table 13.1).

It seems clear from table 13.1 that most voters are not trying to create a minority government. Given a choice of election outcomes they would prefer, more respondents to surveys after the last three federal elections opted for a majority government in preference to a minority, although they differed as to which party should be occupying the government benches. This preference for majority culminated in a total of 69 per cent of those surveyed in 2025 who chose one of the Liberals, Conservatives, or NDP to form the majority. Those wanting one of those three parties to form a government with a minority of the seats constituted only 24 per cent. And while the 2025 figures show that the context does matter somewhat, the

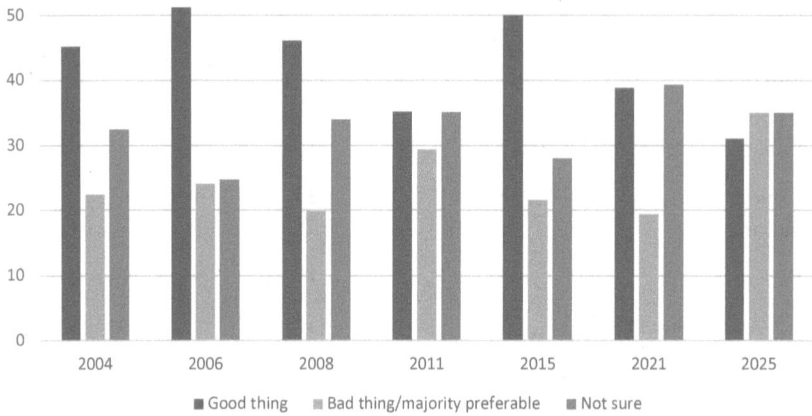

Figure 13.3 | Are minority governments good or bad?

Note: 2004–2021 CES. (2019 Question not asked). "Are minority governments a good thing or a bad thing?" 2025 Abacus. "Since 2000, 6 of 9 federal elections have resulted in minority governments (where the winner has fewer than half the seats in Parliament). Do you think that, in general, minority governments are a good thing or majority governments are preferable?"

preference for majority government over minority in the two previous elections is still substantial.

Even though Canadians prefer majority governments, an additional question asked in a number of past Canadian election studies shows that they do not think that minorities are a bad thing. Figure 13.3 gives the distribution of opinion back to 2004.

Canadian election surveys conducted during the minority government years between 2004 and 2011 indicate that the public was seemingly quite happy to be governed in a minority government situation. This belief culminated in a figure of 51 per cent who felt this was true after the Stephen Harper victory in 2006. Then, when Harper precipitated the 2008 election to try to achieve a majority, most of the public with an opinion (46 per cent) thought the continued minority that resulted was a good thing. Even when Harper achieved his majority in 2011, 35 per cent thought a minority might have been better. Perhaps surprisingly, there is little difference between those who cast their votes for different parties in holding this opinion. For example, 46 per cent of Liberal voters in 2015 thought minority governments were a good thing; Conservative voters were at 47 per cent.

The situation was a bit different in the Abacus survey conducted after the 2025 election. As the bars show in figure 13.3, the approval of minority government as in general a good thing was somewhat lower, at 31 per cent, in spite of (or perhaps because of) the Liberal-NDP supply agreement. We decided to word the other alternative to ask whether majority government would be preferable, and a slight plurality (35 per cent) said it would have been. In a sense, the fact that both the Conservatives and Liberals were insistent in their campaign messages that they needed a strong majority to deal with the United States and with the nation's economic problems likely had an effect on public attitudes towards a potential minority situation. Interestingly, despite the fact that the Liberals won the election, once again those voting Liberal and Conservative had identical patterns of responses to this survey item (31 per cent thinking minorities are a good thing). Only NDP voters were high on this item; understandably, a full 44 per cent of them liked minorities better.

Overall, it seems a fair assessment of public opinion to say that, even if minority government is not their first preference, particularly on occasions like 2025 when much of the rhetoric was arguing for a strong government to coordinate a response to threats from the US, many Canadians are willing to put up with it, to the point of concluding that it is "a good thing."Part of this positive attitude toward minority government may have to do with a Canadian willingness to compromise. To this end, in the Abacus 2025 survey, we asked a simple follow-up question about this. It read: "In a minority government situation, governing parties usually need to compromise to stay in power. Are such compromises a good thing or a bad thing for the country?" Answers were quite one-sided here, with 41 per cent saying the compromises minority government make are good for the country, and only 14 per cent saying they are a bad thing. We do need to mention that this may not be a question many people have considered very much, because 46 per cent took the position that it was "hard to say." Nevertheless, the initial reaction was not hostile to the uncertain legislative environment that comes with minority government.

And what of logistics? What should a minority government do to stay in power, along with compromises? We asked people to choose between formal agreements and ad hoc support-seeking strategies. The results show a clear preference for the statement: "The largest party seeks support for their policies as they go along" (63 per cent) as opposed to "the largest party forms a long-term coalition with another party" (37 per cent). This aversion to formal coalitions may simply be a result of the scarcity of such arrangements throughout Canadian history. Even the "confidence and supply" agreement the NDP negotiated with the Liberals after the 2021 election was not such a coalition, even though Jagmeet Singh announced in fall 2024 that he was "ripping up the agreement." The result, however, is evidently a tolerance for the uncertainty that comes from seeking ad hoc agreements to stay in power, and the compromises inevitably included in such behaviour.

CONCLUSION

The tolerance Canadians appear to show toward minority governments is fortunate, because all indications are that the future may see many more of them. The Liberals and Conservatives seem likely to maintain substantial support in the next few years. The NDP was severely hit by defections of its potential supporters in 2025 but will likely rebound toward more of its usual vote in upcoming elections, particularly if social issues on which its support is based push to the fore. The Bloc Québécois, which revived in 2019 with new leadership following its disastrous results in the 2011 and 2015 elections, now seems positioned for longer term relevance in Quebec politics, alongside an increasingly popular PQ party, especially if a new independence referendum takes place. Short of a collapse by one of the major parties, it may well be that the 2025 federal election was as close as we are likely to get to a majority government for many elections to come.

NOTES

1 Faron Ellis, "The More Things Change ... the Alliance Campaign," in Jon H. Pammett and Christopher Dorrnan (eds), *The Canadian Federal Election of 2000* (Toronto: Dundurn Press, 2001), 59–89.

2 A summary of the findings behind this concept are summarized in Harold D. Clarke et al, *Absent Mandate: Strategies and Choices in Canadian Elections* (Toronto: University of Toronto Press, 2019), chapter 2.

3 For a more extensive account of the reasons for the decline and the occasional reversals of it, see Jon H. Pammett and Lawrence LeDuc,

"Voting Turnout in 2019: The Long and the Short of It," in Jon H. Pammett and Christopher Dornan (eds), *The Canadian Federal Election of 2019* (Montreal and Kingston: McGill-Queen's University Press, 2020), 246–64.

4 Harold D. Clarke et al., *Political Choice in Canada* (Toronto: McGraw-Hill Ryerson, 1979), 359–65.

5 Royal Commission on Electoral Reform and Party Financing, *Final Report* (Ottawa: Canada Communication Group – Publishing, 1991).

6 Lawrence LeDuc and Jon H. Pammett, "The Elusive Liberal Dynasty," in Jon H. Pammett and Christopher Dornan (eds), *The Canadian Federal Election of 2021* (Montreal and Kingston: McGill-Queen's University Press, 2022), 329–33.

7 Lawrence LeDuc and Jon H. Pammett, *Dynasties and Interludes: Past and Present in Canadian Electoral Politics Second Edition* (Toronto: Dundurn Press, 2016). A third edition of this book will be published in 2026.

APPENDIX

Results of the 2025 Canadian Federal Election

	Canada		NL		PEI		NS		NB		QC		ON		MAN		SAS		ALB		BC		Terr
	Seats	Votes	S	V	S	V	S	V	S	V	S	V	S	V	S	V	S	V	S	V	S	V	S
BQ	22	6.3									22	27.7											
CPC	144	41.3	3	39.7		36.9	1	35.3	4	40.7	10	23.3	52	43.8	7	46.4	13	64.6	34	63.6	19	41.2	
GPC	1	1.2		0.1		2.2		0.9		1.7		0.9		1.1		0.7		0.5		0.4	1	2.1	
LPC	169	43.7	4	54.1	4	57.6	10	57.4	6	53.6	45	42.6	70	49.2	6	40.7	1	26.6	2	27.8	20	41.8	2
NDP	7	6.3		5.5		2.4		5.1		2.9	1	4.5		4.8	1	11.0		7.5	1	6.3	3	13.0	1
PPC	0	0.7		0.2		0.5		0.9		0.8		0.8		0.7		0.9		0.5		0.9		0.4	
Other		0.3		0.4		0.4		0.4		0.3		0.3		0.2		0.2		0.2		0.8		0.4	
Total	343	100%	7		4		11		10		78		122		14		14		37		43		3

(Source: Elections Canada Official Results)

Contributors

CHRISTOPHER ADAMS is the rector (college president) of St Paul's College and adjunct professor in the Department of Political Science at the University of Manitoba. For twenty years he served in senior positions in the public opinion research industry. He currently lectures and writes on polling and politics and is a regular commentator and election desk analyst for CBC, CTV, and other media outlets. Dr Adams holds three degrees including a PhD in political science from Carleton University.

DAVID COLETTO is the founder and CEO of Abacus Data and an adjunct professor in the Arthur Kroeger College of Public Affairs at Carleton University.

CHRISTOPHER DORNAN taught at Carleton University for thirty-three years, where he served for nine years as director of the School of Journalism and Communication and six years as director of the Arthur Kroeger College of Public Affairs. He holds a bachelor of journalism from Carleton University, an MA in the history and philosophy of science from the University of Cambridge, and a PhD in communication from McGill University. He has worked as a reporter for the *Edmonton Journal*, an editor and editorial writer for the *Ottawa Citizen*, and a columnist for CBC National Radio. His academic work has been published in *Critical Studies in Communication*, *Science as Culture*, *Media Information Australia*, *Topia*, the *Canadian Medical Association Journal*, the *Media Studies Journal*, and the research reports of the Royal Commission on Electoral Reform and Party Financing. He was a principal writer of the

Public Policy Forum's 2017 report on the state of the Canadian news media, *The Shattered Mirror: News, Democracy and Trust in the Digital Age,* and its follow-up, *The Shattered Mirror 5 Years On*. This is the ninth volume of Canadian election studies he has co-edited with Jon H. Pammett.

FARON ELLIS is an Alberta political scientist who taught politics at Lethbridge Polytechnic for twenty-seven years. He is a graduate of the University of Calgary (BA '87 and PhD '97) and Carleton University (MA '89) political science programs. This is his eleventh contribution to the Canadian Federal Election book series.

ADRIAN HAREWOOD is a writer and broadcaster and associate professor of journalism at Carleton University in Ottawa. He is the host of the current affairs podcast *In Bed with The Elephant*. He was host of CBC Ottawa's drive-home radio show *All in a Day* for three years and anchor of *CBC TV Ottawa News at Six* for thirteen years. He has hosted CBC's *The Current*, *As It Happens*, *Sounds Like Canada, Metro Morning, The House, Counterspin, Hot Type,* and *Power & Politics*. He was also the host of programs on PBS and BRAVO. He has won a Canadian Screen Award for Best Local News Anchor and was nominated for Best Interviewer. His writing has appeared in the *Globe and Mail*, *Ricochet*, *Toronto Star*, *Canadian Dimension* and the Halifax *Chronicle Herald*. His academic work is published in *Facts and Frictions*.

BROOKE JEFFREY is professor of political science at Concordia University, where she served for many years as director of the Graduate Program in Public Administration and Public Policy, and is past president of the Canadian Association of Programs in Public Administration (CAPPA). A former senior Liberal adviser, she is the author of six books on Canadian politics including *Divided Loyalties: The Liberal Party of Canada 1984–2006* (2010) and *Road to Redemption: The Liberal Party of Canada 2006–2019* (2019), both published by University of Toronto Press. This is her eighth contribution to this book series.

RICHARD JENKINS (PhD, University of British Columbia, 1999) is recently retired after twenty-five years working in senior roles in the market research industry in Canada. He is now focused on travel, cycling, and cooking while continuing his passion for understanding and writing about public opinion.

LAWRENCE LEDUC is professor emeritus of political science at the University of Toronto. His publications include *Absent Mandate: Strategies and Choices in Canadian Elections* (with Harold D. Clarke, Jane Jenson, and Jon H. Pammett), *Comparing Democracies* (with Richard G. Niemi and Pippa Norris), *Dynasties and Interludes: Past and Present in Canadian Electoral Politics* (with Jon H. Pammett, Judith I. McKenzie, and André Turcotte), and *The Politics of Direct Democracy* as well as articles on voting, elections, and related topics in North American and European political science journals. In 2015, Professor LeDuc received the Mildred A. Schwartz lifetime achievement award from the Canadian politics section of the American Political Science Association.

LOUIS MASSICOTTE is a retired professor who taught in the departments of political science of Université de Montréal and Université Laval until 2018. Since retirement, he has served as a federal boundary commissioner for Quebec and has also acted as an expert witness in four court cases dealing with election law issues at both levels of government.

ERIC MONTIGNY is a full professor at Université Laval. Co-director of the PARDUR international associated laboratory with the University of Lausanne, he teaches Canadian and Quebec politics, nationalism, political parties, and populism. In 2025, he published the books *Populism in Canada* and *Artificial Democracy,* a collective work on the effects of digital technology on democracy. He is also a researcher with the Groupe de recherche en communication politique, the Center for the Study of Values, Attitudes, and Societies, and the research chairs on democracy and parliamentary institutions, as well as on Démocratie, le vivre-ensemble et les valeurs communes au Québec.

GALA PALAVICINI is a doctoral student in the Department of Political Science at the University of Alberta and a research assistant with the Common Ground Research Initiative. Her research focuses on Canadian and comparative legislative studies, political elites, and democratic representation. Her work has been published in the *Canadian Parliamentary Review* and *West European Politics*. Gala is also currently a research assistant with the Jarislowsky Chair in Trust and Political Leadership at Acadia University.

JON H. PAMMETT is distinguished research professor in political science at Carleton University. He is co-author of *Dynasties and Interludes: Past and Present in Canadian Electoral Politics* (with Lawrence LeDuc) to be published in a third edition in 2026 by Dundurn Press and *Absent Mandate: Strategies and Choices in Canadian Elections* (with Harold Clarke, Jane Jenson, and Lawrence LeDuc). He has co-edited and contributed to the Canadian Federal Election series since 1988.

BRETT POPPLEWELL is an author and associate professor of journalism at Carleton University in Ottawa. His latest book, *Outsider: An Old Man, a Mountain and the Search for a Hidden Past*, was a #1 national bestseller and the winner of the 2024 Edna Staebler Award for Creative Non-Fiction. He is a contributing writer for *The Walrus* and a winner of multiple national magazine awards in Canada. His work has also appeared in *Bloomberg Businessweek*, *Mother Jones*, the *Globe and Mail*, the *Toronto Star*, Sportsnet, *Maclean's*, *Best American Sports Writing*, and *Best Canadian Essays*, among other publications.

JACOB ROBBINS-KANTER is an associate professor of political science at Bishop's University. He is author of *Local Campaign Behaviour in Canadian Elections: The Contours of Centralization* (University of Toronto Press) and co-editor of *The Working Class and Politics in Canada* (UBC Press).

LORI TURNBULL is a professor in the Faculty of Management at Dalhousie University and a senior advisor at the Institute on Governance. Her research, teaching, and public commentary focus on politics and government in Canada, with a specific focus on parliament, elections, political ethics, and public trust. Dr Turnbull was a member of the research council for the Public Inquiry into Foreign Interference. She is a frequent political commentator on television and radio in Canada and around the world. She has authored many peer-reviewed articles and book chapters. Her book *Democratizing the Constitution: Reforming Responsible Government*, co-authored with Mark D. Jarvis and the late Peter Aucoin, won the Donner Prize in 2011 for the best book written on public policy in Canada.

KATRYNE VILLENEUVE-SICONNELLY is a PhD candidate in the Department of Political Science at the Université Laval. Her main research interests include anti-system parties, nationalism, populism, and the institutionalization of political parties. Her work is funded by the SSHRC Bombardier Doctoral Fellowship and she has received the 2020 Prix du Livre politique, awarded by the National Assembly in Quebec, as well as the National Assembly Medal. She has presented at numerous academic conferences and has published peer reviewed articles in the *American Review of Canadian Studies*, the *Catalan Journal of Communication and Cultural Studies*, *French Politics*, the *Canadian Journal of Political Science* and *Politique et Sociétés*.

DANIEL WESTLAKE is a term assistant professor in the School of Public Policy at Simon Fraser University and a consultant researcher with Politikos Research. His research focuses on Canadian parties and elections and multiculturalism and immigration policy. His work has been published in journals including the *Canadian Journal of Political Science*, *Party Politics*, and the *Journal of Ethnic and Migration Studies*.

PATRICK WHITE has been a professor of journalism at Université du Québec à Montréal (UQAM) since 2019. Prior to that, he was founder and managing editor at Huffington Post Quebec, as well as senior news manager at the Canadian Press, Sun Media, and Canoe.ca. He also been senior correspondent at the Reuters news agency and field producer for CTV National News at the Quebec National Assembly.